BALLPARKS

A Journey Through the Fields
of the Past, Present, and Future

Eric Enders

chartwell
books

© 2018 Eric Enders

First published in 2018 by Chartwell Books,
an imprint of The Quarto Group
142 West 36th Street, 4th Floor
New York, New York 10018, USA

T (212) 779-4972 F (212) 779-6058

www.QuartoKnows.com

12

ISBN: 978-0-7858-3616-2

A Green Tiger Book

Designed by Kevin Baier, www.kjwork.com

Photo credits can be found on the final page.

Printed in China

HOUSTON   MONARCHS
VS.
So. Pacific at East End Park.
Aug 8th 1926.
Paid Admission 1,000 — Score 9-8 Favor

ACKNOWLEDGMENTS

It doesn't take a village to produce a book, exactly, but it takes a whole lot more people than just the author. Two people who worked just as hard as I did on this book are editor Jennifer Boudinot and art director Kevin Baier. Jen expertly shepherded the project from beginning to end, and did so with good humor and extraordinary efficiency. She's one of my favorite people to work with. So is Kevin, whose great eye and attention to detail really bring these pages to life. The three of us have worked together on several books now, and it's always a pleasure.

Thanks also to proofreader Leah Zibulsky, who did an excellent job saving us from mistakes. A nonfiction book is nothing without a great index; hearty thanks to Sherri Dietrich for providing that. Many thanks to Michelle Faulkner for believing in this project and helping us get the photos to make it great. Thanks also to Leeann Moreau for getting this whole thing organized. Larry Lester, one of the finest baseball historians around, read the manuscript and offered his valuable insight. Mark Townsend and Dave Stark were extremely generous in providing us with old ticket stubs, pennants, and the other interesting ephemera contained herein. John Horne of the Baseball Hall of Fame, an old softball teammate of mine, helped us find photos in the Hall's vast archives. So did many other librarians across the country, who are too numerous to name here but whose assistance is greatly appreciated. Most importantly, thanks to my family, whose interest in my work helps keep me going. When I was a kid, there were two places I never tired of visiting. My father would take me to the ballpark, and my mother would take me to the library. That combination helped create a baseball writer, so thanks to them for that. And lastly, thanks to Vin Scully, just because.

The Houston Monarchs, Bayou City's most prominent Negro League team, face the Southern Pacific Railroad team for the city's African-American championship in 1926. The Monarchs defeated Southern Pacific 9-8 to win the title. The name of this ballpark, if it had one, has been lost to history, but it was located at the intersection of Cline and Grove Streets, near where Interstates 10 and 59 meet today. The Monarchs were owned by a pair of white grocers, John and James Liuzza, and the two-story house visible behind the grandstand was their family home.

Contents

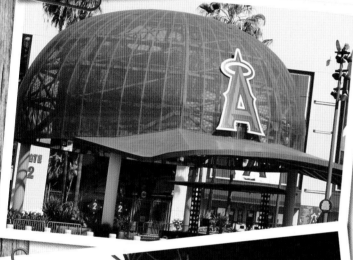

OPPOSITE PAGE, TOP TO BOTTOM: Shibe Park, America's first modern ballpark, was heralded as a phenomenon when it opened in Philadelphia in 1909. "It is the most remarkable sight I have ever witnessed," one attendee said.

Fans at Pittsburgh's Exposition Park watch Game 4 of the first modern World Series, played in 1903 between the Pirates and the Red Sox.

The seats at Nationals Park have been empty surprisingly often since the ballpark opened in 2008. Despite topping ninety-five wins four times, the team has never drawn as many as three million fans in a season.

One of the best features of Milwaukee's Miller Park is Bernie Brewer and his slide in the outfield, a team tradition for more than thirty years.

THIS PAGE: Brooklyn's Ebbets Field hosted its first World Series in 1920, and hot dog vendors did a brisk business outside the ballpark.

The renovated version of Angel Stadium has become one of baseball's biggest draws during the twenty-first century, with Anaheim topping 3 million in attendance every year from 2003 through 2017.

Nicollet Park in Minneapolis, pictured here in 1941, was one of America's most charming minor league parks for six decades, serving as home of the Minneapolis Millers from 1896 through 1955.

Dodger Stadium, the third-oldest major league park, is known for its zigzagging pavilion roof.

Growden Memorial Park looks like pretty much any ballpark you've seen before. It has aluminum bleachers, ads for local businesses on the outfield fence, and a rickety old press box behind home plate. There's nothing extraordinary about it at all, except for one thing: It's located in Fairbanks, Alaska, where the sun shines for twenty-two hours on the first day of summer. Every June 21, Growden Park becomes the most magical place in sports when the Alaska Goldpanners take the field for the Midnight Sun Game. The annual contest has been played every year since 1906, and not once have lights ever been used. It always starts at 10 p.m., and when the clock strikes midnight, play pauses while several thousand fans sing the Alaska flag song in unison. The sun sets around 1 a.m., but it doesn't go far, dipping below the mountains for a two-hour sunset before popping back up. Goldpanners manager Ed Cheff told the *New York Times* that the Midnight Sun Game's "history is special," saying, "The weather is great. The atmosphere is fantastic. In all of sports, there is nothing that can match this game."

That's the thing about ballparks: Context matters. An otherwise ordinary ballpark can become a place where the extraordinary happens.

The renovated version of Yankee Stadium was widely viewed as a colossal mistake, but when Reggie Jackson and Derek Jeter were performing their heroics as Mr. October and Mr. November (respectively), it became a palace filled with mystique and aura. In many ways, the best ballpark in the world is the one you happen to be sitting in at the moment. Even the worst stadiums in this book (we're looking at you, Tropicana Field) are pretty good places to spend a few hours watching baseball.

Ordinary ballparks may be fun, but so are the truly bizarre ones. Clark Field, home of the Texas Longhorns for forty-seven years, had a steep limestone cliff running through the middle of its outfield. The center fielder had to choose whether to play on top of the cliff or 30 feet below

TOP: Clayton Kershaw fires a pitch at Dodger Stadium in 2011, the first of his three Cy Young Award–winning seasons. During the 2010s, Kershaw and Anaheim's Mike Trout established themselves as all-time greats, providing Southern Californians with two huge reasons to go to the ballpark.

BOTTOM LEFT: The Philadelphia Quakers—the team now known as the Phillies—pose at Recreation Park in 1884. Note the alarm bell mounted on the third post from the left, a reminder that the era's wooden ballparks were liable to catch fire at any time.

BOTTOM RIGHT: A vendor sells snow cones at Kauffman Stadium. Although it's unknown exactly when the treats were first sold at ballparks, *snow cone* has been part of baseball's terminology—meaning a catch where the ball sticks up out of the glove—for decades.

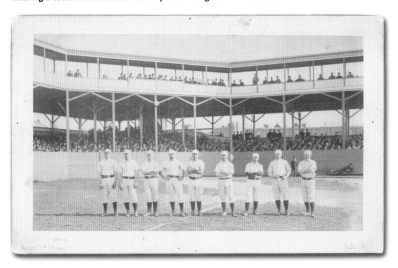

at the base, as only a narrow goat path connected the two halves. Johnstown, Pennsylvania, meanwhile, built its ballpark on The Point, the narrow spot of land where a river-borne tsunami famously crashed into the town in 1889. In order to squeeze a ballpark onto this tiny peninsula, the builders had to create a 250-foot right field foul line but a massive 395-foot power alley in right-center. Examples abound of ballparks like these whose quirks were dictated by their surroundings. In these pages you'll read about the major league park that always smelled like hops and yeast (page 10) and the one that always smelled like dead fish (page 170). You'll read about a stadium carved out of a mountain (page 229), one that closed after a year because it was too foggy (page 236), and an impromptu field built in the middle of the Egyptian desert (page 300).

The way pro ballparks are financed today tends to be underhanded and sleazy, and you'll read some horror stories about that. But the reason such fiascos keep happening is that ballparks are important to people. Folks want to have a nice stadium in their town, and they're usually willing to do what it takes—even if it means donating a billion dollars to a private business, as is the case with the New Yankee Stadium. In El Paso, Texas, where I'm from, the local government imploded its own City Hall to make room for a Triple-A ballpark. That's the urban equivalent of a farmer plowing under his corn to build a baseball field—which, of course, has also happened, both in the movies and in real life. (You can read about it on page 162.) Citizens and governments are often willing to go to great lengths to get ballparks built, and rarely do they regret it.

In countries where baseball is part of the culture, going to the ballpark is such a universal experience that it enters our everyday speech without us realizing it. Perhaps you've asked your auto mechanic to give you a ballpark estimate on repairs...and maybe the answer seemed to come out of left field. And if you've ever worked hard on something you've had a lifelong love for, you definitely tried to cover all the bases. That's certainly what we've done with this book—we hope we've knocked it out of the park. So find your seat, and let us take you out to the ballpark. 🌭

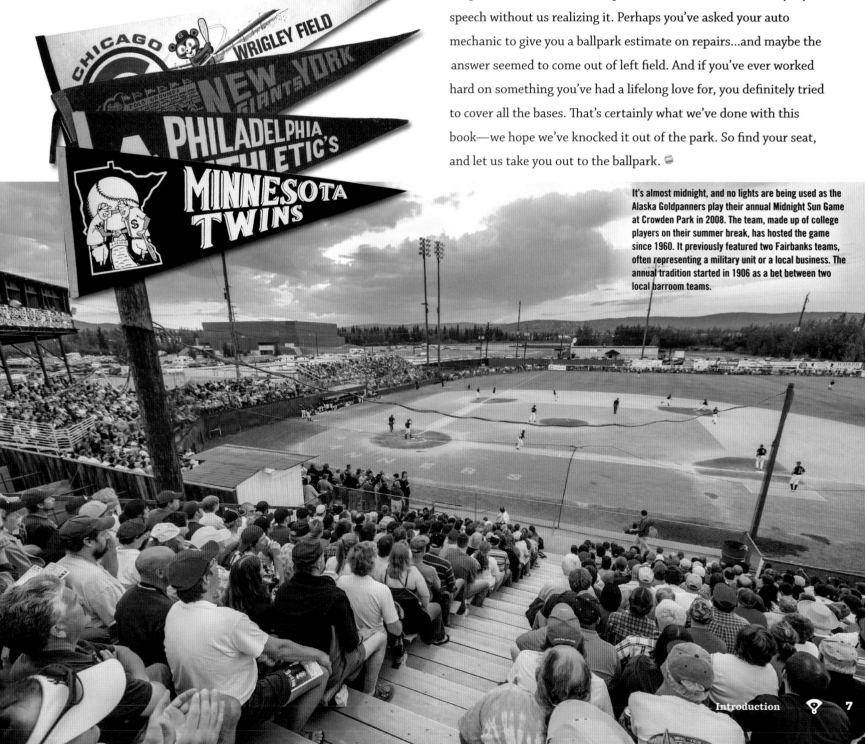

It's almost midnight, and no lights are being used as the Alaska Goldpanners play their annual Midnight Sun Game at Crowden Park in 2008. The team, made up of college players on their summer break, has hosted the game since 1960. It previously featured two Fairbanks teams, often representing a military unit or a local business. The annual tradition started in 1906 as a bet between two local barroom teams.

PHILADELPHIA

BAKER BOWL

TEAM: Philadelphia Phillies (1887–1938)

LOCATION: Corner of W. Huntingdon St. and N. 15th St., Philadelphia

FIRST MLB GAME: April 30, 1887

LAST MLB GAME: June 30, 1938

NOTABLE FEATURES: Tiny dimensions conducive to home runs; huge right field wall with Lifebuoy Soap ad.

SHIBE PARK

TEAMS: Philadelphia Athletics (1909–1954)
Philadelphia Phillies (1938–1970)

NAMES: Shibe Park (1909–1953)
Connie Mack Stadium (1953–1976)

LOCATION: Corner of W. Lehigh Ave. and N. 21st St., Philadelphia

FIRST MLB GAME: April 12, 1909

LAST MLB GAME: October 1, 1970

NOTABLE FEATURES: First-ever steel and concrete stadium; rotunda at home plate entrance; "spite fence" in right field (after 1935).

VETERANS STADIUM

TEAM: Philadelphia Phillies (1971–2003)

NICKNAME: The Vet

LOCATION: Corner of Pattison Ave. and Broad St., Philadelphia (in the South Philadelphia Sports Complex)

FIRST MLB GAME: April 10, 1971

LAST MLB GAME: September 28, 2003

NOTABLE FEATURES: Artificial turf with football markings; city jail in the basement.

PENMAR PARK

TEAM: Philadelphia Stars (1933–1952)

NAMES: Penmar Park, 44th & Parkside Ballpark, PRR YMCA Athletic Field

LOCATION: Corner of 44th St. and Parkside Ave., Philadelphia

NOTABLE FEATURES: Lights installed in 1933; railroad roundhouse behind right field fence that often emitted black smoke and forced games to pause.

CITIZENS BANK PARK

TEAM: Philadelphia Phillies (2004–present)

LOCATION: Corner of S. 11th St. and Pattison Ave., Philadelphia (in the South Philadelphia Sports Complex)

FIRST MLB GAME: April 12, 2004

NOTABLE FEATURES: Neon Liberty Bell in center field; conduciveness to home runs.

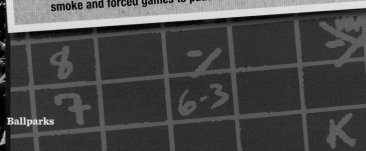

One of America's first cities, Philadelphia is also one of America's first baseball cities. In 1871, the Philadelphia Athletics won major league baseball's first pennant, which they proudly flew from a flagpole outside Jefferson Street Grounds, their small wooden ballpark. Opened in 1864 and renovated in 1871 and 1883, the grounds featured the major leagues' first swimming pool, which was situated behind the right field fence.

The Philadelphia Phillies, meanwhile, were founded in 1883 and played at Recreation Park, which they left after three seasons because they were hitting too many of their valuable baseballs into the Corinthian Reservoir next door. They moved to Baker Bowl on Huntingdon Avenue, where they would play for the next fifty-two years. A renowned hitters' paradise, Baker Bowl was also used by the powerful Hilldale Club during its victory in the 1925 Negro League World Series. (Ordinarily the Hilldales played at their own 8,000-seat ballpark, Hilldale Field, which they built in 1910 in the suburb of Darby.)

A new Philadelphia A's franchise was born in 1901, playing its games at Columbia Park in the Brewerytown neighborhood, where the smell of hops and yeast wafted through the air during games. The A's changed the course of baseball history in 1909 when they opened Shibe Park, the first steel and concrete stadium ever built. They played in that legendary facility until leaving town for Kansas City in 1955.

The Phillies, longtime co-tenants with the A's at Shibe Park, continued to play there until 1970, when they moved to a new multipurpose facility, Veterans Stadium. The Vet was a disaster from the start, but the Phils enjoyed much on-field success there, including their first-ever World Series title in 1980. The team moved into a new retro ballpark, Citizens Bank Park, in 2004. 🌑

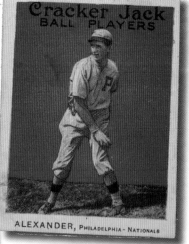

TOP LEFT: Philadelphia's two major league teams may have been inept during most of the early twentieth century, but community and recreational baseball was a thriving pastime in the city. Here, two semipro teams face off at a rec league field on North Street in the Spring Garden neighborhood, sometime in the 1920s.

TOP RIGHT: Grover Cleveland Alexander, called "Ol' Pete" by everyone he knew, pitched the first seven seasons of his career at Baker Bowl, during which he led the league in wins five times. In 1915, he led the Phillies to their first-ever World Series with a 33-10 record and a ridiculous 1.22 earned run average. In 1952, Ronald Reagan played him in the movie *The Winning Team*.

BOTTOM: If you look closely at this image of Baker Bowl, you can see a small hump in deepest center field. This outfield incline was a feature common to early ballparks, including ones in Boston, Cincinnati, and El Paso, Texas. In Baker Bowl's case, it was because a tunnel for the Philadelphia and Reading Railroad ran underneath center field.

OPPOSITE PAGE, TOP AND MIDDLE: In 1924, Baker Bowl hosted the opening two games in the first Negro League World Series ever played. Most of the fans were passionate supporters of the Hilldale Daisies, who played only 10 miles away in the suburb Upper Darby. In Game 1, pictured here, the 5,366 fans went home disappointed as Hilldale lost to Kansas City 6-2. They would also lose the series 5 games to 4.

OPPOSITE PAGE, BOTTOM: Baker Bowl's right field bleachers are overflowing for Game 1 of the 1915 World Series, in which Phillies ace Pete Alexander bested the Red Sox 3-1. These fans didn't know it, but they were witnessing history—the Phillies would go sixty-five years before winning another game in the Fall Classic. Note the absence of a foul pole, which must have made things difficult for the umpires. This image also illustrates how much baseball crowds have changed over the past century: Of the several hundred fans visible here, only one is a woman. (She's next to the man waving a newspaper in the back row.)

BAKER BOWL

PHILADELPHIA PHILLIES 1887–1938

FOR HALF A CENTURY BAKER BOWL hosted the most hapless franchise in baseball, and fittingly enough, it was built on the site of a former dump in North Philadelphia. A bandbox whose cozy dimensions made it the era's most notorious hitter's park, Baker Bowl was the only ballpark built in the 1800s that was still being used well into the twentieth century. During the fifty-two years the Phillies played there, they posted only twenty winning seasons, most of them before 1900. During the park's final two decades, the home team stumbled to ninety or more losses fifteen times. In the first of its many calamities, the wooden park burned to the ground in 1894. It was rebuilt in just twelve days using concrete, steel, and wood, but the stands would catastrophically collapse twice in the ensuing years. The left field bleachers fell down during a game in 1903 and the right field bleachers did the same in 1927; the two incidents killed a total of thirteen fans and injured hundreds more.

Baker Bowl's most notable feature was its 60-foot-tall right field wall, which featured a massive ad for Lifebuoy soap. At just 272 feet away, the wall was an inviting target for hitters, particularly Gavvy Cravath, a right-handed slugger who knocked opposite-field fly balls over it so frequently that he briefly became baseball's modern career home run leader. In 1915, with Cravath leading MLB in homers for a third consecutive season, Baker Bowl hosted its only World Series. Alas, Cravath went homerless and Boston trounced Philadelphia four games to one. The Phillies wouldn't win their first title until sixty-five years later, by which time Baker Bowl had long since become a parking lot. 🌐

SHIBE PARK

PHILADELPHIA ATHLETICS 1909-1954 **PHILADELPHIA PHILLIES 1927, 1938-1970**

WHEN CLASSIC BALLPARKS are discussed, the first names mentioned are usually Ebbets Field, Fenway Park, and Wrigley Field. Shibe Park may lack the name recognition of those beloved stadiums, but it was markedly more important than its famous cousins. By building the first steel and concrete stadium in baseball, Philadelphia A's executives Ben Shibe and Connie Mack essentially invented the concept of the modern ballpark. Before Shibe Park, even the most lavish ballparks had been temporary and ephemeral. After Shibe Park, ballparks often lasted for decades and became touchstones for multiple generations of fans.

Before 1909, baseball parks were made of wood. The stands were wooden, the seats were wooden, the stairs were wooden, and the fences were wooden. This meant that every time someone lit a cigarette or a lantern, the entire structure was at risk. Ballparks of the 1800s tended to be hastily built and used for only a few years before an accidental fire burned them to the ground. Then they were rebuilt and used for a few more years until fire struck again. The cycle repeated itself in almost every major league city. In 1894 alone, four major league parks burned. But in 1904, the world of construction changed dramatically. That year, an engineer named Henry Hooper designed the Ingalls Building, a 16-story skyscraper in Cincinnati that was built using the brand new concept of reinforced concrete. Regular concrete, being crumbly and brittle, was unsuitable for use in buildings. But concrete reinforced

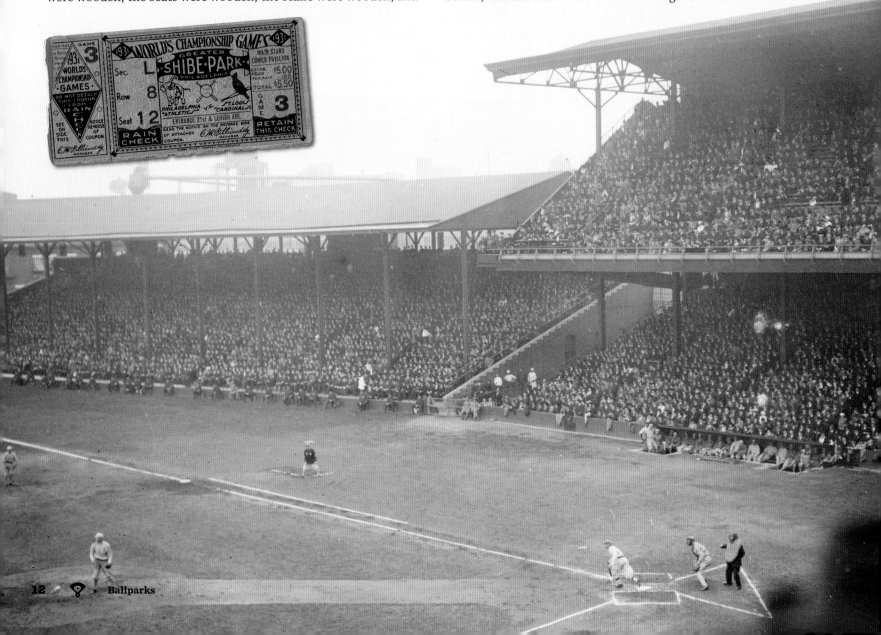

with embedded steel beams offered nearly limitless possibilities, enabling buildings to be built much bigger and taller than ever before. In 1908, Shibe, the Athletics' majority owner, and Mack, the team's manager, decided to try using reinforced concrete to build a baseball park. The sport would never be the same again.

Shibe found a property in what was then the northern outskirts of Philadelphia, and was able to purchase it cheaply because it was next-door to the Philadelphia Hospital for Contagious Diseases. To build his new steel stadium he hired the aptly named firm William Steele and Sons, which was known for steel-frame buildings as well as for inventing the cement mixer. Shibe Park would be a lavish building, but not as lavish as some of its successors. Its budget was a then-unprecedented $500,000, although that figure would be surpassed within a few years by Forbes Field, the Polo Grounds, Ebbets Field, and others.

From the outside, Shibe Park resembled something from the Italian Renaissance, or perhaps Montmartre. Ionic columns, segmented arches, and elaborate brickwork were abundant. The grandstand was covered by a green slate mansard roof trimmed with copper, and a distinctive corner cupola housed Connie Mack's office. The team's script *A* logo was carved above the entrances. Baseball-themed gargoyles depicted bats, baseballs, and one of the game's newer inventions, catchers' masks. A restaurant and a team store, two developments that remain staples of stadiums today, were built in. As things turned out, the Athletics would be plagued by financial troubles throughout their tenure at Shibe Park, but they would be a poor man's team playing in a rich man's ballpark.

The shape of the field was determined by the rectangular city block that contained it. Rather than a semicircular outfield, the left and right field walls were straight lines that met in the middle in dead center field, 515 feet away from home plate. With such a spacious field, overflow crowds were often seated in fair territory on the deep outfield grass, where few hits traveled anyway. "The grounds are so large it is improbable that any batsman, even if he is a stalwart hitter like Cobb, Crawford, or Harry Davis, will be able to drive the ball over the fence," one journalist wrote.

The opening of Shibe Park on April 12, 1909, was an event of such magnitude that all sixteen major league team owners attended. So did 31,000 others, all of them squeezing into a 23,000-seat ballpark, the largest capacity ever seen in baseball at that time. "As a game of ball it was not much," one writer opined. But "as spectacle, it will linger long in the memory of those who were fortunate enough to gain admittance." The reaction to the ballpark itself was one of universal awe. "Shibe Park is the greatest place of its character in the world," one reporter

OPPOSITE PAGE: Shibe Park is packed for Game 2 of the 1913 Fall Classic, which *Sporting Life* called "the most remarkable pitchers' duel in the record of modern World's Series." It was a matchup of baseball's two winningest active pitchers, with Christy Mathewson (shown here on the mound for the Giants) facing Philadelphia's Eddie Plank. Both men pitched ten-inning complete games, and Mathewson won it for New York by breaking the scoreless tie with an RBI single in the tenth. Incidentally, since baseball's color line was still in place then, you may be surprised to see that the leftmost person in the Giants dugout is an African-American man. That's Ed Mackall, who was the team's trainer from 1902 through 1922.

THIS PAGE: The rooftops of 20th Street, which ran behind Shibe Park's right field wall, are hopping with activity during Game 1 of the 1914 World Series. Note that the second house from the right is flying a flag with a white elephant on it. That's a reference to a derogatory comment made by Giants manager John McGraw in 1902, when he called the Athletics franchise "a big white elephant." Instead of being insulted, Connie Mack and Ben Shibe responded defiantly, adopting a white elephant as their team's logo. It can still be seen on the A's uniforms today. By the way, although Shibe Park was torn down in 1976, the buildings seen here are all still standing today—but none of them have bleachers on top anymore.

gushed. George Wright, the retired shortstop who was then baseball's most revered figure, said, "It is the most remarkable sight I have ever witnessed." Shibe's success inspired a ballpark-building frenzy, as nearly every team scrambled to build its own steel and concrete structure. Shibe Park was easily the most spectacular ballpark in the world when it opened, but three months later it was no longer even the most spectacular in Pennsylvania. Pittsburgh's palatial Forbes Field debuted on June 30, 1909, followed in quick succession by the Polo Grounds, Comiskey Park, Fenway Park, and many others.

Ben Shibe had built Philadelphia's ballpark, as one local newspaper put it, "for the masses as well as the classes." Seats in the lower deck were a bit pricey at $1, but seats in the outfield bleachers could be had for a mere quarter. The majority of the seats—13,000 out of 23,000—were actually bleacher seats. "Those who live by the sweat of their brow should have as good a chance of seeing the game as the man who never rolled up his sleeves to earn a dollar," Shibe said.

Some fans avoided paying even the quarter for the bleachers. Almost immediately after Shibe Park opened, fans began watching games from the rooftops of two-story homes on 20th Street that loomed over the outfield wall. Such scenes later became commonplace at Wrigley Field, but Shibe Park was where rooftop, or wildcat, bleachers got their start. For big events like the 1913 World Series, wildcat

THIS PAGE: Connie Mack Stadium as it appeared in the early 1970s, after both of its baseball teams had moved out and the building had become a target for window breakers and graffiti artists. Even then, its original charm was still in evidence, including the grand cupola that once housed Connie Mack's circular office. On the second floor, next to the two Ionic columns, is a gargoyle featuring a pair of crossed baseball bats and a catcher's mask. The latter was a tribute to Mack, who was a catcher during his playing days in the 1880s.

OPPOSITE PAGE, LEFT: Two respected elder statesmen, Boston's Johnny Evers (left) and Philadelphia's Eddie Plank, shake hands before the 1914 World Series at Shibe Park. In what would turn out to be his last full big league season, Evers won the Chalmers Award as the National League's best player that year after helping the Braves climb from last place to first place in thirty-seven days. Plank, the crafty lefty known as "Gettysburg Eddie," would lose a 1-0 heartbreaker to the Braves in his only game of the Fall Classic. Boston swept the A's in four games.

OPPOSITE PAGE, RIGHT: A's pitcher Albert Bender—who, like all Native American players of his era, was nicknamed "Chief"—is shown here finishing off the Giants in the ninth inning of Game 4 of the 1913 World Series at Shibe Park. After retiring this batter, Doc Crandall, Bender would retire two more Giants to wrap up a 6-5 complete game victory. One of the best pitchers ever to toe the rubber at Shibe Park, Bender won 61 career games there, including four in the World Series.

bleachers were deliberately built, with homeowners charging admission fees and selling hot dogs and lemonade. By the time the 1929 and 1930 World Series were played here, rooftop tickets were selling for $7 to $25 apiece and the City of Philadelphia was even taking a $30 cut from each property owner for a permit. Of course, all this unofficial seating infuriated the Athletics, who understandably believed the rooftop seats deprived them of paid admissions. Eventually, Connie Mack and the Shibe family decided they'd had enough. They erected a "spite fence," 38 feet tall and made of green corrugated metal, on top of the existing 12-foot wall. The wildcat bleachers were instantly put out of business. The A's played a dozen more years at Shibe Park after putting up the spite fence, and in what some surely viewed as karma, they finished in last place during nine of those seasons.

By 1935, the year Connie Mack put up the spite fence, the nation was in the throes of the Great Depression and the A's had been forced to sell off all their great players. So in 1938 Mack found a rent-paying tenant: He invited the Philadelphia Phillies to move in. At the time, the Phillies were in the midst of a stretch in which they finished last place sixteen times in twenty-seven years. The A's, by contrast, were one of the sport's marquee franchises, with nine American League pennants to their credit. Almost as soon as the two teams started sharing a ballpark, however, their roles reversed. By the late 1940s it was the A's who were finishing last every year, while the Phillies were a promising young team. In 1950 the Phils drew 1.2 million fans to Shibe Park, while the Athletics barely cracked 300,000.

In 1953 Mack's children, who were by then running the Athletics, changed the ballpark's name from Shibe Park to Connie Mack Stadium. It was a fitting tribute to the man who had co-owned the A's for thirty-eight years and managed them for fifty. But by then the writing was already on the wall: There was room for only one team in Philadelphia, and that team was the Phillies. The Mack family sold the A's in 1954 to a new owner who promptly moved them to Kansas City. The Phillies were now Connie Mack Stadium's sole occupants, awkwardly stuck playing in an aging ballpark named after another team's manager. They continued to play there for sixteen more years, finally moving to Veterans Stadium in 1971. Later that year, two young arsonists set Connie Mack Stadium ablaze, burning the upper deck down and collapsing the roof. The stadium sat in a half-burned state for five years until it finally met the wrecking ball in 1976. 🍂

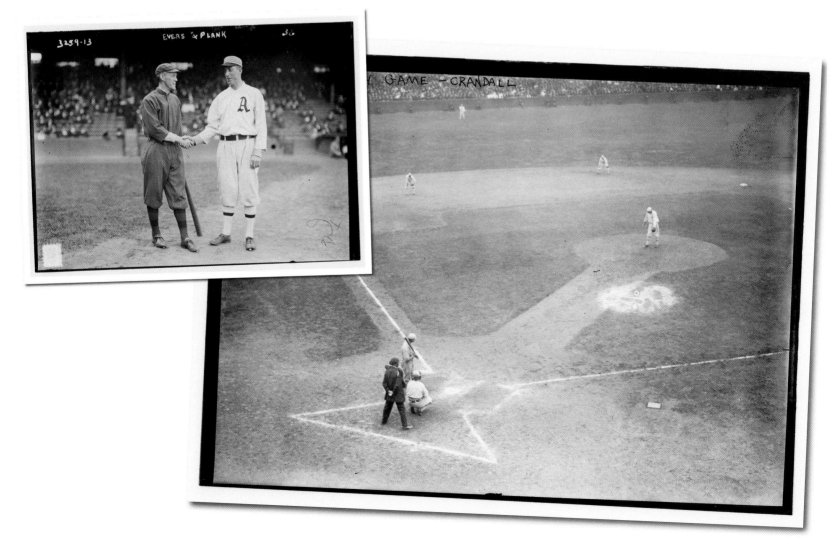

PENMAR PARK
PHILADELPHIA STARS 1933–1952

IN 1892 THE PENNSYLVANIA RAILROAD, whose laborers were mostly African American, built a company-funded YMCA for its workers on Westminster Avenue in West Philadelphia. It quickly became an important neighborhood institution, but it lacked a place to play baseball and football, so in 1903 the company added a large grassy field a couple of blocks away, next to the roundhouse where its engines were serviced. This company field, named Penmar Park, would eventually become home to the city's powerful Negro League team, the Philadelphia Stars.

Located at 44th Street and Parkside Avenue—and often referred to simply by naming that intersection—the field became a true ballpark during the 1920s when a grandstand was built. Lights were added in 1933 when Eddie Gottlieb, the white owner of the Philadelphia Stars, began leasing the stadium

from the Y. (Gottlieb, nicknamed "Mr. Basketball" thanks to his NBA career, would become better known during the 1950s as the Philadelphia Warriors coach who drafted Wilt Chamberlain.) Every morning, according to legend, a piece of Penmar Park's grandstand went missing when a woman named Hattie Williams used a hatchet to chop some pieces of wood from it, which she then used to heat the washtub behind home plate where she boiled hot dogs for that day's game.

Boasting charismatic players like the lanky fireballer Slim Jones, the Stars drew fans to Penmar Park from all over Philadelphia—including, frequently, a biracial youngster named Roy Campanella who dreamed of one day playing for the Stars. (Instead he would grow up to play for the Baltimore Elite Giants and Brooklyn Dodgers.) Baseball was popular enough in Philly that Penmar was chosen as a site for the 1945 Negro League World Series even though neither participating team (the Homestead Grays and Cleveland Buckeyes) was from

Philadelphia. Undoubtedly its most memorable game, though, was a 1947 contest that showcased Satchel Paige's incomparable showmanship. After pitching a perfect game for eight innings, Paige intentionally walked the first three batters in the ninth—thereby ending his perfect game and loading the bases. Then, he ordered his outfielders to lie down on the grass. With his entire outfield horizontal, Paige proceeded to strike out the final three batters on nine pitches, finishing off his no-hitter in style.

OPPOSITE PAGE, TOP: Before the Philadelphia Stars, the city's top African-American club was Hilldale, which played in the suburb of Upper Darby 10 miles west of Center City. Prominent players in this 1921 photo include heavy-hitting catcher Louis Santop (wearing chest protector), diminutive pitcher Phil Cockrell (front row, far right), and forty-two-year-old shortstop Bill Francis (front row, third from right), who also managed the team. Hilldale's founder and owner, Ed Bolden, is at left, wearing a suit.

OPPOSITE PAGE, BOTTOM: The 1939 Philadelphia Stars pose at Penmar Park. They were run by local postal worker Ed Bolden (in suit), the same man who'd founded the Hilldale club three decades earlier. The team's best player was Jud Wilson (front row, third from left), a barrel-chested slugger who was one of the greatest hitters in Negro League annals. Famous for both his prodigious strength and his uncontrolled temper, Wilson was said to be a .370 lifetime hitter. "He was dangerous!" outfielder Clint Thomas once said. "All ballplayers were scared of him."

TOP: Roy Campanella, who grew up attending games at Penmar Park, is shown catching there with the Baltimore Elite Giants during the 1940s. Campanella, the son of an Italian-American father and African-American mother, grew up 4 miles away in the working-class neighborhood of Nicetown. The Elite Giants signed him when he was still a teenager. "I knew I had a lot of friends in those stands," Campanella wrote of the first time he played at Penmar. "They were pulling for me. I was nearly fifteen [but] I felt a lot older and bigger and stronger and wiser than fifteen."

BOTTOM: Dr. Hilda Bolden, owner of the Philadelphia Stars, chats with the team's manager, Oscar Charleston (left), and a couple of players, sometime around 1950. Bolden, a prominent pediatrician and a University of Pennsylvania graduate, inherited the team when her father, Ed Bolden, died. Charleston was retired by this time, but during his playing days he had been perhaps the best player in Negro Leagues history. "The greatest ballplayer I've ever seen in my life was Oscar Charleston," Crawfords outfielder Ted Page once said. "I'd rate Charleston over Joe DiMaggio, over Willie Mays."

VETERANS STADIUM
PHILADELPHIA PHILLIES 1971–2003

WITH THE NEGLECTED Connie Mack Stadium falling apart in its final seasons, the Philadelphia Phillies were happy in 1971 to move into a $43 million government-funded stadium built to house them and the Philadelphia Eagles. Unfortunately, Veterans Stadium turned out to be even more of a disaster than most of its multi-purpose brethren. Most seats were far removed from the action, creating a cold and impersonal environment, and the nosebleed section was even higher up than at most modern superstadiums.

The Vet was ill-suited for both sports it hosted, and its Astro-Turf playing surface was particularly reviled. With exposed seams, unsightly water stains, and dangerous dead spots, it was frequently voted the NFL's worst field and caused career-ending injuries to at least two football players. In 2001, a game was even cancelled when the Baltimore Ravens refused to allow their players onto the unsafe field. Meanwhile, the turf's football markings—which other parks removed during baseball season—proved unable to be erased, resulting in the spectacle of major league games being played on a field crisscrossed with unsightly yard lines and hash marks.

18   Ballparks

Fan misbehavior at Veterans Stadium was so rampant that the city was forced to open a police precinct and jail inside the stadium, a first for a pro sports facility. Wrote Jere Longman in the *New York Times:* "The Vet is a place of leaky pipes, unreliable heat, and glacial elevators, a dank arena where a mouse-chasing cat once fell through the ceiling onto the desk of an assistant coach; where visiting players looked through a peephole into the dressing room of the Eagles' cheerleaders; and where the upper deck has gained a reputation as a hostile tier of taunting, public urination, fighting, and general strangeness." Veterans Stadium was mercifully imploded in 2004, falling to the ground in a mere sixty-two seconds. ☕

OPPOSITE PAGE: The *New York Times* once referred to The Vet's upper deck as "a hostile tier of… public urination," but at least the seats were already yellow.

TOP LEFT: Every fourth day, Veterans Stadium was owned by Steve Carlton, the ace left-hander who won four Cy Young Awards while pitching here. Known for his prickly personality and decades-long policy of not speaking to the media, Carlton did all his talking on the mound. His best season with the Phillies was his first, 1972, when he won 27 games with a stellar 1.97 earned run average. All told, he pitched 242 career games at The Vet, winning 138 of them. He's shown here pitching during the 1980 World Series, when he won two games with a 2.40 ERA and helped the Phillies capture their first-ever championship.

TOP RIGHT: When the Phillies moved into Veterans Stadium in 1971 they also intro- duced a pair of new mascots, Philadelphia Phil (seen here) and Philadelphia Phillis. "They are part of my home run spectac- ular," team president Bill Giles boasted. "When a Phillie hits a homer, Philadelphia Phil will appear between the boards in center field and hit a baseball. It will travel toward the message board in right center and strike a Liberty Bell. The bell will glow and its crack will light up. The ball will continue and hit little Philadelphia Phillis in the fanny and she will fall down." Mercifully, the duo was replaced by the Phillie Phanatic in 1978. Giles somehow managed to keep his job for another forty-four years.

BOTTOM: No, this isn't a scene from the final season of *Mad Men*, but rather the executive offices at Veterans Stadium in 1971. Tom Hudson, the Phillies' director of ticket sales, is seen here leering at his secretary, Ronnie Gibbons. Gibbons was also a member of the "Hot Pants Patrol," a team of 140 female ushers introduced at The Vet that year. Applicants were instructed in a letter to "wear your shortest skirt and your tightest blouse" to the job interview. "The patrol's 'uniforms' raised the ire of conservatives and feminists alike," historian Dan Epstein wrote. "Still, the Phillies managed to draw more than twice as many fans in 1971 as they had during the previous season."

TOP: Three happy fans show off the tickets they've just purchased for Game 2 of the 1980 World Series at Veterans Stadium. It was the Phillies' first appearance in the Fall Classic in thirty years, and the ballpark was packed to its capacity of 66,000 for each of the three games played there. The fans pictured here were luckier than most, because of the 198,000 total tickets available, only 8,000 went on sale to the general public. The rest were reserved for season-ticket holders, corporations, and MLB officials.

BOTTOM: The Phillies on Opening Day 1978. Winners of three straight division titles through 1978, they wouldn't advance to the World Series until 1980. Pictured (from left) is the Opening Day batting order: right fielder Arnold "Bake" McBride, shortstop Larry Bowa, third baseman Mike Schmidt, left fielder Greg Luzinski, first baseman Richie Hebner, center fielder Garry Maddox, catcher Tim McCarver, second baseman Ted Sizemore, and pitcher Steve Carlton.

OPPOSITE PAGE: Phillies baserunner Shane Victorino flies down the line, barely getting thrown out on a bunt attempt on Opening Day 2008 at Citizens Bank Park. Victorino and Jimmy Rollins—seen here rounding third base—were the two sparkplugs of the Phillies team that won the World Series that year.

OPPOSITE PAGE, INSET: The Phillie Phanatic made his debut as the Phillies' mascot in 1978. Ever since, he's been dancing on top of the dugout, mocking the Phillies' opponents, and shooting hot dogs into the crowd. In 1988, the Phanatic was wrestled to the ground by Dodgers manager Tommy Lasorda, who was upset because the Phanatic had been pummeling a Lasorda effigy.

CITIZENS BANK PARK

PHILADELPHIA PHILLIES 2004–PRESENT

AFTER THIRTY-THREE DEPRESSING YEARS in Veterans Stadium, even the most mundane new ballpark would have made Phillies fans happy. Unfortunately, a mundane new ballpark is exactly what they got. Designed by local architect Stanley Cole with assistance from HOK, Citizens Bank Park made thoroughly unimaginative use of the paint-by-numbers retro template. The $458 million stadium opened in 2004 in the South Philadelphia Sports Complex, which was also home to the city's NFL, NHL, and NBA teams.

Of all the retro stadiums built in the wake of Camden Yards, Citizens Bank Park was the most shameless in blatantly copying the features of Baltimore's gem. Both parks featured stately redbrick exteriors, old-fashioned clocks and bilevel bullpens in the outfield, greenery behind the center field fence, and taller-than-normal right field walls displaying large scoreboards. Baltimore's Eutaw Street, the thoroughfare behind right field where all manner of food and souvenirs are sold, was echoed by Citizens Bank's Ashburn Alley. The Phillies even mimicked the Orioles' idea of having a rotund former slugger hawk barbecue sandwiches at a food stand. (In Baltimore it was John "Boog" Powell; in Philly, Greg Luzinski.) Still, there was one thing about Citizens Bank Park everyone loved: It wasn't Veterans Stadium. "It was absolutely fabulous to see The Vet in a pile of rubble," one Phillies fan told the *New York Times* on the new ballpark's opening day. One of the park's signature features is a neon replica of the Liberty Bell that blinks whenever a home run is hit, accompanied by a loud clang from the stadium's loudspeakers. The bell rang frequently during the ballpark's opening season, as the Phillies took advantage of its cozy dimensions to hit 215 home runs, smashing the previous franchise record. ✍

TOP: Jimmy Rollins bats at Citizens Park during a 2009 game. That year the Phillies uniform contained two special patches. On the right sleeve was a patch celebrating their 2008 World Series title, and on the left breast was a black patch bearing the initials of beloved broadcaster Harry Kalas, who died in April 2009. Rollins turned in one of his poorest seasons with the bat in 2009, but he still stole thirty-one bases and won his third career Gold Glove. By the time he retired in 2016, he was the Phillies' all-time leader in hits and ranked second in stolen bases.

MIDDLE: This 10-foot-tall statue of Mike Schmidt stands outside the left field entrance gate at Citizens Bank Park. It's one of four matching sculptures of Phillies legends; the others—Robin Roberts, Richie Ashburn, and Steve Carlton—are located at the other three entrance gates. All four were sculpted by local artist Zenos Frudakis. A fifth statue was added in 2011, with longtime broadcaster Harry Kalas being immortalized in bronze by sculptor Lawrence Nowlan.

BOTTOM: The Phillies locker room facilities have come a long way from the days of Shibe Park, where the players dressed at basic metal lockers in a cramped room. The home team's clubhouse now features forty-four oak lockers, each containing a safe. Adjacent to the locker room are sixteen showers, a sauna, a doctor's office, a weight room with twenty-five exercise machines, and a dining room.

Williamsport, Pennsylvania

Home of the Little League World Series

Although no major league game has ever been played at Howard J. Lamade Stadium, it's nevertheless one of America's most beloved ballparks. Home to the Little League World Series since 1959, this classic stadium in Williamsport, Pennsylvania, is the site of an annual pilgrimage every August, when tens of thousands of fans make their way here to watch a new champion get crowned. A number of major league stars—including Gary Sheffield, Todd Frazier, and Cody Bellinger—first gained national attention while playing at Lamade Stadium as twelve-year-olds.

Lamade Stadium looks like any vintage Triple-A stadium, except everything is two-thirds normal size. The pitcher's mound is 46 feet away from home plate; there are 60 feet between bases; and the outfield fences, originally 205 feet away, were increased to 225 feet in 2006 after youngsters started hitting too many home runs. As one of the rare ballparks with identical dimensions to all fields, its fair territory forms one-fourth of a perfect circle. Lamade is also one of the few surviving ballparks in America with obstructed-view seats. Its grandstand roof is supported by eighteen steel columns, giving the park an aesthetic reminiscent of, say, 1929 rather than its actual construction date of 1959. (Incidentally, many are surprised when they learn that Lamade isn't even the oldest stadium in Williamsport. That distinction belongs to Bowman Field, a minor league ballpark that opened in 1927 and hosted a regular-season MLB game between the Pirates and Cardinals in 2017.)

Lamade Stadium's most notable feature is its outfield seating, which consists of a giant grassy berm stretching from foul pole to foul pole. While the actual grandstand holds only 3,300 fans, around ten times that many can fit on the berm. Refreshingly, admission to the Little League World Series is always free. Grandstand tickets are first-come, first-served on game days, while tickets aren't even required for the berm; fans can just show up, go through a metal detector, and spread out their blankets on the lawn.

As the Little League organization has grown over the years, Lamade has expanded from a stand-alone stadium into a vast complex featuring practice fields, dormitories, and a 10,000-square-foot museum. Lights were erected in 1992. In 2001, a second stadium, 5,000-seat Volunteer Stadium, was built next door, enabling multiple games to be played at the same time.

The Little League World Series received a huge bump in prestige when ESPN began airing its games in 1987. The network paid Little League $90.5 million for the rights to televise the event from 2007 through 2022, a huge financial windfall, but one that also required Little League to renovate Lamade Stadium to make room for ESPN's horde of production trailers, satellite trucks, and catering operations. "We used to scrunch them in right here, right next to the stadium," Little League CFO Dave Houseknecht told *Sports Business Daily*. "It took up an incredible chunk of our property.... They outgrew what we could provide. They knew it and we knew it. It was just a question of finding a solution." In 2014 Little League spent $1.3 million to build a self-contained compound for ESPN next to the stadium, with space for satellite trucks and everything else the network requires. With its financial future secure and its facilities now up to date, Lamade Stadium seems poised to remain one of the sport's most cherished venues for years to come.

With a capacity of 30,000, Lamade Stadium is the largest non-MLB ballpark in the United States. Most fans sit on the grassy berm behind the outfield fence, where they watch the best young players in the world face off every August. "Playing in front of 28,000 to 30,000 fans as an eleven- or twelve-year-old is pretty spectacular," Cody Bellinger, who played in the 2007 Little League World Series, told MLB.com. "It was probably the most fun I had playing baseball."

NEW YORK

 ## HILLTOP PARK

TEAM: New York Highlanders (1903–1912)
LOCATION: Ft. Washington Ave. and W. 165th St., Manhattan
FIRST MLB GAME: April 30, 1903
LAST MLB GAME: October 5, 1912
NOTABLE FEATURES: Location on Manhattan Island's highest point; bull-shaped sign for Bull Durham Tobacco on right field wall.

 ## POLO GROUNDS

TEAMS: New York Giants (1911–1957), New York Yankees (1912–1922), New York Mets (1962–1963)
LOCATION: Corner of W. 157th St. and Harlem River Dr., Manhattan
FIRST MLB GAME: June 28, 1911
LAST MLB GAME: September 18, 1963
NOTABLE FEATURES: Unusually shaped playing field, with nearby foul poles but distant center field fence; the last of five stadiums called Polo Grounds, three of which were on this site.

 ## DYCKMAN OVAL

TEAMS: Cuban Stars (1920–1932), New York Cubans (1935–1936)
LOCATION: Corner of Academy St. and Nagle Ave., Manhattan
NOTABLE FEATURES: Lights installed in 1930; elevated subway tracks running 20 feet outside the main entrance; beer garden located on the premises.

 ## EBBETS FIELD

TEAM: Brooklyn Dodgers (1913–1957)
LOCATION: Corner of Sullivan Pl. and McKeever Pl., Brooklyn
FIRST MLB GAME: April 9, 1913
LAST MLB GAME: September 24, 1957
NOTABLE FEATURES: Ornate exterior with repeating arches; unusual right field wall made of various materials; intimate atmosphere with seating close to field.

 ## YANKEE STADIUM

TEAM: New York Yankees (1923–1973, 1976–2008)
NICKNAME: The House That Ruth Built
LOCATION: Corner of Ruppert Pl. and E. 157th St., The Bronx
FIRST MLB GAME: April 18, 1923
LAST MLB GAME: September 21, 2008
NOTABLE FEATURES: Copper frieze around grandstand; monuments in play in deep center field; short porch in right field measuring 296 feet.

 ## SHEA STADIUM

TEAMS: New York Mets (1964–2008), New York Yankees (1974–1975)
NAME: William A. Shea Municipal Stadium (1964–2009)
LOCATION: Corner of Grand Central Parkway and Roosevelt Ave., Queens (in Flushing Meadows Corona Park)
FIRST MLB GAME: April 17, 1964
LAST MLB GAME: September 28, 2008
NOTABLE FEATURES: Noise from jets approaching nearby LaGuardia Airport; Home Run Apple behind center field fence.

 ## NEW YANKEE STADIUM

TEAM: New York Yankees (2009–present)
NAME: Yankee Stadium (2009–present)
LOCATION: Corner of Macombs Dam Bridge and E. 161st St., The Bronx
FIRST MLB GAME: April 16, 2009
NOTABLE FEATURES: White-painted steel frieze around grandstand, Monument Park behind center field fence; unprecedented number of restaurants & retail outlets.

 ## CITI FIELD

TEAM: New York Mets (2009–present)
LOCATION: Corner of Roosevelt Ave. and 126th St., Queens (in Flushing Meadows Corona Park)
FIRST MLB GAME: April 13, 2009
NOTABLE FEATURES: Panoramic view of Queens; many features copied from Ebbets Field; Jackie Robinson Rotunda honoring MLB's first modern African-American player.

It's difficult to pinpoint the first true baseball field. However, it's easy to identify the greater New York area as the place where baseball was largely developed, and as such, it had some of America's earliest baseball diamonds. During the mid-1800s, games were played at racetracks, polo fields, or wherever players could find enough space. In 1858, the Fashion Course Racetrack in Queens (located near where Citi Field stands today) was the site of the first baseball game with a paid admission; spectators forked over 50¢ to watch all-star teams from Brooklyn and New York (then two different cities) face off. The experiment was so successful that in 1862, an entrepreneur named William Cammeyer opened the first baseball grounds to be fully enclosed by a fence, so that he could charge admission for every game. Cammeyer's ballpark, the Union Grounds in Williamsburg, Brooklyn, served as home to three early major league teams: the Brooklyn Atlantics, Brooklyn Eckfords, and New York Mutuals.

In 1864, an even nicer park, the Capitoline Grounds, was opened in Brooklyn, featuring a bandstand, a ladies' sitting room, and a building where "cranks" (as fans were then called) could stable their horses. One of baseball's most fabled games was played at the Capi-

toline Grounds in 1870, with the Atlantics defeating the Cincinnati Red Stockings in extra innings to end the latter's 84-game winning streak. In 1886 and '87, meanwhile, Staten Islanders flocked to watch the New York Metropolitans play at the St. George Cricket Ground. The lavish park offered a panoramic view of New York Harbor so fans could simultaneously watch the ballgame and, in the background, the brand-new Statue of Liberty being hoisted onto its pedestal.

As the game evolved in New York, so did the ballfields. The New York Giants opened the original Polo Grounds in 1883, and eventually played in four different ballparks of that name. The final one, built in 1911, lasted until the team moved to San Francisco. Meanwhile, a new team called the New York Highlanders debuted in 1903, playing for a decade at Hilltop Park. By 1923, they were known as the Yankees and opened the largest venue in baseball, Yankee Stadium, in The Bronx. After the Brooklyn Dodgers abandoned Ebbets Field and the Giants also moved west, the Yankees had a monopoly over New York baseball for a scant four years. In 1962, the Mets were born, moving soon thereafter into Shea Stadium. Finally, in 2009, both the Yankees and Mets opened new ballparks next to their old ones, bringing ballpark construction in New York to a conclusion—at least for now. ✎

THIS PAGE: The Brooklyn Tip-Tops (in white) partake in Opening Day festivities with the Buffalo Bisons (in black) before playing their first home game at Brooklyn's Washington Park in 1914. That year a new major league, the Federal League, tried to crash MLB's party by placing the Tip-Tops at Washington Park, which the Dodgers had just vacated. Note the unusual message on the outfield wall reminding fans that "base ball players are all human."

OPPOSITE PAGE: In 1912, the Polo Grounds hosted one of the most exciting World Series ever played, with the Giants beating the Red Sox in eight games. Here, a Giants hurler—probably Jeff Tesreau—pitches in Game 4. This version of the Polo Grounds was noted for its intricate terra cotta frieze, the upper tier of which contained coats of arms for all eight National League teams. The frieze was removed during renovations in 1923.

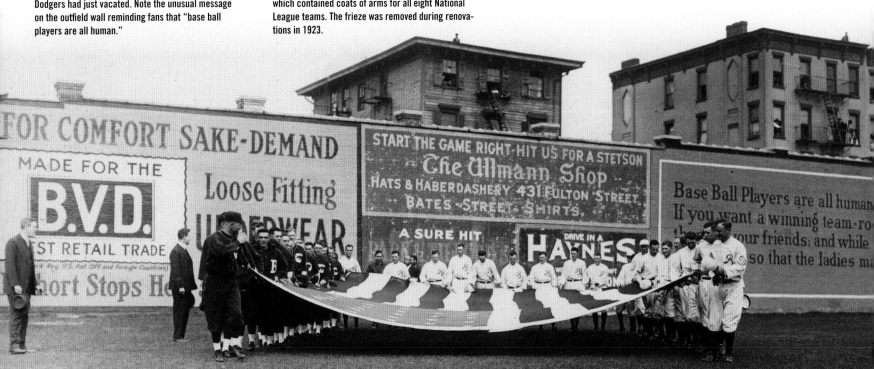

POLO GROUNDS

NEW YORK GIANTS 1889–1957   NEW YORK YANKEES 1913–1922
NEW YORK METS 1962–1963

WHEN THEY HEAR THE WORDS *Polo Grounds,* most people think of the massive horseshoe-shaped stadium where Willie Mays made his famous catch in the 1954 World Series. But that Polo Grounds was actually the last of five different major league ballparks known by that moniker. The final three of these were all built on the famous site at Coogan's Bluff alongside the Harlem River that we think of as "the Polo Grounds" today. But the first two versions of the Polo Grounds were located some forty blocks south, at 5th Avenue and 110th Street. They were built right next to each other, with Polo Grounds I in the southeast corner of the property and Polo Grounds II in the southwest corner.

Polo Grounds I, built in 1880, housed the team that eventually became the Giants, while Polo Grounds II was erected hastily in 1883 for a short-lived team called the New York Metropolitans. Polo Grounds II was one of the worst parks ever constructed, built by using raw garbage as landfill to level the playing surface, and it hosted only thirteen major league games before its much-deserved demise. Polo Grounds I, on the other hand, was a good ballpark, although it lacked outfield fences, and hard-hit balls sometimes bounded past the outfield and onto the other playing field. (Polo Grounds I, incidentally, was the only version of the Polo Grounds where polo was actually played; it had previously been the home of the Westchester Polo Association.)

In 1889, the Giants were kicked out of Polo Grounds I when city officials decided to build a street through the property. The club moved uptown to Harlem, securing a site at 157th Street and Harlem River Drive, in the shadow of a 175-foot-tall rocky outcropping called Coogan's

TOP: Polo Grounds I is festooned with bunting as the New York Giants (at right, wearing fancy collared jerseys) pose with their opponents, the Boston Beaneaters, on Opening Day in 1886. This image is historically significant because it's the earliest known photograph of a human being giving the middle finger salute. Boston's Charley Radbourn, the mischievous pitcher known as "Old Hoss," can be seen at top left slyly flipping off the photographer. This wasn't the only time he did it, either; Radbourn is also shown flipping the bird on his 1887 Old Judge baseball card.

MIDDLE LEFT: No two men were more beloved at the Polo Grounds than manager John McGraw (left) and pitcher Christy Mathewson, who are shown here in the special black uniforms the Giants wore during the 1911 World Series. They were an odd couple—McGraw was known for his frequent brawls and profane vocabulary, while the straitlaced Mathewson was nicknamed "The Christian Gentleman"—but the two became the closest of friends during their fifteen years together with the Giants.

MIDDLE RIGHT: A group of forty-four jubilant Giants fans—forty-three men and one woman—root for the home team on Opening Day 1911 at Polo Grounds IV. Unfortunately, about thirty-six hours after this photo was taken, a fire started underneath the grandstand and burned the twenty-one-year-old ballpark to the ground in just eighty minutes. The Giants immediately began construction on Polo Grounds V, which opened just seventy-five days later.

BOTTOM: A capacity crowd at the Polo Grounds watches Philadelphia's Chief Bender pitch against the Giants in Game 5 of the 1905 World Series. Christy Mathewson threw a shutout in this game to clinch the championship for New York. Overflow fans can be seen everywhere: on the outfield grass, on tops of fences and poles, and lining the streets and ledges of Coogan's Bluff behind the ballpark. In the outfield, policemen are mounted on both horses and special white observation poles. This was the era when the automobile was in the process of replacing the horse and carriage, and both methods of transportation can be seen parked behind the outfield fence.

Bluff. This location, too, housed two major league diamonds adjacent to one another. On the southern end of the property was Polo Grounds III, home to both the Giants and the Brooklyn Gladiators, a franchise that went belly-up after just ninety-nine games. On the northern end of the property was a much nicer ballpark, Polo Grounds IV, which was built by the New York team in the Players' League, an upstart league that began as a labor protest by MLB players unhappy with their salaries. The Players' League quickly folded, though, and the Giants jumped at the chance to move next door to the now-vacant Polo Grounds IV.

It was with their 1891 move to Polo Grounds IV that the Giants finally found a long-term home. They would play on the same diamond at the same location for the next sixty-six years, establishing themselves as one of the most accomplished franchises in the game. Polo Grounds IV was a simple, well-built wooden ballpark, with the grandstand sporting an upper deck between first and third bases. Its most distinctive feature was its oddly elongated shape, necessary because the park was squeezed in between the Harlem River to the east, Coogan's Bluff to the west, and Polo Grounds III to the south. The stands were shaped like a horseshoe and the playing field like a racetrack, with the

TOP: Giants catcher Roger Bresnahan is shown at the Polo Grounds in 1908 wearing an item he'd just recently invented: catchers' shin guards. In 1907, after a rough collision at home plate, Bresnahan began wearing the shin guards seen here, which were modeled after the pads worn by cricketers. One player in the league—Pittsburgh's Fred Clarke, who, coincidentally, is the batter in this photo—strenuously objected to Bresnahan's invention, arguing that the shin guards posed a danger to sliding baserunners. Clarke lost his argument, and shin guards have been a part of baseball ever since.

BOTTOM: Polo Grounds IV as seen from the lower slopes of Coogan's Bluff in 1909. (The higher up you climbed on the bluff, the better your view of the playing field got.) The leafless trees, as well as the whitewashed outfield walls awaiting new advertisements, indicate that this photo was taken during the off-season. The Polo Grounds was notable for how close it was to the elevated subway tracks; the four subway cars visible behind the left field bleachers appear to be only about thirty feet away from the outfield grass. Meanwhile, the Macomb's Dam Bridge, built over the Harlem River in 1895, can be seen behind left-center field.

center field fence located an astounding 500 feet from home plate. Behind this fence was a dusty lot where well-heeled fans could park their horses and carriages.

One early morning in April 1911, Polo Grounds IV burned to the ground, with only the outfield bleachers left standing. Giants owner John T. Brush vowed to rebuild it bigger and better, this time using fireproof steel and concrete. By June, the Giants were back using their field as the construction of Polo Grounds V proceeded around them. When finished, it was a crown jewel, highlighted by a distinctive frieze ringing the grandstand roof, which displayed bas-relief coats of arms for all eight National League teams. Polo Grounds V held 32,000 fans, making it the biggest ballpark in the sport when built, and the addition of outfield bleachers in 1923 raised the capacity to 55,000.

The Polo Grounds clubhouses, unusually, were located in a large building that formed part of the center field fence. In 1951, Giants players famously stole signs by peering through the windows of this building with binoculars, allowing them to cheat their way to the National League pennant. As with the earlier version of the ballpark, the center field wall remained impossibly far away—so far away, in fact, that a gravestone-size monument to World War I hero Eddie Grant was actually built on the playing field in deep center, where it posed few risks because fly balls almost never traveled that far. The left and right field walls, by contrast, were unusually close to home plate—which was great news for Babe Ruth, who hit 75 home runs here during the three seasons it was his home ballpark. (The Yankees were tenants at the Polo Grounds from 1913 through 1922, when Yankee Stadium was completed.) It was also the short left field porch that enabled Bobby Thomson to hit "The Shot Heard 'Round the World," one of the most famous homers in baseball history, in 1951.

During the years they called Coogan's Bluff home, the Giants won fourteen pennants and five World Series, and employed such memorable personalities as Christy Mathewson, John McGraw, and Willie Mays. By the 1950s, though, white fans were less willing to venture

into Harlem for games, and owner Horace Stoneham decided to move the team to California. In 1962, an expansion team, the New York Mets, was created, and used the Polo Grounds as a temporary refuge while their own stadium was being constructed in Queens. In their first season the Mets lost 120 games, a modern record. They moved out in 1963, and a few months later, the Polo Grounds were razed to make way for public housing.

Although the old ballpark at Coogan's Bluff is long gone, a small piece of it blossomed anew in the twenty-first century. The John T. Brush Stairway—built in 1913 and named after the former team owner—once allowed fans to climb from the Polo Grounds home plate entrance at Harlem River Driveway all the way to the top of Coogan's Bluff, from where they could take in a panoramic view of the Polo

Grounds, Yankee Stadium, and the Harlem River. During sold-out Giants games, the perch at the top of the steps filled up with fans seeking a distant view of the action. After the stadium was torn down, the existence of the staircase was all but forgotten, and it fell into extreme disrepair. In 2008, though, a *New York Daily News* editorial urged the city's parks department to restore the historic staircase, which was now part of Highbridge Park. Donations were received from all five pro sports teams that once called the Polo Grounds home—the San Francisco Giants, plus the New York Yankees, Mets, Jets, and football Giants—and in 2015 the renovated Brush Stairway was reopened to the public. These days the eighty steps don't really lead anywhere, but they do offer nostalgic fans an opportunity to literally walk in the footsteps of baseball history.

OPPOSITE PAGE: Willie Mays races back to make what many thought an impossible catch in Game 1 of the 1954 World Series. The distance marker painted on the wall in deepest center field read 483 feet, so Vic Wertz's drive probably traveled about 450 feet before dropping into Mays's glove for an out. The play happened with two runners on base, so the catch played a huge role in New York's eventual 5-2 win. This image also shows a well-known Polo Grounds landmark, the gravestone-like marker on the field of play honoring Eddie Grant, a former Giants infielder who died while rescuing soldiers under his command in the Argonne Forest during World War I. The building behind the Grant monument, meanwhile, housed the home and visiting clubhouses. It was from these windows that the Giants conducted the infamous sign-stealing operation that helped them win the 1951 pennant.

THIS PAGE: Willie Mays hangs around the Polo Grounds batting cage with his teammates. During his early years with the Giants, Mays lived at 155th Street and St. Nicholas Place, just two blocks away from the Polo Grounds, where he played impromptu stickball games with the neighborhood kids. "Every morning, kids would knock on my window," he told *GQ.* "I had to go out and play with them before I went to the ballpark in the morning. Then, in the afternoon, I would sleep a little bit and they would knock on my door. So I would come out and play with them at four to around five.... We had a car for first base, a car for second base, and then a building for third base. If you hit it over the building, you were out. [Afterward], everybody that played with me and played in that area went to a drugstore on the corner. I bought everybody ice cream. It was a joy to have all the kids come around."

TOP: New York baseball's past and future are both visible in this 1962 image of the Polo Grounds taken from Coogan's Bluff. As the snowbound Polo Grounds prepares to host its final season of baseball, the fan in the foreground is holding a game program featuring a picture of Shea Stadium, the new ballpark that would open in Queens in 1964. During the early sixties, the hapless Mets were the worst and most chaotic team imaginable. "The Mets were almost like a zoo, with players coming and going," outfielder Elijah "Pumpsie" Green said. "If you got three hits you played the next game; if you didn't, you were gone."

BOTTOM: The New York Mets (right) and Pittsburgh Pirates watch as a marching band plays before the Mets' first-ever home opener on April 13, 1962. Notables visible here include manager Casey Stengel (No. 37 for the Mets), third baseman Don Zimmer (No. 17 for the Mets), and outfielder Roberto Clemente (No. 21 for the Pirates). New York's new franchise got off to an inauspicious start, as only 12,000 fans showed up for the first home game. The Mets lost this game, 4-3, as well as 119 others to set a modern record for most losses in a season.

OPPOSITE PAGE: A large Opening Day crowd watches the first pitch of the 1909 home season at Hilltop Park, with Otis Clymer batting for Washington and Red Kleinow catching for the New York Highlanders. Note that Kleinow isn't wearing shin guards, but he is wearing the Yankees' iconic "NY" logo on his sleeve. Although the team wouldn't be renamed the Yankees until 1913, and wouldn't start wearing pinstripes until 1915, they began using the classic logo with interlocking letters in 1909. This was the first home game they ever played wearing the logo.

HILLTOP PARK
NEW YORK HIGHLANDERS 1903–1912

IN THE EARLY 1900S THE UPSTART American League sought to place a team in Manhattan to compete with the National League's powerful New York Giants, but they faced a tough problem: Almost every empty lot where a ballpark could be built was owned by the real estate mogul Andrew Freedman, who also owned the Giants. This issue was finally solved when the infamous Tammany Hall political machine agreed to finance the construction of a ballpark in the Washington Heights neighborhood—as long as ownership of the new team was awarded to one of Tammany's bigwigs, Joseph Gordon. Thus was born Hilltop Park and its featured tenant, the New York Highlanders.

The chosen site at 168th and Broadway was a sketchy one. Located on a hill that was supposedly the highest point in Manhattan, the empty lot was rocky and uneven, and was a fifty-minute train ride from downtown. Many fans, therefore, arrived using their own transportation, and the fenced-in grounds included a parking lot for horses, carriages, and newfangled automobiles. Capacity was a robust 16,000, but attendance was hampered by the penny-pinching ways of Tammany officials, who spent only $75,000 to build the rickety ballpark. The Highlanders nearly won a pennant in 1904, but in the most famous game ever played at Hilltop Park, New York's star pitcher, Jack Chesbro, uncorked a ninth-inning wild pitch on the last day of the season that gave the flag to Boston.

By 1912 Hilltop Park was already sliding into disrepair, and the team moved to the humongous new Polo Grounds in 1913, renaming themselves the Yankees in the process. The former site of Hilltop Park has been occupied by Columbia-Presbyterian Hospital since 1925.

TOP: Members of the New York Highlanders (in dark caps) and Philadelphia Athletics (in white caps) relax in the outfield during Opening Day ceremonies at Hilltop Park in 1909. At far right is Albert "Chief" Bender, the Ojibwe pitcher who won 212 games in his Hall of Fame career. Another Hall of Famer in the shot is "Wee Willie" Keeler, owner of the second-longest hitting streak in baseball history at 45 games. He's sitting with his mouth open under the letter *i* in *White Rock*.

BOTTOM: A bustling crowd gathers outside Hilltop Park in 1912 as a cigar-chomping man whizzes by in his car. Among the crowd are two ladies wearing fancy hats, two policemen with nightsticks, and a youngster in short pants carrying a catcher's mitt. Signs on the wall advertise grandstand seats for 75¢, general admission for 50¢, and bleacher seats for a quarter. Although the park's exterior seems to be in good repair here, this would be the last season Hilltop Park was used for major league baseball.

OPPOSITE PAGE: "The marble rotunda was the main entrance to Ebbets Field, and on a busy ballday was like getting into a merry-go-round," Brooklyn fan Bill Reddy told the author Peter Golenbock. "The ticket sellers stood behind gilded cages like circus boxes. People would be pushing and shoving, trying to figure out which gate to go through, which ticket seller had the best seats left."

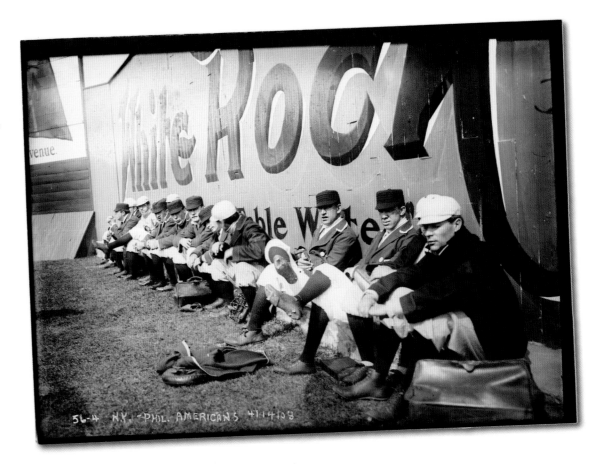

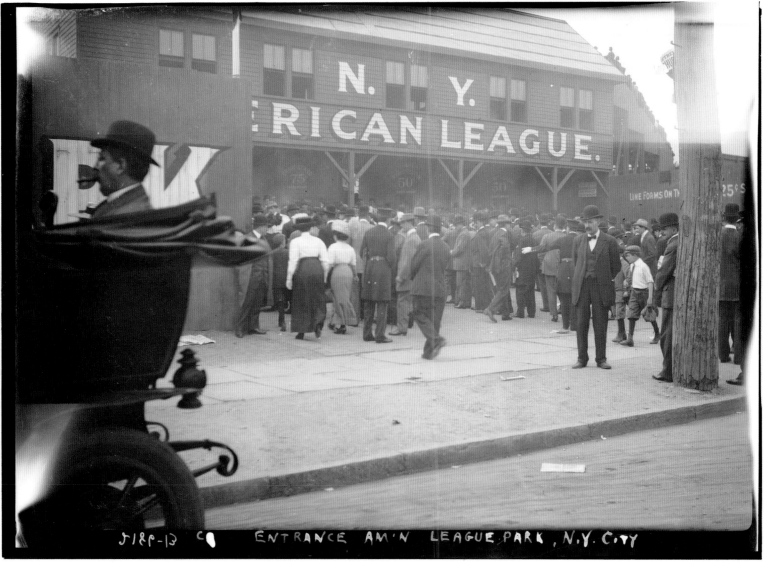

EBBETS FIELD

BROOKLYN DODGERS 1913–1957

ARGUABLY THE MOST BELOVED ballpark in baseball history, Ebbets Field was the home of the famously bumbling Brooklyn Dodgers for three decades before the team finally came of age in the 1940s and blossomed into a great dynasty. Although the little ballpark in Flatbush was used for only forty-five seasons—far fewer than the Dodgers have played at Dodger Stadium—it became baseball's most potent example of a ballpark becoming a living part of a vital community. More than a half century after its demise, Ebbets Field remains a cherished part of the sport's collective memory.

During the 1910s, the Dodgers were battling with the Yankees to become New York's second-best baseball team. (The Giants, with four pennants during the decade, were the clear number one.) With the Giants moving into the spectacular new Polo Grounds in 1911 and the Yankees doing the same the following year, the Dodgers were at risk of fading into irrelevance if they continued to play at their provincial home field, Washington Park. In 1912, the Dodgers had drawn an average of just 3,197 fans per game to the ramshackle old ballpark in Brooklyn's Park Slope neighborhood. Their clubhouse was so old it had literally served as George Washington's headquarters during a Revolutionary War battle.

The Dodgers clearly needed a new stadium, and they were in good position to build one, given that team owner Charles Ebbets was a former architect. Ebbets had abandoned that profession to make a go of it in baseball, hiring on with the Dodgers as a clerk in 1883, when

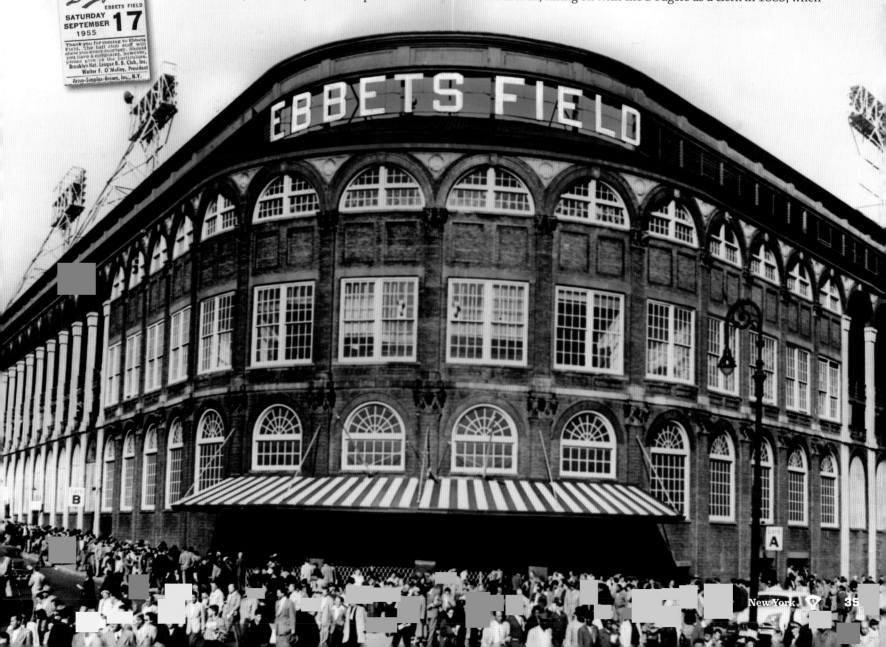

TOP: A group of enthusiastic Dodger fans—some of whom had traveled hundreds of miles to be there—share a pot of coffee outside Ebbets Field after Game 4 of the 1949 World Series. One young Dodger fan, Ray Natiello, recalled that Ebbets Field was sometimes bitterly cold. "It was very cold—so cold that I think it was the first time I had a cup of coffee," Natiello told author John Zinn. "The neighbor who took me was embarrassed buying a young boy coffee, but I needed it to keep out the chill."

BOTTOM: Taken the same day as the photo above it, this image shows Don Newcombe delivering a pitch during Game 4 of the 1949 World Series. The Yankees' Tommy Henrich is about to single to right field, sending baserunner Phil Rizzuto to third. This shot shows Ebbets Field's famous right field wall in all its eccentric glory, although the right fielder pictured is not Carl Furillo but Gene Hermanski, who was replacing the injured Furillo. This was the first World Series to be televised nationally, with the broadcast playing in forty-five markets. The TV cameras can be seen hanging from the underside of the upper deck.

OPPOSITE PAGE: A capacity crowd packs Ebbets Field for a night game in August 1939. The lights were still a novelty at this point, as the Dodgers had installed them just a year earlier. "As they piled into the tiny ballpark that chilly, damp night, they speculated on how the lights would affect the players and what the cool night breezes would do to a pitcher's sensitive arm," *Sports Illustrated* wrote of Ebbets' first night game. It turned out that the lights didn't hamper the pitchers at all, as Cincinnati's Johnny Vander Meer pitched a no-hitter in that first night game. A few days after this photo was taken, Ebbets Field would witness another historic moment: It hosted the first televised game in baseball history on August 26, 1939.

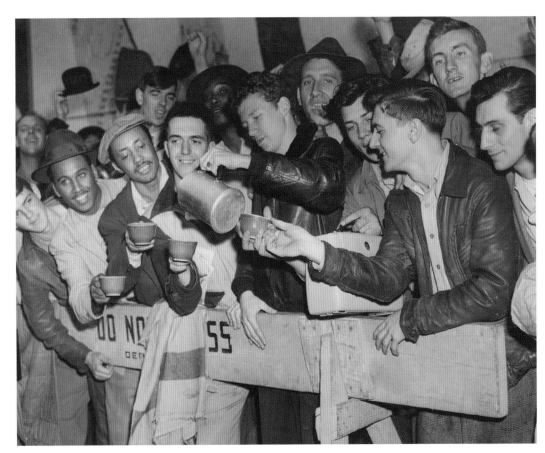

they were still a minor league franchise. Now, having risen through the ranks and bought the club himself, he set his sights on a spectacular new stadium. He decided to build it on top of a garbage dump in a neighborhood known as Pigtown, selecting this inauspicious-sounding property because it was near nine trolley lines. The new ballpark would be reachable in forty-five minutes or less from any location in New York City. Over a period of thirty-nine months beginning in 1908, Ebbets quietly purchased individual parcels of land until he accumulated 4.5 acres, enough to build the concrete and steel masterpiece that would soon be known as Ebbets Field.

In an era of shockingly rapid construction, Ebbets Field was notable for the unusual amount of time and planning that went into it. Work began in March 1912 and took a leisurely thirteen months. (Contrast this with the Polo Grounds, which opened a mere two months after its construction began.) Ebbets wanted to make sure he got it right, so he and architect Clarence Van Buskirk took a cross-country train trip to visit the best of the nation's new steel and concrete ballparks. They picked up ideas at Forbes Field, Redland Field, Comiskey Park, and Sportsman's Park before taking a look at the Polo Grounds across town. "The team took something away from each ballpark," the New York historian Suzanne Spellen wrote. "Charlie Ebbets was elated. His stadium would have the best of the other major stadiums, and would be better than all of them."

The stadium project took a mighty toll on its architect, however. Van Buskirk suffered a nervous breakdown after his railroad tour with Ebbets. During Ebbets Field's construction, Van Buskirk's father died and his wife left him. Soon afterward, his business partner sued him for allegedly taking illicit payments from Ebbets under the table. He never designed another notable building after Ebbets Field.

But the stadium he had built was glorious. It wasn't perfect—Van Buskirk had forgotten to build a press box, for one thing—but it was exactly the baseball paradise Charles Ebbets had been pining for. Its exterior was distinguished by dozens of Roman arches, with *Ebbets Field* spelled out in giant block letters atop the façade. Just inside the main entrance was a classical rotunda 27 feet tall, with a chandelier made of a dozen baseball bats. A double-decked grandstand brought the ballpark's capacity to 25,000 fans, whose transit needs were easily accommodated. Not only was Ebbets Field near many streetcar lines, but it was also the first ballpark built with dedicated parking garages. It also laid claim to some other notable firsts. It was the first ballpark to issue rain checks for postponed games. In 1948, in an effort to protect the oft-injured outfielder Pete Reiser, Ebbets became the first ballpark with padded walls and a warning track in the outfield. And it was the Ebbets Field faithful who created Stan "The Man" Musial's famous nickname, groaning "Here comes the man again!" whenever their famed nemesis came to bat.

Like most parks of its era, Ebbets Field's unusual dimensions were dictated by its surroundings. The left field fence was 419 feet away from home plate, but the right field distance was only 301. That short porch tapered away quickly, however, as the right-center field power alley was a mind-blowing 501 feet away. The spacious dimensions would be shortened in later years, turning Ebbets Field into a power-hitting haven for the lefty slugger Duke Snider, as well as right-handers Gil Hodges, Roy Campanella, and Jackie Robinson.

Among Ebbets Field's unique features was its bizarre—and iconic—right field wall. A slapdash hodgepodge of concrete, metal, plywood, and chicken wire, the wall was famous for its unpredictable ricochets. It was a nightmare for every right fielder in the league except Brooklyn's remarkable Carl Furillo, who made the study of its eccentricities his life's work. "That wall, a mystery of dead spots, bounces, angles, and planes, was a wonder of baseball," wrote Roger Kahn, who covered the Dodgers for the *New York Herald Tribune*. "Plane geometry remained a mystery to [Furillo]. But he knew every angle, every carom. The way Furillo played the wall describes an art form."

The right field wall also contained two iconic advertisements. The scoreboard featured an ad for Schaefer Beer in which the *H* and *E* lit up to let fans know whether a play had been ruled a hit or an error. Even more famous was the ad for Abe Stark, a local clothier, which enticed batters with the slogan "Hit Sign, Win Suit." The sign went up in 1931, and it wasn't until 1937 that someone actually hit it. "That was almost impossible to hit because it was so low to the ground," slugger Ralph Kiner later remembered. "And Carl Furillo would stand in front of it and make it nearly impossible to hit, and we would always joke that Furillo should get a suit because of that." Legend has it that Furillo actually received three suits from Stark—one for preventing fly balls from hitting the sign and two more for hitting it himself.

During its first few decades, Ebbets Field was known for the comical ineptitude of the home team, featuring such lovable losers as

OPPOSITE PAGE: Jackie Robinson runs the bases at Ebbets Field in 1956, his final season in the majors. Although he batted just .275 that year, he remained one of the most respected and feared players in the game. "Jackie Robinson was a helluva player even in 1956, his last season," Braves pitcher Bob Buhl said. "He still gave 110 percent all the time and would do anything to beat you…. He was a team player and we thought he was the leader of the Dodgers."

TOP: As fans arrive early for the game, the 1952 Dodgers pose for a team photo at Ebbets Field. This team would come painfully close to winning the World Series, losing Game 7 to the Yankees in a 4-2 nailbiter. Notable players include Duke Snider (second row, far left), Roy Campanella (fourth row, second from left), Gil Hodges (fourth row, third from left), Pee Wee Reese (third row, third from left), and Don Newcombe (third row, fourth from left). Jackie Robinson was at the center of the team both literally and figuratively; he's in the middle of the third row.

BOTTOM LEFT: Rachel Robinson (center) roots for her husband, Jackie, during Game 7 of the 1952 World Series at Ebbets Field. Sitting next to her, wearing sunglasses, is her friend Caroline Wallerstein. Rachel was a constant presence in the stands throughout Jackie's career, and was often treated savagely by crowds on the road. "I sat through name calling, jeers, and vicious baiting in a furious silence," she wrote in her memoir. "My only response was to sit up very straight, as if my back could absorb the nefarious outbursts and prevent them from reaching him." Rachel, a registered nurse, had first met Jackie in 1940.

BOTTOM RIGHT: The lovably eccentric Casey Stengel was a Dodgers outfielder from 1912 to '17 and the team's manager from 1934 to '36. In 1919, after being traded to Pittsburgh, Stengel pulled a memorable stunt during a return to Ebbets Field. After receiving the usual mixture of boos and cheers a player might expect at his former ballpark, Stengel ostentatiously bowed and doffed his cap—at which point a live sparrow flew out from underneath it.

Casey Stengel and Babe Herman. (In one apocryphal tale, a fan was leaving Ebbets Field and a cab driver asked him how the game was going. The fan said the Dodgers had three men on base. Replied the cabbie: "Which base?") But in the 1940s, two brilliant executives—first Larry MacPhail, then Branch Rickey—transformed the Dodgers into a baseball powerhouse. MacPhail built a pennant winner in 1941 and also hired the beloved broadcaster Red Barber, who did more than anyone to make Ebbets Field an integral part of Brooklyn's cultural identity. Rickey, of course, brought Jackie Robinson to the Dodgers in 1947, breaking the color line that had plagued MLB for sixty-three years. With Robinson serving as the engine driving the machine, the Dodgers won six pennants in ten seasons from 1947 through 1956, including their memorable World Series triumph in 1955. "The sense of cohesion and joy on the field and in the clubhouse was reflected in the stands of Ebbets Field," Robinson's widow, Rachel, later wrote.

Moreso than any other sports franchise in America, the Brooklyn Dodgers were deeply intertwined with their community. The players mostly lived in the neighborhood; it wasn't unusual to run into a Dodger while you were out grocery shopping or pumping gas. The small dimensions and lack of foul territory meant fans at Ebbets were closer to the action, giving the park an intimacy unmatched elsewhere. Brooklyn fans were louder, rowdier, and—most of the time—more supportive than any other fans in baseball. A number of fans became famous themselves. There was Hilda Chester, with her famed cowbell and booming voice. There was Happy Felton, the vaudeville personality who filmed his *Knothole Gang* TV show on the field before games. Entertainment was provided by the musically inept Dodger Sym-Phony Band ("with the emphasis on *phony*," as Red Barber always said). These and thousands of other personalities brought a vibrancy to Ebbets Field that was unique in baseball. That made it all the more painful when the Dodgers moved away in 1957, abandoning the by-then dilapidated and outdated ballpark for the greener pastures of Los Angeles.

TOP: Three young Brooklyn fans cheer on their beloved Dodgers at Ebbets Field before Game 4 of the 1949 World Series. "In 1949, when [Branch] Rickey looked at the Dodger roster, he said, 'This is the best team I have ever been associated with,'" Peter Golenbock wrote in *Bums*. Nevertheless, the Dodgers lost the World Series to the Yankees in five games. They had also lost to New York in 1941 and '47, and would do so again in 1952, '53, and '56.

BOTTOM: The Dodgers Sym-Phony Band was a fixture in Section 8 of Ebbets Field, right behind the Dodgers' first base dugout. They weren't professional musicians or even competent amateurs; the six members included a grocer, a paper cutter, a maintenance man, a beer distributor, and two truck drivers. What they lacked in musical talent they made up for in enthusiasm. They were known for, among other things, playing "Three Blind Mice" whenever the umpires missed a call.

DYCKMAN OVAL

CUBAN STARS 1920-1932   NEW YORK CUBANS 1935-1936

DYCKMAN OVAL, IDENTIFIED AS "the Negro Leagues' nicest stadium" by historian Philip Lowry, began as a modest ballfield inside Manhattan's Inwood Hill Park in 1920. It was the home of the Cuban Stars, a Negro National League team owned by Alejandro Pompez, a Cuban-born numbers runner who became one of the key figures in African-American baseball. Pompez drew thousands to Stars games by scheduling pregame concerts by such luminaries as Louis Armstrong, Cab Calloway, and Count Basie. (He also leased out the Oval for other sports; a billboard on the outside wall read *Field For Rent: Baseball – Boxing – Wrestling – Football – Soccer.)* But Dyckman Oval's heyday turned out to be regrettably brief.

In 1936 Pompez fled the country to escape a racketeering indictment, and two years later Dyckman Oval was torn down by the city government. Despite his criminal record, the African-American community remained grateful to Pompez for building a place they viewed as an oasis of baseball. "He has sacrificed time and money to build up Negro baseball in New York and to give his teams a home ground," the *New York Age* wrote in 1938. With Yankee Stadium usually off limits to Negro League teams, promoters of African-American baseball in New York often had to scramble to find adequate places to play. The ambitious Pompez eventually transformed Dyckman Oval into "Harlem's amusement park," as one historian put it. He built enough seats for 4,600 fans, added a beer garden, and in 1930 he installed lights, making Dyckman one of the nation's first ballparks to host night baseball.

TOP: Although not all members of the Cuban Stars were actually Cuban, Martín Dihigo was one who fit the description. Nicknamed "El Inmortal" ("The Immortal"), he's still widely considered the best ballplayer ever born in Cuba. Dihigo came to New York as a seventeen-year-old in 1923, and he astonished fans at Dyckman Oval with his ability to expertly play eight of the nine positions on the field—all except catcher. "Dihigo was just a big old kid," teammate Frank Duncan recalled. "Got along with everybody, full of fun all the time."

MIDDLE: Dyckman Oval as it appeared in 1919, several years before Alejandro Pompez renovated it into one of Negro League baseball's premier stadiums. The Treat 'Em Rough Baseball Club was a team of ex–major leaguers who played several exhibition games against Negro League teams at Dyckman Oval in 1919. The team's name came from a military magazine, *Treat 'Em Rough,* that was published by the team's owner. Note the message on the wall promising to donate game proceeds toward artificial limbs for World War I veterans.

BOTTOM LEFT: Dyckman Oval was torn down in 1938 while its owner, Alejandro Pompez, was mired in legal troubles. By the time this photo of New York Cubans outfielder Lorenzo Cabrera was taken in the late 1940s, the team was playing at a variety of other local ballparks, including Yankee Stadium.

BOTTOM RIGHT: Dyckman Oval drew African-American and Latino fans in almost equal numbers during the 1930s, and its prestige was bolstered by the frequent presence of celebrities in the crowd. "Dyckman Oval is rapidly gaining the right to the title of Manhattan's amusement center," Lewis Dial wrote in the *New York Age.* "Every branch of sports from races to cricket have been exhibited at Pompez's beautiful miniature stadium."

YANKEE STADIUM

NEW YORK YANKEES 1923-1973, 1976-2008

NO STADIUM IN BASEBALL HISTORY has ever been as closely associated with one player as Yankee Stadium has with Babe Ruth. Although the ballpark bore witness to extraordinary feats by Lou Gehrig, Joe DiMaggio, Mickey Mantle, Derek Jeter, and other legends, it was known as "The House That Ruth Built" throughout its eighty-four years of use. This is somewhat ironic given that Ruth actually posted his best seasons while playing at Fenway Park (1918) and the Polo Grounds (1920 and '21). But the need for a venue to properly showcase The Bambino's exploits did lead directly to the building of Yankee Stadium, and no other player ever dominated the proceedings there quite like Ruth did.

The Yankees were tenants of the Giants at the Polo Grounds from 1913 through 1922. During the teens the Yanks were also-rans, and the Giants were happy to accept their $65,000 annual rent payment. But when Ruth arrived in 1920 and the Yankees began outdrawing their landlords, the Giants soon evicted them. "To boot, the Giants were annoyed by the loud, unmannered class of followers the Yankees attracted," the journalist Bob Klapisch wrote. In 1922, Yankees owner Jacob Ruppert purchased a lumberyard in the Bronx from the Astor family for $675,000. The property provided not only a great locale for a stadium, but also an opportunity to needle the rival Giants, since it was just across the Harlem River from the Polo Grounds.

Ruppert hired Osborn Engineering of Cleveland to design the stadium. Over a nine-month period, 3 million board feet of lumber, 20,000 tons of concrete, and 3,100 tons of steel were put to use building what was, at the time, the largest sports stadium ever constructed. In fact, Yankee Stadium was the first baseball facility to even be called a stadium, a word borrowed from the grand sports palaces of ancient Greece and Rome. Among Yankee Stadium's unique features was a 15-foot-deep underground vault directly beneath second base. This hidden room housed telegraph, telephone, and electrical wiring, and allowed the stadium to easily be refitted to host such events as boxing matches.

TOP: Babe Ruth (right) and Lou Gehrig yuk it up in the Yankee dugout during a road game. Ruth hit 259 career home runs at Yankee Stadium, the second-most of any player, while Gehrig's 251 ranked third. (Mickey Mantle is the leader with 266.) Teammates for a dozen years, Ruth and Gehrig were the best of friends until 1934, when Gehrig began to suspect his wife, Eleanor, of infidelity during an all-star trip to Japan. "When he found his bride, half drunk, talking with Ruth in Ruth's stateroom on the *Empress of Japan*, the barrier between the two Yankees stars grew insurmountable," Leigh Montville wrote in *The Big Bam: The Life and Times of Babe Ruth*. The two stars didn't reconcile until 1939, when Gehrig was dying of amyotrophic lateral sclerosis.

BOTTOM: Yankee Stadium as it appeared during the 1927 World Series, with Babe Ruth visible in the foreground playing right field. The fearsome Yankees batted .308 as a team in 1927, and their 158 home runs were nearly triple the total of the next-best team in the league. "The New York Yankees and their practically hopeless adversaries came to town today to continue the one-sided World Series of 1927," the *Pittsburgh Post-Gazette* wrote before Game 3 at Yankee Stadium. Games 3 and 4 weren't any better for the Pirates, as the Yankees completed a four-game sweep and outscored them 23-10.

TOP: Fans watch intently during a Negro League game at Yankee Stadium during the 1930s or early '40s. The ballpark was off-limits to African-American baseball until 1930, when the ban ended thanks in part to the friendship between Babe Ruth and John Henry Lloyd, the first baseman and manager of the New York Lincoln Giants. "Lloyd and Babe are great friends and often discuss close plays during the progress of the game," journalist Alvin Moses wrote in *Abbott's Monthly* in 1933. Though the details are murky, Ruth's influence was likely a factor in Lloyd's Lincoln Giants becoming the first African-American team allowed to play at Yankee Stadium. They faced the Homestead Grays in a doubleheader there on July 5, 1930, and from then on Yankee Stadium was used frequently for Negro League games.

BOTTOM: Satchel Paige warms up at Yankee Stadium on May 11, 1941, as another Hall of Fame pitcher, Pete Alexander, looks on. Paige, signed by the New York Black Yankees for this game only, arrived in town "driving a long car, squiring a pretty girl, and 'thinking about' signing a Black Yankee contract," one reporter wrote. Paige's appearance drew a crowd of more than 20,000—a higher attendance than eight of the nine MLB games played that day—and Mayor Fiorello La Guardia threw out the first pitch. Paige pitched a complete game victory over the Philadelphia Stars, limiting them to five hits.

OPPOSITE PAGE: Mickey Mantle takes a massive swing at Yankee Stadium. The handsome blond switch-hitter took over Joe DiMaggio's center field job in 1952, and his stupendous power hitting made him an immediate fan favorite. "The excitement surrounding Mantle goes beyond numbers," Robert Creamer wrote in *Sports Illustrated* in 1956. "Like Ruth, his violent strength is held in a sheath of powerful, controlled grace. Like Ruth, he makes home run hitting simple and exciting at the same time."

Yankee Stadium's exterior featured various bas-relief designs in the terra cotta, including a distinctive seal featuring an eagle clutching baseball bats. Inside, the signature visual element was a 15-foot-tall decorative frieze (often incorrectly called a façade) spanning the grandstand roof from foul pole to foul pole. The copper frieze, which unfortunately turned green soon after it was erected, seemed to evoke some Greek or Roman past but was actually devised from scratch. "The shape of it came from out of nowhere," architectural critic John Pastier told the *New York Times*. "It was quite original. It's not like they copied a classic design."

Workers were still busy putting the finishing touches on Yankee Stadium when it hosted its first game on April 23, 1923, before a then–major league record 74,200 fans. The stadium's first home run, appropriately, was hit by Babe Ruth, a three-run shot that provided the winning margin in the Yankees' victory over the Red Sox. Over the final dozen seasons of his Yankee career, Ruth would bat .349 with 259

home runs at The House That Ruth Built. "Actually, it would've been more accurate to say Yankee Stadium was 'The House Built for Ruth' thanks to its 295-foot dimension at the right-field foul pole," Klapisch wrote. During the stadium's first season the team drew over a million fans. The Yankees' already-considerable financial advantage over their competitors was enhanced by playing in this cash cow of a stadium, and the team would build a decades-long dynasty by reinvesting revenue in player salaries and a top-notch farm system.

The different areas of the stadium would witness countless important moments in baseball history. On the grass in deep center field, Al Gionfriddo famously robbed Joe DiMaggio of a homer in the 1947 World Series. In the left field corner, Sandy Amoros's extraordinary catch in 1955 helped the Brooklyn Dodgers clinch their first (and only) championship. In the right field stands, a teenage fan caught Roger Maris's record-breaking 61st homer in 1961. In the middle of the infield, a temporary boxing ring hosted a bevy of glamorous fights, including the historic Joe Louis–Max Schmeling bout in

TOP: Whitey Ford, "The Chairman of the Board," fires a pitch in 1963. Thanks to tremendous run support from the likes of Mickey Mantle and Yogi Berra, Ford won games at a higher rate than any pitcher in modern history. His .674 lifetime winning percentage is the best of any pitcher with at least 1,500 innings, a smidge ahead of Pedro Martinez and Clayton Kershaw.

BOTTOM LEFT: Joe DiMaggio signs autographs at Yankee Stadium during the mid-1950s, a few years after his retirement. The occasion was probably Old-Timers' Day, a Yankee Stadium tradition dating to 1948. DiMaggio attended almost every year, missing the event only once from 1952 to his death in 1999. At his request, he was always introduced as "Baseball's Greatest Living Player," though his career accomplishments paled in comparison to those of Ted Williams, Hank Aaron, Willie Mays, and Mickey Mantle.

BOTTOM RIGHT: Reggie Jackson holds court at his locker in Yankee Stadium, basking in the afterglow of the greatest game of his career. Jackson swung his bat only three times during Game 6 of the 1977 World Series, but he hit a home run on each swing, tying Babe Ruth's 51-year-old record for most homers in a Series game. "Jackson is beyond argument the top media draw in baseball," wrote one of the reporters surrounding Jackson's locker, *Sports Illustrated*'s Ron Fimrite. "The space around his cubicle after even far less consequential games looks like the site of a crap game or a rugby scrum."

OPPOSITE PAGE, TOP: Organist Eddie Layton delighted Yankee Stadium crowds with his colorful performances for thirty-eight seasons, from 1967 until his death in 2004. "It was Eddie's request that since he wasn't going to be buried near Yankee Stadium, they point his coffin away from Shea," his rabbi said.

OPPOSITE PAGE, BOTTOM: This image from September 30, 1961, provides a rare color glimpse of the pre-renovation Yankee Stadium, with its signature frieze on the roof of the upper deck. The center fielder in the middle of the photo is Roger Maris, who the following day would hit his 61st homer to break Babe Ruth's single-season record.

1936 and its rematch in 1938. The expansive foul territory behind home plate was where Babe Ruth stood in 1947 to bid an emotional farewell to Yankee fans, his voice ravaged by the throat cancer that would soon kill him. And, of course, the pitcher's mound was where Don Larsen stood in 1956 when he pitched the only perfect game in World Series history.

No event at Yankee Stadium, however, was as powerful as the ceremony honoring Lou Gehrig between games of a 1939 double-header. Two months earlier, with his motor skills mysteriously failing him, Gehrig had taken himself out of New York's lineup after a record 2,130 consecutive games. He would soon die of the rare disease that today bears his name. At the time, though, fans were unaware of the full extent of Gehrig's illness. So, for that matter, was Gehrig himself, whose wife and doctors had mostly kept him in the dark regarding his impending death. But Gehrig could read between the lines, and he knew something was terribly wrong as he stood at the microphone that July 4, reading a hastily

prepared speech scrawled on the back of an envelope. "You've been reading about a bad break," he told the crowd of 61,000. "But today, I consider myself the luckiest man on the face of the earth. I have been in ballparks for seventeen years and have never received anything but kindness and encouragement from you fans... I might have been given a bad break, but I've got an awful lot to live for." A month after his death, the Yankees placed a monument to Gehrig on the playing field in deepest center field, where it eventually became part of Monument Park, a memorial garden of sorts celebrating great Yankees of the past.

During their first forty years in the stadium, the Yankees won an astonishing twenty world championships. By the 1970s, however, the Yankees' dynasty was beginning to crumble, and so too was their ballpark. After the 1973 season, new owner George Steinbrenner somehow convinced the New York City government to buy the Yankee Stadium from him and spend $24 million to renovate it. The renovation plan was so drastic that it required the Yankees to relocate to Shea Stadium, home of the Mets, for two full seasons.

Soon after the final game of 1973, bulldozers began their work and The House That Ruth Built was no more. In its place rose a generic new stadium that possessed none of its predecessor's charm or grandeur. The Yankees' remodeled home had cozier dimensions and a smaller seating capacity, but the seats themselves were much farther away from the action, making the experience much more impersonal. The stately green seats were replaced by plastic blue ones. Most distressingly, Yankee Stadium's signature copper frieze was sold for scrap metal, replaced by a smaller, cheap-looking concrete version in the outfield.

Historian Philip Lowry called the scrapping of the frieze "a horrible architectural mistake," and the same might well be said of the entire renovation project. The Yankees insisted that the ballpark they opened in 1976 was a renovation, not an entirely new stadium, but fans could tell the difference. The new version was Yankee Stadium in name only. "I always feel sad because that's really The House That Ruth Built," Yankees pitcher Fritz Peterson said of the version torn down in 1973. "The other place, it could be anywhere."

The Yankees would play in their new McStadium for thirty-three years, enjoying almost as much on-field success there as they had at the original. It was here where Reggie Jackson hit three home runs in one game of the 1977 World Series, and where the Yankees of Joe Torre and Derek Jeter won four championships in a five-year period. An entirely new generation of Yankee fans grew up attending games here, perfectly content with the ballpark because they didn't have the original to compare it to. Finally, this version of the Yankee Stadium also began to show wear and tear, and the team threatened to move to New Jersey unless they received a new government-funded stadium. The gambit worked, and the Bronx Bombers played their final game at Yankee Stadium on September 21, 2008. 🖾

TOP: Mariano Rivera and Derek Jeter, seen here in 2003, were the mainstays of the Yankees dynasty that won seven pennants and five World Series titles between 1996 and 2009. Rivera was the team's greatest postseason weapon, posting an astounding 0.70 ERA in 141 career playoff innings while converting 42 of 47 save opportunities. "Probably not since Koufax have we seen anyone leave the game with so much respect," Joe Torre said when Rivera retired in 2013.

BOTTOM: Yankee Stadium as it appeared during its final years in the early 2000s. Unfortunately, the ballpark's one major renovation began in 1973 during the heart of the concrete bowl era, and the original Yankee Stadium was essentially torn down and rebuilt as a cookie-cutter stadium. The monuments were removed from the playing field, the copper frieze was sold and replaced with the concrete facsimile seen here, and the once-delightfully-quirky field dimensions were standardized. "We're not going to change it to some cookie-cutter ballpark like Shea Stadium," architect Perry Green said, before doing exactly that.

OPPOSITE PAGE: Shea Stadium was built on the same site in Flushing Meadows that Walter O'Malley had rejected in the mid-1950s, harrumphing that "if my team is forced to play in the borough of Queens, they will no longer be the Brooklyn Dodgers." The Mets, however, were happy to make Queens their home, and they soon began drawing a younger, more energetic crowd than the staid Yankees. "Mets fans flocked to Shea as if they were off to a neighborhood block party," write John Florio and Ouisie Shapiro in their book *One Nation Under Baseball: How the 1960s Collided with the National Pastime*. "They showed up with tambourines, hoisted flags on fishing poles, hung banners, blew trumpets, and lit firecrackers."

SHEA STADIUM
NEW YORK METS 1964–2008

FEW BALLPARKS HAVE SQUEEZED as much action into so short a lifetime as Shea Stadium. In its four and a half decades, the giant ballpark in Flushing Meadows hosted a World's Fair, a mass given by Pope John Paul II, and concerts by the Beatles, The Rolling Stones, and Billy Joel. In baseball, Shea housed the best of teams (the 1986 Mets), the worst of teams (the mid-1960s Mets), and everything in between. But it's best remembered as the backdrop for the 1969 Mets, perhaps the most lovable and unlikely World Series champion of all time.

New York had lost two-thirds of its major league teams in 1958, but it didn't take long to get one back. Mayor Robert Wagner appointed corporate lawyer Bill Shea to head a commission charged with returning the National League to New York, an effort that succeeded in 1962 when the Mets were born. While the team was playing its first two seasons at the Polo Grounds, the city built a new, $25.2 million stadium on the same site in Queens that had been rejected by the Brooklyn Dodgers a few years earlier. The ballpark's opening was timed to coincide with the 1964 World's Fair, being held in the adjacent Flushing Meadows–Corona Park. Shea Stadium would briefly house the Yankees, as well as football's Jets and Giants, but it would always be synonymous with the New York Mets.

Although it superficially resembled Dodger Stadium, Shea was outfitted with hydraulically movable stands so football teams could also play there. In an effort to differentiate themselves from the buttoned-down Yankees, the Mets made a conscious effort to imbue the ballpark experience with sound and color. A large scoreboard in right field featured a faux New York City skyline. In center field, a big apple would emerge from a top hat and light up whenever a Met homered. Mets fans were younger and more raucous than Yankees

fans, and they started a tradition of bringing homemade banners and signs to the ballpark. The circus atmosphere was augmented by brightly colored plastic seats: yellow at field level, beige in the loge, white in the club level, blue in the mezzanine, and green in the upper deck. Even the Mets' uniforms were a colorful mishmash, borrowing blue from the Dodgers, orange from the Giants, and pinstripes from the Yankees.

The fan-friendly effort worked, as the Mets outdrew the Yankees in each of Shea's first twelve years, even though the Yankees were a winning team and the Mets were usually awful. The fans didn't even mind the deafening roar of jets landing at nearby LaGuardia Airport.

When New York defeated Pittsburgh to clinch the 1973 pennant, a joyous mob rushed the field, ripped up the turf, and made off with the bases, turning the playing surface into a wasteland before the ensuing World Series. Thirteen years later, when the Mets won the 1986 World Series, a similar scene occurred. It was a small price to pay for such unbridled fan enthusiasm. Mets fans continued to flock faithfully to Shea Stadium until 2008, when the team moved into new Citi Field next door. 🌭

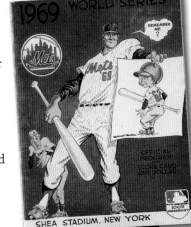

OPPOSITE PAGE: A few hours after winning the 1969 World Series, pitchers Tom Seaver (No. 41) and Gary Gentry survey the damage done by the thousands of jubilant fans who stormed the field at Shea Stadium after the game. "They immediately touched off one of the great, riotous scenes in sports history, as thousands of persons swarmed from their seats and tore up the patch of ground where the Mets had made history," Joe Durso wrote in the *New York Times*. In the aftermath, thirty-one fans were treated for injuries at the ballpark and five more were rushed to the hospital.

TOP: Twenty-year-old Dwight Gooden throws a pitch in 1985, the year he turned in one of the greatest pitching seasons of all time. Boasting an overpowering fastball and a cartoonish curve, Gooden went 24-4 with a 1.53 ERA, the best mark in the majors since 1968. "It was almost surreal, like an out-of-body experience," Gooden later said. "Every game I felt totally in control. I could put the ball where I wanted it. Before the hitter even gets in the box I've got him defeated. That was a great feeling."

MIDDLE: "Sign Man"—whose real name was Karl Ehrhardt—holds up a sign taunting Cincinnati's Pete Rose (No. 14). From 1964 through 1981 Ehrhardt was a ubiquitous presence at Shea Stadium, always toting a large bag filled with different signs. Whenever a big play happened, "he was able to reach into his bag and pull out something appropriate without missing a beat," Mets ticket manager Bob Mandt told the *New York Times*. Rose became a target of New Yorkers' ire during the 1973 playoffs when he brawled with Mets shortstop Bud Harrelson after a collision at second base.

BOTTOM: The Beatles played what became their most celebrated concert at Shea Stadium on August 15, 1965, beginning their set with "Twist and Shout" and ending it eleven songs later with "I'm Down." It was one of the first outdoor stadium concerts ever held, and it grossed $304,000, believed to be a record at the time. "There is no more famous gig in rock & roll history than when the Beatles played Shea Stadium, an orange and blue ass pit of a venue," Colin Fleming wrote in *Rolling Stone*. "Chances are if you've seen footage of a single Beatles gig, it is this one."

CITI FIELD

NEW YORK METS 2008-PRESENT

DURING THE EARLY 2000s, the Mets and Yankees convinced—or, more accurately, coerced—the New York City government to build two opulent new baseball stadiums. Neither ballpark was strictly necessary, but the new venues (and the luxury suites therein) would give the Big Apple's ball teams an economic advantage over their competitors in smaller markets. The local government contributed $614 million in cash, tax breaks, and infrastructure costs to the Mets' new home, and naming rights were sold for $400 million to the banking giant Citigroup—which was on the brink of collapse as a prime offender in the subprime mortgage crisis. The funds to name the park Citi Field came from a federal government bailout.

Its sleazy origin story notwithstanding, Citi Field was relatively well-received. There was nothing original or breathtaking about it, but it cost only half as much as the new Yankee Stadium, and was decidedly less martial and imposing. "The park has a casual feel,

with warm red brick inside, lots of amenities, great sight lines, and a layout that's easy to navigate," the *New Yorker* architecture critic Paul Goldberger wrote. "There are 42,000 seats, 15,000 fewer than Shea had, all a calm dark green and arranged in somewhat irregular tiers, bringing you much closer to the field than before."

The stadium was notable for its conscious mimicry of Ebbets Field, where Mets owner Fred Wilpon had attended many games as a child. "The Mets, having no ancient ballpark of their own to evoke, have appropriated someone else's," Goldberger quipped. Wilpon's Ebbets Field obsession made a certain amount of sense: As New York's underdog team, the Mets are the spiritual descendants of the Brooklyn Dodgers, and many older Mets fans were originally Dodgers supporters. From the outside, Citi Field is virtually an exact re-creation of Ebbets, with the same pattern of redbrick archways and windows. The right field wall also echoes Carl Furillo's famous

wall in Brooklyn. Wrapping snakelike around the bullpen while getting shorter as it nears the foul line, it presents a daunting challenge for opposing right fielders, as well as a nifty home field advantage for any Mets right fielder who learns its nuances.

Citi Field's first base entrance is named after Gil Hodges, the beloved Dodgers first baseman. The Ebbets-esque home plate entrance, meanwhile, is named The Jackie Robinson Rotunda after the Dodgers hero, who is buried only a few subway stops away. Robinson's name is inlaid in the marble and granite floor, and a giant sculpture of his number, 42, serves as the rotunda's centerpiece. Adorning the walls are quotations, photographs, and reminders of the values Robinson held dear.

OPPOSITE PAGE: Citi Field's exterior bears a remarkable resemblance to that of Ebbets Field, as can be seen by comparing this photo to the one of Ebbets on page 35. One things Ebbets Field didn't have, though, was a home run apple, the mechanized fruit that emerges from a top hat every time a Mets player homers. The apple pictured here is the original one from Shea Stadium, which was retired and placed in front of Citi Field after Shea was torn down. A newer and larger version is now in active use behind the center field wall.

TOP: The first thing fans see when they enter Citi Field is the Jackie Robinson Rotunda, which includes photos of Robinson etched into the tiles and quotes by him inscribed on the walls. "When we're not here anymore, this will be," Mets owner Fred Wilpon said at the rotunda's 2009 dedication ceremony.

BOTTOM LEFT: This sculpture of the number 42 is the centerpiece of Citi Field's Jackie Robinson Rotunda. The number was retired throughout baseball in 1997, but all players using it at the time, including Mets outfielder Butch Huskey, were allowed to wear it for the rest of their careers. The last player to wear it regularly was Mariano Rivera in 2013.

BOTTOM RIGHT: This version of the Mets logo and city skyline appears on top of Citi Field's most popular concession stand, Shake Shack. It's modeled after Shea Stadium's old scoreboard, which featured a silhouette of the Manhattan skyline. After the 9/11 attacks, the team covered the silhouette of the World Trade Center with a yellow ribbon.

THIS PAGE: This panoramic image shows Citi Field during its debut season of 2009, with Mets left-hander Johan Santana pitching to Colorado's Dexter Fowler. In 2012, seeking to give their moribund offense a boost, the Mets reduced the outfield distances seen here, bringing the left-center field wall 14 feet closer to home plate and the right-center wall 25 feet closer. Apparently that wasn't enough, as in 2015 the right-center field wall was moved another 10 feet closer. "We're talking about creating a little more excitement, a little more entertainment at the ballpark, which I think goes hand-in-hand with scoring," team president Sandy Alderson said. "That's not going to appeal to baseball purists. But we need more than baseball purists to fill the ballpark."

TOP INSET: David Wright takes a big swing at Citi Field. Wright, the Mets' all-time leader in hits, runs, RBIs, and wins above replacement, was a mainstay in New York's lineup from 2004 until 2016, when his career came to an abrupt end thirty-seven games into the season. In 2015, Wright had been diagnosed with spinal stenosis, a chronic narrowing of the spinal column. He managed to hit a dramatic home run in Game 3 of the 2015 World Series, but multiple surgeries on his back, neck, and shoulder failed to alleviate the pain, and he was reduced to spending the 2017 through 2019 seasons on the disabled list so the Mets could collect on an injury insurance policy. "You take for granted how much you enjoy it until you can't do it anymore," Wright said in 2018.

BOTTOM INSET: Mr. Met performs at Citi Field in 2010. The much-loved mascot was introduced in cartoon artwork in 1963, and the live-action version debuted at Shea Stadium the following season, making him baseball's first sentient mascot. Mr. Met has survived many trials and tribulations over the years. During the late 1970s, the Mets phased him out, replacing him with a live barnyard animal named Mettle the Mule. Mr. Met was reintroduced in 1994, but not long afterward, he was nearly assassinated by the Secret Service when he embraced President Bill Clinton a bit too enthusiastically. Perhaps most memorably, he flipped off some Mets fans in 2017, although technically he didn't use his middle finger since he only has four. During a hard day at the office—and a rough season in the standings—it seems the mascot just snapped when some hecklers went too far. "The fans were cursing at Mr. Met with the F-word and saying derogatory things about Mr. Met's mom," said a fan who witnessed the incident.

NEW YANKEE STADIUM

NEW YORK YANKEES   2009-PRESENT

AFTER FIFTY-ONE MEMORABLE YEARS in the original Yankee Stadium, and thirty-three more in the renovated version, the New York Yankees finally abandoned the House That Ruth Built in 2009. The new edition of Yankee Stadium, located right next door to where the old one once stood, is the most lavish, ambitious, and expensive ballpark ever constructed, at a cost of $1.5 billion. With a listed capacity of 52,325, it's also the second-largest ballpark in the majors after the Dodger Stadium.

In 2005, after years of threatening to move to New Jersey, Yankees owner George Steinbrenner struck a deal with mayor Michael Bloomberg for a new stadium to be financed via tax-exempt municipal bonds, and ground was broken in 2006. Yet, despite the sweetheart deal, Steinbrenner remained unhappy. As late as October 2008, when the New Yankee Stadium was nearly complete, the team was still issuing hollow threats about moving to New Jersey unless it received more financial help from the government. Although the team is responsible for paying back $1.2 billion in bonds, economists expect the stadium

will eventually cost taxpayers an additional $1.2 billion in tax breaks, infrastructure, and interest. The stadium is also officially owned by the city so as to exempt the Yankees from paying property taxes.

Designed by Populous (as HOK Sport was now called), the New Yankee Stadium wisely hearkened back to the original Yankee Stadium instead of the trashy, renovated version. Two notable features that had been destroyed in the 1976 renovation—the famous copper frieze, and the words *Yankee Stadium* carved in granite at the main entrance—were rebuilt in a manner resembling the original. (The new frieze lacked the detail of the original and used steel instead of copper, but at least they tried.) The original Monument Park was also moved in toto from the old stadium, although it was squeezed into a less-than-ideal location behind the center field wall. "Best of all," wrote *Times* architecture critic Nicolai Ouroussoff, "the slot that separated the scoreboard from the right field stands in the old stadium has been re-created, so you can still catch glimpses of the subway

OPPOSITE PAGE: New Yankee Stadium's entrance is decidedly martial and imposing, as if striving to embody Dante's warning, "Abandon hope all ye who enter here." It's loosely modeled on the entrance to the original Yankee Stadium, although the new version is much, much larger. "The towering arched windows that dominated the original exterior, an echo of the Roman Colosseum, have been recast in a mix of limestone, granite, and cast stone, and they are as imposing as ever," *New York Times* architecture critic Nicolai Ouroussoff wrote.

TOP: New Yankee Stadium's Monument Park is shoehorned into center field, as if the architects forgot to set aside space for it. Whereas the original Monument Park had abundant greenery that helped it live up to the name "Park," the new version is dominated by gray brick and concrete, earning it the derisive nickname "Monument Cave." In theory, fans can visit up to forty-five minutes before game time, although in practice, you've got to show up much earlier than that to actually get in. The park contains plaques celebrating the twenty-three Yankees whose numbers have been retired, plus larger, gravestone-sized tributes to Lou Gehrig, Miller Huggins, Babe Ruth, Joe DiMaggio, Mickey Mantle, George Steinbrenner, and the 9/11 victims.

BOTTOM: People look like ants scurrying about the floor of New Yankee Stadium's massive Great Hall, which covers nearly three quarters of an acre. Old Yankee Stadium was sometimes criticized for being too cramped, but the new ballpark swings the pendulum far in the other direction, as if preparing for a future in which human beings are 40 feet tall. "HOK has reincarnated the old stadium," *New Yorker* architecture critic Paul Goldberger wrote. "It has tried hard, very hard, to make us think of its predecessor, with sumptuous architectural effects that have the self-important air of a new courthouse."

rumbling by—a reminder that the stadium has been carved out of the heart of a living, thriving city."

Although its architecture mimicked the original Yankee Stadium, the new structure is three times larger—24 acres instead of 8. Essentially, the New Yankee Stadium was designed to function as a giant ATM from which the team withdraws as much money as possible. When the vast stadium opened, its concourse housed (among other things) a candy store, a pastry shop, a butcher shop, an art gallery, a conference center, eight team stores, and seventeen kitchens, several of them bearing the names of celebrity chefs. Although the stadium offered any amenity one could want, its vast scale gave the ballpark a cold and impersonal feel. "The new stadium, in contrast [to the old one], has too often had a desultory vibe," the *New York Times* noted.

Part of the problem was that the Yankees abandoned all pretense of attracting families and everyday fans to the ballpark. New Yankee Stadium was unapologetically a park of the wealthy, by the wealthy, and for the wealthy. According to the Team Marketing Report, a family of four sitting in non-premium seats paid an average of $410.88—about one percent of the average family's yearly income—to attend a game at New Yankee Stadium in 2009. As state assemblyman Richard Brodsky put it, "You have a stadium paid for by taxpayers that taxpayers can't afford to get into." The stadium's fifty-two luxury suites cost as much as $850,000 per season. The cheapest lower-deck ticket between the bases ran $350 per game. The best box seats cost a whopping $2,625, and sales were so poor that the new stadium became famous for how empty it always appeared on television.

By 2017, the New Yankee Stadium's novelty had worn off, and it was looking even emptier—the team was selling only 78 percent of available seats, with an even smaller percentage actually attending. Ticket revenue was $166 million less than it had been eight years earlier, throwing the team's ability to pay its debts into doubt. "When they entered into the new Yankee Stadium in 2009, they were overpricing the average fan, the working-class families who were the bedrock of the franchise," said Wayne McDonnell, chair of NYU's Tisch Institute for Sports Management, Media, and Business. "And that rubbed a lot of people the wrong way, because they felt as if the new Yankee Stadium wasn't for them."

Alex Rodriguez hits the 562nd homer of his career at New Yankee Stadium in 2009, the ballpark's debut season. Rodriguez's thirteen-year tenure with the Yankees was chaotic and controversial, but when he retired he ranked in the franchise's all-time top ten in home runs, runs scored, and wins above replacement. A-Rod won two MVP awards with the Yankees and helped lead them to the 2009 World Series title. He also won praise for his stellar glovework after converting to third base so the defensively inferior Derek Jeter could remain at shortstop.

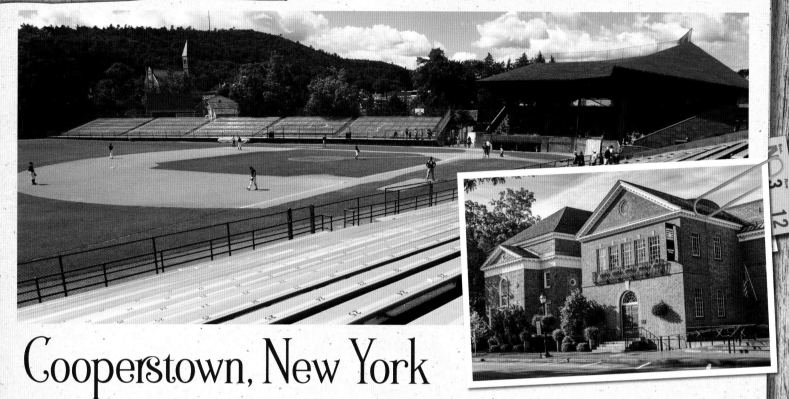

Cooperstown, New York

The Baseball Hall of Fame and Doubleday Field

According to legend, baseball was invented in Cooperstown, New York, on a sunny summer's day in 1839, when a young man named Abner Doubleday devised the rules and held the first game in a cow pasture belonging to farmer Elihu Phinney. Unfortunately, this story is completely false—it was fabricated by a old man suffering from dementia in 1905—but that hasn't stopped millions of baseball fans from making their pilgrimage to the old ballpark that now stands on the site of Phinney's cow pasture.

In 1920, the Cooperstown Chamber of Commerce purchased the faux-historic site from the Phinney family for $5,000. The village had grown up to surround the pasture; by 1924, when a 250-seat wooden grandstand was built on the site, the pasture was located on a much-trafficked part of Main Street. The site didn't really reach prominence, though, until 1939, when the brand new National Baseball Hall of Fame and Museum opened its doors two blocks down the street. Major League Baseball was planning a weekend of festivities in conjunction with the Hall's grand opening, and it needed a modern baseball stadium to use. The Works Progress Administration agreed to build a new steel and concrete stadium on Phinney's pasture, costing $10,000. This is the structure that still stands today.

Doubleday Field is a small, unpretentious ballpark that would probably collapse if it were ever filled to its listed capacity of 9,791. Its most elaborate flourish is its entrance gate made of brick, wrought iron, and a peaked white wooden roof. The ballpark fits snugly into its tree-lined neighborhood; behind the outfield wall, residents on Elm Street and Susquehanna Avenue can see the playing field from the second story of their homes.

The first event at the new stadium was a game between two area high schools on May 12, 1939. Two months later, in conjunction with the Hall of Fame's grand opening, an all-star game was played between two teams of then-current MLB stars, including Lefty Grove, Mel Ott, and Hank Greenberg. In 1940, Doubleday Field began hosting the Hall of Fame Game, an annual tradition wherein two major league teams played an exhibition game in Cooperstown on Hall of Fame Weekend. Played every year from 1940 through 2008, the game brought such luminaries as Ted Williams, Hank Aaron, Willie Mays, and Cal Ripken Jr. to Doubleday Field. Today Doubleday Field is used by youth teams, adult leagues, and whoever else is willing to pay the $550 rental fee to play a game there.

THIS PAGE: Doubleday Field, once the site of a famous cow pasture, is now located in the middle of Cooperstown. Visible in the background are the historic Otsego County Courthouse, built in 1880, and Irish Hill, settled by immigrant hop pickers in the mid-nineteenth century.

INSET: The Baseball Hall of Fame opened on Cooperstown's Main Street in 1939, the same year as Doubleday Field. The first induction ceremony, featuring Babe Ruth, Cy Young, and nine others, took place on the steps pictured here. The ceremonies were moved to the nearby town of Middlefield starting in 1992.

PITTSBURGH

FORBES FIELD

TEAM: Pittsburgh Pirates (1909–1970)

LOCATION: Corner of Boquet St. and Sennott St., Pittsburgh

FIRST MLB GAME: June 30, 1909

LAST MLB GAME: June 28, 1970

NOTABLE FEATURES: Modern exterior with exposed steel; redbrick outfield wall covered with ivy; deep outfield gaps conducive to triples.

GREENLEE FIELD

TEAMS: Pittsburgh Crawfords (1932–1938), Homestead Grays (1935–1938)

LOCATION: Corner of Bedford Ave. and Junilla St., Pittsburgh

NOTABLE FEATURES: Sloping embankment in right field topped by 12-inch-high concrete wall; operated jointly with the famed Crawford Grill, a 1-mile streetcar ride away (down Bedford Avenue).

THREE RIVERS STADIUM

TEAM: Pittsburgh Pirates (1970–2000)

LOCATION: Corner of W. General Robinson St. and Stadium Circle, Pittsburgh

FIRST MLB GAME: July 16, 1970

LAST MLB GAME: October 1, 2000

NOTABLE FEATURES: Location at the convergence of Pittsburgh's three rivers; first outdoor ballpark to feature artificial turf.

PNC PARK

TEAM: Pittsburgh Pirates (2001–present)

LOCATION: Corner of W. General Robinson St. and Mazeroski Way, Pittsburgh

FIRST MLB GAME: April 9, 2001

NOTABLE FEATURES: Proximity to Allegheny River; panoramic view of Roberto Clemente Bridge and downtown Pittsburgh; intimate setting with seats close to field.

During the early 1900s Pittsburgh was known as The Smoky City due to the overwhelming amount of coal-burning smoke churned out by its many factories, steamboats, and furnaces. City streets were dark even when the sun shone overhead, and streetlights were sometimes necessary during the middle of the day. The problem was worst in an area of downtown known as the Golden Triangle, where the Allegheny and Monongahela rivers converged to form the Ohio. Hundreds of steamboats routinely loitered there, belching out thick clouds of smoke that made the simple act of breathing a risky undertaking.

It was in the heart of this sooty neighborhood where the Pittsburgh Pirates played the earliest years of their existence, in small wooden firetraps known as Recreation Park and Exposition Park. The latter ballpark, opened in 1882, was so close to the Allegheny that it flooded whenever the river did, which was often. On the bright side, the team's star player, Honus Wagner, was known for "accidentally" leaving the ballpark gate open whenever there were youngsters around in need of free admission.

In 1909, the Pirates' visionary owner, Barney Dreyfuss, conceived what was then the largest and most beautiful baseball park the world had ever seen—and built it as far away from downtown as humanly possible. The Oakland district, with its clean air and stately oak trees, was only 4 miles away as the crow flies but a light-year's distance in every other respect. The Pirates played there at majestic Forbes Field for six memorable decades, but by the early 1970s the air was clean enough for them to return downtown. The team opened Three Rivers Stadium in 1970 on nearly the exact spot where Exposition Park had once stood. After three decades there, the Pirates moved next door to breathtaking PNC Park, one of the finest ballparks ever built. 🌑

TOP: Exposition Park is packed for Game 4 of the 1903 World Series, the first Fall Classic of the modern era. The fence-like structure on top of the grandstand is a screen to prevent foul balls from striking unsuspecting passersby.

BOTTOM: A standing-room-only crowd fills Exposition Park for a doubleheader between the Pirates and Giants in 1904. The hazy, smoky environment was a constant annoyance and one of the main reasons the Pirates fled to the distant Oakland neighborhood in 1909.

FORBES FIELD

PITTSBURGH PIRATES 1909–1970

FORBES FIELD, HAILED AS the grandest ballpark ever built at the time of its opening, was the brainchild of Pittsburgh Pirates owner Barney Dreyfuss, a German immigrant who had amassed his large fortune distilling bourbon in Kentucky. In 1908, with the help of his friend Andrew Carnegie—who was developing the neighborhood at the time—Dreyfuss purchased 7 acres of real estate in the Oakland district of Pittsburgh. The site was immediately adjacent to Schenley Park, a 300-acre wonderland of sculpted gardens. Also nearby were four institutions recently founded by Carnegie: the Carnegie Public Library, the Carnegie Museum of Art, the Carnegie Museum of Natural History, and the Carnegie Technical Institute (known today as Carnegie Mellon University).

Construction on the Pirates' new ballpark began on New Year's Day 1909 when workers began filling and leveling the ravine that ran through the property. Meanwhile, the University of Pittsburgh was simultaneously building its own new campus right next door. By the time this orgy of construction was complete, virtually every important civic and educational institution in Pittsburgh was located within a few blocks of Forbes Field.

Dreyfuss hired a landscape engineer named Charles Leavitt Jr. to design the ballpark, with input from Pirates manager Fred Clarke. (Clarke, a tinkerer in his spare time, had devised and patented many inventions, including a device for rolling the tarp onto the field during rain delays.) Leavitt's experience lay mostly in building parklands, racetracks, and cemeteries; Forbes Field would be the only ballpark he ever built. And yet, it turned out to be an unquestioned masterpiece. What's more, its construction took only six months from start to finish, thanks to workers toiling in double shifts.

Leavitt used his $2 million budget—three times the cost of Comiskey Park—to great effect. Forbes Field was the second ballpark to use steel and concrete as materials; the first, Shibe Park, opened just two months earlier. But unlike Shibe's designers, Leavitt did not attempt to hide his steel behind bricks and mortar. He ostentatiously showed it off, using exposed steel cross-bracing beams as a center-piece of the building's façade. A stately steel awning shaded the main entrance behind home plate, and ground level was marked by a suc-cession of intricate window panes framed by stilted arches. Whereas Shibe Park, with its Italian Renaissance cupola, attempted to evoke the past, Forbes Field was sleek, modern, and forward-looking.

In a surprisingly self-effacing move for a baseball owner, Barney Dreyfuss named the new park not after himself but after General John Forbes, a hero of the French and Indian War who had captured nearby Fort Duquesne for the British. Before the stadium even opened, some took to calling it "Dreyfuss' Folly," believing that his lavish spending was an investment unlikely to be repaid. Among the park's exorbitant features was a street-level promenade underneath the stands that allowed fans to take shelter when rainstorms hit. "Many thought Mr. Dreyfuss was making a mistake," his son-in-law William Benswanger, a team executive, later recalled. "He was called 'crazy' for taking such a step and was told 'the park will never be filled.' It was filled the first day."

PREVIOUS PAGE: The triple-decked Forbes Field was a revelation when it opened in 1909, combining architectural beauty with a generous seating capacity of 24,000. The stands were never segregated here, as is made clear by the presence of many African-American fans in the foreground of this image. These cheap bleacher seats were not considered an appropriate place for ladies, however. Although women can be seen in this photo sitting in all three decks of the main grandstand, there are no female fans whatsoever in the bleachers. The ballpark's most expensive tickets were the private boxes in the third deck, which went for $8.75 per eight-seat box.

THIS PAGE: Nine men—enough to form their own baseball team—climb a telephone pole outside Forbes Field in order to get a glimpse of the 1909 World Series. The large building in the background is the Carnegie Library of Pittsburgh, completed in 1895, which still serves as the city's main library.

OPPOSITE PAGE, TOP: Baseball's two best players, Ty Cobb (right) and Honus Wagner, talk hitting at Forbes Field during the 1909 World Series. Most fans around the country were rooting for Wagner, the jovial thirteen-year veteran, to prevail over Cobb, the brash and abrasive twenty-two-year-old. Wagner did indeed outhit Cobb in the series, .333 to .231, and his Pirates outlasted Cobb's Tigers four games to three. The Pirates thus became the first team ever to win a World Series title in their first season at a new ball-park. Three other teams—the 1912 Red Sox, 2006 Cardinals, and 2009 Yankees—have done it since.

OPPOSITE PAGE, BOTTOM: The 1896 Pirates pose at Exposition Park, thirteen years before the team moved into Forbes Field. The lone mustachioed player is "Eagle Eye" Jake Beckley, a Hall of Fame first baseman who "at the time of his retirement was one of only three men in the majors who still sported facial hair," historian David Fleitz wrote. Next to Beckley, in the middle of the middle row, is the team's thirty-three-year-old manager, Connie Mack, who was in his final season as an active player.

PITTSBURGH BASE BALL CLUB

ADMIT ONE | BOX 263

1913

Sep. 24

Barney Dreyfuss, Prest.

In fact, it was overfilled the first day. Forbes Field had a generous capacity of 25,000, but for its first game a then–major league record 30,388 swarmed through the turnstiles. Among the dignitaries in attendance was Al Pratt, the Civil War veteran who had founded the Pirates in 1882. Dreyfuss himself stood at the gate shaking the hands of fans as they entered. Once inside, everyone realized the magnitude of what Dreyfuss had accomplished. "The formal opening of Forbes Field…was an historic event," Francis Richter, a preeminent sportswriter of the era, wrote. "Words must fail to picture in the mind's eye adequately the splendors of the magnificent pile President Dreyfuss erected as a tribute to the national game, a beneficence to Pittsburgh and an enduring monument to himself. For architectural beauty, imposing size, solid construction, and public comfort and convenience, it has not its superior in the world."

Barely three months after Forbes Field opened, the Pirates won their first World Series, propelled by the all-around brilliance of shortstop Honus Wagner. In ensuing years the park would be the backdrop for many notable moments in baseball, including the mud-splattered Game 7 of the 1925 World Series, the titanic home runs of Josh Gibson, and the brilliant early career of Roberto Clemente. Oddly, no pitcher ever threw a no-hitter at Forbes Field, but its distant and angular outfield wall made it a notorious haven for triples. Only eleven teams in modern baseball have ever hit 110 triples in a season; six of them were Pirates teams that played at Forbes Field. In 1912, an obscure Pittsburgh outfielder named Owen Wilson hit 36 three-baggers in one season, far more than any big leaguer before or since.

The most famous spectacle to take place at Forbes was, of course, the 1960 World Series, during

which the Pirates' Bill Mazeroski hit what remains the only Game 7 walk-off homer in Series history. The Yankees brutally dominated Pittsburgh throughout the series, outscoring them 55-27, but Pittsburgh got the big hits when it mattered. Game 7 was a contest full of unforgettable visuals—Mazeroski being mobbed by fans as he rounded the bases, Yogi Berra futilely watching the ball sail over the ivy-covered left field wall—but the most indelible image was captured by George Silk, a photographer for *Life* magazine. Silk snapped an extraordinary photo of students cheering on the Pirates from their bird's-eye perch on the 42nd story of the University of Pittsburgh's main building, 535 feet above the playing field. The image remains one of the most iconic photographs in baseball history. ✑

TOP: It's 3:36 p.m. on October 13, 1960, and these University of Pittsburgh students are cheering on Bill Mazeroski, who has just hit a walk-off home run to win Game 7 of the World Series for the Pirates. They've got a great view of the action from the 42-story Cathedral of Learning, which opened in 1939 virtually next door to Forbes Field. In the years since, the university has grown to encompass the ballpark's former location; the onetime site of home plate is now in the lobby of another university building, Posvar Hall.

BOTTOM: Forbes Field as it appeared during its debut season of 1909. The park was universally hailed as a masterpiece, a work of breathtaking architectural beauty that was also, at the time, the largest ballpark ever built. The gorgeous exterior was made of buff-colored terra cotta, which is also used in the Pirates' current home, PNC Park. The intricate steel trusses and beams were painted green, while the awning over the main entrance contained rust-colored slate tiles.

OPPOSITE PAGE, TOP: Josh Gibson grew up on Strauss Street in Pittsburgh's Pleasant Valley neighborhood, about 4 miles north of the site where Greenlee Field would later be built. When he was sixteen, Gimbels department store hired the strapping young Gibson as an elevator operator, mostly so he could play on the store's baseball team. In 1932, when Gus Greenlee decided to turn his Pittsburgh Crawfords into black baseball's biggest juggernaut, one of his first moves was luring the twenty-year-old slugger away from the crosstown Homestead Grays.

OPPOSITE PAGE, BOTTOM: This photo of Greenlee Field was snapped during the 1930s by Charles "Teenie" Harris, a pioneering African-American photographer. Harris was taught the business by his uncle and older brother, who were also professional photographers. During the mid-1920s Harris co-founded a semipro baseball team, the Pittsburgh Crawfords, for whom he also played shortstop. After the team was sold to Gus Greenlee, Harris opened his own photography business, Flash Studio, with money he'd saved working as a chauffeur. He devoted the rest of his life to documenting African-American life in Pittsburgh, including baseball.

OH, YOU PIRATES

IN 1930, GUS GREENLEE, a Pittsburgh numbers kingpin who also owned the legendary jazz club the Crawford Grill, decided to enter the baseball business—and when Greenlee started a business, he did it in style. Within a few years he had not only built one of the greatest teams ever assembled, but also opened Greenlee Field, one of the few stadiums that was black-owned, and purpose-built for Negro Leagues baseball.

First, Greenlee bought a local semipro team and renamed it the Crawfords after his nightclub. Then he purchased an empty lot at 2500

Bedford Avenue that was often used for sandlot games. On this site he built an attractive, workmanlike stadium at a cost of $100,000. Sporting a handsome façade of red brick, Greenlee Field contained 75 tons of steel and fourteen railcars' worth

of cement. Notably, it included spacious locker rooms for both home and visiting teams, a feature prized by African-American players. "No longer did black players have to dress and shower in the dingy surroundings of the YMCA because the white owners of Ammon Field and Forbes Field refused the use of their accommodations," historian James Bankes wrote. The players were also impressed by the quality of the playing surface. Recalled outfielder James "Cool Papa" Bell: "It was beautiful. It had lots of grass. It felt like you were playing in a major league park. The best thing for me was the big outfield. Plenty of room to run."

Greenlee Field's opening on April 10, 1932, was a grand affair attended by Pittsburgh's mayor and most of the city council. "Gus made his entrance in a red convertible," the historian Mark Ribowsky wrote. "Surrounded by a marching band, he received a standing ovation from the capacity crowd of 6,000. Clad in a white silk suit and tie, Gus walked to the pitching mound and threw out the first pitch." The Crawfords won the game 1-0 behind a Satchel Paige shutout, scoring the lone run in a dramatic ninth inning. By year's end, some 119,000 fans had passed through the Greenlee Field turnstiles—65,000 for baseball and the rest for various

other events, including a memorable football game between Wilberforce University and West Virginia State for the black college championship.

Offering lucrative contracts to the nation's biggest African-American stars, Greenlee assembled a star-studded roster that included Paige and Bell, as well as fellow luminaries Josh Gibson, Judy Johnson, and Oscar Charleston (who also served as manager). Soon the Crawfords were drawing 200,000 fans a year during the heart of the Great Depression. Greenlee installed lights for night games and kept fans entertained with bizarre promotions like a pregame race between Jesse Owens and a racehorse (Owens won). However, "the ballpark Greenlee built never achieved the level of patronage to turn a profit," wrote Rob Ruck in *Sandlot Seasons: Sport in Black Pittsburgh*. Greenlee's tendency to hire white employees to work at the ballpark, Ruck asserts, turned off the African-American audience. Also, "the Depression undercut attendance, as did the failure of builders to install an awning over the grandstand, which could have shielded fans from inclement weather." In 1938 Greenlee Field, after just six years of existence, fell victim to the wrecking ball. It was replaced by a housing project, the Bedford Dwellings. Never again would a ballpark be built specifically for a Negro League team. ☕

TOP: This photo of the Greenlee Field stands may have been taken on a Sunday afternoon, as these Crawfords fans—mostly African-Americans, but also a few white folks—are dressed in their churchgoing finest. Like the image on the previous page, this photo was taken by the famed local photographer Teenie Harris.

BOTTOM: The Pittsburgh Crawfords were so proud of Greenlee Field that they had the ballpark's name painted on their bus, which was actually a Mack truck custom-fitted as a touring bus. We know this photo was taken sometime around May 27, 1937, because that was the date of the heavyweight fight between John Henry Lewis and Charlie Massera advertised in a poster on the stadium wall. Among the many outstanding players on the Crawfords were first baseman and manager Oscar Charleston (far left), left fielder Sam Bankhead (fourth from left), third baseman Judy Johnson (eighth from right), center fielder Cool Papa Bell (seventh from right), catcher Josh Gibson (fourth from right), and pitcher Satchel Paige (second from right).

OPPOSITE PAGE: Three Rivers Stadium, which opened in 1970, was the second ballpark in MLB history to forgo a dirt infield, instead installing small sliding pits around each base. (The first was Riverfront Stadium in Cincinnati, which opened sixteen days earlier.) Pittsburgh's new ballpark was located on the same picturesque site as Exposition Park—see page 62—but unfortunately, fans got to see the dramatic skyline pictured here only if they sat in the very last row of the upper deck. Three Rivers was a completely enclosed concrete bowl, blocking off all views of its surrounding environs.

THREE RIVERS STADIUM

PITTSBURGH PIRATES 1970-2000

ALTHOUGH THREE RIVERS STADIUM got positive reviews upon its opening, Pirates fans never fully warmed to the huge concrete bowl on the north bank of the Allegheny River. Pittsburgh ranked in the top half of the league in attendance only three times in the stadium's thirty-one-year history, despite finishing in first place nine times during that period. Those fans who did show up, however, were entertained by the prodigious power hitting of Willie Stargell and Barry Bonds, and by the final three seasons of Roberto Clemente's peerless career.

The Pirates had wanted a new stadium as early as 1958, when they sold Forbes Field to the adjacent (and expanding) University of Pittsburgh. The school allowed the team to stay until they could get a new park built, a wait that would turn out to be more than a decade. In 1968, ground was finally broken on a $55 million multipurpose facility designed by Osborn Engineering to house the Pirates and the NFL's Steelers. Three Rivers Stadium opened in July 1970.

Like many of its peers, Three Rivers featured movable seating blocks that eased the transition between baseball and football configurations. About 8,000 box seats along the baselines were shifted to become 50-yard-line seats for football. The concrete stadium's round shape and red-and-yellow plastic seats gave it a cookie-cutter feel, but some were pleased by the novelty of its space-age appearance. "Seeing the stadium for the first time from just beyond the outer walls is an experience in itself," wrote Dan Smrekar, of the *New Castle News*. "At first it resembles something from the future or maybe even another planet. The huge circular building with spiraling ramps makes you stop in awe."

Three Rivers Stadium resembled its multipurpose brethren in almost every respect, but its idyllic location set it apart. Its name derived from the stadium's proximity to Pittsburgh's Golden Triangle, where the Allegheny and Monongahela rivers converge to form the Ohio. The site was just across the Allegheny from downtown Pittsburgh, within walking distance for office workers, and also a stone's throw from Fort Pitt, the colonial-era bastion from which the city derived its name. But the completely enclosed upper deck necessary for football made all this scenery invisible to those sitting in the stands. Still, upon its opening, the park received mostly hosannas. "This sort of makes you forget about Forbes Field in a hurry," said one opening-night attendee.

Three Rivers' capacity was about 48,000, but by the 1990s, ticket demand had dwindled enough that the Pirates felt they needed to reduce supply by covering many upper-deck sections with unsightly tarps. During this era, the team was even uglier than the ballpark. In 1993, the Pirates began a streak of losing seasons that would eventually reach twenty in a row, an all-time baseball record. The team sought to alleviate its woes by constructing a new stadium next door, and the Pirates played their last game at Three Rivers on October 1, 2000. The ballpark was imploded the following February, and the site is now a parking lot for the Pirates' beautiful new home, PNC Park. 🦜

OPPOSITE PAGE: Ace lefty Jerry Reuss throws a pitch at Three Rivers Stadium in 1976. "One of the unique features of Three Rivers Stadium...was the field-level Plexigas window behind home plate," Reuss wrote. "Used by television cameras and photographers, it was also a great place to sneak a hot dog during the game!" Reuss pitched five seasons for Pittsburgh, reaching a career high of 18 wins and making the All-Star team in 1975. With playing time in the 1960s, '70s, '80s, and '90s, he's one of just ten pitchers in MLB history to compete in four different decades.

TOP LEFT: Pirates manager Danny Murtaugh poses with an unidentified youngster before the 1971 World Series at Three Rivers Stadium. This photo nicely illustrates the innovative changes the Pirates made to their uniforms in 1970 to coincide with the opening of their new stadium. The team got rid of its traditional flannel button-down jerseys, replacing them with pullover tops made of a nylon blend. They also jettisoned belts in favor of elastic waistbands. Here Murtaugh is sporting the new getup, while his young companion is dressed in the old uniform. The nylon-pullover look would become emblematic of the cookie-cutter-stadium era, and within a few years most other teams would make similar changes to their uniforms.

TOP RIGHT: This shot of Roberto Clemente was taken at Forbes Field shortly before the Pirates moved into Three Rivers Stadium. Clemente was very much at home in both ballparks. He batted .329 in 1,070 career games at Forbes and .334 in 136 career games at Three Rivers. In all other big league ballparks, he batted a collective .306. "I'm going to miss certain fans at Forbes Field," Clemente said in 1970 as the team prepared to move to its new ballpark. "I know Three Rivers Stadium will be beautiful, but I have wonderful memories of Forbes."

BOTTOM: Only the great Willie Stargell could pull off the yellow-pants look with such style. Stargell, seen here batting at Three Rivers Stadium during the 1979 World Series, was the elder statesman of the Pirates that year, when he won the National League MVP award despite batting just .281 with 82 runs batted in. Stargell's well-documented leadership skills, voters believed, more than made up for what he lacked in numbers. "Willie was our crutch," teammate Bill Robinson said. "Anything you needed, any problems you had personally or in baseball, he took the burden."

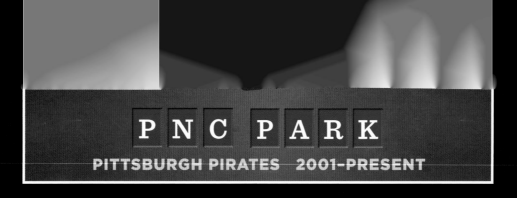

P N C P A R K
PITTSBURGH PIRATES 2001–PRESENT

PNC PARK, OPENED BY the Pittsburgh Pirates on the north bank of the Allegheny River in 2001, is everything a baseball stadium could hope to be. With inspired architecture, tremendous sightlines, a breathtaking city view, and an invigorating neighborhood surrounding it, PNC became an immediate contender for the title of best baseball park ever built. Unfortunately, this perfect new stadium debuted during a seemingly endless string of losing seasons by the Pirates, prompting *The Onion* to run the satirical headline "PNC Park Threatens to Leave Pittsburgh Unless Better Team Is Built."

The ballpark's construction was controversial from start to finish. "Those involved in cutting the deal to finance PNC Park went on a wild ride," wrote Robert Dvorchak in the *Pittsburgh Post-Gazette*. "Running counter to much of the public's sentiment, they climbed, hurtled, dipped, careened, nearly derailed, and zoomed like they were in a roller coaster car." Citizens in the eleven-county area surrounding Pittsburgh voted down a publicly funded park in 1997, but local politicians decided to ignore the voters' wishes, creating a funding plan that sidestepped voter approval. By a one-vote margin, Allegheny County's commissioners approved covering $143 million of the park's $262 million budget, with the rest of the money coming from the state government, the sale of naming rights, and a tiny amount from the Pirates. The two county commissioners who'd shepherded the project were voted out of office by the angry citizenry, but nevertheless, ground was broken on April 7, 1999. Twenty-three labor unions joined forces to build the park, including scuba divers who built a sea wall to protect the park from flooding by the Allegheny. PNC Park was completed in just twenty-four months, reportedly the fastest construction time for any ballpark in the modern era.

PNC's location next to the Pirates' old park was stunning. For years, the enclosed upper deck of Three Rivers had prevented fans from taking in the awe-inspiring view of downtown Pittsburgh just across the river. The Sixth Street Bridge, a stately 442-foot span erected in 1928, was renamed the Roberto Clemente Bridge. Painted Pirates yellow, the bridge forms the centerpiece of the magnificent vista seen from the grandstand, and it's closed to automobiles on game days so pedestrians can walk from downtown to the game. Alternatively, fans can park across the river and arrive at the game by water taxi. "Pittsburgh didn't plant its ballpark away from the heart of the city, as Atlanta and Seattle did, or in the suburbs, like the Texas Rangers did," wrote architecture critic Patricia Lowry. "Framed by the Allegheny River and three city streets, PNC Park is part of the urban fabric."

It's also astoundingly beautiful. In a 2003 ranking of MLB ballparks, ESPN.com rated PNC ahead of Pacific Bell (now AT&T) Park and Camden Yards as the best stadium in baseball, even comparing it to a nearby Frank Lloyd Wright masterwork. "*Fallingwater* is regarded as the perfect blend of art, architecture and environment—or at least it was until PNC Park opened," ESPN's Jim Callis wrote. "Pittsburgh hasn't seen anything this beautiful since Clemente unleashed throws from right field."

The Steel City's ballpark appropriately contains artfully exposed steel beams throughout, along with detailed latticework. An intricate steel frieze, similar to the copper one torn down at Yankee Stadium in 1974, rings the top of the grandstand. The beams and seats are navy blue as a tip of the cap to Forbes Field. Behind the left field foul pole, a decorative canopy and walkway rise high in the air, giving fans who choose to leave their seats a unique perspective on the action. Other popular features include a brew pub in left field and a party deck overlooking the river behind the center field fence.

In right field, the 21-foot-high wall contains a hand-operated scoreboard. Behind that, the Allegheny River flows just 443 feet from home plate, reachable by a long blast from a

OPPOSITE PAGE: With its lights turned off for a postgame fireworks show, PNC Park is a glowing apparition on the Allegheny. A great way to get to the ballpark is to walk over the Roberto Clemente Bridge, which becomes a pedestrian bridge on game days. Formerly called the Sixth Street Bridge, the span is one of the "Three Sisters," three matching yellow bridges built in the 1920s to connect downtown Pittsburgh to the Golden Triangle. After PNC Park opened, all three bridges were renamed after famous Pittsburghers. (The other two are now the Rachel Carson Bridge and the Andy Warhol Bridge.)

TOP: With his ebullient smile, bouncing dreadlocks, and five-tool baseball skills, Andrew McCutchen gave the Pirates franchise a jolt of energy when he arrived in the major leagues in 2009. He played nine seasons for the team and topped twenty homers in seven of them. In 2013, the year Pittsburgh finally made the playoffs after a twenty-year drought, McCutchen posted a .911 OPS and was named National League MVP.

BOTTOM: PNC Park's buff-colored terra cotta is a tribute to Forbes Field, whose façade was made of the same material. The statue of Honus Wagner outside PNC's main entrance, meanwhile, has lived a long and circuitous life. Sculpted by local artist Frank Vittor, it was erected in Schenley Park across from Forbes Field in 1955, seven months before the legendary shortstop died. After the Pirates moved to Three Rivers Stadium, the statue was relocated to that ballpark's right field entrance. Finally, when PNC Park opened, the statue was uprooted once again and moved to its current location. Now it stands a long fly ball away from the site of Exposition Park, where Wagner played much of his career.

left-handed slugger. Over in left field, meanwhile, the fence is only 6 feet high, making it the shortest in baseball except for the one at Dodger Stadium, and allowing fleet-footed outfielders to leap into the stands to rob home runs.

Of the first ten retro ballparks built after Camden Yards, eight featured redbrick exteriors. PNC bucked that trend by using large limestone slabs and buff-colored artificial stone with terra cotta ornamentation. The green steel roof was another feature meant to evoke Forbes Field, and statues of Pirates legends Clemente and Honus Wagner were salvaged from Three Rivers Stadium and placed outside the entrance. They were later joined by a pair of newer statues honoring Willie Stargell and Bill Mazeroski.

For all its aesthetic magnificence, the best thing about PNC may be its coziness and outstanding views of the playing field. The park is tiny. It was the first major league stadium built with only two decks since Milwaukee's County Stadium in 1953, and there is nothing resembling a bad seat in the house—the upper deck's highest seats hover only 88 feet above the playing field. In 2008, after the Red Sox added seats to Fenway Park, PNC became the smallest ballpark in the majors with a capacity of just over 38,000. (The Athletics, Marlins, and Rays had smaller listed capacities, but all three had closed off vast sections of their ballparks to artificially reduce ticket supply.)

Though Pittsburghers quickly fell in love with PNC Park, the Pirates tried their best to make it difficult. The club lost 100 games in PNC's inaugural season, and in 2012 it posted a losing record for the twentieth consecutive year—the longest such streak (by far) in baseball history. Yet that season more than 2 million Pirates fans streamed through the turnstiles anyway. Clearly the attraction was the beautiful ballpark and not the wretched team. In 2013, led by the exciting young center fielder Andrew McCutchen, the Pirates finally broke through with a winning season. That October 6, PNC Park hosted the first playoff game in its history. With the stadium packed to the gills, the deafening roar of the home crowd spurred the Pirates to a 6-2 victory over Cincinnati. "That was amazing," Pirates catcher Russell Martin said. "I've never heard a crowd so loud in my life." 🌀

TOP: Stealing a page from Milwaukee's playbook, the Pirates created the Great Pierogi Race in 1999. After the fifth inning, the contestants—from left, Sauerkraut Saul, Oliver Onion, Cheese Chester, and Jalapeño Hannah—race around the basepaths to the delight of the crowd. Pierogies (boiled dumplings filled with potatoes or meat) are just one of the many local delicacies found at PNC Park's concession stands. The best-known item is probably the Primanti Brothers sandwich, which consists of a massive pile of pastrami or corned beef, French fries, and cole slaw, packed between two slices of bread.

BOTTOM: This Roberto Clemente statue, sculpted by Pittsburgher Susan Wagner, was first placed outside Three Rivers Stadium in 1994. In 2001 it was moved to this spot near the foot of the Roberto Clemente Bridge, where it now serves as a gathering place for Pirates fans. In 2012 residents of Essex County, New Jersey, raised $110,000 to build a smaller but otherwise identical copy of this statue. That version now stands at Branch Brook Park in Newark, less than a mile away from Roberto Clemente Elementary School.

Pilot Field, Buffalo

A Minor League Park Fit for the Majors

During the late 1980s, the Chicago White Sox and San Francisco Giants, among other teams, were shopping around for new cities to call home. Buffalo went all in to lure them to town, spending $56 million to build Pilot Field, the nation's largest minor league ballpark, with the intention of eventually expanding it to major league size. Buffalo hadn't had major league baseball since 1915, and although the city had slid lower in the nation's population rankings every decade since then, residents still longed for a major league team of their own.

Unlike most stadiums of its era, Pilot Field was built in the heart of downtown, surrounded by bustling city streets. (The location at Washington and Swan Streets had once been the site of the Statler Hotel, a landmark 12-story edifice built in 1907 and torn down in 1968.) As construction neared completion in the spring of 1988, the excitement in town was as palpable as the wind chill. Opening Day tickets went on sale to the public on a snowy March morning and sold out in eighty-four minutes. Season tickets were in such high demand that the team had to cut off sales after 9,000. By season's end Buffalo had shattered every minor league attendance record in existence, drawing an astonishing 1.19 million fans—a higher attendance than three major league teams that year, despite the fact that the MLB season was a month longer.

Pilot Field was designed by HOK, the Kansas City–based firm that would become famous for building Camden Yards four years later. With its exposed structural steel and arched doorways, Pilot was the company's first attempt at a retro ballpark design, laying the groundwork for a generation of big league stadiums to follow. "It's a brand-new building, but it looks like an old-time baseball field," Buffalo Bisons co-owner Mindy Rich said. "You've got to give a lot of credit to the city, the preservationists, and the architects for coming up with a design that not only fit, but that complemented the area and looked so perfect here." The amenities were many, including thirty-eight luxury suites, a full-service restaurant, and clubhouses and bullpens built to MLB's exacting standards. The park contained 19,500 seats, expandable to 40,000 if and when a major league team arrived.

Alas, major league baseball never did come to Buffalo. The Giants and White Sox stayed put, and when MLB created two expansion teams in 1993, it picked Denver and Miami. However, three decades after its opening, Pilot Field is still thriving as America's largest—and one of its best—minor league ballparks. After a series of several name changes, it is known today as Coca-Cola Field.

TOP: Pilot Field—now called Coca-Cola Field—has been praised for the way it seamlessly fits in with the historic architecture of downtown Buffalo. The 244-foot-tall tower behind third base looks like part of a church, but it's actually the Old Post Office, which served as Buffalo's main post office from 1901 through 1963. It now houses an Erie Community College campus.

BOTTOM: Buffalo's baseball history goes back to the nineteenth century, when they had a National League team called the Bisons. The 1882 Buffalo Bisons were led by outfielder and manager Jim O'Rourke (center), who was nicknamed "Orator Jim" due to his penchant for delivering grandiose soliloquies at the drop of a hat.

WASHINGTON, DC

GRIFFITH STADIUM

TEAMS: Washington Senators I (1911–1960), Washington Senators II (1961)

NAMES: National Park (1911–1921), Griffith Stadium (1922–1965)

LOCATION: Corner of Georgia Ave. and W St. NW, Washington

FIRST MLB GAME: April 12, 1911

LAST MLB GAME: October 2, 1960

NOTABLE FEATURES: Crooked outfield fence zigzagging around stately houses; piecemeal appearance with the auxiliary grandstand being larger than the main grandstand.

RFK STADIUM

TEAMS: Washington Senators II (1962–1971), Washington Nationals (2005-2007)

NAMES: D.C. Stadium (1962–1968), Robert F. Kennedy Memorial Stadium (1969-present)

LOCATION: Corner of Capitol St. NE and 22nd St. NE, Washington

FIRST MLB GAME: April 9, 1962

LAST MLB GAME: September 30, 2007

NOTABLE FEATURES: Massive upper deck containing far more seats than the lower deck; eerie back-and-forth swaying of stands when filled to capacity.

NATIONALS PARK

TEAM: Washington Nationals (2008–present)

LOCATION: Corner of South Capitol St. SW and Potomac Ave. SE, Washington

FIRST MLB GAME: March 30, 2008

NOTABLE FEATURES: Presidents Race on field during fourth inning; first MLB ballpark to be LEED-certified by the US Green Building Council.

In its debut season of 1871, the first-ever pro baseball league, the National Association, boasted two Washington-based teams. In fact, the first major league baseball game ever played took place between these two clubs, the Olympics and the Nationals, on April 22, 1871. It was played at Olympic Grounds, a 500-seat wooden ballpark that featured a restaurant underneath the stands. However, the Nationals somehow failed to pay their $10 league dues that year, so their membership in the National Association was revoked after just five games. Their game results were also nullified, so modern record books no longer recognize that April 22 game as the first MLB game ever played.

Eight different short-lived MLB teams called Washington home during the nineteenth century, five of them called the Nationals. One of these, the 1884 Nationals, played in a ballpark located on the lawn of the US Capitol building. Another, the 1891 Nationals, built themselves a new ballpark on Georgia Avenue, felling 125 large oak trees to construct Boundary Field. This park would later be rebuilt as Griffith Stadium and would host major league games through 1961. A giant multipurpose stadium, RFK, was built for the expansion Washington Senators in 1962 and also housed the new Washington Nationals when they first arrived from Montreal in 2005. Now the Nationals have a beautiful home aptly named Nationals Park (for now).

TOP: Before Griffith Stadium was built in 1911, the site was occupied by this small wooden park known as either National Park or American League Park. This was the ballpark where William Howard Taft threw out the first-ever presidential first pitch in 1910. Not visible in the image, unfortunately, is a doghouse that was in play in center field, where the grounds crew stored the American flag between games. An outfielder once got his head stuck retrieving a fly ball that bounced into the doghouse, resulting in an inside-the-park home run.

BOTTOM: Firemen hose down the remains of National Park, which burned down on March 17, 1911, when a plumber accidentally lit it on fire with a blowtorch. The ballpark that replaced it—which would eventually be named Griffith Stadium—opened that April 12, only eleven days after construction began.

OPPOSITE PAGE: National Park had just been renamed Griffith Stadium when this photo was taken in the early 1920s. Washington fans must have been a well-dressed bunch, as seven different billboards on the outfield wall advertise some form of menswear. The ad next to the right field foul line promises a free silk shirt to any batter hitting the sign.

LIKE SO MANY BALLPARKS of its era, Griffith Stadium was born hastily and unexpectedly when a fire burned down its predecessor, National Park, in 1911. In only eleven days, construction on the new ballpark was complete enough for the Senators to begin playing games there. Also known initially as National Park, the park was given a new name in 1920 when Senators manager Clark Griffith became team president. Griffith immediately built two huge new grandstands down the left and right field lines, which towered over the tiny existing grandstand behind home plate, giving the park an unusual, piecemeal appearance.

Griffith was a notorious penny-pincher, and his stadium therefore lacked the architectural flourishes of its peers, such as Forbes Field. Indeed, few photographs of its exterior even exist, as if everyone collectively decided there wasn't much worth documenting. Inside, the park was distinctive for its meandering center field wall, which zigzagged around five houses and a massive oak tree. With a left field fence more than 400 feet away and a right field fence 30 feet tall, Griffith Stadium was probably the toughest park in baseball to hit home runs in.

That was just fine with the Senators' best player, the legendary pitcher Walter Johnson, who won exactly 200 games at Griffith Stadium in his career—the most wins of any pitcher in history

at one ballpark. It was Johnson who recorded the win in the stadium's most memorable game, Game 7 of the 1924 World Series, which the Senators won in twelve innings to clinch their first and only championship. Ironically, it was poor groundskeeping that won them the title. Two key hits for Washington, including the Series winner, were routine grounders that bounced over infielders' heads after hitting pebbles in the infield.

During Griffith Stadium's early years, the population of Washington was about 25 percent African American, and black fans were a sizable part of the audience. "The ballpark, located at 7th Street and Florida Avenue in northwest Washington, stood in the heart of a thriving black residential and commercial district," the historian Brad Snyder wrote in his book *In the Shadow of the Senators*. "It also was just down the street from Howard University, the 'Capstone of Negro Education. …With an affluent black population in their own backyard, the Senators boasted one of major league baseball's largest and most loyal black fan bases." Nonetheless, Griffith Stadium was one of just two segregated ballparks in major league baseball. Segregation here was merely by custom, whereas in St. Louis it was a written rule, but either way, black Washingtonians were limited to sitting in the right field stands. According to Snyder,

that didn't deter the team's African-American fans, who during the 1920s and '30s, generally preferred to attend Senators games instead of Negro League games played in the same ballpark.

By the 1940s, though, that equation had completely reversed. The Senators' slide into mediocrity, combined with an increasing social consciousness, now made the Negro National League's Homestead Grays the preferred team of the African-American community. Two big reasons were Josh Gibson, the catcher whose power hitting became the stuff of legend, and Buck Leonard, a sweet-swinging first baseman and perennial .300 hitter. In 1943, Gibson hit ten home runs at Griffith Stadium, more than all American League hitters combined.

"The best team in the Negro Leagues played in the same ballpark as one of the worst teams in the major leagues, highlighting the illogic of maintaining separate leagues," Snyder wrote. Even as he kept Senators games segregated, Clark Griffith happily rented out his ballpark for African-American cultural events ranging from church revivals to drill competitions. Most notably, it became the site of the annual Thanksgiving Day football game between Lincoln and Howard Universities, a cherished local tradition.

For all these reasons, many saw Washington as the likeliest team to integrate major league baseball. Led by Sam Lacy of the *Baltimore Afro-American*, black sportswriters consistently pressured Griffith to sign Gibson, Leonard, and other black stars. He never did. In retrospect, integrating early might have saved the franchise, but instead, the Senators withered away into mediocrity. In 1960 they left for Bloomington, Minnesota, and renamed themselves the Twins. Clark Griffith was dead by then, but the new owner, his nephew Calvin, offered one last parting insult to the black Washingtonians who had put so much money in the family's pocket. Upon landing in Minnesota, he told an assembled crowd: "We came here because you've got good, hardworking white people here."

In 1961, a new Washington Senators franchise was created, using Griffith Stadium for one season while its new ballpark was being built. After that, the old stadium stood vacant for several years, falling into a state of extreme disrepair. Shoulder-high weeds choked the infield, steel beams fell from the upper deck, and piles of garbage were strewn everywhere. "The inside of the stadium looked like a disaster area," the *Washington Post* wrote. Mercifully, Griffith Stadium was finally torn down on February 11, 1965. 🌐

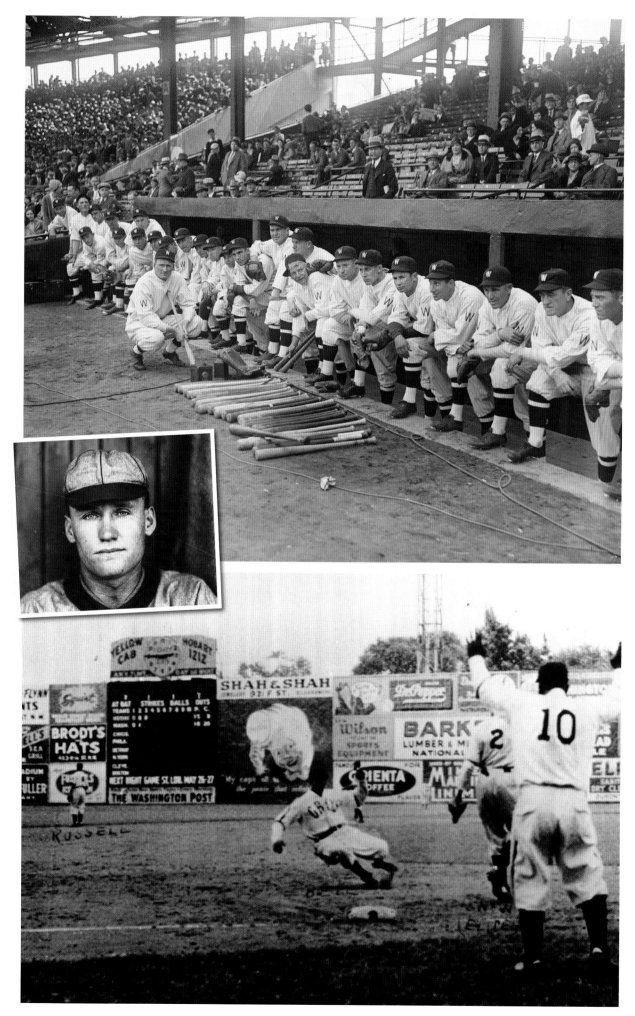

OPPOSITE PAGE, TOP: Connie Mack played his first major league game on September 11, 1886, when he debuted as the catcher for the Washington Nationals. Sixty-four years later, on October 1, 1950, he managed his final big league game—this time against Washington.

OPPOSITE PAGE, BOTTOM LEFT: It's hard to imagine a better lineup than the one the American League fielded during the 1937 All-Star Game at Griffith Stadium. From left are Lou Gehrig, Joe Cronin, Bill Dickey, Joe DiMaggio, Charlie Gehringer, Jimmie Foxx, and Hank Greenberg. With Gehrig holding down first base, Greenberg and Foxx had to start the game on the bench. To no one's surprise, the AL bludgeoned the NL into submission, 8-3.

OPPOSITE PAGE, BOTTOM RIGHT: One of the greatest hitters ever to play at Griffith Stadium was Buck Leonard, who used his textbook left-handed swing to bat an estimated .320 during his eighteen-year career in the Negro Leagues. The soft-spoken Leonard entered pro ball as a last resort in 1933 after losing his job as a railroad laborer. He then played seventeen straight years for the Homestead Grays. "During the war when people couldn't get much gas, that's when our best crowds were," he once said. "People couldn't travel, so they would have to stay in Washington on weekends."

TOP: The Washington Senators pose in Griffith Stadium's dugout in 1931, with manager Walter Johnson (kneeling in dirt with bat) perhaps imparting some words of wisdom. At the time, the Senators were the only major league team to employ what they called a "comedy coacher," an ex-player named Nick Altrock whose job was partly to coach and partly to entertain the crowd with comic antics. While coaching first base, the irrepressible Altrock (visible in the middle of the photo with a sideways cap) would mock the umpire, pantomime the opposition's movements, and generally keep everyone in good spirits.

MIDDLE: Walter Johnson is the only pitcher in baseball history to win 200 games in one ballpark, which he did at Griffith Stadium. He's pictured here in 1911, the year the ballpark opened. Thirteen years later he would be the winning pitcher when the Senators won their only championship, pitching four innings of scoreless extra-inning relief to win Game 7 of the 1924 World Series.

BOTTOM: Cool Papa Bell slides into third base at Griffith Stadium in 1946. During the 1940s the Homestead Grays, usually based in Pittsburgh, played about half their games in Washington, bringing top-shelf Negro League baseball to a community that hadn't previously had it. Also visible here are umpire Silk Lee, Baltimore shortstop Frank Russell (No. 4), third baseman Felton Snow (No. 2), and Grays manager "Candy Jim" Taylor (No. 10). Though he isn't pictured, we know Josh Gibson was catching this game for Homestead because his number, 20, is listed on the outfield scoreboard.

TOP: President Franklin Roosevelt gets up from his wheelchair to throw the first pitch at the Senators' 1934 home opener. "Roosevelt enjoys himself at a ball game as much as a kid on Christmas morning," *Baseball Magazine* once wrote. This was the third of eleven MLB games FDR would attend as president, all but one of them at Griffith Stadium. To Roosevelt's left, with his mouth open laughing, is team owner and stadium namesake Clark Griffith, who had once been a star pitcher himself. Next to Griffith is the Senators' manager and shortstop, Joe Cronin, who kept the gossip columnists busy because he was dating Griffith's niece.

MIDDLE: President Lyndon Johnson stuffs his face with popcorn at the Senators' 1964 home opener. Sitting to his right are Speaker of the House John McCormack and House Majority Whip Hale Boggs. This was LBJ's first ballgame as president, but he'd been a frequent presence at Griffith Stadium when he was a congressman from Texas. "He used to come out and eat hot dogs," Clark Griffith once said. "I used to go out and sit with them and tell them about all these new ballplayers and who was coming. Of course, that's when he was minority leader. When he became majority leader he had to change his style of living."

BOTTOM: Richard Nixon watches Washington's home opener in 1969 with Senators owner Bob Short (in the navy suit) and baseball commissioner Bowie Kuhn (wearing glasses and a red tie). This was DC Stadium's first game under its new name, RFK Memorial Stadium. Sitting behind Nixon, for some reason, is actor Robert Taylor of *Death Valley Days*. Though Dwight Eisenhower and both George Bushes were also huge baseball fans, no president loved the national pastime as much as Nixon, who followed the game intensely, sometimes at the expense of running the country. "He made the effort, in the midst of his schedule, to research and compile lists of the greatest baseball players," Nixon biographer John Farrell wrote.

RFK STADIUM

WASHINGTON SENATORS II 1962–1971 WASHINGTON NATIONALS 2005–2007

RFK MEMORIAL STADIUM, HOME TO TWO eternally moribund baseball teams, is notable as the earliest example of a multipurpose stadium—the concrete doughnuts that purported to accommodate both baseball and football, but in reality, accommodated neither. Opened in 1962 as home of the Washington Senators and Washington Redskins, the stadium had a "formal, pretentious, martial, classically antiseptic, and cold style" which gave the impression that it had been "designed by Stalin," historian Philip Lowry wrote. In its thirteen years as an MLB facility, RFK housed only one winning team, and even that club, the 1969 Senators, finished fourth.

DC Stadium, as it was called until 1969, was the first ballpark ever owned by the federal government. It was intended to be a thoroughly modern structure, with movable stands on rollers allowing the seats to be repositioned between baseball and football games. A hydraulic lift even allowed the pitcher's mound to be raised and lowered. However, the movable stands meant that there was no lower deck of bleachers. Instead the only outfield seats were in the upper deck, far from the action. Because of the space necessary for football, the regular grandstand seats were also much farther away than usual, giving the stadium a distant and impersonal feel.

The Senators left for Texas in 1972, leaving the stadium without baseball until 2005, when the Montreal Expos moved in and renamed themselves the Washington Nationals. Local baseball fans were so enthused to have a team, they didn't mind the stadium's flaws. During Nats games RFK Stadium's atmosphere was often electric, and when it was full, one could feel the stands swaying back and forth, an eerie artifact of the grandstand's hollow (but safe) construction. The baseball team moved to new digs in 2008, but RFK enjoyed continued relevance as the home of soccer's DC United, who played there until 2017. 🌀

LEFT: Manager Ted Williams (far left) and his Washington Senators are introduced at RFK Stadium on Opening Day 1971, which would turn out to be the team's final season in Washington. The day's ceremonies included a first pitch by President Richard Nixon, a close friend of Williams'. The following year, as Nixon was enduring withering criticism over the Vietnam War, Williams wrote him a letter of support. "Coming as it does from one whose own military record is a source of inspiration…your understanding of why these steps had to be taken means a great deal to me," Nixon wrote in reply.

NATIONALS PARK

THREE YEARS AFTER THE OTHER twenty-nine major league teams banded together to move the Montreal Expos to Washington, DC, the team acquired a stately new ballpark in 2008. After spending its entire forty-year existence playing in three dysfunctional venues, the franchise finally had a legitimate major league stadium to call home. Situated on a riverbank surrounded by cherry trees, and within sight of a number of national landmarks, Nationals Park was the final reward for patient Washingtonians who had pined for baseball's return since 1972.

After two years of contentious negotiations that included accusations of bad faith on both sides, the DC Council approved the $611 million stadium in 2004 by a margin of one vote. Using city tax dollars to build the ballpark was a hugely controversial issue, particularly since most of the ballpark's patrons were expected to come from affluent suburbs, which didn't contribute to the funding. The government made the deal despite opinion polls that showed that Washingtonians opposed the deal by as much as a two-to-one margin. Voters eventually booted out three city council members who had supported the project.

For architectural firm HOK Sport, Nationals Park represented an opportunity to bounce back from the self-plagiarism that had characterized so many of its recent creations. The designers eschewed the redbrick retro look, instead using steel and glass. The straight lines and right angles of the exterior were meant to evoke DC's public buildings, particularly the acclaimed East Wing of the National Gallery of Art designed by I.M. Pei. Inside, the main colors were white (the color of the steel beams) and navy blue (the color of the seats). The playing field was 24 feet below street level, meaning that the majority of fans walked down, not up, to their seats after entering. A whopping 4,000 club seats and seventy-eight luxury boxes provided ample tax write-offs and dealmaking space for the city's many lobbyists.

The park's location on the Anacostia River is ideal. Just a few blocks northeast is the Tidal Basin, which serves as home to the Washington Monument, Jefferson Memorial, Lincoln

The higher up you go in the stands at Nationals Park, the better your view of the iconic monuments surrounding the ballpark. Fans in the upper deck on the first base side can see both the Washington Monument (2 miles northeast) and the US Capitol (1 mile north). After only a few years of existence, Nationals Park has itself become something of a local icon, to the point that it's prominently featured in the opening credits of the show *House of Cards.* "The Nationals being in the neighborhood is a huge sense of pride and enthusiasm for the community," Meredith Fascett, a neighborhood commissioner, told the *Washington Times* in 2018.

Memorial, and other public monuments. From the upper deck, fans have a view of the US Capitol behind the left field foul pole.

When it opened, the team boasted that the ballpark would help renew what had become a blighted area of town, but nearby residents were skeptical. "The projects are still here, the drugs are still here, the shooting is still here," business owner Eglon Daley told the *New York Times*. "I don't see where people on this side are getting a job over there [at the ballpark]." Reviews of the park itself were mixed. "It is a machine for baseball and for sucking the money

out of the pockets of people who like baseball, and it makes no apologies about its purely functional design," *Washington Post* culture critic Philip Kennicott wrote. "Although it is positioned on one of the most symbolically significant and potentially beautiful axes of the city, aligned with the Capitol and next to the Anacostia River, it all but fades into the landscape. Two disastrously situated parking garages—reserved for high-paying ticketholders—obscure the front entrance, and its other three sides present a bland face to the world."

Nationals Park is the first "green" sports stadium in the country, as certified by the US Green Building Council. Among its environmentally friendly features are energy-efficient lighting, low-flow restroom faucets, 100 recycling bins, and special parking spaces for hybrid vehicles. The ballpark's signature feature, however, is without question the fourth-inning Presidents Race, a wildly popular adaptation of Milwaukee's famed sausage race. In the DC version, four team employees race around the bases wearing caricature costumes of the four presidents who appear on Mount Rushmore. (William Howard Taft, Herbert Hoover, and, for some reason, Calvin Coolidge, have also made cameo appearances.) The race features a delightful running gag, as Roosevelt is never allowed to win. Often Teddy's pratfalls are the talk of the ballpark. He has frequently been tripped mid-race or become sidetracked talking to fans, and once was disqualified for driving a motor scooter to the finish line. On October 3, 2012, the long-suffering Teddy finally won a race, ending his losing streak at 525 games.

TOP: Nationals Park was energized in 2011 by the arrival of Bryce Harper, the brash nineteen-year-old who may have been the most-hyped prospect in the history of baseball. Harper quickly endeared himself to Nats fans with his all-out hustle and prodigious power. The best illustration of Harper's fearless attitude came in a road game at Philadelphia. During Harper's eighth game in the majors, Phillies ace Cole Hamels purposely plunked him with a pitch, just to put the rookie in his place. Harper responded by coolly walking to first—and moments later, he shocked the Phillies by stealing home.

BOTTOM: Six presidents are hanging out in a tunnel beneath Nationals Park, although one of them appears significantly shorter than the rest. From left are George Washington, Thomas Jefferson, Barack Obama, William Howard Taft, Teddy Roosevelt, and Abe Lincoln. According to former White House photographer Pete Souza, the president's motorcade had been driving away from the 2015 Congressional Baseball Game when Obama spotted the presidential mascots and asked his driver to stop for this photo op.

BOSTON

HUNTINGTON AVENUE GROUNDS

TEAM: Boston Red Sox (1901–1911)

LOCATION: Corner of Huntington Ave. and Bryant Ave. (now Forsyth St.), Boston

FIRST MLB GAME: May 8, 1901

LAST MLB GAME: October 7, 1911

NOTABLE FEATURES: Toolshed in play in deep center field; 50-foot embankment in left field.

FENWAY PARK

TEAM: Boston Red Sox (1912–present)

LOCATION: Corner of Yawkey Way and Van Ness St., Boston

FIRST MLB GAME: April 20, 1912

NOTABLE FEATURES: 37-foot-tall left field wall dubbed The Green Monster; hill in left field known as Duffy's Cliff (razed in 1934).

BRAVES FIELD

TEAM: Boston Braves (1915–1952)

NAMES: Braves Field (1915–1935, 1941–1952), National League Field (1936-1941)

LOCATION: Corner of Babcock St. and Commonwealth Ave., Boston

FIRST MLB GAME: August 18, 1915

LAST MLB GAME: September 21, 1952

NOTABLE FEATURES: Huge capacity fueled by large bleacher sections down both foul lines; "jury box" seating in right field underneath massive scoreboard.

FENWAY PARK

When business failures forced the legendary Cincinnati Red Stockings to leave Ohio in 1871, the team moved en masse to Massachusetts, keeping the Red Stockings moniker and moving into a cozy wooden ballpark in Boston's South End neighborhood. Naturally dubbed South End Grounds, this park would be rebuilt in 1883 and 1894. The stunning 1883 version, known as the Grand Pavilion, was the most beautiful and elaborate ballpark of its era. The double-decked grandstand resembled a medieval castle, with seven gables and seven prominent spires, each flying a huge flag. Tragically, this landmark of ballpark construction was destroyed on May 15, 1894 by the Great Roxbury Fire, which started underneath the right field stands. Boston players tried in vain to put out the blaze, which eventually destroyed 200 buildings.

The ballpark was rebuilt in two months, but in a decidedly less lavish manner. This new, more pedestrian South End Grounds served as home of the Boston Braves until 1915, when the team moved into a massive new home, Braves Field. Another major league team, the Red Sox, was founded in 1901 and initially played at Huntington Avenue Grounds in North Roxbury. That quaint wooden ballpark was replaced in 1912 by Fenway Park. The venerable Fenway has undergone massive changes throughout its century of use, and was saved from the wrecking ball in the early 2000s when the Red Sox decided to pour millions into renovating it instead of moving to a new ballpark. Yet much of its original charm remains, and it's now the oldest park in the majors. 🔲

BOTTOM: Four major league ballparks burned down in 1894, and the most tragic loss was undoubtedly Boston's South End Grounds, where the famous grandstand known as the Grand Pavilion was reduced to cinders. The most opulent grandstand of its day, the Grand Pavilion (the edge of which can be seen at right) featured conical spires, elaborate wooden arches, and a rare upper deck. In the 120-plus years since, there has never been another Boston ballpark built with an upper deck (although one was added to Fenway years after it opened).

THE BOSTON BASE BALL CLUB.
1888.

COPYRIGHT. 1894.
BY
W. B. DAVIDSON.

THE SITE OF THE FIRST WORLD SERIES GAME ever played, Huntington Avenue Grounds was the home of the Boston Red Sox—or the "Americans," as they were originally called—during the franchise's first eleven years of existence. When the American League rebranded itself as a major league in 1901, a healthy franchise in Boston—as well as a suitable ballpark there—were seen as keys to the new league's success. For this reason, league officials formed a special committee to choose the best site for Boston's ballpark, with Philadelphia A's manager Connie Mack as serving as chairman. After touring a variety of possible locations, Mack's committee chose a site in North Roxbury just across the train tracks from the South End Grounds, where the other local team, the Boston Beaneaters, had played since 1872.

The Huntington Avenue Grounds was built on a grassy field where the circus usually set up when it came to town. "There was a fairly large pond on the property that children would splash into during summer months," Bill Nowlin wrote in his book *Red Sox Threads*. "In the winter, of course, people could ice skate there, but this was no high society skating pond. The area was largely bounded by rail yards, a huge Boston Storage Warehouse behind the length of the left field bleachers, some stables, breweries, and a pickle factory. The United Drug Company was situated near enough to the park that one could often smell the chemicals."

Huntington was built of wood and concrete, with four entrance gates and enough seats to accommodate 9,000 fans. The vast outfield measured 530 feet to dead center, and left field featured a sloping embankment, 50 feet deep, designed to accommodate overflow crowds during well-attended games. That overflow seating became necessary in 1903 when more than 16,000 fans packed in to watch the Americans face the Pittsburgh Pirates in

Cab. 23.50.15

OPPOSITE PAGE, TOP LEFT: The 1878 Boston Red Stockings (left) and Providence Grays pose for a portrait at Messer Street Grounds in Providence, Rhode Island. The Red Stockings employed two of early baseball's most influential figures, brothers George and Harry Wright. George, a star shortstop, is lounging on the grass in the center of the photo. Harry, the team's manager, is seated with a top hat and cane. Two years after this photo was taken, Messer Street Grounds became the site of MLB's first perfect game, pitched by a young Brown University student named Lee Richmond.

OPPOSITE PAGE, TOP RIGHT: Much has changed in baseball since this lithograph depicting the Boston Beaneaters was made in 1888. Note that the pitcher is only 50 feet away from home, the plate is square rather than pentagonal, and the catcher, King Kelly, isn't wearing a mask. This image takes the perspective of a fan sitting in the lower deck of Boston's Grand Pavilion—the same structure depicted in the photograph just underneath it.

THIS PAGE: Huntington Avenue Grounds is an absolute madhouse in this photo taken before Game 3 of the 1903 World Series. Police, despite wielding rubber hoses and baseball bats, are unable to keep the crowd off the field. People are standing on top of carriages and climbing fences, and a crowd is mobbing the poor infielders, preventing them from warming up.

the first modern World Series game ever played. Despite the extra space, thousands of fans were turned away, and many climbed fences and lampposts to get any view they could. Boston lost that contest 7-3, but behind superlative pitching from Bill Dineen and Cy Young, the Americans won the Series in eight games.

When the Red Sox moved to the much larger Fenway Park in 1912, they took the sod from Huntington with them and installed it on their new field. The Huntington Avenue site was eventually purchased by Northeastern University, which built a large gymnasium called the Cabot Center on it in 1954. Today an exhibit inside the Cabot Center recounts the site's baseball history, while a plaque on the gym's outside wall marks the former location of the left field foul pole. In 1993, a bronze statue of Cy Young was erected on the spot where home plate once stood.

TOP: Huntington Avenue Grounds in 1911. A billboard on the fence indicates that a musician, "Creatore and His Band," played here every night after the game was over. (Giuseppe Creatore, born in Naples, was a trombonist who combined music with circus-style gymnastics; if you're curious, his recordings can be easily found online.) Visible in the foreground is a stand selling cigars for 10¢ and popcorn for 5¢, while a cluster of men and boys is gathered behind the left field fence, perhaps gambling. Most interestingly, if you look straight up from the pitcher's mound, you can see the grandstand of South End Grounds, Boston's other major league ballpark. It was right across the railroad tracks.

BOTTOM: The Red Sox paid a huge sum—$3,500—to lure Cy Young away from the National League in 1901, when he was thirty-four years old. He won 33, 32, and 28 games, respectively, in his first three seasons with Boston.

INSET: This 1916 season ticket book belonged to one of Boston's sports icons, Mike "Nuf Ced" McGreevy. A gregarious local saloonkeeper, McGreevy was known as Beantown's number one baseball fan. He ran the Third Base Saloon—so named because it was "the last stop before home"—and was known to end drunken arguments with the simple phrase 'nuff said. He was one of the founders of the Royal Rooters, the influential fan club that supported first the Beaneaters, then later the Red Sox.

OPPOSITE PAGE: Fenway Park as it appeared in 2017. Many of its twenty-first-century changes are visible here, including seats on top of the left field wall, additional seating on the grandstand roof, and a vast increase in the number of ads painted on the Green Monster.

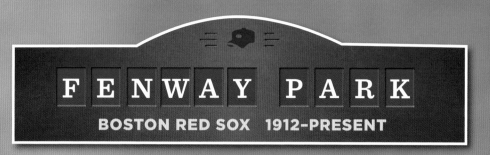

FENWAY PARK

BOSTON RED SOX 1912-PRESENT

IN THE SPRING OF 1912, the Boston Red Sox unveiled what would become the most enduring ballpark in baseball history, and did so to shockingly little fanfare. On the day of Fenway Park's scheduled opening, locals' minds were not on the Red Sox. Instead they were processing the news, first published the previous day, that the largest and most famous ship in the world—the supposedly unsinkable *RMS Titanic*—had hit an iceberg and sunk in the North Atlantic. Among the 1,500 who perished were seventeen Massachusetts residents, and it was the maritime tragedy, not the opening of the ballpark, that dominated the headlines.

In any case, Wednesday, April 17, was a dreary, rainy day, and the opening game was postponed. The next day, it was postponed again. The next day, it was rained out once more. Finally, on April 20, 1912, Fenway Park hosted its first baseball game. The festivities kicked off with an odd new practice that would soon become commonplace in baseball: a ceremonial first pitch. It was thrown by the team's most famous fan, Boston Mayor John Fitzgerald, known to everyone as "Honey Fitz." (Half a century later Fitz's grandson and namesake, John Fitzgerald Kennedy, would be elected president.) In that inaugural game the Red Sox committed six errors and left eighteen men on base, but they managed to pull out a thrilling twelve-inning win over the Yankees—not that anyone noticed. Attendance was 24,000, just 70 percent of capacity, and the grand opening didn't even make the front page of Boston's newspapers. Everyone was still reading about the *Titanic*.

At its opening, Fenway Park looked remarkably similar to the ballpark we know today. The outfield was oddly shaped, with a tiny left field and a massive expanse of grass in right. The main grandstand was covered by a steel roof stretching from foul pole to foul pole, and a massive section of 50¢ bleachers lay beyond the right field wall. A large press box was built on top of the roof, and photographers roamed free on the rooftop waiting to capture the action. Most notably, a 25-foot left field wall loomed over everything, though it was not yet

painted green. Instead it was plastered with ads, most of them for popular beverages of the day: Coca-Cola, Budweiser, Mumm's Extra Rye Whiskey, and Pureoxia ginger ale. A hilly incline at the base of the wall was dubbed "Duffy's Cliff" after Sox left fielder Duffy Lewis, who learned to climb the hill as deftly as if he'd been born on it.

Fenway's right field wall, on the other hand, was so distant at 380 feet away that it proved an unreachable target for left-handed hitters. In 1939, the arrival of a left-handed prodigy named Ted Williams prompted the Red Sox to make the park a little less daunting for lefties. After Williams's rookie season, the bullpens were relocated from the baselines to right field, reducing the home run distance by 23 feet. The bleachers there became known as "Williamsburg," and today a lone seat in row 37 is painted red to mark the spot where the longest home run of Williams's career landed.

In 1934, after owner Tom Yawkey bought the team, Duffy's Cliff and the wooden left field wall were both razed. The wall was rebuilt using a wooden frame covered by tin sheeting, and its height was raised to 37 feet, the same height it maintains today. A couple of years later netting was installed on top, so home run balls wouldn't break the windows of businesses across the

street. In 1947, the wall was finally painted the distinctive color of green that gave it its famous "Green Monster" nickname.

In 1976, field-level padding was added to the Green Monster, and the tin sheeting was replaced with melamine, a durable hard plastic commonly used to make cafeteria trays. While the sound of balls hitting the wall remains as loud as ever, the noise is now more of a sharp thud than a metallic clang. For decades, the caretakers of the Monster's hand-operated scoreboard sat on folding chairs inside the wall, peering at the game through 1-inch-high slits cut into the wall. The area inside is dark and dingy, 5 feet wide by 40 feet long, and rats have been known to make an occasional appearance. The scoreboard contains 127 openings for numbers, and an inventory of heavy tin panels with painted numbers hangs on the back wall, ready and waiting in case the score should change.

Remarkably, Fenway Park cost only $650,000 to build in 1912, but as baseball marched into the modern era, the team was compelled to add improvements.

OPPOSITE PAGE: This statue of Carl Yastrzemski was erected outside Fenway Park's right field entrance in 2013. Sculpted by Maryland artist Toby Mendez, it shows Yaz tipping his helmet after the final at-bat of his career in 1983.

TOP: Babe Ruth (left) poses with three of his Red Sox teammates—Ernie Shore, Rube Foster, and Del Gainer—in what appears to be the dugout of Washington, DC's Griffith Stadium. During the six years Ruth called Fenway Park home, he hit only eleven home runs there, as opposed to thirty-eight in road games.

MIDDLE: Fenway Park's red seat (inset) marks the spot where the longest home run in the stadium's history landed. Blasted by Ted Williams on June 9, 1946, the ball reached the thirty-third row of the right field bleachers, where it struck an elderly fan in the head. "How far away must one sit to be safe in this park?" the fan, Joseph Boucher, complained. "I didn't even get the ball. They say it bounced a dozen rows higher, but after it hit my head I was no longer interested."

BOTTOM LEFT: Yankees reliever Chad Green signs the inside of the Green Monster in 2017. One of Fenway Park's most fascinating areas, this dingy but hallowed space is where the park's two scoreboard operators ply their trade. Few are allowed to visit, but those who do usually sign their names on the wall, a tradition that goes back decades. During the early 2000s, Yankees pitcher David Wells added "Fenway Sucks" next to his signature.

BOTTOM RIGHT: Fenway Park still contains many vintage seats, including these from the 1930s. None of the park's original seats still exist, however; most were burned when the park caught fire in 1934 and were replaced by the blue chairs seen here. These seats date from an era when Americans were decidedly slimmer. They're only 15 inches wide, whereas some seats in new Yankee Stadium are as wide as 24 inches.

Lights were erected in 1947, an LCD message board in 1976, and a private club behind home plate in 1988. Still, by the mid-1990s Fenway was beginning to fray around the edges. More importantly, it was now one of the smallest ballparks in the majors, limiting the amount of revenue per game it could generate. With the retro-ballpark craze sweeping through baseball, Red Sox owner John Harrington sought a way to cash in with a new stadium of his own. In the time-honored tradition of baseball owners, Harrington tried to emphasize the need for a new ball-park by letting the old one fall into as much disrepair as possible.

Various sites across Boston were proposed to replace Fenway, but the idea that gained traction was a "New Fenway Park" located one block south of the old one. The proposed new park was essentially a copy of the old one, with the same unusual dimensions and monstrous left field wall—with the main difference being 12,000 additional seats and 100 luxury suites. But a fan organization called Save Fenway Park hired an architect to draw up plans for what a renovated Fenway might look like, and, facing entrenched opposition, Harrington finally gave up in 2001, announcing he was selling the Red Sox to the highest bidder. The winning bid of $700 million was submitted by John Henry—who also happened to be the only bidder who wanted to save Fenway Park.

Henry decided to renovate Fenway in stages, with construction taking place each offseason over a ten-year period. The final cost would be $285 million, and Henry smartly hired Janet Marie Smith, the Orioles executive who'd supervised the construction of Camden Yards, to oversee the renovations. The first order of business was making a deal with the city to close a neighboring street, Yawkey Way, so it could function as an open-air concourse on game days. In 2003, a manual out-of-town scoreboard was added, as were 269 barstools on top of the Green Monster—seats that quickly became the most coveted in Fenway Park. Seating atop the right field roof was added in 2004, and in 2005, the

INSET: This pennant was printed during the 1975 World Series, but of course it was never sold, because the Red Sox lost Game 7 to Cincinnati. Boston fans would have to wait another twenty-nine years for their next title.

TOP: Luis Tiant Jr. throws a pitch at Fenway during the 1975 World Series. That Fall Classic was a special one for El Tiante, as his father—the illustrious Cuban pitcher Luis Tiant Sr.—received special dispensation from Fidel Castro to travel to Boston and watch his son pitch.

BOTTOM: Reliever Koji Uehara pitches during Game 2 of the 2013 World Series at Fenway. Boston won the series to capture its third title in ten years.

playing field and home clubhouse were replaced. More than 1,000 standing-room-only spots were added in 2006, and in 2007, an underground batting cage and locker rooms for team employees were built. In 2009, the right field rooftop seating, which had proven a big hit, was nearly tripled in size. In 2010, a statue was unveiled depicting four Red Sox stars of the 1940s: Ted Williams, Bobby Doerr, Johnny Pesky, and Dom DiMaggio. The decade-long project was capped off in 2011 with the installation of three large HD video boards.

The renovations increased seating capacity from 33,933 to 37,731. Between 2003 and 2013 the Red Sox sold out 820 consecutive games, the longest such streak in sports history. Meanwhile, Smith's sure-handed shepherding of the renovation came to be regarded as one of the great accomplishments in ballpark-building history. She made Fenway a marquee venue again, not only for baseball fans,

but also for hockey and football games, and concerts by the likes of Bruce Springsteen and Pearl Jam. After baseball's oldest venue was refurbished so successfully, the owners of the second- and third-oldest ballparks—Wrigley Field and Dodger Stadium—decided to undertake similar projects. In 2012, Los Angeles even hired Smith away from the Red Sox to work on the Dodger Stadium renovations.

"For years, Fenway was destined to go in a different direction," Smith told the *Worcester Telegram*. "We felt like it was for us to reel it in, like a save, pull it off the brink, from jumping off the cliff. The challenge was how to sustain excitement and enthusiasm about that scale of investment over a ten-year period. That's a long time for an organization to have to take a deep breath every September and get ready to start construction, millions of dollars of construction, and then finish in April. It wasn't always certain what the outcome would be." ⚾

TOP: Officially, Fenway Park's Green Monster seats sell for anywhere from $135 to $500, although they can fetch much higher prices on the secondary market. Originally installed in 2003, the seats have gained a reputation for having one of the best vantage points in baseball. "I can't imagine a better place to watch," Sox fan Ken Husler told the *Denver Post*. "You're sitting right on top of everything. You've got a great perspective on how deep a ball's hit, and you're really close like you're sitting on the left fielder's shoulder."

BOTTOM: Red Sox owner John Henry once presented David Ortiz with a plaque declaring him "the best clutch hitter in Boston Red Sox history," and few would disagree. Ortiz's career included 191 home runs that gave his team the lead, 46 more that tied the score, and 11 walk-offs that ended the game instantly. His greatest moment, though, had little to do with baseball. In 2013, before the Sox played their first home game since the Boston Marathon bombing, Ortiz made a fiery speech to the Fenway faithful. "This is our f-cking city," he reminded Bostonians, in a statement that was credited with galvanizing the city's recovery efforts.

THIS PAGE: Fenway Park as it appeared in 2008, with Texas Rangers outfielders Milton Bradley (left) and Josh Hamilton warming up between innings. Almost nothing in this photo would be recognizable to a fan attending a game in 1912, the year Fenway opened. The left field wall wasn't green back then, but was instead filled with colorful ads for such products as Budweiser and Coca-Cola. There was no seating on top of the wall back then, but there was some at the bottom, with bleacher seats on the outfield grass. The long ladder visible here was added in 1936 so home run balls could be retrieved, and lights were installed in 1947. The iconic Citgo sign, now designated by the city as a historic landmark, was built two blocks away from the ballpark in 1940. From 1947 through 1999, advertisements weren't allowed on the historic Green Monster, a prohibition that ended with an ad promoting the 1999 All-Star Game. Advertising has been re-infiltrating the wall ever since, and by the time this photo was taken in 2008, there were eight large ads on the wall and three more behind it.

TOP INSET: Fenway Park's exterior boasts banners celebrating the team's pennant-winning seasons. The red banners represent World Series titles, while the blue ones denote years when Boston won the pennant but not the World Series. There are eleven banners in all, seven red and four blue. In 1977, the street where they hang was renamed Yawkey Way after the industrial heir who owned the Red Sox for forty-three years. However, after a white supremacist riot in Charlottesville, Virginia, prompted a nationwide re-examination of racist monuments, Red Sox management asked the city to rename the street. Tom Yawkey had been baseball's most stubborn practitioner of segregation, refusing to employ African-American players for a dozen years after Jackie Robinson debuted with Brooklyn. In April 2018 Yawkey Way was officially reverted to its original name, Jersey Street.

BOTTOM INSET: This statue of Ted Williams with a young fan was erected on Yawkey Way (now Jersey Street) in 2004. Sculpted by Florida artist Franc Talarico, it commemorates Williams' charitable work on behalf of children. "Williams made hundreds of trips, most unreported, to local hospitals to visit sick children during his playing career," the Associated Press wrote. "His support was critical to the founding and continued success of the Jimmy Fund, which raises money for the Dana-Farber Cancer Institute."

BRAVES FIELD

BOSTON BRAVES   1915–1952

ONE OF THE MOST MASSIVE BALLPARKS ever constructed, Braves Field was built in the heady days after the 1914 "Miracle Braves" had pulled off perhaps the unlikeliest World Series title of all time. The stadium was the brainchild of team owner James Gaffney, who had made a fortune as a corrupt contractor and a leader in New York's Tammany Hall machine. Gaffney, like all MLB owners, desperately wanted his own version of the hugely successful Shibe Park. Within four years of Shibe's 1909 opening, twelve of the sixteen MLB clubs were playing in new steel stadiums; the four exceptions were the Cubs, Cardinals, Phillies, and Braves.

Bostonians had been thrilled by the Braves' miracle championship, but Gaffney's blood boiled at having to rent brand-new Fenway Park for the World Series games because it was so much bigger than the Braves' aging ballpark. Gaffney became determined to build an even better ballpark than Fenway and wrest the title of Boston's favorite team away from the Red Sox. "The birth and subsequent demise of Braves Field serves as a 'pivot point' in ballpark history, one that distinguishes two very different approaches to how baseball parks should be built and how they should relate to their host city and its citizens," historian Bob Ruzzo wrote in the *Baseball Research Journal*.

Gaffney bought a plot of land for $100,000, called a press conference to announce his plans, and then began work on the new stadium, serving as his own contractor. Instead of pouring money into the ballpark as the owners of the Pirates and Giants had, Gaffney's guiding principle was cutting corners wherever possible. He saved money by leaving the first- and third-base stands without a roof, and

Braves Field—Home of the Boston Braves, Boston, Mass.

by making the exterior façade utilitarian rather than decorative. An aficionado of inside-the-park homers, Gaffney made sure the playing field was gigantic; the power alley in right-center field was 520 feet away from home plate. "This is the only field in the country on which you can play an absolutely fair game of ball without the interference of fences," Ty Cobb said, when he first saw the completed Braves Field.

Braves Field was always intended to be functional, not magical. As far as Gaffney was concerned, the park achieved the only two goals he cared about: It cost relatively little, and it held a huge number of fans—40,000, to be exact. The owner was delighted when, a year after he'd gone crawling to the Red Sox to rent Fenway Park for the World Series, the tables were suddenly turned. In 1915 the Red Sox had to ask him for permission to play their World Series games at Braves Field, since it was much larger than even Fenway Park. Gaffney happily accommodated them, and the Sox won that Fall Classic with spectacular play from outfielders Duffy Lewis, Tris Speaker, and Harry Hooper. Ironically, that would be the only victorious World Series a Boston team would ever play at Braves Field. The Braves called it home for thirty-eight years, during which time they made only one World Series—and lost. The large seating capacity so prized by James Gaffney turned out to be wholly unnecessary, as the Braves averaged fewer than 10,000 fans per game thirty-three times in the stadium's existence. In 1953, having long since lost their battle with the Red Sox for Boston's heart, the Braves moved west to Milwaukee. Braves Field was purchased by Boston University, which eventually renovated it, renamed it Nickerson Field, and still uses it today for lacrosse and soccer.

OPPOSITE PAGE, TOP: The 1914 "Miracle Braves" didn't play at Braves Field, but their unexpected World Series victory was the impetus for building it. Playing at the dilapidated South End Grounds, the Braves charged from last place on July 19 all the way to first place by August 25. Then, in the World Series, they dismantled the Philadelphia Athletics so thoroughly that some observers believed the A's were throwing the series.

OPPOSITE PAGE, BOTTOM: Most of Braves Field's 40,000 seats were in the huge sections of uncovered seating down the left and right field lines. The fans seen here are actually Red Sox rooters attending Game 2 of the 1916 World Series, played at Braves Field because it had a much larger capacity than Fenway Park. It turned out to be an extraordinary game, with two lefty pitching aces—Boston's Babe Ruth and Brooklyn's Sherry Smith—going toe-to-toe for fourteen innings. The Sox finally won it on a walk-off single by pinch hitter Del Gainer.

TOP: This postcard shows Braves Field sometime after May 1946, which is when lights were installed for night baseball. Earlier that same year, about 5,000 fans left the 1946 home opener with green paint on their clothing, because the seats hadn't yet dried after being repainted earlier in the day. The Braves eventually paid the irate fans $6,000—an average of $1.20 each—in compensation.

MIDDLE: First baseman Art Shires signs autographs for kids at Braves Field in the summer of 1932. In those days most young baseball fans kept small autograph books in which they collected the signatures of their favorite ballplayers.

BOTTOM: Morrie Arnovich, the Phillies' All-Star first baseman, takes a big swing at Braves Field in 1939. Behind the plate catching is Al López, the namesake of Al López Field in Tampa, which is discussed on page 293.

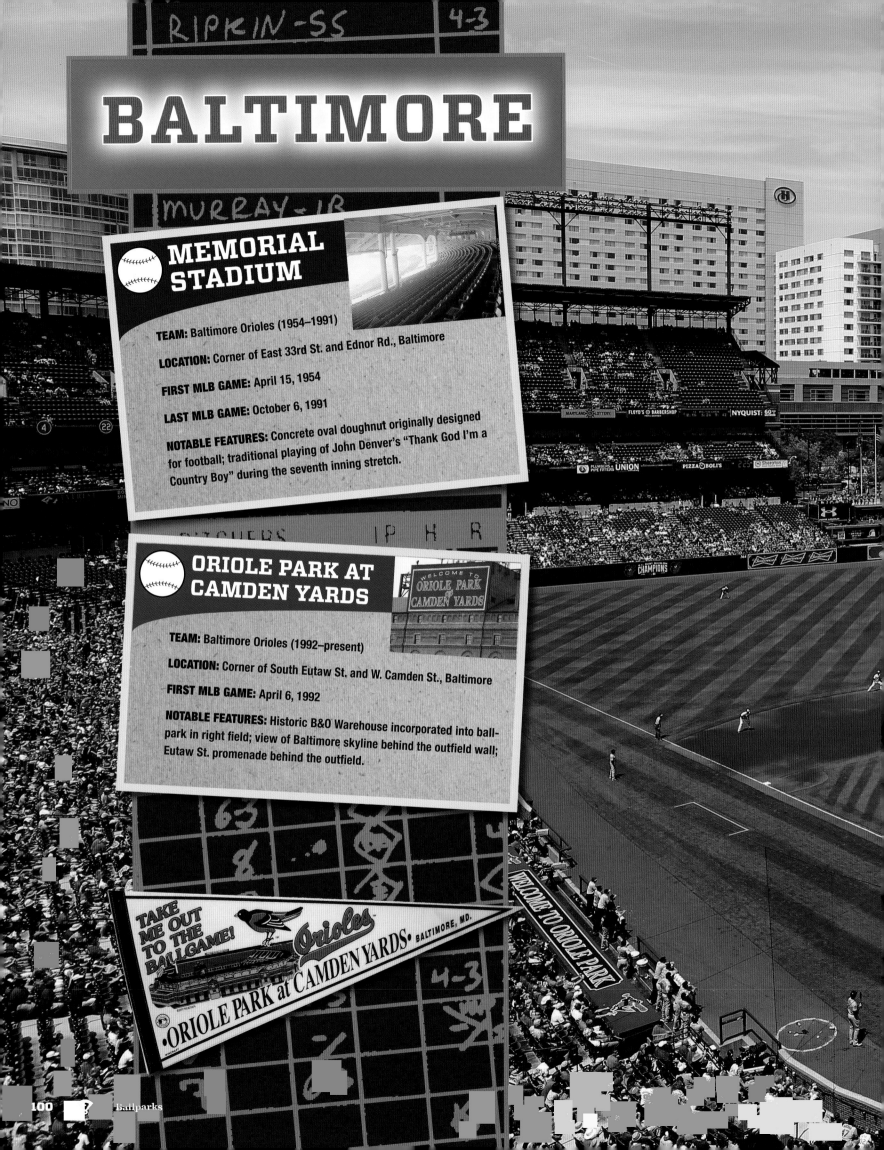

BALTIMORE

MEMORIAL STADIUM

TEAM: Baltimore Orioles (1954–1991)

LOCATION: Corner of East 33rd St. and Ednor Rd., Baltimore

FIRST MLB GAME: April 15, 1954

LAST MLB GAME: October 6, 1991

NOTABLE FEATURES: Concrete oval doughnut originally designed for football; traditional playing of John Denver's "Thank God I'm a Country Boy" during the seventh inning stretch.

ORIOLE PARK AT CAMDEN YARDS

WELCOME TO ORIOLE PARK at CAMDEN YARDS

TEAM: Baltimore Orioles (1992–present)

LOCATION: Corner of South Eutaw St. and W. Camden St., Baltimore

FIRST MLB GAME: April 6, 1992

NOTABLE FEATURES: Historic B&O Warehouse incorporated into ball-park in right field; view of Baltimore skyline behind the outfield wall; Eutaw St. promenade behind the outfield.

TAKE ME OUT TO THE BALLGAME! Orioles • ORIOLE PARK at CAMDEN YARDS • BALTIMORE, MD.

nown today as the home of the iconic Oriole Park at Camden Yards, Baltimore has a major league history that dates all the way back to 1871. Although the city didn't yet have a team, a local ballpark served as a neutral site for a game between Washington and Fort Wayne. Later, a number of different Baltimore teams, most of them called the Orioles, played at different short-lived stadiums around town throughout the nineteenth century. One of these, Oriole Park I, was built next to an amusement park that offered discounted admission for baseball fans.

The famed Baltimore Orioles of the 1890s, led by "Wee Willie" Keeler and John McGraw, annually packed thousands of fans into Oriole Park III, built in 1891 near Druid Hill Park. Right field in this ballpark was an adventure, featuring both a small hill and a creek that often overflowed onto the playing field.

In 1914, the minor league Baltimore Orioles boasted a gregarious teenage pitcher named Babe Ruth, but their attendance at Oriole Park

IV suffered because a short-lived major league team, the Terrapins, set up shop that same year in a new ballpark just across 29th Street. After the Terrapins went belly-up, Baltimore was a minor league town for three more decades until the city lured the St. Louis Browns to town by building massive Memorial Stadium. The Browns were renamed—you guessed it— the Baltimore Orioles, and enjoyed four decades of success at Memorial before moving into a spectacularly innovative retro ballpark in 1992. Officially named Oriole Park at Camden Yards, it is the sixth Baltimore ballpark to be called Oriole Park.

TOP: Four members of the Baltimore Elite Giants—from left, Henry Kimbro, Butch Davis, Lester Lockett, and Lenny Pearson— pose at Bugle Field in 1949. Baltimore won the Negro American League pennant that year thanks to these four men plus Jim Gilliam and Joe Black, who would both go on to play for the Brooklyn Dodgers. Incidentally, the Elite Giants and their fans pronounced the word *elite* unusually, as if it rhymed with *tea light*.

BOTTOM: On September 27, 1897, more than 30,000 fans packed Oriole Park III for one of the biggest games in Baltimore history. The Orioles, aiming for their fourth straight National League pennant, entered the day half a game behind the rival Boston Beaneaters. Boston won a wild game, 19-10, and the vaunted Orioles finished in second place. The disjointed lettering visible on the back of Oriole Park's outfield fence indicates that the planks had probably been salvaged from some other structure.

MEMORIAL STADIUM

BALTIMORE ORIOLES 1954–1991

A MINOR LEAGUE BALLPARK that was gradually expanded into a major league facility, Memorial Stadium was the home of the Orioles from their arrival in Baltimore until the building of Camden Yards. The first ballpark on this site was built in 1922 as a football stadium, and in 1944 was adapted to house minor league baseball. This iteration of the ballpark went by a variety of names, including Babe Ruth Stadium.

In 1950, in an attempt to attract a major league team, the City of Baltimore (which owned the facility) financed a $2.5 million rebuild, tearing down the entire structure and building a new one. The new horseshoe-shaped grandstand, now called Memorial Stadium, had a seating capacity of 31,000. Four years later, when the St. Louis Browns appeared to be looking for a new home, an upper deck was added, increasing the total cost to $6.5 million and the capacity to 46,000. The Browns moved in in 1954 and renamed themselves the Baltimore Orioles after the venerable former minor league franchise.

Perennial losers as the Browns, the Orioles quickly became a winning franchise in Baltimore, capturing their first World Series title in 1966. From 1968 through 1985, they had a winning record every year. A number of beloved players became Baltimore civic institutions while playing here, including Brooks Robinson, Boog Powell, Eddie Murray, and Cal Ripken Jr. The team moved to the extraordinary new Camden Yards in 1991, leaving behind a bevy of fond memories on 33rd Street. Memorial Stadium was torn down in 2002, but in 2010 the Ripken family's charity, the Cal Ripken Sr. Foundation, donated $1.5 million to build a YMCA field on the site. Today, youth players come up to bat in the exact same spot where Cal Ripken Jr. once did. 🖾

Shortstop Cal Ripken Jr. (No. 8) shares a moment with his father, third base coach Cal Ripken Sr. during the 1983 World Series. The younger Ripken spent much of his youth at Memorial Stadium, as his father worked in the Orioles organization for thirty-six years. "It does make you think of all the memories you have of playing here," Ripken Jr. said in 2010 when a new youth field was built on the former site of Memorial Stadium. "My favorite one is hitting my first home run and shaking Dad's hand."

TOP: Brooks Robinson (left) jumps into the arms of pitcher Mike Cuéllar after the final out of the 1970 World Series, as shortstop Mark Belanger looks on. Cuéllar pitched a complete game in the clinching Game 5, but it was Robinson's defensive heroics that would linger in fans' memories for decades to come. His glovework was so spectacular that in the eighth inning, the Memorial Stadium crowd gave him a standing ovation even after he struck out. "It was the most touching thing that has ever happened to me on a baseball diamond," Robinson said.

BOTTOM: Opened in 1950, Memorial Stadium was expanded in stages until 1964, when its capacity reached 54,000 for baseball and 65,000 for football. The ballpark was named to honor the deceased veterans of World Wars I and II; the lettering on the façade is a dedication. The stainless-steel letters of the final line—"Time will not dim the glory of their deeds"—were salvaged before the ballpark's demolition and placed at Camden Yards.

OPPOSITE PAGE: Manny Machado bats against the Red Sox in 2014, when Camden Yards was already the ninth-oldest ballpark in baseball. Almost every ballpark built since 1992 is, to some degree, an attempt to re-create the retro feel that the Orioles and architectural firm HOK pioneered. The ornate ironwork on top of the scoreboard, which advertises the *Baltimore Sun*, may be the classiest advertisement in baseball.

ORIOLE PARK AT CAMDEN YARDS

BALTIMORE ORIOLES 1992-PRESENT

IT ALL BEGAN SO INNOCENTLY. In the mid-1980s, the Baltimore Orioles, who had spent their entire existence playing in a nondescript football stadium, decided they wanted a new home. What they got was a palace: a ballpark that seamlessly blended into the urban landscape, and was so jaw-droppingly beautiful that almost every team in baseball eventually attempted to mimic it. Built for a relatively modest $110 million and funded by the state of Maryland via a new instant lottery game, Oriole Park at Camden Yards was like nothing fans had seen before—and also like everything they'd seen before. Its meticulously curated atmosphere was such a success that it spurred the largest ballpark-building movement in history. In terms of influence, Camden Yards is rivaled only by Shibe Park for the distinction of the most important ballpark ever constructed.

In the decade prior to Oriole Park's debut, only two new stadiums had opened in the major leagues: SkyDome, an AstroTurf-covered behemoth in Toronto, and Comiskey Park II, a middling attempt to rebuild Charles Comiskey's 1910 palace. Baltimore's new ballpark was completely unlike either one. Whereas the concrete bowls and domes of the past had sealed fans off from the urban environment surrounding them, Oriole Park at Camden Yards embraced and utilized that environment.

The Camden Yards area had been floated as a potential stadium site before, most notably by Bill Veeck Jr. when he attempted to buy the Orioles in the 1970s. It was within walking distance of the revitalized Inner Harbor area, the Babe Ruth Museum, and the supposedly haunted grave site of Edgar Allan Poe. It seemed a perfect site, particularly since it was literally Ruth's childhood home. Before being dispatched to reform school, the young Bambino had lived with

TOP: The B&O warehouse, built in 1905, almost met the wrecking ball before an architecture student named Eric Moss convinced the Orioles to save it. "No one cared about it," Peter Richmond wrote in *Ballpark: Camden Yards and the Building of an American Dream*. "The warehouse—so oddly disproportioned and squat…was like the other ingredients of Baltimore's once-delightfully eccentric skyline, fine for the legend, but not right for the new age."

BOTTOM: Although ninety-seven regular-season home runs have been hit into Eutaw Street, not a single one has ever struck the B&O warehouse. This photo illustrates why it's so difficult—a ball has to clear not only the 21-foot-tall right field wall and an adjacent standing-room area, but also this 60-foot-wide thoroughfare. Only Ken Griffey Jr. has ever done it, in the 1993 Home Run Derby. The tall building visible to the left of the warehouse is the Bromo-Seltzer Tower, a local icon constructed in 1911. It was once visible from the Camden Yards stands before an unsightly Hilton hotel blocked the view.

OPPOSITE PAGE: A crowd of 40,000—many of them Yankee fans—watches the Orioles face New York in 2013. During the early twenty-first century, with Baltimore finishing in fourth place seemingly every year, Camden Yards earned the nickname "Yankee Stadium South" as throngs of New Yorkers streamed in to fill the vacant seats every time the Bronx Bombers were in town. "We definitely feel it," Yankees manager Joe Girardi once said. "It's nice to have your fans travel wherever you go."

his parents in an apartment above his father's tavern at 406 Conway Street. That was smack in the middle of what would become center field at Camden Yards, and the remains of Ruth's Café were unearthed during construction.

Another building in the abandoned Baltimore & Ohio rail yards, this one still standing, was the B&O warehouse. Completed in 1905, the tan brick edifice was supposedly the longest building on the East Coast at the time, at 1,016 feet long (but just 51 feet wide). For decades, the building sheltered all manner of cargo entering Baltimore via train, but by the late 1980s it had lain vacant for decades. The Orioles at first viewed the warehouse as a nuisance, an obstruction that interfered with their otherwise ideal plan for the site. According to architect Richard deFlon, Orioles President Larry Lucchino was adamantly opposed to leaving the building standing. "No way," Lucchino reportedly said. "This is stupid. You don't want this ugly old building." So the architectural firm the Orioles hired—Kansas City–based Hellmuth, Obata, and Kassabaum (HOK)—created a model that involved tearing the warehouse down. But in 1987, the *Baltimore Sun* and *City Paper* both ran articles hyping a brilliant design by Eric Moss, a Syracuse University architecture student who had ingeniously incorporated the warehouse into the stadium's structure behind the right field wall. Moss's idea became the talk of the town.

The Orioles decided to keep the warehouse. Its inclusion made Camden Yards, as author Peter Richmond noted, "the oldest ballpark in America, as well as its newest." It also changed the team's entire concept of what the ballpark could become. Keeping the warehouse was not only practical—the Orioles could use it as office space—but also served as a

tip of the cap to America's historic urban ballparks, which had usually been squeezed into existing city blocks amongst existing buildings. Two long-ago ballparks, Huntington Avenue Grounds in Boston (page 89) and the Baker Bowl in Philadelphia (page 10), had featured warehouses behind the left field fence. The Orioles began studying photographs of old parks, seeking to distill the features that had made them so beloved to fans. In one remarkable note, Orioles Vice President Janet Marie Smith instructed HOK on what the team wanted done:

> Compatible with the warehouse and Baltimore's civic buildings in terms of scale, configuration, and color…[t]he outer wall of the upper roof concourse should be designed so fans can see the city. Move the upper deck closer to the playing field. Reduce the height of the second deck. Reduce the height of the third deck…. Turn the upper deck seating where it abuts the warehouse to face home plate. The rail at field level should be ornamental ironwork. Trees, plants, and other greenery are critical to designing this facility as a ballpark, not a stadium.

It was a critically important memo. For the first time in generations, a ballpark was being constructed with the fan experience as the central consideration. Previous stadiums had focused on amenities— concessions, parking, souvenirs—but Camden Yards, while providing no shortage of amenities, focused on aesthetics. Above all, the park was designed to be beautiful. "If Major League Baseball offered awards for architecture, this team would win hands down," *New York Times* architecture critic Paul Goldberger wrote in 1989, as construction was about

to begin. The blueprint, Goldberger said, was "the best plan for a major league baseball park in more than a generation....This is a building capable of wiping out in a single gesture fifty years of wretched stadium design.... It makes every sprawling concrete dome sitting in a sea of parked cars look bloated, fat, and tired."

The finished stadium was a revelation, particularly in its attention to detail. Its façade consisted of brick arches and wrought iron instead of concrete. The foul poles had small steel bars aligned in a stately cross-bracing pattern. Aisle seats were adorned with ironwork designs recalling the 1890s Orioles, winners of three NL pennants. A unique two-tiered set of bullpens was built in left-center field.

Even the advertising was great. "Here, unlike other stadiums, the ads are part of the architecture," one local ad executive told the *New York Times*. Atop the scoreboard sat an antique-style clock sponsored by the local newspaper, on which the twelve hours, instead of numbers, were represented by the twelve letters "B-A-L-T-I-M-O-R-E-S-U-N." Below that, old-timey lettering spelled out *The Sun,* with the *H* and *E* lighting up to denote a hit or an error.

And of course, for the first time in modern history, a historic building was incorporated into a ballpark's design. Eutaw Street, the thoroughfare running between the B&O warehouse and the ballpark, was closed to auto traffic and turned into a pedestrian walkway. Brass plaques embedded in the ground marked the spots where home runs reached the street. (Through 2017, ninety-one homers had landed in Eutaw Street, but the warehouse itself, with its nearest corner 439 feet from home plate, has never been hit by a home run. The only ball to reach it on the fly was a batting-practice blast by Ken Griffey Jr. during the 1993 Home Run Derby.) On game days, Eutaw Street becomes a hub of activity where you can watch batting practice, purchase souvenirs, play carnival games, relax in a shady beer garden, or eat the signature barbecue sold by Orioles legend Boog Powell. Near the entrance gate is a striking statue of Babe Ruth as he appeared during his teenage years—although the sculptor failed to do his homework, depicting the left-handed Babe as a righty.

For all its architectural virtuosity, one of the stadium's signature elements is simply the view. Fans looking toward the outfield are treated to a stunning city skyline including the landmark Emerson Bromo-Seltzer Tower, built in 1911. Unfortunately, this panoramic view was partially ruined in 2008, blocked by the construction of a massive taxpayer-funded Hilton hotel behind left field. This monstrosity was widely protested by baseball fans, who believed it robbed the stadium of some of its charm. Karma seemed to side with the fans, as the hotel began losing money like a sieve as soon as it opened.

Most Orioles fans, though, didn't let the loss of the city view lessen their love for their ballpark. The most joyous moment there came on September 5, 1995, when Cal Ripken Jr. played in his 2,131st consecutive game, breaking the "unbreakable" record set by Lou Gehrig. Fittingly, Ripken hit a home run, and play-by-play of the big hit was provided by President Bill Clinton, who happened to be sitting in as a guest in the broadcast booth. Even if Camden Yards hosts baseball for another century, it will likely never see another moment as exhilarating as the beloved Ripken high-fiving hundreds of Orioles fans while taking an impromptu victory lap around the field.

Camden Yards was so universally praised upon its opening that other teams moved quickly to mimic it, sparking the largest and most expensive cycle of ballpark building in the history of the game. Twenty-four new major league ballparks opened between 1994 and 2017, almost all of them attempting (with varying degrees of success) to echo the retro feel of Camden Yards. Most of these were also built by the firm HOK, which was renamed Populous in 2009. Some of the new stadiums, such as PNC Park in Pittsburgh, would surpass Oriole Park in terms of sheer beauty. But Baltimore's park remained both a gem and a groundbreaker, the retro ballpark without which all the others would not have existed. "Camden Yards helped baseball fans and architects and urban designers—and municipal leaders—realize that this was a very attractive alternative to the stadium in the middle of a sea of cars," Howard Decker, curator of the National Building Museum, told the *Sun*. "It had a huge impact in helping us realize that the old-style stadiums that our parents and grandparents grew up with really represented something of extraordinary value."

OPPOSITE PAGE, TOP: At some ballparks, a gate is just a gate. At Camden Yards, it's a miniature work of art. The bird illustration found on all the stadium entrances is a reproduction of the logo the Orioles wore on their caps when they first moved to Baltimore in 1954. While the B&O warehouse and the ballpark's gorgeous sightlines get all the attention, it was also the little touches like this that led so many fans to fall in love with Camden Yards.

OPPOSITE PAGE, BOTTOM: The Orioles' mascot—rather uncreatively named The Oriole Bird—tries to fire up the fans at Camden Yards in 2013. The mascot made his major league debut in 1979, when he was publicly hatched out of an egg at Memorial Stadium. Like most major league mascots, The Oriole Bird doesn't speak, but he does have a surprisingly verbose Twitter account. He can also be hired to, um, not speak at your corporate event for $350 per hour.

THIS PAGE: It's likely that no baseball fan who witnessed it will ever forget the night of September 6, 1995, when Cal Ripken Jr. broke Lou Gehrig's record of 2,130 consecutive games played. After speeches were made and tears were shed, Ripken was persuaded by teammate Rafael Palmeiro to take a victory lap around the ballpark. "It was an amazing experience," Ripken told Reuters. "When I went to shake hands with the fans, it became very intimate, personal, one-on-one. I remember recognizing faces, people, and sometimes names. By the time I got a quarter of the way around, it didn't matter anymore to me that the game was still going on. I was enjoying it. It was a people moment, not a baseball moment."

New Jersey

A Historic Flirtation with the Majors

Baseball in New Jersey has a long and storied history, including The Elysian Fields in Hoboken often cited as the birthplace of baseball. It was here on June 19, 1846, that the New York Knickerbockers were clobbered by a team called the New York Nine, 23-1, in a contest popularly considered to be history's first baseball game. In reality, this wasn't the first game ever—baseball was well-established by then—but it was the first game played under actual written rules. Nine months earlier the Knickerbockers had codified the sport's first list of twenty rules, including rule number one: "Members must strictly observe the time agreed upon for exercise, and be punctual in their attendance." After several more decades of use as an athletic field, the Elysian Fields site eventually became part of a Maxwell House coffee plant.

Another notable ballpark was Roosevelt Stadium in Jersey City, where the aptly named Jack Roosevelt Robinson broke pro baseball's color barrier in 1946. Built in 1937 with a gorgeous art deco façade, Roosevelt Stadium seated 24,000 patrons and was home to the Jersey City Giants, New York's Triple-A team. On April 18, 1946, it became the site of the first integrated minor league game in more than fifty years when Robinson took the field with the visiting Montreal Royals. Jackie's first game was a smashing success with four hits including a three-run homer, plus four runs scored and two stolen bases. Robinson later returned to Roosevelt Stadium as a member of the Brooklyn Dodgers, who played fifteen "home" games there in 1956 and '57. Although Dodgers owner Walter O'Malley hoped to use the games as proof the Dodgers could leave Brooklyn, attendance was disappointing, and to make matters worse, the Jersey fans constantly heckled Robinson, who responded by lambasting them in the newspapers. Instead of moving to Jersey City, the Dodgers moved to Los Angeles, and Roosevelt Stadium was razed in 1985.

Another New Jersey landmark—and one of the few government-funded stadiums of its era—was Hinchliffe Stadium, built by the city of Paterson as a public works project in 1932. The stadium was laid out in a classical amphitheater style reminiscent of the Los Angeles Coliseum. A horseshoe-shaped grandstand, sunken below street level, contained concentric rows of wooden bench seating. The exterior was decorated with art deco–style terra cotta.

Hinchliffe Stadium was best known as the home of the New York Black Yankees, the Negro National League team owned by tap-dancing legend Bill "Bojangles" Robinson. The Black Yankees called Hinchliffe home from 1933 through 1945, with the exception of the 1938 season, when they played one year on Randall's Island. In 1933, the Black Yankees played a game at Hinchliffe for the unofficial championship of African-American baseball, losing to the Philadelphia Stars. Hinchliffe Stadium was also used frequently by another Negro League team, the New York Cubans, who played here periodically from 1933 through 1950. Hinchliffe was one of the few stadiums of its era where white, Latino, and African-American fans all attended in large numbers, sitting together in the integrated grandstand.

Conceived as an all-purpose sports stadium, Hinchliffe also hosted boxing matches, auto racing, concerts by the likes of Duke Ellington, and comedy shows by the famed local duo Abbott and Costello. It even hosted local high school football. In the early 1940s, Paterson's Eastside High School played here with their star player, Larry Doby, who would later break the color barrier in the American League.

During the late twentieth century, Hinchliffe Stadium became abandoned and neglected, its grandstand crumbling and overgrown with weeds. Recognizing its historic value, Paterson voters in 2009 approved a bond issue to cover half the money needed to save it, including such repairs as the exterior façade, terra cotta work, four ticket booths, and the metal gates. In 2015, the US Congress passed a bill that added Hinchliffe Stadium to Great Falls National Historical Park, making it the first baseball stadium to become part of the National Park Service. 🖂

OPPOSITE PAGE: The Elysian Fields, site of the first baseball game played under written rules, was a popular weekend pleasure ground for New Yorkers in the mid-1800s. Manhattanites would take the ferry there to watch cricket matches and bare-knuckle prizefights, eat fresh oysters, or simply enjoy a stroll around the grassy meadow.

TOP: Four members of the New York Black Yankees—from left, manager Tex Burnett, third baseman Harry Williams, right fielder Tom Parker, and left fielder Dan Wilson—pose in the dugout in 1942. The Black Yankees used Hinchliffe Stadium as their home ballpark from 1934 to 1945.

MIDDLE: The art deco ticket windows at Hinchliffe Stadium as they appeared in 2015 before renovations began. Named after John Hinchliffe, the mayor and local brewery owner who was responsible for its construction, Hinchliffe Stadium was laid out in a classical amphitheater style reminiscent of the Los Angeles Coliseum (page 224) and built on a rocky bluff overlooking the Great Falls of the Passaic River.

BOTTOM: The Skyliners Drum and Bugle Corps performs at Jersey City's Roosevelt Stadium in 1972. In addition to hosting minor league baseball for eighteen years, the stadium was also used for concerts, boxing matches, soccer games, and other community events.

MONTREAL

JARRY PARK

TEAM: Montreal Expos (1969–1976)

NAME: Stade Parc Jarry

LOCATION: Inside Parc Jarry, a municipal park at the corner of Rue Jarry and Boulevard Sainte-Laurente, Montreal

FIRST MLB GAME: April 14, 1969

LAST MLB GAME: September 26, 1976

NOTABLE FEATURES: Location inside a picturesque city park; swimming pool known as *"la piscine de Willie"* behind right field wall.

OLYMPIC STADIUM

TEAM: Montreal Expos (1977–2004)

NAME: Stade Olympique

NICKNAME: The Big O (later, The Big Owe)

LOCATION: Corner of Avenue Pierre-De Coubertin and Rue Pie-IX, Montreal

FIRST MLB GAME: April 15, 1977

LAST MLB GAME: September 29, 2004

NOTABLE FEATURES: Bright orange, chronically malfunctioning retractable roof; 583-foot inclined tower leaning over the stadium; part of a vast Olympic complex that included a velodrome and a natatorium.

MONTREAL
expos

The Montreal Royals, the city's beloved minor league team for six decades, were born accidentally in 1897 when a team from Rochester, New York, relocated to Montreal after their own stadium burned down. From 1928 through 1960, the Royals played at Delorimier Downs (later renamed Hector Racine Stadium), a single-decked minor league ballpark in the working class Sainte-Marie neighborhood. The club reached its zenith when it was the Brooklyn Dodgers' top farm team, winning seven Triple-A pennants between 1945 and 1958.

The most memorable Royals season came in 1946, when the Dodgers chose Montreal as the city to break pro baseball's color barrier. Jackie Robinson enjoyed a transcendent season in Montreal, batting .349 with 40 steals, as the Royals won the 1946 Little World Series. After the clinching game, a mob of elated fans chased Robinson as he jogged from Delorimier Downs back to his apartment. "It was probably the only day in history," wrote Sam Malton of the *Pittsburgh Courier*, "that a black man ran from a white mob with love, not lynching, on its mind." Robinson was promoted to Brooklyn the following season.

The Royals moved to Syracuse in 1960, and Montreal then set its sights on major league status, which it achieved in 1969 when the expansion Expos were born. Scrambling to find a suitable venue, city officials ended up transforming a recreational ballfield inside a city park into a big league stadium that held 28,000 fans. Eight years later, the Expos moved into giant Olympic Stadium (*Stade Olympique* in French), which was infamously plagued with all manner of problems throughout its twenty-eight-year tenure. In 2005, after local voters declined to provide funding for Labatt Park, a proposed open-air stadium in downtown Montreal, MLB relocated the Expos to Washington, DC, where they became the Nationals. 🖤

PREVIOUS PAGE: Olympic Stadium sits amid the Montreal skyline as the St. Lawrence River flows in the background. During the 1976 Summer Olympics held here, American sprinter Edwin Moses set a world record in the men's 400-meter hurdles, while Caitlyn (then known as Bruce) Jenner won a gold medal in the decathlon.

THIS PAGE: Jarry Park is packed for Opening Day in 1970, its second season as home of the Montreal Expos. Note the spring snow on the ground behind the stadium. The following year, Opening Day would be even colder, with fans standing on giant piles of snow behind the outfield fence in order to watch the game for free.

OPPOSITE PAGE: The Montreal Expos and St. Louis Cardinals line up at Jarry Park on April 14, 1969, before the first major league baseball game ever played outside the United States. It was also the first major league game where two national anthems were played, which is what's happening in this photo. (The program for the game can be seen on the next page.) Though the Expos moved out in 1976, the press box and grandstand seen here are still in use. They've been incorporated into the tennis stadium that now stands on the site, Stade IGA.

JARRY PARK

MONTREAL EXPOS 1969–1976

WHEN JARRY PARK STADIUM WAS BUILT in 1960, it was a modest community field inside an idyllic public park, with a grandstand accommodating just 3,000 fans. Intended to be used for youth league games, it was built amid an urban oasis of trees, ponds, flowers, and fountains. By the end of the decade it had been transformed into a makeshift big league stadium and hosted the first major league games ever played outside the United States. Though intended as a short-term solution, Jarry ended up serving as the home of the Montreal Expos for their first eight seasons.

In preparation for the Expos' arrival, the park's capacity was expanded nearly tenfold, to 28,450. The city paid 75 percent of the $4 million expansion cost, with the club picking up the rest. The original grandstand was extended all the way down the foul lines, a block of 7,700 bleacher seats was added in left field, and a press box was constructed as a mini upper deck behind home plate. A large scoreboard was built behind right field, and beyond that was a previously existing municipal swimming pool. On July 16, 1969, Pittsburgh slugger Willie Stargell hit what was believed to be the longest home run at Jarry Park, a clout that landed in the pool with a gigantic splash. The pool, which still exists, is referred to by locals as *"la piscine de Willie."*

OLYMPIC STADIUM
MONTREAL EXPOS 1977-2004

MONTREAL'S OLYMPIC STADIUM enjoyed a banner debut year, hosting a number of important events as the main stadium for the 1976 Summer Olympics. Soon afterward, however, it became a running joke, a bureaucratic money pit, and a disaster of such proportions that it led to the demise of baseball in Montreal three decades later. The Expos, like their stadium, were the laughingstock of baseball for a decade before their departure for Washington, DC, in 2005. But during the glory years of the 1980s, both team and ballpark enjoyed a memorable heyday.

After Montreal was awarded the 1976 Olympics, a special tax on cigarettes generated $134 million (Canadian) for a massive domed stadium designed by French architect Roger Taillibert. It was to feature a revolutionary retractable roof, opened and closed by cables attached to a 583-foot tower that was reputed to be the tallest inclined structure in the world. The vast complex would also include promenades, a velodrome, and the Olympic swimming pool. When some worried that the project would lose money, Montreal mayor Jean Drapeau famously responded that "the Olympics can no more have a deficit than a man can have a baby." But by the time the stadium was finally fully paid off in 1996, the Olympics were gone, the Expos no longer existed, and interest and repairs had driven the stunning pricetag to an estimated $1.86 billion, an amount that is still rising today. Initially nicknamed "The Big O," the spelling of the stadium's moniker was eventually changed sarcastically to "The Big Owe."

After thirty-eight months of construction, the building was still incomplete, with the roof nowhere near being finished, when the stadium hosted the Olympic opening ceremonies on June 17, 1976. After also hosting track and field, soccer, swimming, and equestrian medal events, it became the Expos' home ballpark in 1977. The stadium's infamous orange Kevlar roof sat unused in a warehouse in France until 1982, and its installation was finally completed in 1987, more than a decade after the stadium's opening. The 60,000-square-foot roof was so bulky that it could not be used in winds of higher than twenty-five miles per hour, so Expos games were occasionally rained out even after it was installed. The roof proved less than durable, too; it was plagued by an endless series of rips and leaks.

In 1992, the Expos decided that opening and closing the roof wasn't worth the hassle, and decided to close it permanently. Six years later they replaced it with a $26 million nonretractable blue roof. This, too, proved unreliable, collapsing in January 1999 under the weight of accumulated snow. After that, tubes of heated water were installed underneath the roof to melt the snow atop it. However, other portions of the park were crumbling too. In 1991, a 55-ton chunk of concrete fell, causing the cancellation of thirteen Expos games.

Though Olympic Stadium turned out to be one of the all-time boondoggles, Expos fans nonetheless loved their team, and proved to be louder and more enthusiastic fans than their American counterparts. During the 1980s, they cheered on a thrilling young club led by Hall of Famers Tim Raines, Andre Dawson, and Gary Carter. The crowds grew smaller in the 1990s when ownership refused to support the team financially, but even during these fallow years the stadium was filled with the deafening roar of fans stomping in unison on the aluminum bleachers. In 2002, Major League Baseball, upset that Montreal voters had declined to pay for a new stadium, tried to fold the Expos out of existence. Legal challenges prevented this, and instead the franchise was moved to Washington, DC, in 2005. Olympic Stadium is still used part-time by the Canadian Football League and Major League Soccer. Remarkably, yet another new roof was approved in 2017, at a cost of $250 million.

TOP: In theory, the 583-foot tower seen here was supposed to support Olympic Stadium's retractable roof, which could be raised or lowered by the attached cables. In practice, the system never really worked, and the roof has remained closed for most of its lifetime. On a brighter note, today you can still take an elevator up to the top of the tower, which offers an outstanding panoramic view of Montreal.

BOTTOM LEFT: Games at Olympic Stadium were made livelier by Youppi!, the delightful orange-haired mascot of indeterminate species. (His name is French for "Yippee!") In 1989, Youppi! became the first mascot ever ejected from a major league game when his playful antics atop the visitors' dugout caused Dodgers manager Tommy Lasorda to complain. When the Expos moved to Washington, many fans worried about Youppi!'s fate, but thankfully he found employment as the mascot of the NHL's Montreal Canadiens.

BOTTOM RIGHT: During the Expos' 1980s heyday, a number of players were beloved by local fans, including the Nicaraguan pitcher Dennis Martínez, nicknamed "El Presidente." Montrealers cheered more loudly and enthusiastically than their American counterparts, creating a joyous atmosphere inside Olympic Stadium. They especially loved pounding their feet on the ballpark's aluminum bleachers, producing a loud metallic sound that literally shook the stadium.

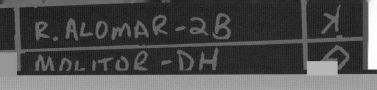

TORONTO

EXHIBITION STADIUM

TEAM: Toronto Blue Jays (1977–1989)

NICKNAME: Prohibition Stadium

LOCATION: Corner of Princes' Blvd. & Ontario Dr., Toronto

FIRST MLB GAME: April 7, 1977

LAST MLB GAME: May 28, 1989

NOTABLE FEATURES: Harsh lake-effect weather from nearby Lake Ontario; many seats located far from the action due to its football-friendly design.

ROGERS CENTRE

TEAM: Toronto Blue Jays (1989–present)

NAMES: SkyDome (1989–2005), Rogers Centre (2005–present)

LOCATION: 1 Blue Jays Way, Toronto

FIRST MLB GAME: June 5, 1989

NOTABLE FEATURES: Built-in hotel with a view of field from guest rooms; first functional retractable roof in MLB; view of CN Tower, once the world's tallest structure, behind right field.

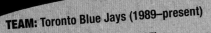

TORONTO BLUE JAYS

The only Canadian city to currently host a major league team, Toronto had its first dalliance with pro baseball in 1885, when it was part of the Canadian League, a short-lived minor league comprised of five Ontario-based teams. The (baseball) Maple Leafs borrowed a local lacrosse stadium, Jarvis Street Grounds, for their games.

Later, the minor league Toronto Maple Leafs played at Hanlan's Point, a ballpark built on an island in Lake Ontario and accessible only by ferry boat. (Conveniently, the ferry company also owned the ballpark.) The single-decked wooden ballpark burned down in 1903, was rebuilt in 1908, burned down again in 1909, and was rebuilt in 1910 as a 17,000-seat jewel. On September 5, 1914, a young pitcher named Babe Ruth hit the first home run of his career at Hanlan's Point Stadium.

In 1926, the Leafs spent $750,000 to build Maple Leaf Stadium, a 23,000-seat facility with a large steel roof covering the grandstand.

Though located within a stone's throw of the old island ballpark, this venue was on the mainland. Lights were installed in 1934, and Maple Leaf Stadium served as Toronto's main baseball venue until the team left town in 1968. Nine years later, Toronto was finally awarded an MLB franchise, and city officials scrambled to repurpose the local football venue, Exhibition Stadium, into a baseball field. The seating layout was awkward and games were often interrupted by snowdrifts, but the Blue Jays endured twelve and a half grueling seasons there before finally moving into the ultra-modern SkyDome in 1989.

TOP: Maple Leaf Stadium is filled to capacity, at 19,000, for Opening Day in 1955. Taking the ceremonial first swing is Fred "Big Daddy" Gardiner, who was then metro chairman of Toronto—essentially mayor of Toronto and all its suburbs.

MIDDLE: Hanlan's Point, located on an island in Lake Ontario, housed pro baseball in Toronto intermittently from 1897 through 1926, with several different ballparks being built on the same site. This photo dates from around 1905. Bizarrely, a bandstand is on the field of play in center field, creating an obstacle. The electrical light hanging in the foreground must have served some non-baseball purpose, since all ballgames were played in the daytime.

BOTTOM RIGHT: Hanlan's Point Stadium on Ward's Island as it appeared in 1919, with a roller coaster and Ferris wheel visible next to it. This was the last and biggest of the three ballparks built on this site.

BOTTOM LEFT: An overflow crowd, including many fans standing on the outfield grass, watches the Toronto Maple Leafs at Hanlan's Point Stadium in 1911. Visible behind the outfield fence is the Old Mill, a popular water chute ride.

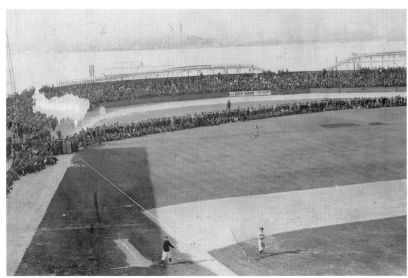

EXHIBITION STADIUM

TORONTO BLUE JAYS 1977-1989

IN 1977, THE BIG LEAGUES ARRIVED in Toronto, where the Blue Jays spent their early years playing on an awkwardly converted football field, where snow and freezing rain were often blown in from Lake Ontario a block away. Exhibition Stadium, the renovated home of the Canadian Football League's Toronto Argonauts, was less than ideal for baseball, but it proved popular enough with fans in the frozen north, who were starved for major league baseball. Despite the horrendous weather, the stadium attracted well over a million fans in every full season it was used.

The site had been used as an athletic field since 1879, with the stadium structure having been rebuilt several times. Because Canadian football fields are 30 yards longer than American ones, Exhibition Stadium was an even worse fit for baseball than most multipurpose stadiums, even after an $18 million renovation. The main football grandstand became the left-field bleachers for baseball games, and a smaller section of seats was added around home plate. Because of this unusual configuration, Exhibition became the only major league park where the bleachers were roofed but the main grandstand was not. Some seats were as far as 820 feet from home, and others had such terrible views that the Jays didn't even bother to sell them.

Expecting intolerable evening temperatures, Toronto scheduled all eleven of its April 1977 home games during the daytime. The harsh weather was nonetheless in full effect on Opening Day, when the wind chill dipped below zero degrees Fahrenheit during the first game in Blue Jays franchise history. Snow gusts blew all over the park, and the Jays even had to borrow a Zamboni from the NHL's Maple Leafs to clear the infield between innings. After thirteen seasons braving the wind and cold, the Jays finally moved indoors to SkyDome in 1989. ⚾

TOP: Workers erect a new scoreboard at Exhibition Stadium in the spring of 1977 as the Blue Jays prepare to make their debut. This bare-bones scoreboard was superseded by a larger, $2.5 million model the following year.

MIDDLE: This pair of teenage Blue Jays fans is bundled up in parkas awaiting the Blue Jays' home opener in 1977. "Checking over the lineups, they still hadn't decided on their favorite players," the *Toronto Star* reported.

BOTTOM: This photo illustrates the dual uses of Exhibition Stadium, with the straight-as-an-arrow football grandstand in the background and the newer, elbow-shaped baseball grandstand in the foreground. Some of the best football seats ended up in deep center field for baseball, and tickets for those sections often weren't even put on sale.

ROGERS CENTRE

TORONTO BLUE JAYS   1989-PRESENT

AFTER ENDURING A DECADE of frequent snowdrifts at Exhibition Stadium, the Blue Jays began making plans for a dome that would set the baseball world on its ear. Once hailed as the vanguard of a new generation of ballparks, Toronto's SkyDome was baseball's most lavish and ambitious stadium at the time it opened. Featuring a retractable dome, a Hard Rock Café, and a built-in hotel whose rooms overlooked the playing field, the giant multipurpose facility attracted enough fans in its heady early days to break baseball's attendance record two years in a row.

Its eventual cost of over $500 million (Canadian) was funded by a special corporation whose investors included the city of Toronto, the province of Ontario, and twenty-five private companies. Some $60 million was raised by presales of luxury boxes. Ground was broken in 1986 in the middle of downtown Toronto, just a block from Lake Ontario. The ballpark sat next door to what was then the tallest building in the world, the CN Tower. From the vantage point of the Toronto Islands as well as watercraft in Lake Ontario, SkyDome's distinctive half-moon-shaped roof would become a signature of the city's skyline, similar to the way the Sydney Opera House dominates views of that city.

SkyDome's roof was retractable, an extravagance deemed necessary in light of the weather problems the team had suffered at Exhibition Stadium. The first retractable dome in baseball that was actually functional (Montreal's Olympic Stadium featured a version that was dead on arrival), SkyDome's massive cover was a remarkable feat of engineering. It could open and close in just twenty minutes. Designed by architects Roderick Robbie and Michael Allen, it owed much to similar roofs at concert halls, although at 310 feet high and weighing 11,000 tons, it was built on a much grander scale. Unfortunately, the structure of the roof mandated a high seating bowl, and some seats were markedly distant from the playing field. The height of the roof also meant that SkyDome, even when packed with fans, never generated the same ear-splitting noise levels as other covered structures, like the Metrodome.

SkyDome (renamed Rogers Centre in 2005) began a trend in the way it markets baseball to the wealthy fan instead of the average Joe. It was baseball's first "mallpark," a structure where the actual ballgame seemed to exist only as a vehicle for selling every consumer product under the sun. In addition to Sightlines restaurant that sits high beyond the center field fence (the Hard Rock Café closed in 2009), various other bars, clubs, and upscale restaurants dot the concourse. More than $5 million in commissioned paintings and sculptures decorate the grounds. With a fitness club, movie theater, and built-in hotel, the Rogers Centre seems the sort of building where you might be able to live your entire life without ever leaving.

The hotel, located above the outfield, has more than 300 rooms, 70 of which contain picture windows overlooking the field (and cost an exorbitant premium). It seems that team officials never considered that while hotel patrons could see the game through their windows, fans in the stadium could also see inside. After 1997, when one amorous couple put on a public and explicit display, future guests were sternly reminded to close their curtains.

The luster began to wear off of the massive SkyDome soon after its opening. Initially fans were seduced by the novelty of the park, and also by the presence of an outstanding Blue Jays team. In 1991, the Jays broke baseball's all-time record by drawing over 4 million fans; the next year, they broke it again. They won the World Series in 1992 and again in 1993. But just as the team's talented roster began to decay, fans also grew weary of the giant dome.

With the opening of Camden Yards in 1992, baseball took a decided turn toward retro ballparks, a style that encompassed everything SkyDome was not. Attendance dropped more than 50 percent during the late 1990s as the Blue Jays settled into a comfortable mediocrity. Alas, underneath all its bells and whistles, SkyDome was just another domed stadium with artificial turf. *New York Times* writer Michael Janofsky compared it to "an airplane hangar or a merchandise mart or a place in which Crazy Eddie might hold a giant warehouse sale." The Orioles' new ballpark was now drawing all the attention, and a stadium construction boom began in which every new park tried to mimic the retro feel of Camden Yards.

Instead of pointing the way to the future, as many had predicted, the 'Dome became an anachronism less than a decade after its opening. In 2005 the stadium was purchased for a mere $25 million, one-twentieth of its original cost, by Rogers Communications, the Canadian media conglomerate that had purchased the Blue Jays five years earlier. The name was changed from SkyDome to Rogers Centre, and a series of gradual refurbishments began, including the installation of a new video board and a better brand of artificial turf. These improvements, however, can do little to alter SkyDome's legacy as a park built a few years too soon, a fad instead of trendsetter. 🔾

OPPOSITE PAGE: The Rogers Centre is at its most gorgeous when viewed at night from the Toronto Islands. This photo was probably taken from the former site of Hanlan's Point Stadium (see page 120).

TOP: A quartet of drummers adds to the festive pregame atmosphere outside the Rogers Centre. Behind them is *The Audience*, a collection of fifteen baseball-fan gargoyles sculpted by local artist Michael Snow.

BOTTOM: The greatest moment in SkyDome's history was surely Joe Carter's walk-off homer against Mitch Williams to win the 1993 World Series. It's one of just two World Series–ending home runs in baseball history. (The other was by Bill Mazeroski.)

ST. LOUIS

SPORTSMAN'S PARK

TEAMS: St. Louis Browns (1909–1953), St. Louis Cardinals (1920–1966)
NAMES: Sportsman's Park (1909–53), Busch Stadium (1954–1966)
LOCATION: Corner of Dodier St., and N. Spring Ave., St. Louis
FIRST MLB GAME: April 14, 1909
LAST MLB GAME: May 8, 1966
NOTABLE FEATURES: Budweiser eagle on scoreboard that flapped its wings after a home run; apartment underneath stands where Browns owner Bill Veeck Jr. lived.

STARS PARK

TEAM: St. Louis Stars (1922–1931)
LOCATION: Corner of Compton St. and Market St., St. Louis
NOTABLE FEATURES: One of the earliest stadiums to host night baseball, with lights installed in 1930; trolley car repair shed located down left field line just 269 feet from home plate.

BUSCH STADIUM II

TEAM: St. Louis Cardinals (1966–2005)
NAME: Busch Memorial Stadium (1966–2005)
LOCATION: Corner of Spruce St. and Stadium Plaza, St. Louis
FIRST MLB GAME: May 12, 1966
LAST MLB GAME: October 19, 2005 (NLCS Game 6)
NOTABLE FEATURES: Artificial turf 1970-1995; built on former site of St. Louis Chinatown.

BUSCH STADIUM III

TEAM: St. Louis Cardinals (2006–present)
LOCATION: Corner of S. 8th St. and Interstate 64 W., St. Louis
FIRST MLB GAME: April 10, 2006
NOTABLE FEATURES: Redbrick façade; view of Gateway Arch behind center field.

aseball was first played in St. Louis on an empty lot at the intersection of Grand and Dodier in the 1860s, and for the next century, an increasingly elaborate series of ballparks would turn that spot into St. Louis' baseball mecca. Throughout the nineteenth century, the wooden ballpark there repeatedly burned down and was rebuilt. In between fires, it served as the home of five different major league teams—three of them named the St. Louis Browns.

The Browns of the 1880s played in the freewheeling American Association, known as the "Beer and Whisky League" after two items sold in large numbers at its ballparks. The Browns were owned by Chris Von Der Ahe, an eccentric young German immigrant who had grown wealthy selling beer at his saloon next to the ballpark. Von Der Ahe turned Sportsman's Park into a glorious drunken playland,

featuring a shoot-the-chute waterslide behind the outfield fence and a beer garden down the right field line. He also became the first baseball tycoon to offer zany promotions before games; in 1885, Sitting Bull made an appearance before the ballgame with Buffalo Bill Cody and his Wild West Show.

In 1909, a grander version of Sportsman's Park was built on the site using steel and concrete. The Browns played there until 1953 and the Cardinals until 1966, when a giant concrete bowl called Busch Stadium II was built downtown in the shadow of the Gateway Arch. For four decades this cookie-cutter park was home to a series of memorable teams with stars like Bob Gibson, Ozzie Smith, and Albert Pujols. In 2006, the Cardinals moved a few blocks away to the retro-style Busch Stadium III. 🐾

TOP: Helene Robison Britton, the first female owner of a major league team, talks with her husband, Schuyler Britton, in 1913. Mrs. Britton inherited the Cardinals when her uncle Stanley Robison died in 1911, and much to the consternation of some baseball executives, she played an active role in running the club, even traveling with the team on road trips. For the first decade of her ownership, the Cardinals played their games at Robison Field, eventually moving to Sportsman's Park in 1920.

BOTTOM: The Sportsman's Park scoreboard as seen during Game 7 of the 1964 World Series. When August Anheuser Busch Jr., universally known as "Gussie," bought the Cardinals in 1953, he installed this huge electronic scoreboard in left field. After every Cardinals home run, the Budweiser eagle would light up and flap its wings. Busch's adept intermingling of his baseball and brewery businesses caused such a stir that it landed him on the cover of *Time* magazine in 1955.

SPORTSMAN'S PARK

ST. LOUIS BROWNS 1909–1953   ST. LOUIS CARDINALS 1920–1966

BY THE EARLY TWENTIETH CENTURY, the beloved St. Louis Browns of the 1880s were out of business, and a different Browns franchise—this one playing in the American League—now called Sportsman's Park home. In 1908 and 1909, they essentially rebuilt the old ballpark from scratch, mostly using the fire-resistant materials of steel and concrete. The outfield bleachers remained wooden, but the renovated double-decked grandstand was billed as being completely fireproof. In 1925, the bleachers were finally modernized and

the upper deck was extended to the foul lines, giving the stadium the appearance it would have for the next four decades.

In 1920, the Browns gained some company when the St. Louis Cardinals moved in. League officials arranged the teams' schedules so that one club was always home while the other was on the road, but the constant use turned the field into one of the worst playing surfaces in baseball. The Browns were the stadium's landlords and the Cardinals merely rent-paying tenants, but nevertheless, the Cardinals proved to be the more successful franchise over time. Three distinct

In 1944, Sportsman's Park was decked out in patriotic bunting for an all–St. Louis World Series between the Browns and the Cardinals. It was the third and final time in history that all games in a given year's World Series were played at the same ballpark. (The others took place in 1921 and '22 at the Polo Grounds.) The Browns won their only pennant ever in 1944, but the Cards triumphed in the Fall Classic, 4 games to 2. Note the large light towers on the grandstand roof, which were relatively recent additions to Sportsman's Park, having been added in 1940.

TOP: Photographer Charles Trefts, left, and his brother-in-law, the painter Martin Kaiser, watch the 1934 World Series from atop the roof of Sportsman's Park. It was common during the first half of the twentieth century for photographers, newsreel cameramen, and broadcasters to ply their trade from the roofs of ballparks. (Another example can be seen in the photo of the 1944 World Series on the previous page.)

BOTTOM LEFT: St. Louis Browns employees carry an oversize birthday cake onto the Sportsman's Park field between games of a doubleheader on August 19, 1951. The giant confection was part of an extravaganza commemorating the American League's fiftieth anniversary, and unbeknownst to the crowd, there was a person hiding inside it. Moments after this image was taken, a 3-foot-7-inch man named Eddie Gaedel popped out of the cake, and team owner Bill Veeck Jr. announced that he'd signed Gaedel to play for the Browns.

BOTTOM RIGHT: Babe Ruth poses with an unidentified girl in the Sportsman's Park stands during the 1934 World Series between the Cardinals and Athletics. Ruth's career with the Yankees had ended a few days earlier, and he attended the Fall Classic in hopes of landing a job as some team's manager. Alas, he received no offers.

OPPOSITE PAGE: Fans in the left field bleachers watch Bob Gibson face the Yankees in Game 2 of the 1964 World Series, the final postseason series played at Sportsman's Park before it closed nineteen months later. The integrated crowd visible here was a relatively recent phenomenon at Sportsman's Park, where the stands had been segregated for decades.

Cardinals dynasties would eventually play at Sportsman's Park. The first, during the 1930s, featured the boisterous Dizzy Dean and his famed "Gashouse Gang." The second, during World War II, was led by the young hitting prodigy Stan Musial. The third, during the 1960s, was powered by superstars Bob Gibson and Lou Brock.

As the nation's southernmost big-league ballpark during most of its existence, Sportsman's Park was also baseball's last bastion of segregation. With KMOX's 50,000-watt radio tower beaming Cardinals games to every Southern state, the Redbirds became the team of choice throughout the former Confederacy. Unlike most ballparks, Sportsman's Park rarely hosted Negro League games, and the local African-American club, the St. Louis Stars, was forced to build its own stadium 2 miles away. Cardinals and Browns games were rigidly segregated, with African-American fans relegated to a section of the right field bleachers. In 1941, however, the fortitude of Satchel Paige changed all that.

On July 4, 1941, some Negro League promoters rented Sportsman's Park for a game between two of the marquee African-American teams in the country, the Chicago American Giants and Paige's Kansas City Monarchs. The main attraction was Paige, the cocky hurler who, at age thirty-five, was already a legend. But as the scheduled date approached, Paige delivered a bold ultimatum: He would refuse to pitch the game unless the Sportsman's Park stands were desegregated. After a contentious standoff, the promoters relented, and an integrated crowd of nearly 20,000 watched Paige dominate Chicago 11-2. Three months later, the stands were again integrated for a barnstorming matchup between Paige and Bob Feller. Paige was always proud, he said, of "having put a little dent in Jim Crow,"

TOP: The indomitable Bill Veeck Jr. poses in front of his office at Sportsman's Park, where he also had his own apartment. Veeck prided himself on remaining accessible to the everyday fan. "The doors came off my office," he wrote in his memoir, *Veeck as in Wreck.* "I put in a direct telephone line—and advertised the number—so that anyone who wanted to call could get me direct without any nonsense about switchboards or screenings.... If a drunk or two called in the early-morning hours, well, that was one of the occupational risks. A drunk has to be pretty interested in the team to call at three in the morning."

BOTTOM: There was no sweeter swing than that of Stan "The Man" Musial, shown here in the early 1950s with Brooklyn's Roy Campanella catching. Musial's stance at the plate looked awkward—it seemed as if he was peering around a corner with one foot stuck in a bucket—but once he started his swing, the mechanics were perfect. Musial played twenty-two years with the Cardinals, all of them at Sportsman's Park, and won seven batting titles and three MVP awards. "Almost all the dents on Stan Musial's bat were by the label," Hall of Famer Ralph Kiner once said. "Bad hitters had dents all over."

and in 1944, Browns and Cardinals games at Sportsman's Park were officially desegregated.

During the 1950s, the most visible figure at Sportsman's Park was Bill Veeck Jr., the eccentric disabled war hero who not only owned the Browns but also lived in a custom-built apartment inside the ballpark. Veeck pulled countless promotional stunts, but none more memorable than the one on August 19, 1951, when he held a fiftieth-birthday celebration for both the American League and Falstaff Beer, the team's main sponsor. Between games of a doubleheader Veeck put on a grand spectacle, with motorcycles zooming around the infield, baseball clown Max Patkin dancing on the mound, and an eight-piece band featuring Satchel Paige, by now a Browns reliever, as the drummer. In the grand finale, a little person named Eddie Gaedel leapt out from inside a 7-foot-tall birthday cake and Veeck announced that Gaedel was the Browns' newest player. Before the game, he'd signed the 3-foot-7 Gaedel to a one-day contract for $100, and had planned on giving him one plate appearance. Wearing a uniform with the fraction $\frac{1}{8}$ on the back, Gaedel used the tiniest strike zone in baseball history to draw a four-pitch walk from Tigers pitcher Bob Cain, who could barely stop laughing long enough to deliver his pitches.

Veeck sold the Browns in 1953 to a group of investors who moved them to Baltimore. He then sold Sportsman's Park to the Cardinals, who were now owned by Budweiser tycoon August Busch Jr. Busch tried to rename the ballpark Budweiser Stadium, but league officials wouldn't allow it. Instead he named it Busch Stadium, then started marketing a new beverage called Busch Bavarian Beer. In 1966, the Cardinals moved to a new Busch Stadium downtown, and within six months, the old ballpark at the corner of Grand and Dodier had been razed.

This photo looking north on Grand Avenue shows Sportsman's Park as it appeared during the late 1950s or early 1960s, after its name had changed to Busch Stadium. Like many classic ballparks, the size and shape of Sportsman's Park were dictated by the city streets surrounding it. Among the businesses visible in this image are a drugstore, a sandwich shop, a haberdashery, a used-car dealership, and a paint store. Today the same intersection lies mostly abandoned, contaminated by asbestos and other toxins left behind by a long-defunct carburetor factory.

STARS PARK

ST. LOUIS STARS 1909–1953

FOR A BRIEF PERIOD DURING THE 1920s, the St. Louis Stars were one of the greatest teams of all time, black or white, and in 1922, the team decided it needed its own ballpark to call home. Located at the corner of Compton Avenue and Market Street in midtown St. Louis, Stars Park became one of the few stadiums ever constructed specifically for Negro League baseball.

In most cities, the local Negro League team simply rented the major league stadium when its occupant was out of town. In St. Louis, however, that didn't work, since Sportsman's Park served as home to both the Browns and Cardinals and was therefore rarely vacant. So on July 2, 1922, the Stars opened Stars Park, a workmanlike, no-nonsense structure built for $38,000. It didn't even have an outer façade, just an open view of the wooden cross-bracing beams that supported the grandstand. A modest banner bearing the name Stars Park hung above the home plate entrance, where a small wooden shack served as a ticket office. Many years after the stadium's demise, ex-Stars outfielder James "Cool Papa" Bell described it to author John Holway:

> It was a wood park. At first it didn't have a top on it. I guess it could seat around 5,000 people. It had a wood fence around it, and people almost cut that fence down by cutting peepholes in it. In right field they had a house sat on a corner there, must have been about 400 feet down the line. In left was a car shed. Down the line was 269 feet, then it would slant off to center around 500 feet. By the car barn was a track running beside there. If a right-hand hitter could pull the ball he could hit it up on that shed, but they had to hit it high—about 30 feet high. The car shed was the wall. Where the car shed ended, there you had a fence. There was plenty of room out there in center field; there wasn't anybody going to hit it out of there.

Despite its vast expanse in center field, Stars Park became famous for the short left field porch described by Bell. Right-handed sluggers such as George "Mule" Suttles and Willie Wells became adept at lofting shallow fly balls over the roof of the trolley car shed, resulting in prolific home run totals. By one count Wells hit twenty-seven homers in eighty-

For many years it was believed that no photographs existed of Stars Park's exterior. But in 2016, an archivist at the Missouri Historical Society, Lauren Sallwasser, found this unidentified photo and, through some historical detective work, was able to confirm that it depicted Stars Park. The first clue was the sagging cloth banner above the wooden ticket office, with lettering that can barely be made out to read *Stars Park*. Since baseballs were expensive during the 1920s, the Stars reused them as often as possible. If you were standing on this street corner and happened to catch a foul ball, you could return it to the box office in exchange for a free ticket.

eight official league games in 1929, reputed to be a Negro League single-season record. Long balls were so prevalent that during some years, balls hit over the trolley shed were considered ground-rule doubles. Aided by their friendly home ballpark, the Stars slugged their way to Negro National League pennants in 1928 and 1930.

Alas, the park's heyday was brief. The Negro National League collapsed in 1931 at the onset of the Great Depression, and the ballpark was sold to the city of St. Louis. Today, the stadium is gone but the site remains a baseball diamond, serving as the home field of the Harris-Stowe State Hornets, a historically black university competing at the NAIA level. 🖰

TOP: The most famous member of the St. Louis Stars was Cool Papa Bell, a former left-handed pitcher who converted to the outfield and became legendary for his extraordinary speed on the bases. Born in Starkville, Mississippi, Bell moved to St. Louis at age seventeen, playing baseball for a living during the day while attending high school classes at night. "The only thing that counted was to be an honest, clean-livin' man who cared about other people," he once said. "I've always tried to live up to those words."

BOTTOM: The 1928 St. Louis Stars were one of the finest Negro League teams ever assembled, featuring three Hall of Famers in their prime: center fielder Cool Papa Bell, shortstop Willie Wells, and first baseman Mule Suttles. Wells, a native Texan who had begun his career as a batboy for the Austin Black Senators, was one of the Negro Leagues' best power hitters despite his small frame. Suttles, a former Alabama coal miner, used his massive 6-foot-4 frame to blast many home runs over Stars Park's short left field fence.

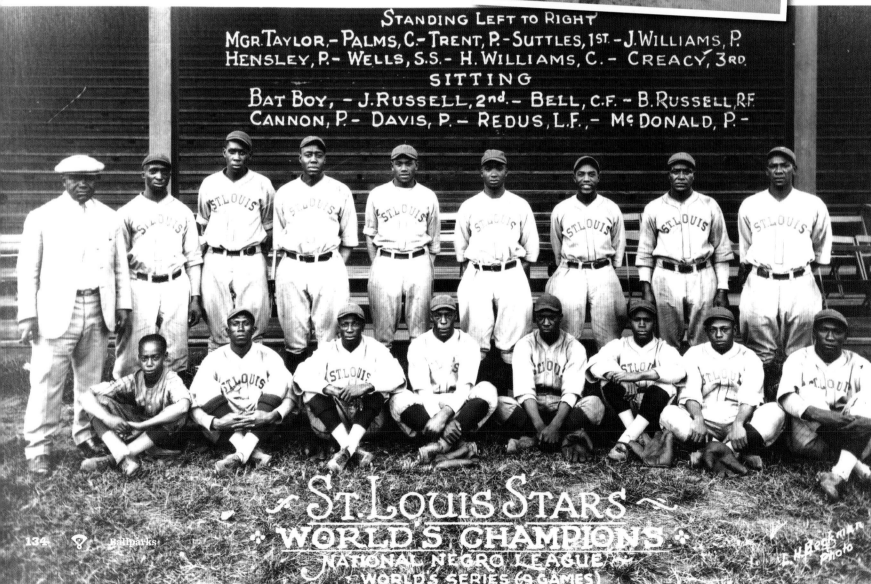

STANDING LEFT TO RIGHT
MGR. TAYLOR, – PALMS, C – TRENT, P – SUTTLES, 1ST – J. WILLIAMS, P.
HENSLEY, P – WELLS, S.S. – H. WILLIAMS, C. – CREACY, 3RD.
SITTING
BAT BOY, – J. RUSSELL, 2ND – BELL, C.F. – B. RUSSELL, R.F.
CANNON, P – DAVIS, P – REDUS, L.F. – McDONALD, P. –

ST. LOUIS STARS
WORLD'S CHAMPIONS
NATIONAL NEGRO LEAGUE
WORLD'S SERIES (9 GAMES)

BUSCH MEMORIAL STADIUM

ST. LOUIS CARDINALS 1966–2005

AS PERHAPS THE LEAST-BAD cookie-cutter stadium ever built, Busch Memorial Stadium was the best possible version of a bad idea. It was home to the St. Louis Cardinals for the finest forty-year stretch in their history, with three distinct eras of winning teams: the first one led by Bob Gibson, the second by Ozzie Smith, and the third by Albert Pujols.

In 1964, the year the Cardinals won their first World Series in nearly two decades, ground was broken for the city's first completely new baseball stadium since 1893. As the second of three St. Louis ballparks named Busch Stadium, this one is often dubbed Busch Stadium II to distinguish it from the structures that preceded and followed it. Completed in 1966, Busch II was the first multipurpose stadium in the National League, also serving as home of the NFL's Cardinals and Rams at various times.

Seeking a distinctive stadium with a Modernist design, the Cardinals hired a prestigious architect, Edward Durell Stone, who had previously worked on Radio City Music Hall and the Museum of Modern Art. The ballpark site was located just a few blocks away from the soaring Gateway Arch, also then under construction, which would become the city's best-known landmark. In a prescient design flourish, Stone topped Busch Stadium's grandstand with ninety-six tiny arches in a 360-degree circle, making the building unmistakably evocative of St. Louis. In most other aspects, however, the perfectly round concrete bowl closely resembled its homogeneous brethren.

Bob Gibson throws a pitch at Busch Stadium II in 1966, the ballpark's debut season. The ninety-six tiny arches in the stadium's roof were designed by architect Edward Durell Stone to mimic the Gateway Arch, which itself had been completed in October 1965. A month after this photo was taken, the Beatles played a concert on the field.

In 1967, Busch Stadium's first full year of use, the Cardinals won a memorable world championship over the Boston Red Sox and set a new franchise attendance record of 2.1 million. Overall, the team would enjoy great success in the ballpark, with eleven first-place finishes in forty years. In 1970, at the behest of the football Cardinals, the grass in the outfield was removed and replaced with artificial turf. The same was done to the infield in 1977. These changes were not only an aesthetic disaster but also caused extreme temperatures in the summer, when heat radiated off the concrete and the plastic grass. However, the turf gave rise to an exciting new Cardinals team that was assembled with the ballpark's characteristics in mind. Utilizing the speed and fielding ability of Ozzie Smith, Willie McGee, and later Vince Coleman, St. Louis won three pennants and a world championship between 1982 and '87.

After the football Cardinals and the Rams both moved out, Busch Stadium was reverted back to a traditional baseball park in 1996 as the artificial turf was replaced by the real thing. A handsome hand-operated scoreboard was also added, and during its last decade of existence Busch became an underrated jewel. The Cards traded for Mark "Big Mac" McGwire, whose thrilling pursuit of the home run record in 1998 drew record crowds even for batting practice. Thanks to a McDonald's sponsorship, the section in left field where many of his hits landed was officially named "Big Mac Land." Led by McGwire and young slugger Albert Pujols, the Cardinals became a powerhouse during Busch Stadium's final years, making the playoffs five times in six seasons. The team moved a few blocks away to new Busch Stadium III in 2006.

The entrance ramps of Busch Stadium II as they appeared in 1967, when the building was brand-new and the concrete had not yet acquired its grimy patina. The stadium was designed by Arkansas native Edward Durell Stone, "a celebrity architect whose wholly unique modern aesthetic of 'new romanticism' played a crucial role in defining middle-class culture," according to his biographer, Mary Anne Hunting.

BUSCH STADIUM III

ST. LOUIS CARDINALS 1966-2005

IN 2006, THE CARDINALS BECAME the first team since 1912 to christen a new ballpark with a World Series title in the park's first season. With a record of 83-79, the '06 Cardinals were by far the worst championship team in baseball history, but that scarcely mattered as they celebrated by spraying cheap champagne all over their state-of-the-art new clubhouse. A $365 million retro park built by HOK, Busch Stadium III was designed with details intended to evoke the city's historic structures, including the Eads Bridge (opened in 1874) and the Anheuser-Busch Brewery (1892). With a playing field sunken below street level and a panoramic vista in the outfield, fans in the stands could catch glimpses of the Gateway Arch and, from some seats, the Mississippi River three blocks away.

While Sportsman's Park was home to Stan Musial, and Busch Stadium II was home to Ozzie Smith, Busch III's most famous denizen so far has probably been a feral cat. On August 9, 2017, a one-pound kitten ran onto the field while the Cardinals were mounting a bases-loaded rally. A young groundskeeper eventually captured the playful kitten, only to be bitten twice as he carried it off the field—much to the delight of the home crowd. Then on the very next pitch, the Cardinals' Yadier Molina hit a go-ahead grand slam, and the legend of the Rally Cat was born.

Over the next few weeks a legal kerfuffle ensued as the Cardinals, the local nonprofit St. Louis Feral Cat Outreach, and a random fan in attendance each claimed to be the rightful owner of the now-famous kitten. In the end the nonprofit kept the Rally Cat, nursed it to full health, and placed it with an adoptive family three months later. Meanwhile, Busch Stadium's remaining feral cats are still biding their time in the stadium's innards, presumably waiting for their own shot at stardom. ⚾

In 2011, just five years after opening Busch Stadium III with a World Series title, the Cardinals won another one, triggering the on-field celebration seen here. Their Game 7 win at Busch Stadium III was exciting, but it was the eleven-inning Game 6, with its game-tying triple by David Freese, that entered baseball lore as one of the finest games ever played. "Last night after Game 6, I told several friends, 'I'm really proud to be the commissioner of a sport that can produce what just happened,'" commissioner Bud Selig said.

The exposed structural steel supporting Busch Stadium III's roof evokes a similar design element featured at Sportsman's Park, which can be seen on page 127. The giant Busch Stadium lettering, meanwhile, mimicks the famous Budweiser sign at the historic Anheuser-Busch brewery 2 miles south of the ballpark. Busch III's design process was a battle between architectural firm HOK Sport, which favored a more modern design, and Cardinals owner Bill DeWitt Jr., who demanded a more retro approach. As usual, the client's wishes won out over the architect's, and Busch is a decidedly derivative ballpark. "We embrace it," HOK executive Earl Santee said. "We're trying to push the design a little bit and give it some original thought and fresh ideas, and he has to understand that."

TOP INSET: Among the modern conveniences at Busch Stadium III are ATM-style ticket dispensers, enabling fans to buy last-minute admission without standing in long lines at the ticket window. The machines get plenty of use, as the Cardinals ranked in the National League's top three in attendance during eleven of the new ballpark's first twelve seasons.

BOTTOM INSET: The Cardinals' most iconic player during the early years of Busch Stadium III was Albert Pujols, who batted .331 with 49 home runs during the park's opening season. Pujols hit 110 of his 600-plus career home runs at Busch III. Shockingly, the franchise icon left St. Louis for Anaheim in 2012, with the Cardinals unwilling to match the enormous $254 million contract offered by the Angels. It turned out to be a wise decision by St. Louis: Pujols' career collapsed almost immediately after the contract was signed.

CHICAGO

SCHORLING PARK

TEAMS: Chicago White Sox 1900–1910, Chicago American Giants 1911–1940

NAMES: White Sox Park/South Side Park 1900–1910, Schorling Park 1911–1931, 1937–1940, Cole's Park 1932–1936

LOCATION: Corner of W. Pershing Road and S. Princeton Ave., Chicago

FIRST MLB GAME: April 24, 1901

LAST MLB GAME: June 27, 1910

NOTABLE FEATURES: Small upper deck dedicated exclusively to luxury boxes; unusual outfield fence that curved inward in straightaway center field.

COMISKEY PARK

TEAM: Chicago White Sox 1910–1990

LOCATION: Corner of W. 35th St. and S. Shields Ave., Chicago (adjacent to and north of Guaranteed Rate Field)

FIRST MLB GAME: July 1, 1910

LAST MLB GAME: September 30, 1990

NOTABLE FEATURES: Arcade of segmental arches ringing outer façade; exploding scoreboard with pinwheels installed by owner Bill Veeck Jr. in 1960.

WRIGLEY FIELD

TEAMS: Chicago Whales 1914–1915, Chicago Cubs 1916–present

NAMES: Weeghman Park 1914–1915, Cubs Park 1916–1926, Wrigley Field 1927–present

NICKNAME: The Friendly Confines

LOCATION: Corner of N. Clark St. and W. Addison St., Chicago

FIRST MLB GAME: April 23, 1914

NOTABLE FEATURES: Ivy covering outfield wall; rooftop bleachers across Waveland and Sheffield Avenues; large manually operated scoreboard in dead center field.

GUARANTEED RATE FIELD

TEAM: Chicago White Sox 1991–present

NAMES: Comiskey Park II 1991–2002, U.S. Cellular Field 2003–2016, Guaranteed Rate Field 2017–present

NICKNAME: New Comiskey

LOCATION: Corner of W. 35th St. and S. Shields Ave., Chicago

FIRST MLB GAME: April 18, 1991

NOTABLE FEATURES: Scoreboard replicating the classic scoreboard from Old Comiskey; music by legendary organist Nancy Faust.

For most of the twentieth century, life was painful if you were a Chicago baseball fan. On the North Side, entire generations of Cubs fans lived and died without knowing what it felt like for their team to win the World Series. On the South Side, the White Sox went eighty-eight years without winning a title—punishment, perhaps, for losing the 1919 Series on purpose. But remarkably, a century of constant losing did little to deter Chicagoans from loving the sport. They continued to fill the local stadiums in large numbers and root lustily for their teams. During the 1970s at Comiskey Park, Chicagoans even invented one of the great ballpark traditions—singing "Take Me Out to the Ball Game" during the seventh inning stretch.

When Mrs. O'Leary's cow allegedly knocked over a lantern on October 8, 1871, she started a cataclysm that cost the Windy City its first Major League Baseball team. The Great Chicago Fire ravaged most of the city, including White Stockings Grounds, a wooden ballpark located on the site where Anish Kapoor's famed *Cloud Gate* sculpture known as "The Bean," now stands. The Stockings were forced to drop out of the league.

TOP: As a brass band practices in the stands behind them, the 1913 Chicago Cubs pose for a team photo at West Side Park. This was one of the team's final seasons in the old wooden ballpark; they would leave for Weeghman Park—now known as Wrigley Field—in 1916. After a decade of immense success, the Cubs franchise was headed downhill by the time this photo was taken. Three star players—Mordecai Brown, Frank Chance, and Joe Tinker—had recently left, and those who remained, like second baseman Johnny Evers (second row, third from right) were past their prime.

BOTTOM: Lake Front Park, home of the Cubs franchise from 1878 through 1884, was located inside a city park that was also called Lake Front Park. Though the stadium had been torn down by the time this photo was taken in 1893, the image nicely illustrates the narrow strip of land the ballpark was squeezed into, with train tracks and Lake Michigan on one side and Michigan Avenue on the other. Lake Front Park's outfield distances were only 180 feet to left field and 196 to right, which enabled four different Chicago players to break the MLB single-season home run record in 1884. Today, the former ballpark site is occupied by Chicago's best-known work of public art, the Anish Kapoor sculpture known as "The Bean." This photo was probably taken from atop the then-brand-new Art Institute of Chicago Building, which opened in late 1893.

OPPOSITE PAGE, TOP: This shot of Wrigley Field was taken during the first game ever played there on April 23, 1914. Work on the ballpark wasn't quite finished yet, as evidenced by the sawhorses and other construction materials visible along the back wall of the outfield. Note the twenty-eight American flags on top of the roof, which were removed when the upper deck was added in 1927.

OPPOSITE PAGE, BOTTOM: West Side Grounds was the home of the Cubs from 1893 through 1915, during which they won four pennants and two World Series titles. This photo shows Cubs pitcher Jack Pfiester facing the New York Giants in 1908, when the Cubs, Giants, and Pirates faced off in one of the most exciting pennant races of all time. (Chicago eventually won the title thanks to the famous baserunning blunder known as "Merkle's Boner.") The renowned double play trio of Tinker, Evers, and Chance are all visible in this photo, playing shortstop, second base, and first base, respectively.

Three years later, the White Stockings returned and reclaimed the site where their park had burned down. The new venue, Lake Front Park, was called "the finest park of the era" by one historian and contained eighteen luxury boxes plus an elaborate bandstand. Because the site was hemmed in by railroad tracks, the distance to left field was a comical 180 feet, and right field wasn't much better, at 196. During some seasons balls hit over the left field fence counted as ground-rule doubles. In 1884, when they counted as homers, four Chicago batters broke the major league home run record, led by Ed Williamson's 27.

During the early 1900s, the White Stockings—who had recently renamed themselves the Cubs—fielded the finest team in baseball at West Side Grounds, where fans paid 50¢ for a bench seat, 75¢ for a chair, or a dollar for a box seat. The park had a massive right field wall, 40 feet tall, which contained perhaps the largest advertisements ever seen at a ballpark. (A billboard erected during the 1906 World Series—*The Tribune Always Makes a Hit with Its Sporting News*—was about 275 feet long.) In 1916, the Cubs left West Side Grounds for Wrigley Field.

A new team called the White Sox, meanwhile, joined the major leagues in 1901, setting up the two-team system that the city has enjoyed ever since. The Sox's first home was South Side Park, which they turned over to the Negro Leagues after opening Comiskey Park two blocks away in 1910. During its eighty-year tenure, Comiskey hosted many of baseball's marquee events, including the annual Negro Leagues East-West Game. The Soxs moved next door to New Comiskey in 1991, and both Chicago teams have now played at their respective sites for more than a hundred years. 🐻

SCHORLING PARK

ALTHOUGH THE NEGRO National League was officially founded in Kansas City, Missouri, the organization's power resided at Schorling Park in Chicago. Andrew "Rube" Foster, a portly, well-dressed Texan who addressed everyone as "darlin'," was the brains behind both the Negro Leagues and its most prestigious franchise, the Chicago American Giants. Schorling Park, an old wooden ballpark on Chicago's South Side that had once been home to the White Sox, was the home field of the American Giants for three decades.

The grassy lot on 39th Street had been used as a cricket field during the famous World's Columbian Exposition in 1893. In 1900, retired ballplayer Charles Comiskey built a wooden grandstand there for the American League team he had just founded, the Chicago White Sox. He named it South Side Park. Comiskey gradually built it into a ballpark of major league quality, adding luxury boxes in 1901 and a roof in 1902. In 1906, South Side Park hosted three games during the much-ballyhooed inter-city World Series between the Cubs and White Sox. (The Pale Hose, despite being heavy underdogs, won in six games.) In 1910, however, Comiskey moved the Sox to Comiskey Park, a humongous steel and concrete stadium three blocks away.

Comiskey leased the now-vacant old ballpark to his son-in-law, a saloonkeeper named John Schorling, who rebuilt the grandstand, added some bleachers, and renamed it Schorling Park. In 1911 Schorling entered into a long and fruitful partnership with Rube Foster, and his ballpark became the new home of Foster's American Giants. For the next several decades Schorling Park was a central part of African-American life in Chicago, and the American Giants usually boasted a loaded roster. The team's best players included shortstop John Henry Lloyd, slugging outfielder Cristóbal Torriente, and left-handed pitcher Willie Foster, Rube's half brother. At Schorling

Schorling Base Ball Park—39th and Princeton Ave., Chicago, Ill.
Home of RUBE FOSTER'S AMERICAN GIANTS
Three Time Champions—The Negro National League

Record attendance of 17,337 see Rube Foster's American Giants
crush Kansas City Monarchs 5 to 4—10 Innings,
with the Great Rogan pitching

How American Giants Forced Their Way to Top of Negro National League

American Giants	3	American Giants	3	
Kansas City	2	Kansas City	2	
		10 INNINGS		
American Giants	5	American Giants	7	
Kansas City	4	Kansas City	4	
10 INNINGS				

HOME OF RUBE F

TOP: White Sox pitcher Nick Altrock faces the Boston Americans at South Side Park (also sometimes called White Sox Park). This was the most extreme pitcher's park of its era, even though the distance to the outfield wall was not out of the ordinary. In 1904, the year this photo was taken, the Sox didn't hit a homer in their home ballpark all season. This was the home field of the 1906 World Series winners who were famously dubbed "Hitless Wonders," although the nickname was a misnomer. Modern statistical analysis shows that the 1906 White Sox were actually an above-average offensive team, but the extreme nature of their ballpark fooled contemporary observers into believing they couldn't hit.

BOTTOM: White Sox Park as it appeared after its name was changed to Schorling Park and it became a Negro League stadium. Note that the small section of rooftop skyboxes, visible in the 1904 photo at left, had been removed by the time this image was taken in the early 1920s. (The Chicago building commissioner had deemed them unsafe and ordered their removal.) Visible behind the outfield are the smokestacks and industrial buildings of the Union Stock Yards, the massive meatpacking facility that led Carl Sandburg to dub Chicago "hog butcher for the world."

ER'S AMERICAN GIANTS.

RUBE FOSTER
The Victor.

TOP: The two men most vital to the success of the Chicago American Giants were half brothers Rube Foster (right, with cane) and Willie Foster (left, in baseball uniform). Rube, who had been a star pitcher at the turn of the twentieth century, was the leading visionary behind Negro League baseball. He founded the American Giants in 1911 and the Negro National League in 1920. Willie, born a quarter century after his half brother, dominated as a left-handed pitcher during the 1920s.

MIDDLE: The Chicago American Giants pose with their team bus in 1950. By the time this photo was taken, the American Giants franchise was on the downswing. Rube Foster had died in an insane asylum in 1930, and Schorling Park burned down in 1940. Manager Ted Radcliffe (in street clothes at far left) had once been a star player for the team, nicknamed "Double Duty" because he played both pitcher and catcher.

BOTTOM: The Cubs and White Sox face off at South Side Park in the 1909 Chicago City Series, played in October after their regular seasons. The City Series, played twenty-six times between 1903 and 1942, was a much-ballyhooed event locally, even though the games were technically exhibitions. South Side Park's rooftop boxes, which had been condemned as unsafe by Chicago's building commissioner in 1907, were apparently being used again by 1909, at least for this game.

OPPOSITE PAGE, TOP: The team poses at Schorling Park in 1927, the year they defeated the Bacharach Giants in the Negro League World Series. Their best players that season included southpaw pitcher Willie Foster (second from left in middle row) and first baseman Dave Malarcher (third from left in front row).

OPPOSITE PAGE, BOTTOM: Played annually at Comiskey Park, the East-West All-Star Game was the biggest event in Negro Leagues baseball from 1933 through the 1950s. In this photo from the 1939 game, Henry Milton of the Kansas City Monarchs slides home as catcher Josh Gibson tries to block his progress. Milton was called out on the play, but his West team rallied in the eighth to win 4-2.

Park on September 29, 1926, Willie Foster turned in one of the most extraordinary pitching performances in history. The American Giants needed to sweep a playoff doubleheader against the Kansas City Monarchs to clinch the Negro National League title. Willie pitched a seven-hit shutout in the first game, then a two-hit shutout in the second game, capturing the pennant in dramatic fashion.

"[Rube] Foster operated the team, Schorling the park," Faye Young, the noted *Chicago Defender* columnist, wrote in 1948. "They worked harmoniously together until Foster died in 1930." After Foster's death, the American Giants were run by a succession of would-be entrepreneurs, including Robert Cole, who briefly renamed the ballpark Cole's Park during the 1930s. During that decade, it also functioned as a dog racing venue. On Christmas Day 1940, the ballpark met its end, burning down after the night watchman's wood stove reportedly overheated.

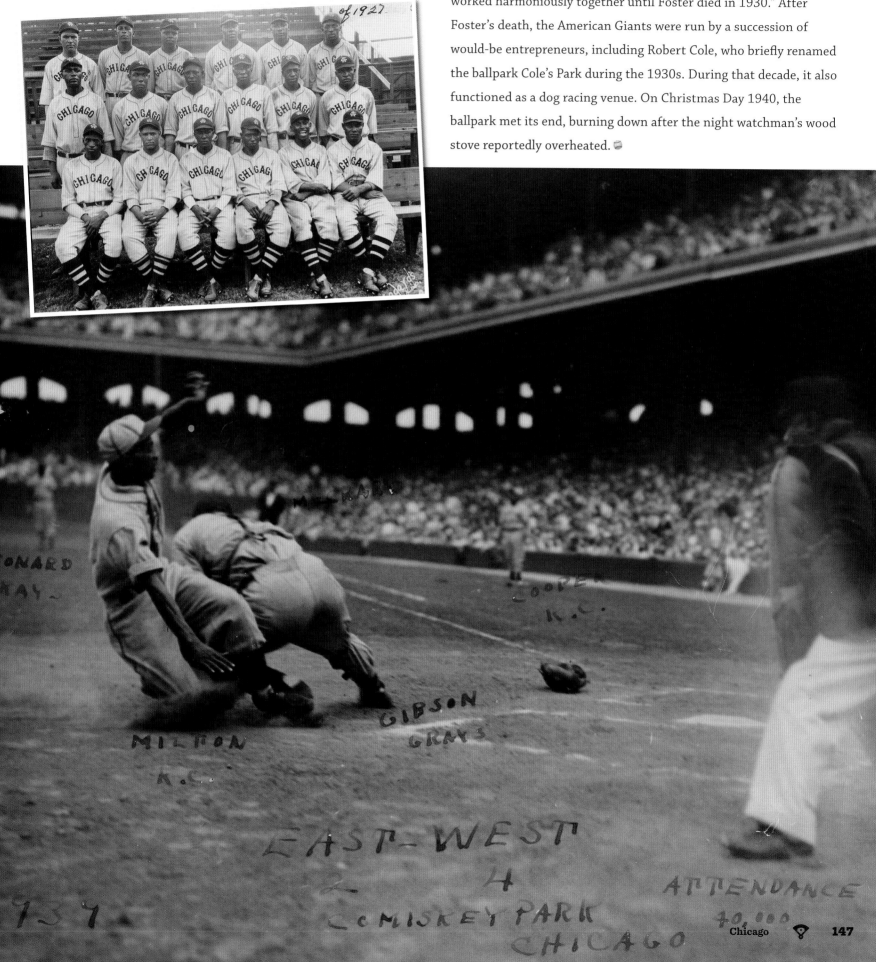

COMISKEY PARK

CHICAGO WHITE SOX 1910–1990

EVEN BEFORE HE ATTENDED Shibe Park's grand opening in 1909, White Sox owner Charles Comiskey had grown jealous of Philadelphia's jewel of a stadium, and decided the South Side of Chicago needed a steel and concrete baseball palace of its own. To accomplish this, Comiskey immediately hired Zachary Taylor Davis, a semi-prominent local architect who would later go on to design Wrigley Field.

Davis originally envisioned an elaborate Roman façade for Comiskey's ballpark, but the owner, in order to save money, scuttled the fancy blueprints in favor of a more utilitarian exterior. Visually, Comiskey Park was distinguished by a series of segmental arches that lined the grandstand 30 feet above street level, providing an instantly recognizable motif that was visible from both inside and outside the ballpark. Taylor's design team tried to talk Comiskey into approving cantilevered decks so as to avoid building pillars that obstructed fans' views, but the penurious owner turned down the idea, which would have added some $350,000 to a budget that

already exceeded $700,000. Another influential voice in Taylor's ear was that of Big Ed Walsh, Chicago's twenty-eight-year-old pitching ace, who successfully lobbied for extremely distant outfield fences. With the center field fence 440 feet away, Walsh posted a career-best 1.27 ERA during the new ballpark's first season.

During its eighty-one years as home of the White Sox, Comiskey Park witnessed precious little winning but plenty of memorable moments. It was where "Shoeless" Joe Jackson purposely misplayed fly balls in an attempt to throw the 1919 World Series. It was where the forty-one-year-old Ted Lyons, "Sunday Teddy," enjoyed one of the most unique pitching seasons ever, hurling nine innings every Sunday in 1942 without fail. It was where the Go-Go Sox of Luis Aparicio and Nellie Fox sprinted their way to the 1959 pennant. It was where owner Bill Veeck Jr. introduced fans to innovations like the exploding scoreboard. And it was where the most ill-conceived promotion in baseball history, Disco Demolition Night, degenerated into a cesspool of arson, rioting, and thinly veiled racism—not to mention a forfeited ballgame.

But as beloved as Comiskey Park was by White Sox fans, the greatest games it ever hosted had nothing to do with the Pale Hose. Comiskey's most important role in history was serving as the permanent

OPPOSITE PAGE: One-year-old Comiskey Park is packed to the gills as fans watch the Cubs and White Sox play in the Chicago City Series on October 9, 1911, the fortieth anniversary of the Great Chicago Fire. This photo is notable for, among other things, the remarkable variety of hats on display. Derbies, fedoras, boaters, newsboys, conductor's hats, and a variety of women's straw and feathered hats are visible—everything, it seems, except baseball caps.

TOP: The Comiskey Park entrance as it appeared in its earliest days, with signs advertising grandstand seats for just 75¢. White Sox owner Charles Comiskey was nicknamed "The Old Roman," and architect Zachary Taylor Davis had initially wanted to build a fancy Roman-style façade for the ballpark. However, the penny-pinching Comiskey demurred, instead settling for the simple brick façade seen here.

BOTTOM: The changes in Comiskey Park's exterior are apparent when comparing this 1985 photo with the one above it, which dates from the 1910s. By the 1980s, the natural brick exterior had been painted white, the stand-alone ticket booths had been removed, an elevator shaft had been built, and the ballpark's name was rendered in paint instead of the raised lettering of the earlier era. The stately windows with flower boxes underneath had also been removed. Still present were the ballpark's signature arched windows, which were visible from nearly anywhere inside or outside the ballpark.

site of the East-West Game, the Negro Leagues' version of the All-Star Game. Fans of color—and a few white folks, too—made annual pilgrimages from around the country to attend the game, which was held for the first time in September 1933, just two months after the first white All-Star Game was played at the same venue. The East-West Game was the brainchild of Roy Sparrow, a Pittsburgh Crawfords executive. "One particular day we were sitting in a restaurant in Pittsburgh," Dave Malarcher, manager of the Chicago American Giants, later recalled, "and [Sparrow] said, 'You know, Dave, we could organize a big game like the major league All-Star Game and call it the East-West Game.' About three weeks later when we came to Chicago, we found that...they had organized the first East-West Game and rented Comiskey Park."

Despite inclement weather, that 1933 contest proved a rousing success. Fans watched the East squad, led by the speedy Cool Papa Bell, lose 11-7 to a West club that featured Turkey Stearnes, Willie Wells, and Mule Suttles, all members of the hometown

Chicago American Giants. "The Depression didn't stop 'em—the rain couldn't—and so a howling, thundering mob of 20,000 souls braved an early downpour and a threatening storm to see the pick of the East's baseball players battle the pick of the West in a Game of Games at the White Sox ball park in Chicago last Sunday afternoon," wrote Al Monroe in the *Chicago Defender*.

TOP: Cubs catcher Gabby Hartnett chats with Al Capone and his twelve-year-old son, Sonny, at Comiskey Park in 1931. In the second row are three of Capone's mob underlings: Sam "Golf Bag" Hunt, "Cowboy Frank" DiGiovanni, and "Machine Gun Jack" McGurn. The Capone gang was attending a Cubs-White Sox charity game benefiting the state's unemployment relief fund, which had been decimated by the Great Depression. When baseball commissioner Kenesaw Mountain Landis saw this image in the next day's *Chicago Tribune*, he fired off an angry telegram to Hartnett: "You are no longer allowed to have your picture taken with Al Capone." Replied Hartnett: "OK, but if you don't want me to have my picture taken with Al Capone, you tell him." Five weeks after the photo was taken Capone was sentenced to prison for tax evasion, ending his life as a free man.

BOTTOM: Comiskey Park hosted the first-ever MLB All-Star Game in 1933. Here, Babe Ruth, Lou Gehrig, and Al Simmons pose with a youngster named Edwin Diamond before the historic event. (Diamond would grow up to become a noted journalist and the author of eleven books.) Note the arched windows in the background, a distinctive feature of Comiskey Park that is much appreciated by historians, since it makes virtually any photo taken there instantly recognizable.

OPPOSITE PAGE, TOP: Shoeless Joe Jackson, an outfielder, fools around with a catcher's mitt for a photographer in the Comiskey Park dugout. This photo was taken in 1919, the year Jackson conspired with six of his teammates to throw the World Series on behalf of gamblers. Although modern-day fans have tried hard to acquit him, the facts aren't really in dispute: Jackson agreed to the fixing scheme, took the gamblers' money, and signed a confession in 1920. (This photo was taken when the White Sox still wore completely white socks; they last did so in 1945.)

OPPOSITE PAGE, BOTTOM: Dan Wilson of the St. Louis Stars is lifted onto the shoulders of his West teammates after hitting a game-winning homer in the eighth inning of the 1939 East-West Game at Comiskey Park. Also joining the celebration are Kansas City Monarchs shortstop Ted Strong, Cleveland Buckeyes third baseman Parnell Woods, and Memphis Red Sox center fielder Neil Robinson.

The East-West Game continued to be played at Comiskey Park virtually every year through 1960, with 20 percent of gate receipts going to Old Man Comiskey's family. The game became a cornerstone not only of Negro League baseball but also of African-American culture in general. Stars turned out by the dozen. Families planned summer vacations around it. "Oh, man, it was quite an affair," Negro Leagues star Buck O'Neil recalled in 2001:

> The Illinois Central train and the City of New Orleans [train] would put on a couple of extra cars, and they would bring people and pick 'em up in Memphis and all the way up. The New York Central would put on a couple of extra cars in New York City, and the Santa Fe Chief would put on a couple of extra cars coming out of California, picking up people along the way. It was quite an evening. I'll tell you what it was like: It was like a Joe Louis prizefight. Everybody was there, all of the dignitaries. I've seen Joe Louis throw out the first ball, I've seen Bojangles throw out the first pitch at the East-West Game, all of the great ones. We'd fill up the ballpark. In fact, they always said we outdrew the major leaguers.

That last claim might sound like bluster, but thanks to excellent record keeping by the Negro Leagues, it's documented. During the first eighteen years, the white and black All-Star games were held concurrently, the African-American version outdrew the white version nine times.

By the 1980s, though, the Negro Leagues were extinct and some white fans were avoiding Comiskey Park altogether due to fear of its South Side neighborhood. A nearby housing project, the Robert Taylor Homes, had become notorious for its poverty, gang violence, and crack cocaine. The White Sox threatened to move to St. Petersburg, Florida, unless the Illinois state legislature approved a new ballpark—which it did in 1988, by a margin of one vote. Immediately afterward, fans seemed to gain a newfound appreciation for Old Comiskey, waxing nostalgic about the ballyard during its final years. Wrigley Field "is more picturesque, a ballpark that could come from the movies," the architecture critic Paul Goldberger wrote. "But Comiskey is more real, a glorious, raunchy old place that has nothing picturesque about it at all. Over the years, Comiskey Park has been pushed and pulled and altered and expanded every which way, and it is so tough it never loses an ounce of its character. Wrigley is the field of dreams, but Comiskey is Chicago."

TOP: Chicagoans riot on the Comiskey Park playing field during what was surely the most ill-conceived promotion in baseball history, Disco Demolition Night, in 1979. Held at the height of the disco backlash of the late seventies, the White Sox offered tickets to a doubleheader for 98¢ if fans brought a disco record with them. All the albums were then piled on the field between games and exploded in a ceremony presided over by a local disc jockey, Steve Dahl. Immediately after the explosion and ensuing bonfire, thousands of young rock fans stormed the field. They threw records like Frisbees, started more fires, and pulled the bases up from the infield. Remarkably, only thirty-nine people were arrested among the thousands of rioters, but the second game of the doubleheader was forfeited to the Tigers.

BOTTOM: A paltry crowd of 12,000 watches the White Sox and Blue Jays play at Comiskey Park during its final season in 1990. By this time few fans were showing up at the crumbling old ballpark, and construction was nearly finished on the new stadium next door, which would open the following spring.

WRIGLEY FIELD

CHICAGO WHALES 1914–1915   CHICAGO CUBS 1916–PRESENT

NO BALLPARK HAS EVER BEEN the scene of quite as much heartbreak as Wrigley Field. For its first 102 seasons of existence, fans filled the ballpark optimistically each summer, only to have their hopes dashed when their team again failed to win the World Series. The songwriter Steve Goodman put it best in his 1983 tune "A Dying Cubs Fan's Last Request." Written as Goodman himself was dying of leukemia, the song tells the humorous and poignant story of a dying Cubs fan who longs for his funeral to be held at Wrigley Field. "I've got season's tickets to watch the angels now / So it's just what I'm gonna do," the dying man sings. "But you, the living, you're stuck here with the Cubs / So it's me who feels sorry for you."

Few fans realize that Wrigley Field wasn't even built by the Cubs but by the Chicago Whales, a team in a competing major league called the Federal League. It was initially called Weeghman Park after the Whales' owner, and was constructed over a six-week period in 1914 for $500,000, a middling sum for the time. After the Whales went belly-up in 1915, the Cubs seized on the opportunity to move in. In 1923, Cubs owner William Wrigley expanded the grandstand and nearly doubled the park's capacity to 30,000. Four years later he added an upper deck, enabling the Cubs to become the first National League team to draw a million fans in one season.

It was in 1937, though, that Wrigley Field came to resemble the ballpark it is today, with the addition of its three most iconic features: the bleachers, the humongous hand-operated scoreboard behind them, and the ivy covering the outfield wall. The latter was the brainchild of a twenty-three-year-old marketing whiz named Bill Veeck Jr.,

Wrigley Field's iconic center field scoreboard has changed little since it was first erected in 1937. Originally a brownish-red, it was painted green in 1944. The ship's mast with the flags of all National League teams has been there from the beginning, but the numberless clock was added in 1941 and the floodlights in 1989. In 2013, the Cubs got special permission from the city's Landmarks Commission to add the advertisement underneath.

INSET: William Wrigley Jr. became majority owner of the Cubs in 1921, purchasing the team with money from the chewing gum empire he had founded in 1892. A jovial, charismatic salesman, Wrigley enjoyed being the public face of the team and could often be found in the box seats of his eponymous ballpark. When he died in 1932, ownership of the team passed to his son Philip.

whose late father had once been team president. Ordered by William Wrigley to come up with "an outdoor, woodsy motif" to beautify the ballpark, young Veeck planted a combination of Boston ivy (which grows fuller) and Japanese bittersweet (which sprouts faster in chilly spring weather). The ivy has been the ballpark's signature ever since.

Though the bleachers were built in 1937, it wasn't until the 1970s that Wrigley's notorious "Bleacher Bums" entered the public consciousness. During that freewheeling decade, there were no night games, so the team's weekday attendance was drawn largely from schoolchildren and the unemployed. The Bleacher Bums, fueled by a seemingly limitless intake of Old Style beer, became known throughout baseball for, among other things, tossing home run balls hit by the visiting team back onto the field.

They heckled opponents mercilessly, but also sometimes targeted the Cubs. In 1983, Cubs manager Lee Elia reached the boiling point, going on an unhinged rant against his own team's fans that has become a staple of baseball lore. "If they're the real Chicago f-ckin' fans, they can kiss my f-ckin' ass," he said in part. "The motherf-ckers don't even work. That's why they're out at the f-ckin' game. They oughta go out and get a f-ckin' job and find out what it's like to go out and earn a f-ckin' living."

On the field, the 1970s were a sort of golden era for Cubs fans, in part because the decade has been romanticized in the work of a number of creative artists who grew up attending games at Wrigley Field. These include Goodman, Bill Murray, Pearl Jam frontman Eddie Vedder, and actor/playwright Joe Mantegna, who wrote a play called "Bleacher Bums" based on the outfield denizens. Two players of this era were particularly revered: Ernie Banks, the sunny "Mr. Cub," and Ron Santo, the fun-loving third baseman who later served as the team's radio announcer. In 1982 that duo was joined by television announcer Harry Caray, whose inebriated butchering of name pronunciations only served to make him all the more lovable. Caray spent just sixteen years with the Cubs, but possessed such force of personality that it seemed like three times that long. Today, all three men have statues honoring them outside Wrigley Field.

OPPOSITE PAGE: The Cubs played two home games in the 1929 World Series, and the paid attendance at both was around 50,000—much larger than Wrigley Field's seating capacity. Overflow fans were seated on the field at the base of the outfield wall (the ivy would be planted eight years later). Balls hit into the roped-off area were ground-rule doubles.

TOP: The Cubs won the 1929 pennant largely due to these five men, who formed the core of an offense that bludgeoned opposing teams into submission. Pictured from left are right fielder Kiki Cuyler, second baseman (and manager) Rogers Hornsby, center fielder Hack Wilson, first baseman Charlie Grimm, and left fielder Riggs Stephenson. Collectively the five star sluggers batted .351 with 611 runs batted in.

BOTTOM LEFT: Cardinals great Dizzy Dean was traded to the Cubs in 1938 after his career had been derailed by a foot injury suffered in the 1937 All-Star Game. Dean altered his pitching mechanics to favor his foot, which resulted in him hurting his arm. He enjoyed a brief renaissance with the Cubs, resting for a week to ten days between appearances to allow his sore arm to recover. He went 7-1 with a 1.81 ERA over thirteen games in 1938.

BOTTOM RIGHT: Ron Santo fields a throw at Wrigley Field during the early 1970s, with Montreal baserunner Rusty Staub bearing down on him. Santo played for the Cubs from 1960 to 1973, hitting 337 home runs and making eight all-star teams. He became even more beloved after his playing days ended, serving as the team's ebullient radio announcer for thirty years. Santo liked to refer to himself as "the single biggest Cubs fan of all time," and few would argue.

From 1981 through 2009, the Cubs and their ballpark were owned by the Tribune Company, publishers of the local newspaper, who generally kept the team in a state of comfortable mediocrity. Knowing that fans were going to fill up Wrigley Field win or lose, Tribune saw little incentive to invest in high-salaried players who would make the club a World Series contender. Instead, the Cubs skated along to what seemed like an endless series of fourth-place finishes.

The Tribune Company did make one important investment in the stadium, however, waging a six-year battle to install lights. For four decades, Wrigley Field had been the only major league stadium without night baseball. Efforts to install lights had blown hot and cold since 1941, the year team owner Phil Wrigley (William's son) purchased 165 tons of steel to erect light towers—and then promptly donated the much-needed materiel to the military when World War II started.

In its quest to host night games, the Tribune Company faced formidable opposition from the residents of Wrigleyville, who feared the specter of drunken Cubs fans invading their neighborhood en masse at night. The residents were both well-heeled and politically connected, and they managed to convince the city council and state legislature to pass laws that effectively banned night baseball in Chicago, with a special exception made for the White Sox. The city council voted against the Cubs by the astonishing margin of 42-2. In response, the Cubs filed lawsuits and made vague threats to move the team if night baseball were not approved. After years of legal wrangling, the team finally reached a compromise with a new, friendlier city government. The Cubs agreed to ground rules stipulating that only eighteen night games a year could be played, no beer would be sold after 9:20 p.m., and no organ music would be played after 9:30. On August 8, 1988, some 40,000 fans and 500 media members packed Wrigley Field for the ballpark's first-ever night game, which was to be played before a national television audience. Appropriately enough, the ballgame was rained out.

As the Tribune's ownership came to an end, Wrigley Field was still one of baseball's crown jewels but was in sore need of an update. The locker rooms were sweltering and infamously tiny, making players reluctant to sign with the Cubs. The bathrooms were both too few and too fragrant; the smell of stale urine constantly wafted through the stands. Deficient concession facilities forced fans to miss huge chunks of the game standing in line. Even the exit ramps were inadequate for the number of people using them, resulting in massive gridlock when fans tried to leave after the game. In 2013, the team and stadium were sold to a family of Nebraska brokerage moguls, the Ricketts, for $1.8 billion. The new owners took their

OPPOSITE PAGE: Harry Caray joined the Cubs broadcast team in 1982, bringing with him a tradition he'd started as a White Sox announcer at Comiskey Park: singing "Take Me Out to the Ball Game" during the seventh inning stretch. After his death in 1998 the Cubs kept the tradition going, with Caray's singing role assumed by a different celebrity each game.

TOP: A woman turns around to grin at the photographer on September 28, 1938, turning her back on one of the most chaotic and memorable scenes in Wrigley Field's history. Somewhere in the mass of humanity behind her is Gabby Hartnett, the Cubs' catcher and manager, who has just touched home plate after hitting his legendary "Homer in the Gloamin'" against Pittsburgh. The walk-off homer didn't technically win the pennant, but it did propel Chicago from half a game behind Pittsburgh to half a game ahead, and three days later they clinched the crown. It was "an afternoon which beggars description," John P. Carmichael wrote of Hartnett's homer in the *Chicago Daily News*. "It was almost too much for human flesh and blood to watch."

BOTTOM: Equipping Wrigley Field for night baseball was a forty-seven-year odyssey, beginning with an aborted attempt to add lights in 1941 and finally ending when the Cubs played their first home night game in 1988. (However, that contest was only the Cubs' first night game at Wrigley. The All-American Girls Professional Baseball League had played its all-star game there under temporary portable lights in 1943.)

stewardship seriously, vowing to update Wrigley Field and put a winning team on the field. They successfully accomplished both.

From 2015 through 2018, the Cubs undertook an extensive renovation that brought Wrigley Field into the twenty-first century. Concession stands and restrooms were added; new bullpens, locker rooms, and training facilities were built; the bleachers were rebuilt with added seats; the press box was renovated; and giant HD video boards were added in right and left field. Other additions were made with an eye toward boosting revenue, including a retail shopping complex, several swanky clubs for high rollers, and even a new team-owned hotel adjacent to the ballpark. All the changes were reflected in exorbitant new ticket prices. A bleacher ticket, which cost $1.25 in 1976, cost $139 for certain premium games in 2017. Even after adjusting for inflation, that's a price hike of 2,500 percent. Needless to say, children are no longer attending Cubs games after school on a lark.

The new owners improved the on-field product by hiring Theo Epstein, the wunderkind who had finally brought a World Series title to Boston, to run the Cubs' baseball operations. In short order Epstein acquired two superstars—Kris Bryant through the draft, Anthony Rizzo through a brilliant trade—and made astute moves to fill out the rest of the roster with quality players. In 2015, the newly revamped Cubs won ninety-seven games. In 2016, they fielded one of the greatest teams of modern times, winning 103 games and

bringing the World Series back to Wrigley Field for the first time since 1945.

The middle three games of the Fall Classic were held at Wrigley, and the environment, unsurprisingly, was one of jubilant bedlam. The streets and bars of Wrigleyville were packed to the gills. Longtime fans openly wept tears of joy. (Scalpers, too, wept tears of joy, as Series tickets sold for an average of $3,500 per game, with the most desirable seats fetching $18,000 apiece.) Stars like Eddie Vedder and Bill Murray led cheers in the stands, giggling like children. For Cubs fans of all ages, a lifetime of waiting came to an end in a paroxysm of nervous energy.

The Cubs ended up winning the title in a dramatic seventh game played on the road in Cleveland, but it might as well have been played at Wrigley Field. Cubs fans gathered there in the street to watch anyway. As soon as Bryant threw the ball to Rizzo for the final out, the crowd erupted as the text on Wrigley's iconic message board was changed to read *WORLD SERIES CHAMPIONS*. Horns honked all across Chicagoland as people spontaneously rushed toward the ballpark to celebrate. Cemeteries were deluged by Cubs fans communing with long-dead relatives. Fans celebrated so vigorously that nine months later, Chicago experienced a baby boom. At that moment, the preceding century of futility seemed entirely worth it. And somewhere, Steve Goodman was surely smiling. ⬤

OPPOSITE PAGE: Wrigley Field's rooftop bleachers in 2010, shortly before their view was blocked by a giant set of video boards. When the Ricketts family bought the Cubs in 2013 they waged war against the wildcat bleachers, reneging on an agreement the Cubs' previous ownership had signed with the rooftop owners. That 2004 deal had required the rooftops to give 17 percent of their revenue to the team; in return, the Cubs promised to never block their view. After the Cubs violated the contract a legal battle ensued; the team won. With their assets devalued, the rooftop owners were forced to sell. The Cubs now own thirteen of the sixteen buildings with rooftop bleachers.

TOP: Kris Bryant, the Cubs' best player, spent most of the 2016 World Series smiling. Here he cracks a grin in mid-swing as he hits a game-tying homer against Cleveland in Game 5. Three days later, he was famously grinning as he fielded a tenth-inning grounder for the last out of the epic Game 7. "I don't remember feeling a smile," Bryant said unconvincingly. "I kind of make that stupid face any time I do anything."

BOTTOM LEFT: The Cubs' 2016 World Series title was celebrated not only in Chicago but across the Midwest, as evidenced by this sign on a radio station building in Marion, Indiana, 177 miles away.

BOTTOM RIGHT: Wrigley Field's iconic marquee has flashed thousands of messages over the years, but none quite as joyous as the one it displayed after the Cubs won the 2016 World Series. Erected in 1934, the marquee was initially painted fern green, then later changed to navy blue. It finally acquired its current shade of brilliant red in the mid-1960s.

"NEW COMISKEY PARK," AS IT WAS KNOWN when it opened in 1991, was immediately like a state-of-the-art bicycle in the age of automobiles—having built the stadium just before the retro-ballpark rage swept through baseball, the White Sox found themselves with a brand-new park, but still left behind.

During the late 1980s, Sox owners Jerry Reinsdorf and Eddie Einhorn had threatened to move the team from Old Comiskey to St. Petersburg, Florida, unless they got a new taxpayer-funded stadium. After some backroom deal-making, a $150 million funding bill passed each house of the Illinois legislature by a margin of one vote. New Comiskey was the first baseball-only park with real grass since Anaheim Stadium opened in 1966. However, with features like upscale concession stands and a members-only stadium club, it seemed to reject the patronage of the hot-dogs-and-beer crowd. "These rich people are just taking over," one fan told the *New York Times* on Opening Day. "You see all these people in suits. You see these limousines.... I'm just a regular steelworker." Said another fan, "You feel like you need a tie to go in."

The ballpark's signature visual feature was borrowed from its predecessor, a larger version of Bill Veeck Jr.'s famous exploding scoreboard with its spinning pinwheels. That was New Comiskey in a nutshell; Its name and best features were borrowed from a park which itself had been deemed expendable. There was nothing terribly wrong with the new stadium; it just lacked identity, and its seats were too far away from the field. The first row in the upper deck was actually farther away from the action than the last row of the upper deck at Old Comiskey. When Camden Yards opened just one year after New Comiskey, the degree to which the White Sox had miscalculated became immediately apparent, and the Sox announced plans for a $41 million in renovations in 2001—when the ballpark was just ten years old. These included replacement of the stadium chairs, a revamped scoreboard, a raft of trendy restaurants and shops, a new roof, and the removal of 6,600 seats to reduce ticket supply and hopefully spur demand. The ballpark's name was also sold, and further renovations followed from 2008 through 2016. These updates certainly made it a better place to watch a game, but Guaranteed Rate Field (as it is now known) still stands as a multimillion-dollar monument to poor timing. 🌭

OPPOSITE PAGE: New Comiskey Park as it appeared between 1991 and 2005, when it was officially known as Cellular One Field. The pinwheel-topped scoreboard in center field was a mostly faithful reproduction of the famous exploding scoreboard installed at Old Comiskey by Bill Veeck Jr. Veeck had conceived the scoreboard as a giant version of a pinball machine. "There will be noises of varying tones and intensities," the *Chicago Tribune* wrote in 1960, when the board made its debut. "Other buttons will produce varying noises, such as thunder and the collision of locomotives. The eight small ladders atop the scoreboard will flash into electrical patterns. Strobe lights are atop the two higher ladders. Bombs and fireworks also will be exploding from the firing platform."

TOP: As this photo demonstrates, Wrigley Field isn't the only Chicago stadium with ivy growing on it. New Comiskey Park was the last ballpark built before the retro-ballpark craze took off, but architectural firm HOK did foreshadow some of the concepts here that it would bring to Camden Yards a year later. Exposed structural steel and arched doorways both became staples of retro-ballpark design, as did the creative use of greenery.

BOTTOM: Like many teams with storied pasts, the White Sox take advantage of any opportunity to celebrate their history. The team's retired numbers were displayed on the outfield wall until 2013, when they were removed and replaced with advertisements.

Dyersville, Iowa

The Field of Dreams: A Beloved Film Come to Life

IN 1989, the movie *Field of Dreams* became an unexpected hit, bringing grown men and women to tears with its themes of family and redemption. The movie earned a modest $64 million, but it became a cultural touchstone and earned an Academy Award nomination for best picture. Three decades have passed since the film's release, but the Field of Dreams itself is still standing in Dyersville, Iowa, a living testament to the power of nostalgia. The film's catchphrase—"If you build it, he will come"—once referred to Shoeless Joe Jackson, but now applies to the thousands of baseball fans who annually visit this out-of-the-way site.

The film crew actually built the Field of Dreams on two adjacent farms, with the property line going from third base to right-center field. The main part of the field, as well as the farmhouse featured in the movie, belonged to Don Lansing, while left and most of center field belonged to Al Ameskamp. After filming ended, Lansing kept his portion intact, but Ameskamp did not, replanting corn in what had once been the outfield. But soon, a funny thing happened. The film touched so many hearts that some 50,000 tourists a year began making pilgrimages to the actual Field of Dreams. They played catch, hit fungoes to each other, and generally just enjoyed geeking out over their favorite movie. Al Ameskamp quickly reversed course, plowing under his corn to rebuild the baseball field—much as Kevin Costner's character had done in the movie. "By conserving the site, Dyersville has built a bizarro time machine on the cheap, one that transports visitors into an actual setting that seems to occupy a mythical place in the American past—the wholesome sandlot we've long outgrown," Adam Doster wrote in *The Atlantic*.

But instead of combining forces to run the field as a single tourist attraction, each family presented its own half of the property as the true Field of Dreams. Neither charged admission, feeling that would violate the spirit of the movie, but each set up their own gift shop. Al Ameskamp, despite owning only a small portion of the field, went all out to attract more tourists. He hired an out-of-state management company, and tried to build batting cages and a corn maze. Don Lansing, meanwhile, wanted less commercialization; he was content to run his small souvenir stand himself. Neither neighbor was willing to cooperate with the other, and neither was willing to sell.

Things continued this way until Ameskamp died. His widow sold her part of the field to the Lansing family in 2007. The field was finally united under a single owner, but

in 2011 the Lansings gave it up anyway, selling to a Chicago company for $3.4 million. (As Iowa farmland, the acreage would have been worth $1.3 million. The site's movie cachet, then, was worth $2.1 million by itself—an impressive amount for a movie a quarter century old.) Unfortunately, the new owner's development plan was essentially Don Lansing's worst nightmare. The company announced that it intended to turn the Field of Dreams into a massive baseball and softball complex, with twenty-four fields, an indoor training facility, and plans to host 2,000 youth teams each summer. The plan has met with derision and widespread local opposition, and the future of the Field of Dreams remains in limbo. It's worth a visit while it still stands in its present form.

OPPOSITE PAGE: Since 1989, an amateur baseball team billing themselves as the "Ghost Players" has played regularly on weekends at the Field of Dreams site. Wearing replica uniforms of the 1919 White Sox, they emerge from the corn before taking their positions on the diamond, much to the delight of visiting tourists.

TOP: For now, the Field of Dreams still appears much as it did in the film, including the small wooden bleachers that Kevin Costner and James Earl Jones once sat on. During filming, the Lansing family had to vacate the first floor of their white farmhouse so the movie company could use it as the Kinsellas' fictional home. The farmhouse initially lacked a porch and swing, both of which were added by the film crew and remain part of the house today.

BOTTOM: Anyone is welcome to play ball on the Field of Dreams free of charge, and more than a million visitors have availed themselves of the opportunity since the film's release in 1989.

Original
FIELD
OF
DREAMS
MOVIE SITE

MAIN ENTRANCE
OPEN DAILY 9AM-6PM

CLEVELAND

LEAGUE PARK

TEAM: Cleveland Indians
(1910–1932, 1934–1946)

LOCATION: Corner of E. 66th St. and Linwood Ave., Cleveland

FIRST MLB GAME: April 21, 1910

LAST MLB GAME: September 21, 1946

NOTABLE FEATURES: Right field only 290 feet from home plate, topped by 40-foot fence.

CLEVELAND MUNICIPAL STADIUM

TEAM: Cleveland Indians (1932–1993)

NICKNAME: The Mistake by the Lake

LOCATION: Corner of W. 3rd St. and Erieside Ave., Cleveland

FIRST MLB GAME: July 31, 1932

LAST MLB GAME: October 3, 1993

NOTABLE FEATURES: Largest stadium ever used long-term for baseball; chilly winds blew in from Lake Erie; fan John Adams banged bass drum in center field bleachers.

PROGRESSIVE FIELD

TEAM: Cleveland Indians (1994–present)

NAMES: Jacobs Field (1994–2008),
Progressive Field (2008–present)

NICKNAME: The Jake

LOCATION: Corner of Carnegie Ave. and Ontario St., Cleveland

FIRST MLB GAME: April 4, 1994

NOTABLE FEATURES: Panoramic view of downtown Cleveland; sold out 455 consecutive games between 1995 and 2001.

Cleveland is a city with a long baseball history. In fact, the first Major League Baseball game ever played, on May 1871, involved a Cleveland team called the Forest Citys—although that contest was actually played on the road in Fort Wayne, Indiana. When at home, the Forest Citys played at a makeshift ballpark at East 55th Street and Central Avenue, but both the team and ballpark went out of business within a few years.

Another major league team, the Cleveland Spiders, was formed in 1887. Spider Park, located east of downtown on Payne Avenue, was noted for its excellent playing surface, but just three years after it opened a bolt of lightning struck and burned it to the ground. The Spiders constructed a new ballpark at the corner of 66th and Lexington, and it was this location that would become the home of Cleveland baseball until 1946. The first ballpark on the site, a wooden structure called League Park, was simple, unadorned, and functional.

The winning pitcher in its inaugural game was a young Spiders right-hander named Cy Young.

The Spiders went out of business after their famously dismal 1899 season, but in 1901 a new club—the team now known as the Indians—was born. In 1910 the Indians hired the local firm Osborn Engineering to rebuild League Park in steel and concrete, which gave it another several decades of use. Between 1932 and 1946, the Indians alternated between League Park and the massive new Municipal Stadium, using the former for weekday games and the latter on nights and weekends. Clevelanders braved Municipal's biting winds for six decades until finally moving into spectacular new Jacobs Field in 1994.

The New Base Ball Park, Cleveland, Ohio.

TOP: As this vintage postcard aptly illustrates, League Park was a small ballpark that fit snugly into the residential Hough neighborhood surrounding it. Known as "Little Hollywood," the neighborhood was home to an ethnic working-class population of mostly Eastern European heritage.

BOTTOM : The 1910 Cleveland Naps pose inside the newly rebuilt version of League Park, which opened that year. The team was named after its manager and best player, Nap Lajoie (who is the only person not wearing a sweater). Cleveland's ace pitcher, Addie Joss, is pictured third from right. Joss had pitched a no-hitter eight days before this photo was taken, but less than a year later he was dead. In April 1911 Joss collapsed on the field before a game, and died soon afterward of tubercular meningitis. The most famous game ever played at League Park was an all-star exhibition held to benefit Joss's widow and children; the participants included Ty Cobb, Walter Johnson, and Shoeless Joe Jackson.

LEAGUE PARK
CLEVELAND INDIANS 1910–1932, 1934–1946

LEAGUE PARK WAS A COMPACT and nondescript ballpark, shaped like a square with one corner cut off at an angle. With the right field fence just 290 feet away, the playing field was barely major league size. The Indians erected a 45-foot fence there to keep home runs from coming too cheaply, but even that huge barrier wasn't enough to stop Babe Ruth, who hit his 500th career homer over it in 1929.

The Indians left League Park for the new Cleveland Municipal Stadium in 1932, only to return in 1934. For the next fourteen years the team used both stadiums: Municipal on weekends and holidays, League Park on dates when smaller crowds were expected. All night games were played at Municipal, since League Park lacked lights. In 1945, during a Cleveland Rams NFL playoff game at League Park, a set of temporary bleachers collapsed and sent 700 fans falling to

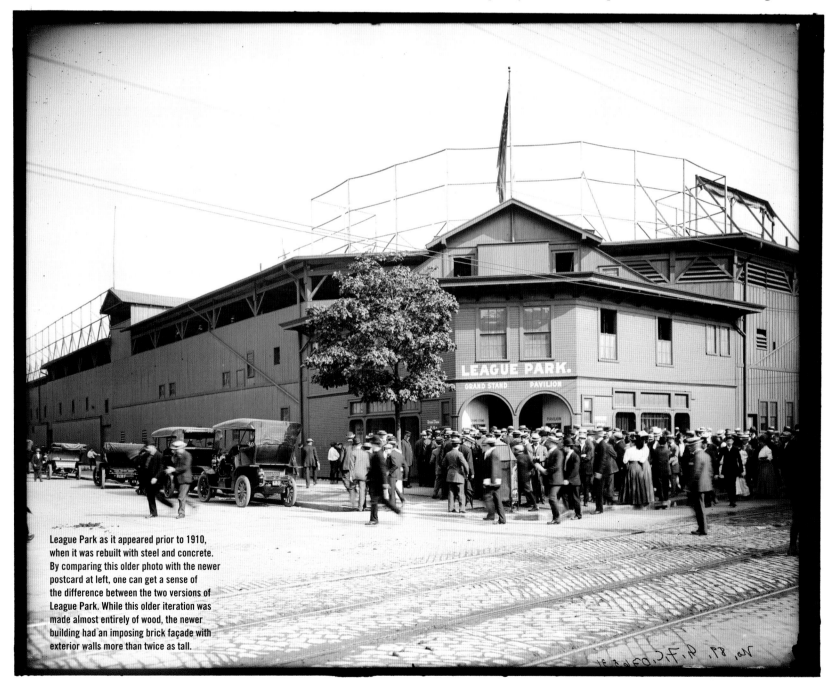

League Park as it appeared prior to 1910, when it was rebuilt with steel and concrete. By comparing this older photo with the newer postcard at left, one can get a sense of the difference between the two versions of League Park. While this older iteration was made almost entirely of wood, the newer building had an imposing brick façade with exterior walls more than twice as tall.

the ground. The accident heralded the end of the ballpark's life. The following year the Rams moved to Los Angeles, while the Indians were purchased by the brilliant promoter Bill Veeck Jr. Envisioning large crowds on an everyday basis, Veeck moved the baseball team permanently to Municipal Stadium.

After the Indians departed, the Cleveland Buckeyes of the Negro American League were left as League Park's only occupants. The Buckeyes folded in 1950, and League Park was partially demolished the next year. Happily, the remaining portion survived for six decades before it was rescued by the Cleveland City Council, which approved a $6.3 million renovation in 2011. Today, the original ticket office houses the Baseball Heritage Museum, and a new baseball diamond sits exactly where the old one did, serving as a community baseball field. 🖐

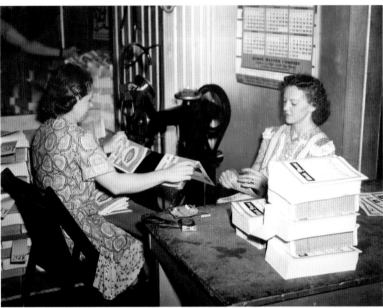

League Park, Cleveland, Ohio.

6950

OPPOSITE PAGE, LEFT: The League Park groundskeeping crew poses in 1932 sitting atop one of the main implements of their trade—the tarp.

OPPOSITE PAGE, TOP RIGHT: In this 1940 photo that the photographer cryptically labeled "In the Scorecard Room," a pair of seamstresses appear to be sewing bindings onto a stack of Indians scorecards.

OPPOSITE PAGE, BOTTOM RIGHT: In the early days of baseball, "knothole gangs" of children often sneaked free peeks at the game though knotholes in wooden outfield fences. When steel and concrete stadiums replaced wooden ones they no longer had the knotholes to work with, so these enterprising young Clevelanders somehow poked a hole in the steel fence.

TOP: A view from the left-center field bleachers at League Park. Almost nothing in this view still exists, but several other pieces of League Park are still standing, including the right field wall and the ticket office outside the main entrance.

BOTTOM: A pensive Nap Lajoie takes a break in 1908 at the wooden version of League Park, which (typically for the era) had plain benches instead of dugouts. This photo was taken by Louis Van Oeyen, the renowned *Cleveland Press* photographer who captured some of the most memorable baseball images of the early 1900s. Lajoie batted .339 over his thirteen-year career with Cleveland, and was so beloved that the team was renamed the Naps for most of his tenure.

CLEVELAND MUNICIPAL STADIUM

CLEVELAND INDIANS 1932–1993

EVOCATIVELY NICKNAMED "The Mistake by the Lake," Cleveland Municipal Stadium was the second-largest ballpark in major league history, and one of the most desolate as well. The first multipurpose stadium in baseball, its design seemed geared toward accommodating football, with Indians games mostly an afterthought. During the late 1940s, it was a thrilling place to watch a ballgame, but by its waning years in the 1980s, it was patronized by only a few hardy souls willing to brave the freezing winds whipping in from Lake Erie.

Municipal Stadium was, as its name indicates, built and owned by the city of Cleveland, the first major league ballpark to be publicly funded. In that respect, it was a trailblazer. Once the Indians demonstrated that government entities could be coerced into paying for stadiums, few ballparks were ever built with private funds again. Voters approved the $2.5 million budget in November 1928, with

an eye on luring the 1932 Olympic Games to Cleveland. But the Olympics went to Los Angeles instead, and by the time the Great Depression hit in 1929, the stadium project was starting to smell like a boondoggle. (It also smelled like dead fish, a scent which routinely wafted in from Lake Erie, where fish carcasses piled up on the shoreline, unable to survive the lake's filthy water.)

Even with the Olympic dream gone, construction on Municipal Stadium began in the summer of 1930. It was erected on what seemed like prime lakefront real estate; in actuality, the property was landfill made from old tires and crushed automobiles. In future years, as the landfill settled, right field would always sag a bit lower than the rest of the playing field. The field itself was colossal, with

the center field fence 470 feet away. Babe Ruth once wisecracked, "You'd have to have a horse to play the outfield there."

The Indians made the huge new stadium their home ballpark, playing seventy-seven games there in 1933, but it was so desolate and empty that they decided to move back to their previous home, League Park, the next year. For the next fourteen seasons, they used Municipal only on weekends and holidays, and for other occasions when large crowds were anticipated. But by 1946, League Park had become so decrepit that the Indians had moved into Municipal Stadium for good. They could pack in more than 85,000 fans, which they did on rare occasions, mostly during the late 1940s, when, for a brief time, the Indians became the hottest ticket in baseball. With owner Bill Veeck Jr. signing players like Satchel Paige and Larry Doby, the club won the World Series in 1948 and another pennant in 1954. Game 5 of the 1948 World Series was attended by a whopping 86,288 fans, a major league record at the time.

TOP: Sixteen-year-old movie star Judy Garland (in the fur coat) was the guest of honor on Opening Day at Cleveland Municipal Stadium in 1939. She's joined by (from left) team owner Alva Bradley, Cleveland Mayor Harold Burton, and manager Ossie Vitt. A month before this photo was taken, Garland had completed shooting *The Wizard of Oz*; she would become an instant super-star when the film was released in August 1939. "I'm crazy about baseball," Garland wrote in a 1937 magazine column. "I love going to baseball games, and I generally cheer myself hoarse whenever anybody makes a home run."

BOTTOM: Cleveland Municipal Stadium as it appeared while under construction in the spring of 1931. The stadium was finished two months later, with its first event being a title bout between heavyweight boxing champ Max Schmeling and challenger Young Stribling. (Schmeling won.)

ND STADIUM
L. 6-1931

During the 1970s and '80s, the Indians were mostly terrible, Municipal Stadium was rapidly decaying, and the mood there was one of despair and even nihilism. Only a few dedicated fans continued to show up, most famously a young computer technician named John Adams, who sat high up in the center field bleachers every night and banged on a bass drum all game long. The atmosphere at Municipal Stadium during these years was perfectly captured in the 1989 film *Major League*, although the movie was actually filmed at County Stadium in Milwaukee. Cleveland Municipal Stadium finally closed after the 1993 season, when the Indians moved to the spectacular new Jacobs Field a mile away. The old stadium was torn down in 1996 and its concrete pieces dumped into Lake Erie, where they serve as a barrier reef. Now Municipal Stadium sleeps with the fishes. 🏺

TOP: Bob Feller, who debuted with the Indians at age seventeen in 1936, may have been the most-hyped pitching prospect in baseball history. That September he struck out 17 batters in a game, becoming the first pitcher ever to post a strikeout total matching his age. In May 1937, with almost a year of big league experience under his belt, Feller left the team for a week so he could attend his high school graduation back in Van Meter, Iowa. The ceremony was broadcast nationwide on NBC radio.

BOTTOM: During the 1970s Municipal Stadium, like many major league ballparks, was plagued by boorish and violent fan behavior. Here Indians reliever Tom Hilgendorf is helped off the field by a security guard after being hit with a metal folding chair thrown by a fan. The incident happened during Municipal's infamous Ten Cent Beer Night promotion in 1974, with drunken fans spending most of the game pelting the players and umpires with rocks, bottles, and other objects. The game was tied in the ninth when the umps decided they'd had enough, declaring Texas the winner by forfeit.

OPPOSITE PAGE: The defining visual characteristic of Progressive Field is the use of exposed structural steel painted white. This is most visible at the park's entrance, seen here, and in its light towers, shown on page 161. The light towers "act as a visual bridge between the smokestacks of The Flats and the skyscrapers of downtown," *Chicago Tribune* architecture critic Blair Kamin wrote. "Elegantly vertical and decidedly functional, because they employ new lighting technology that eliminates the need for cumbersome horizontal bands of fixtures, the towers subtly recall baseball's romantic past while firmly moving it into the realities of the present."

PROGRESSIVE FIELD

CLEVELAND INDIANS 1994–PRESENT

THE OPENING OF JACOBS FIELD IN 1994 sent a clear signal that the retro ballpark had become the new standard in baseball. Although it wasn't as explicit a throwback as Camden Yards (which had opened two years prior), Jacobs had the same natural grass, the same intimate feel, and a similar urban setting, which made it the bustling centerpiece of rejuvenated downtown Cleveland. The park's opening also dovetailed nicely with the arrival of a masterfully constructed roster of young players. These homegrown stars, abetted by increased revenues from the new stadium, propelled the Indians to a decade so prosperous that Cleveland became baseball's most-imitated model for how to run a franchise. A quarter century after its opening, the ballpark (now called Progressive Field) remains a beloved hub of Cleveland's sports scene.

The area along Huron Road between Ninth and Ontario Streets had long been an eyesore in downtown Cleveland. The site was once occupied by the Central Market, a bustling marketplace that became a civic landmark in the late 1800s before burning down in 1940. It sat vacant until 1990, when Cleveland voters were asked to approve the construction of the Gateway Sports Complex on the site. The complex would include a new baseball-only park as well as an adjacent basketball arena for the NBA's Cavaliers. Nearly half of the ballpark's $175 million pricetag would come from alcohol and cigarette taxes, with the other

half privately financed. Days before the vote, MLB Commissioner Fay Vincent subtly threatened that Cleveland would lose its team if voters failed to approve the funding. The measure passed.

Located within walking distance of Lake Erie and the soon-to-open Rock & Roll Hall of Fame, Jacobs Field was an urban delight. Author Jonathan Knight noted that "the most important and impressive visual feature of the new park wasn't anything that was constructed—it was what wasn't constructed. No matter where you were in Jacobs Field, you could see some hint of the Cleveland skyline or some architectural reminder of where you were." Unlike other ballparks, Cleveland's stadium sought to highlight the city's industrial heritage rather than hide it. The exposed steel latticework that surrounded the park (and also held up the floodlights) was intended to evoke the city's many bridges, while its granite and limestone foundation lent an aura of stability. A life-size statue of Bob Feller stood in center field.

The park contained a whopping 119 luxury suites, but regular fans found plenty to enjoy too. Extra space between rows allowed for more leg room, and wider-than-normal aisles made for a comfortable experience. The chairs, painted a classic dark green, were 2 inches wider than those at Municipal Stadium had been. Moreover, the seats down the baselines were angled toward the infield, something

TOP: LeBron James (left), Richard Jefferson (in green shirt), JR Smith (far right) and other members of the Cleveland Cavaliers celebrate an Indians victory during the 2016 playoffs at Progressive Field. James had once trolled Cleveland fans by wearing a Yankees cap to a 2007 Indians-Yankees playoff game, but by 2016, the Ohio native was back on Cleveland's bandwagon, becoming a constant and enthusiastic presence at Progressive Field during the team's run to Game 7 of the World Series. Of course, with the Cavaliers' home arena located only a few dozen steps from the ballpark, it was an easy trip for the basketball legend.

BOTTOM: Progressive Field is distinguished by its creative use of exposed white structural steel, which is visible in the light towers, grandstand roof, left field pillars, and scoreboard support structure. The scoreboard has been replaced twice since the ballpark's 1994 opening; the version seen here was installed in 2016 and measures 59 feet tall and 221 feet wide.

rarely seen in previous ballparks. This simple yet hugely helpful feature could never have been pulled off in a multipurpose stadium, where seats must face straight ahead for football purposes. In the years since Jacobs Field's debut, angled seats have become the standard in baseball-only parks.

Jacobs Field's dimensions strongly favored hitters, particularly right-handed ones, with a 19-foot-high left field wall standing just 325 feet away from home plate. With three warmup mounds for each team instead of two, the ballpark also acknowledged the increasing prevalence of specialized relief pitchers. The natural turf, a Kentucky bluegrass blend, had been grown in Indiana for a year before being transported to Cleveland. It was planted in a 12-inch-deep bed of sand, which itself sat on a 2-inch layer of loose gravel. Some 18 inches below the playing surface was a series of drainpipes capable of clearing water from the field at a rate of 12 inches per hour.

Two inches of snow fell the day before Jacobs Field's 1994 grand opening, but the weather cleared in time for Cleveland to pull off a dramatic eleven-inning victory. The win marked the beginning of the greatest period of success in franchise history. Between 1994 and 2001, the Indians finished in first place six times and second place twice. The team hosted a remarkable thirty postseason games at "The Jake," winning seventeen of them. The Indians also sold out Jacobs Field 455 consecutive times, a then–major league record that has since been broken by Boston and San Francisco. When the sellout streak ended in 2001, the team retired uniform number 455 in honor of its rabid fans.

In a city famed for sparse crowds—the Indians had once drawn 365 fans for a game at 73,811-seat Municipal Stadium—Jacobs Field was a revelation, demonstrating just how quickly a terrific stadium and a winning record could reverse a team's fortunes. In 2008, the Progressive Insurance Company paid $58 million for the park's naming rights through 2023. The 2014–15 offseason, meanwhile, saw the twenty-year-old ballpark undergo its first renovations. Most of the changes were minor ones that sought to implement baseball's latest stadium fad: replacing rows of far-away bleacher seats with terraced restaurant seating. Today, The Jake remains a phenomenal venue for baseball, even when there's no actual game being played there. When the Indians went on the road to play the middle three games of the 2017 World Series, an average of 22,000 fans per night packed into Progressive Field anyway, paying $5 apiece to watch the games on the ballpark's video board. ⚾

CINCINNATI

CROSLEY FIELD

TEAM: Cincinnati Reds (1912–1970)

NAMES: Redland Field (1912–1933), Crosley Field (1934–1972)

LOCATION: Corner of Findlay St. and Western Ave., Cincinnati

FIRST MLB GAME: April 11, 1912

LAST MLB GAME: June 24, 1970

NOTABLE FEATURES: 4-foot-high terrace at base of left field wall; site of first major league night game; known for the best-tasting lemonade in baseball.

RIVERFRONT STADIUM

TEAM: Cincinnati Reds (1970–2002)

NAMES: Riverfront Stadium (1970–1996), Cinergy Field (1996–2002)

LOCATION: Corner of of E. 2nd St. and Mehring Way, Cincinnati

FIRST MLB GAME: June 30, 1970

LAST MLB GAME: September 22, 2002

NOTABLE FEATURES: Home of "Big Red Machine" dynasty during 1970s; located on north bank of Ohio River.

GREAT AMERICAN BALL PARK

TEAM: Cincinnati Reds (2003–present)

LOCATION: Corner of 2nd St. E. and Joe Nuxhall Way, Cincinnati

FIRST MLB GAME: April 10, 2006

NOTABLE FEATURES: Fake riverboat in center field; exposed steel beams painted white; located on north bank of Ohio River.

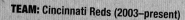

The Cincinnati Reds love to claim that they're the oldest team in baseball—a claim that's unequivocally false. The current Reds franchise is completely unrelated to the Cincinnati Red Stockings of the nineteenth century, the first official professional team in baseball. During the late 1860s, many baseball teams routinely paid their star players under the table while publicly maintaining a posture of amateurism. In 1869, Cincinnati became the first club to abandon the pretense, deciding to openly pay its ten players, with star short-stop George Wright drawing the largest salary at $1,400 per year.

The Red Stockings scheduled most of their games on the road, but when home in Cincinnati, they played at Union Grounds, a cricket field next to the railroad tracks northwest of downtown. Today, the site is the Cincinnati Museum Center. The Stockings put $10,000 into renovating the grounds, but in 1869, the year they went pro, the club turned a profit of only $1.39. The Red Stockings relocated to Boston in 1871; today they are known as the Atlanta Braves.

From 1884 through 1970, the epicenter of Cincinnati baseball was the corner of Findlay Street and Western Avenue, where a succession of different ballparks housed the Reds for eighty-seven years. Baseball didn't exactly have an auspicious beginning there;

during the very first game the stands collapsed, injuring dozens of fans. The park was rebuilt in 1884, 1894, 1902, and 1912, and it was the 1912 version, Crosley Field, that would last the longest and become beloved by generations of fans. However, the version built in 1902—called Palace of the Fans—was perhaps the most significant. With a grandstand modeled after a Greek temple, Palace of the Fans featured hand-carved Corinthian columns, opera-style private boxes, and special beer-drinking sections down the foul lines, making it the most lavish ballpark of its era.

TOP: Architect John Thurtle designed Palace of the Fans to resemble a Greek temple, although he was probably equally inspired by the famed White City at the 1893 World's Columbian Exposition in Chicago.

MIDDLE: A construction crew tears down Palace of the Fans in November 1911 to make way for the construction of new Redland Field, which would open the following spring.

BOTTOM: A crowd of 12,000 fills Palace of the Fans on opening day 1905. There are at least 103 columns visible in this photo, which must be a record for a major league stadium. The small screened-in area under the main grandstand was known as "Roooter's Row," and was row-dier than the rest of the park because it offered access to a bar where whiskey was sold. The small right field grandstand at the left edge of this photo was actually the only surviving remnant from the Reds' previous ballpark. League Park had burned down in 1900, leaving only its home plate grandstand behind, which the Reds repurposed as the right field stands. When Palace of the Fans was built they simply rotated the diamond ninety degrees clockwise, so what had previously been the home plate grandstand was now located in the right field corner.

CROSLEY FIELD

CINCINNATI REDS 1912–1970

CROSLEY FIELD, KNOWN AS REDLAND FIELD when it opened in 1912, was the longest-lasting of the four ballparks built at the corner of Findlay Street and Western Avenue in Cincinnati. Built for $225,000, it was a fairly typical example of the era's steel and concrete stadiums, with a grandstand extending from foul pole to foul pole, an upper deck stretching from first to third base, and a generous set of bleachers behind the right field fence. The field's most unique feature was a gentle incline at the base of the left field wall that sloped to a height 4 feet above the playing field, causing frustration for many an outfielder. The incline was popularly known as the Crosley Field terrace, but that was a misnomer; it was actually a sloping hill that ended at the fence. The terrace existed because York Street, which ran behind left field, was about 6 feet higher than the playing surface, and it was easier and cheaper to leave the slope the way it was than to level it. "It still resonates in the lore here," Reds team historian Greg Rhodes told MLB.com in 2015. "If you were to launch into a conversation with any random person who saw a game at Crosley, it would take about a minute before the terrace came up. It was such an odd little feature, and everyone remembers it."

In 1934, the Reds were purchased by Powel Crosley Jr., a local businessman who had made his fortune selling radios and spare auto parts. Crosley immediately renamed the ballpark after himself,

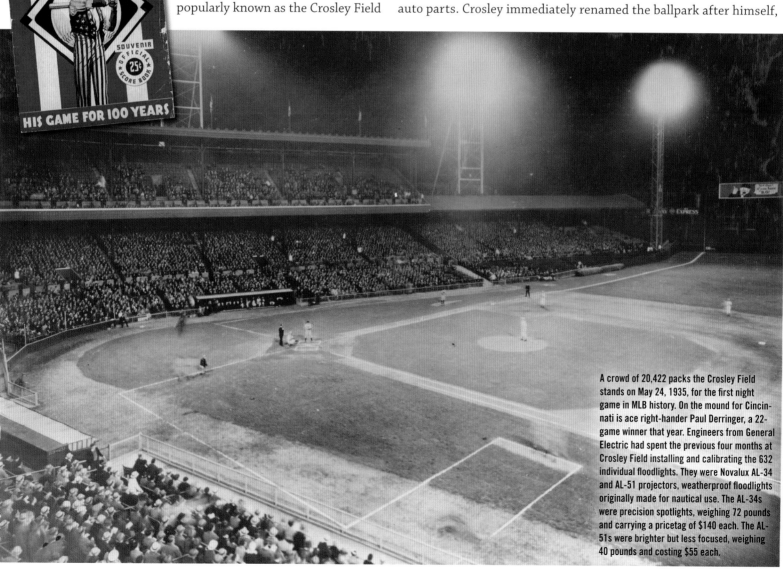

A crowd of 20,422 packs the Crosley Field stands on May 24, 1935, for the first night game in MLB history. On the mound for Cincinnati is ace right-hander Paul Derringer, a 22-game winner that year. Engineers from General Electric had spent the previous four months at Crosley Field installing and calibrating the 632 individual floodlights. They were Novalux AL-34 and AL-51 projectors, weatherproof floodlights originally made for nautical use. The AL-34s were precision spotlights, weighing 72 pounds and carrying a pricetag of $140 each. The AL-51s were brighter but less focused, weighing 40 pounds and costing $55 each.

TOP: The famous Crosley Field terrace—a slight incline at the base of the left field wall—is barely distinguishable in this photo taken in 1956. During the 1950s, the Cubs accused the Reds of stealing signs by placing players with binoculars inside the large Crowe Engineering building behind the fence, although the allegations were never proven.

BOTTOM: Christy Mathewson warms up at Redland Field on July 26, 1916, six days after being traded to the Reds. Mathewson's legendary pitching career was mostly finished by then, but Giants skipper John McGraw traded him to the Reds so he could serve as Cincinnati's manager. Mathewson pitched just one game for Cincinnati—the only game he ever pitched for a team other than the Giants—before retiring to concentrate on his managerial career.

INSET: This plaque near the intersection of Findlay Street and Western Avenue marks the spot where Crosley Field's home plate used to be, although some ballpark historians have claimed that the plaque is not located exactly on the correct spot.

OPPOSITE PAGE, TOP: Frank Robinson was one of the best players ever to take the field at Crosley Field (although this photo was actually taken at Ebbets Field). Robinson is pictured here as a fresh-faced twenty-year-old in 1956, the year he broke the MLB record for most home runs by a rookie, with 38. The photo can be dated exactly because 1956 was the only year Cincinnati wore its "Mr. Redlegs" logo on the front of its jerseys.

OPPOSITE PAGE, BOTTOM: Reds manager Fred Hutchinson watches nervously as the Reds face the Yankees in the 1961 World Series at Crosley Field. Hutchinson had good reason to worry, as the '61 Yankees were an offensive juggernaut, clubbing a then–major league record 240 home runs. New York scored twice as many runs as Cincinnati in the Fall Classic, winning easily in five games. Three years after this photo was taken, Hutchinson died at age forty-five of lung cancer caused by his three-packs-a-day smoking habit. His older brother William, a prominent surgeon, founded the Fred Hutchinson Cancer Research Center in 1972.

and more importantly, he hired a hard-drinking, bombastic visionary named Larry MacPhail to be the general manager. MacPhail implemented many innovations, two of which would change baseball forever. First, he hired broadcaster Red Barber to call the games on the radio, thumbing his nose at the conventional wisdom that free games on the radio would deter fans from coming to the ballpark. (As everyone quickly discovered, exactly the opposite was true.)

MacPhail's other big innovation was one he borrowed from the Kansas City Monarchs: night baseball. People had been experimenting with various lighting methods for night games since the 1880s, but nobody had made it work until the Monarchs did, surviving the Great Depression by barnstorming from town to town with portable floodlights. MacPhail took the idea and ran with it, convincing Crosley that installing permanent light fixtures for night baseball would increase attendance significantly, enabling working people to come to weeknight games. On May 24, 1935, President Franklin Roosevelt flipped a switch inside the White House that turned the lights on 400 miles away at Crosley Field. In the first night game in major league history, the Reds defeated the Philadelphia Phillies 2-1. The lights would burn at Crosley Field for thirty-five more years, until the team moved across town to Riverfront Stadium in 1970. 🍥

RIVERFRONT STADIUM

CINCINNATI REDS 1970-2002

RIVERFRONT STADIUM, a multipurpose doughnut on the north bank of the Ohio River, was home to some of the greatest teams in the history of baseball during its heyday in the 1970s. The Big Red Machine of Pete Rose, Johnny Bench, and Joe Morgan won four National League pennants and two world championships in the ballpark's first seven seasons, but after that, the Cincinnati franchise fell into a slump that saw it make only one World Series appearance in its final two-and-a-half decades at Riverfront.

After Cincinnati voters passed a $40 million bond issue for a new stadium in 1962, construction began in 1968 and was completed in 1970. The stadium's purpose was to attract a pro football team to town, and it succeeded in 1967 when the Cincinnati Bengals were created as an expansion franchise in the American Football League.

The Reds moved in to the new stadium as well, but there was never any doubt that this was a football venue first and foremost.

A monument to unoriginality, Riverfront had most of the same features as the multipurpose stadiums that preceded it: a symmetrical bowl shape, artificial turf, plastic seats color-coded according to price level, movable stands on wheels, and a huge parking garage built in. It also had an idyllic waterfront backdrop; the park was easily visible from across the Ohio River in Covington, Kentucky. It was one of the first major league stadiums ever to feature a flood wall. After a few years of enthralling baseball, though, the novelty of the cookie-cutter experience wore off for Cincinnatians and attendance began to drop. In 2002, the Reds left Riverfront Stadium for a new retro-style ballpark next door. ⚾

OPPOSITE PAGE: A gleaming Riverfront Stadium creates a spectacular reflection on the Ohio River as seen from the shoreline of Northern Kentucky. Riverfront's exterior was considerably more attractive than its interior, and its primary asset was its idyllic waterfront location. Although it eventually came to be seen as an architectural misstep, the ballpark initially received rave reviews. "On the whole, Riverfront Stadium should be the master blueprint for all cities considering new stadia," the Montreal Gazette's Ted Blackman wrote, when it opened in 1970. "I'd have to rate [it] as the most practical and eye-pleasing in existence."

TOP: Fan favorite Pete Rose waits in Riverfront Stadium's on-deck circle on July 9, 1978. Earlier in the game, Rose had singled twice against the Giants to extend his hitting streak to twenty-five games. By the time it was over, Rose's hitting streak would reach 44 games, the third-longest streak in history.

BOTTOM: Johnny Bench is congratulated by his Reds teammates, including Tom Hume, Pete Rose, and Ray Knight, after hitting a home run at Riverfront Stadium in 1977 or 1978. Rose and Bench were teammates from 1967 through 1978, during which time they combined for 4,034 hits, 423 home runs, 4 pennants, and 2 World Series titles.

GREAT AMERICAN BALL PARK

CINCINNATI REDS   2003–PRESENT

ONE OF THE NEWER AND LESS ORIGINAL entries in the retro-ballpark series, Great American Ball Park seemed to arrive a day late and a dollar short. Though the park itself was inoffensive enough, it was emblematic of an emerging problem with retro stadiums: In rejecting the aesthetics of the 1970s cookie-cutter parks, the new ballparks were so homogenous that they risked becoming cookie cutters themselves. "The retro trend has grown stale, as if the architects are simply going through the retro motions," *New York Times* architecture critic Christopher Hawthorne wrote. "The low point came this spring in Cincinnati.... Great American's historical touches, like the reproduction riverboat smokestacks that sit behind the center-field fence, have a bland, even rote, feel."

Although Great American Ball Park is a very pleasant place to watch a game, there's little about it that's original. The white structural steel and vertical light standards were lifted directly from Cleveland's new ballpark, as one can see when comparing this image with the photo of Progressive Field on pages 164–165.

INSET: Great American Ball Park is in many respects a shrine to Pete Rose. The stadium is located on Pete Rose Way, his retired number 14 is on display inside, a statue of him sliding headfirst stands outside the ballpark, and he is the central figure in the Reds Hall of Fame and Museum located on-site.

Great American Ball Park did have attributes. For one thing, it made effective use of color. The exposed steel beams, the dominant architectural feature, were painted white, nicely offsetting the green of the playing field and the deep red of the seats. The ballpark's setting on the north bank of the Ohio River was also ideal, although at

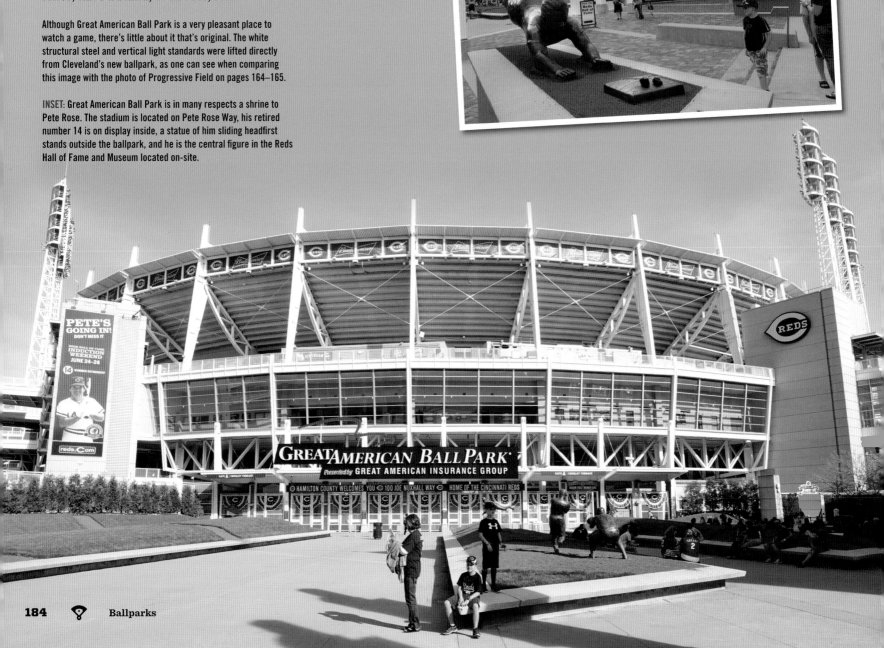

580 feet from home plate, the river was unreachable by even the hardest-hit home runs.

Great American was within easy walking distance of many other civic landmarks, including an NFL stadium, a hockey arena, and the National Underground Railroad Museum. Unfortunately, in 2007, the Reds obliterated the young ballpark's best feature: its panoramic vista of the Ohio River and the Kentucky hills on the other side. The team blocked this stellar view by building what it called the Riverboat Deck, a giant faux steamship in center field that served as a venue for private parties and also contained office space for the local phone company. Still, the stadium makes for a great day at the ballpark if you're a Reds fan. ☕

TOP: No player has hit more home runs at Great American Ball Park than Joey Votto, who slugged 141 balls over its fences between 2007 and 2017. Despite leading the National League in on-base percentage six times, Votto remains shockingly under-appreciated in Cincinnati. He is routinely ripped on the air by the team's cantankerous play-by-play broadcaster, Marty Brennaman, who takes issue with Votto's hitting approach, leadership qualities, and salary. "If I could trade him, I'd trade him yesterday," Brennaman said in 2017.

BOTTOM: One of Great American Ball Park's signature features is the pair of faux riverboat smokestacks behind the right-center field fence, which shoot fireworks whenever a Reds batter hits a home run. During a 2015 game, the right smokestack suddenly burst into flames due to a faulty propane valve. Fortunately, nobody was injured and the game continued uninterrupted.

DETROIT

TIGER STADIUM

TEAM: Detroit Tigers (1912–1999)

NAMES: Navin Field (1912–1937),
Briggs Stadium (1938–1960),
Tiger Stadium (1961–2009)

LOCATION: Corner of Michigan Ave. and Trumbull Ave., Detroit

FIRST MLB GAME: April 20, 1912

LAST MLB GAME: September 27, 1999

NOTABLE FEATURES: Playing field shaped like a square with rounded corners; unique outfield bleachers that hung directly over the playing field.

MACK PARK

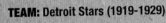

TEAM: Detroit Stars (1919-1929)

LOCATION: Corner of Mack Ave. and Fairview St., Detroit

NOTABLE FEATURES: Wooden stands roofed with tin sheeting; tall right field wall with a wire screen on top.

COMERICA PARK

TEAM: Detroit Tigers (2000–present)

LOCATION: Corner of John R St. and E. Montcalm St., Detroit

FIRST MLB GAME: April 11, 2000

NOTABLE FEATURES: Snarling tiger statues at the entrance gate; large outfield with distant fences; adjacent to Ford Field, home of the Detroit Lions.

The phrase may mean little to the rest of us, but to Detroiters of a certain age, the words *Michigan and Trumbull* trigger a variety of Pavlovian responses: childhood, longing, the smell of hot dogs and stale beer, and most of all, bright white baseball uniforms with the Old English *D*. For more than a century, the Detroit Tigers played at the corner of Michigan and Trumbull Avenues, first at a cozy wooden structure called Bennett Park, then at a massive yet intimate shrine known variously as Navin Field, Briggs Stadium, and, finally, Tiger Stadium.

Bennett Park was built in 1896 on the site of a former dog pound. It was named after a beloved local player named Charlie Bennett, whose career had ended when he slipped on a train platform and a speeding locomotive sliced off his legs. The park was cramped and rickety, and in 1912, the Tigers replaced it with a larger steel and concrete version that they would use for the next eighty-eight years. Tiger Stadium was renovated and remodeled many times, and served as home to a trio of beloved teams—the 1930s Tigers of Hank Greenberg, the Al Kaline–Willie Horton club of the late 1960s, and Sparky Anderson's 1984 world champions. In 1999, the Tigers finally bid farewell to Michigan and Trumbull, moving to Comerica Park 1 mile away.

CHAS. W. BENNETT.
ALLEN & GINTER'S
RICHMOND. *Cigarettes* VIRGINIA.

TOP: Bennett Park was named after Charlie Bennett, the catcher for the Detroit Wolverines from 1881 to '88. Bennett and his wife, Alice, are credited with inventing baseball's first rudimentary chest protector—a vest that Alice modified by sewing pieces of cork into the lining.

BOTTOM: Tigers outfielder Matty McIntyre poses in the Bennett Park outfield sometime between 1905 and 1910. Note the ad on the wall promising fifty free La Azora cigars to any player who hit a home run—a good indication of how rare homers were during the Deadball Era. The rickety seats behind the fence here are wildcat bleachers, a term for unofficial seating located outside the ballpark property and run by a third party. At Bennett Park, the bleacher owners charged anywhere from a nickel to 15¢, depending on the importance of the game.

OPPOSITE PAGE: This photo taken during the 1935 World Series shows a hectic scene on both sides. On the left, fans inside Navin Field are cheering on the Tigers against the Cubs. On the right, bustling Trumbull Avenue is filled with ticket buyers, ticket sellers, and mounted policemen.

TIGER STADIUM

DETROIT TIGERS 1912-1999

WHEN THE STEEL AND CONCRETE stadium craze began in 1909, Detroit Tigers owner Frank Navin was among the first to hop on the bandwagon. At the end of the 1911 season, he tore down Bennett Park and hired a Cleveland firm called Osborn Engineering to construct a new park by the following spring. (Osborn was the preeminent ballpark design firm of its day; its other credits included Forbes Field and the Polo Grounds.) Six months of nonstop construction later, Navin Field opened on April 20, 1912—coincidentally the same date as Fenway Park. Appropriately enough, Ty Cobb stole home in the first game.

Ballparks of the steel and concrete era can be roughly divided into two groups: those whose owners spared no expense on their construction, and those whose owners guarded each nickel like it was the last coin on earth. In the former category were Forbes Field and the Polo Grounds; in the latter were Griffith Stadium and Navin Field. Frank Navin spent only $250,000 on his new ballpark, and he got what he paid for: a perfectly serviceable but undistinguished venue. "Navin Field as it looked in 1912 bore little resemblance to the ballpark that eventually became Tiger Stadium," the historian Scott Ferkovich wrote. "The multiple expansions that resulted in the familiar double-decked, fully-enclosed classic were still far in the future." The park's 23,000 bright yellow seats would not stand the test of time, but one element did: a 125-foot-tall flagpole in center field

TOP: No figure in Tigers history is more beloved than Ernie Harwell, the announcer who enchanted Detroiters with his mellifluous Georgia drawl for forty-two years. He's pictured here during the 1970s with his longtime broadcast partner, Paul Carey, on the right.

BOTTOM: Tiger Stadium's appearance changed dramatically over its eighty-eight seasons; this is how it looked during its final years in the late 1990s. By this point, ownership had allowed the stadium to become dilapidated, but fans still loved going to games, especially in the right field bleachers, which were some of the most fun seats in baseball because of their unique overhang.

OPPOSITE PAGE, TOP: Tiger Stadium was known as Briggs Stadium from 1938 through 1960, when the team was owned by Walter Briggs. This postcard was produced prior to 1948, because the light towers added that year are not present in the image. The Tigers were the fifteenth of the sixteen "original" MLB teams to embrace night baseball; only the Cubs were slower.

OPPOSITE PAGE, BOTTOM: Hank Greenberg takes a mighty swing at Tiger Stadium, but based on the direction he's looking, he probably just hit a pop-up. He didn't hit many of them. An RBI machine, Greenberg played only seven full seasons with Detroit, but he drove in at least 113 runs in all of them. As the first star player drafted into the military during World War II, he missed parts of five seasons serving his country.

that was actually on the field of play. While the rest of Navin Field transformed rapidly around it, the flagpole remained in place for all eighty-eight years of the ballpark's existence.

During Navin Field's first decade, the population of Detroit more than doubled as it became the headquarters of the new automobile manufacturing industry. Frank Navin attempted to keep pace with the higher demand for tickets by adding an upper deck in 1923. By the mid-1930s, Navin not only had a larger ballpark, but also an outstanding team to play in it, led by slugging first baseman Hank Greenberg. The Tigers won the pennant in 1934, but they lost the winner-take-all Game 7 of the World Series, 11-0. Frustrated at seeing the championship fall through their grasp, Detroiters in the Navin Field bleachers pelted the

opposing St. Louis Cardinals with so much rotten fruit and other sundries that the game had to be temporarily suspended. Three weeks later, Frank Navin died of a heart attack while horseback riding.

Navin's family sold the Tigers to a new owner, Walter Briggs, who initiated an extensive renovation in 1937 and '38. (Naturally, he also changed the name to Briggs Stadium.) The upper deck, which had previously existed only in the infield, was extended 360 degrees around the playing field, giving Briggs Stadium the wraparound bowl-like appearance commonly associated with football stadiums today. The stadium, however, was not actually round. Rather, it was shaped like a square with rounded corners, with home plate, the two foul poles, and center field each located at one corner. This peculiar configuration meant the distance down the foul lines was unusually short (340 feet to left field and 325 to right), while the distance to dead center field was a whopping 440 feet.

Because the playing field was extremely close to the streets running behind the outfield, a creative solution was required to build an upper deck in left and right field. While the stadium's footprint couldn't be widened, the upper deck itself could—so the top level was constructed such that it hung over the lower deck by 10 feet. This unusual overhang eventually became the stadium's signature, and the first rows of the upper deck were the most unique and intimate seats in baseball. Fans in

the upper deck might actually be closer to home plate than the outfielders were, depending on how the defense was positioned. "Most visiting outfielders' recollections include chasing a ball to the warning track and waiting for it to land in their glove, only to have it land in the overhang of the upper deck," wrote Jason Beck for MLB.com.

The stadium had its final name change in 1961, becoming known as Tiger Stadium. During the 1980s, the ballpark housed an exciting team with a plethora of stars, including the intense outfielder Kirk Gibson and the grandfatherly manager Sparky Anderson. The Tigers won the World Series easily in 1984. By then, though, the players were in much better shape than their ballpark. A fire had destroyed the press box in 1977. Paint was peeling, steel pillars were rusting, and the green wooden seats were rotting away in Detroit's harsh winters. A few cursory renovations were undertaken, including new plastic seats in 1980, but during the 1990s, the stadium continued to descend into decrepitude. Team ownership, intent on securing funding for a new ballpark, steadfastly refused to allocate any resources toward the upkeep of Tiger Stadium. Even the chairs began disappearing one by one. At one point, a ratty old couch was plunked down in the bleachers to replace a stolen row of seats.

During the 1990s team owner Mike Ilitch allowed Tiger Stadium to fall into disrepair, hoping it would bolster his case for a new stadium. The gambit eventually succeeded. "Tiger Stadium was old and decrepit, but just about every single memory from there is positive," wrote Eric Adelson for Yahoo! Sports.

In September 1999, Tiger Stadium finally hosted its last game, a contest fondly remembered for the ballpark's final hit, a massive grand slam onto the rooftop by Detroit catcher Robert Fick. The stadium was bulldozed in 2008, and today memories are all that remain. "I'll always remember things like the short right field porch with the overhang," Kirk Gibson said in 2013. "The small dugout, where you'd always bump your head when you were excited and jumped up. The proximity of the fans to the players. Things that were incredible and probably will never be recaptured."

MACK PARK

DETROIT STARS 1919–1929

MACK PARK, HOME OF THE ILLUSTRIOUS Detroit Stars for more than a decade, was built in 1914 by John Roesink, a white haberdasher and semipro baseball promoter. Located in the heart of Detroit's working-class German community, the wooden structure held between 6,000 and 10,000 fans. During its first few seasons, it hosted mostly semipro games, but in 1919, the ballpark found a permanent tenant in the city's newly founded African-American team. During the 1920s, the Detroit Stars would become a powerhouse in the Negro National League, the sport's first successful African-American league. The Stars featured many memorable players, but fans particularly loved Norman Stearnes, the slugging center fielder who was nicknamed "Turkey" for the awkward way he ran. Roesink figured that since he already owned the ballpark, he might as well buy the team, too, so he did, in 1925.

On the night of July 6, 1929, it rained heavily in Detroit. The next afternoon, Roesink found himself with a soaking wet playing field— and worse, 2,000 waiting in the stands whose money would have to be refunded if the game wasn't held. So Roesink walked to a gas station and bought two five-gallon cans of fuel, intending to soak the playing field in gasoline and light it on fire, thereby evaporating the moisture. What exactly happened next is unclear, but an ear-splitting explosion rocked the right field bleachers. Within minutes, fire had also spread to the left field bleachers. Terrified fans leapt 30 feet from the stands to the ground, some of them suffering broken legs and fractured skulls. In the main grandstand, people tried to escape by fleeing onto the field, but were prevented from doing so by the wire screen that protected fans from foul balls. Twenty minutes after the fire started,

Workers help clear debris after the 1929 fire that devastated Mack Park. Mack could have been repaired, but Detroit Stars owner Joe Roesink chose instead to move 6 miles away to Hamtramck Stadium, which was closer to the team's fan base.

the entire right field grandstand collapsed. By then, players from both teams had knocked down the stadium's wooden outer wall, allowing people to escape.

Astoundingly, nobody died in the fire, although 220 fans were injured, 103 of them badly enough to be hospitalized. Damage to Mack Park was estimated at $12,000. Instead of rebuilding, Roesink moved the Stars to a new $100,000 ballpark, Hamtramck Stadium, in 1930. Mack Park was getting old anyway, and the new stadium was closer to the burgeoning African-American neighborhood of Paradise Valley. The Detroit Stars folded just two years later, decimated by the Great Depression. Mack Park, ironically, lasted much longer, continuing to host high school and semipro games until the 1960s. ☕

TOP LEFT: Fans watch a game at Mack Park in an undated photo.

TOP RIGHT: Turkey Stearnes, the power-hitting center fielder who was the linchpin of the Detroit Stars' lineup during the 1920s, takes some practice swings at Tiger Stadium in 1979. Though Stearnes was never allowed to play for the Tigers, he followed the team avidly in his retirement years, sitting in the stands among fans who probably had no idea who he was. "He never missed a game," his daughter Rosilyn Brown said. "He always sat in the bleachers because he said that's where the fun was."

MIDDLE: The Detroit Stars in 1920, the year they became charter members of the Negro National League. The Stars boasted some of the best African-American players in the country, including slugging outfielder Pete Hill (middle row, second from left), strong-armed catcher Bruce Petway (back row, third from left), lefty junkballer Bill Holland (back row, far left), and spitball pitcher Big Bill Gatewood (back row, third from right). The manager, wearing a sweater with a star on it, was Tenny Blount, a local gambling kingpin.

BOTTOM: The Detroit Tigers relax in the Mack Park dugout. Though the exact circumstances of this photo are unknown, the Tigers were probably visiting Mack for a game against the Detroit Stars. Exhibitions pitting major league teams against Negro League clubs were a common occurrence, particularly during the early 1920s, which is probably when this photo was taken.

COMERICA PARK
DETROIT TIGERS 2000–PRESENT

COMERICA PARK'S BIGGEST PROBLEM has always been that it had a hard act to follow. Opened in 2000 as the successor to legendary Tiger Stadium, Comerica was one of the better retro ballparks built in the wake of Camden Yards. The memory of its predecessor proved difficult to escape, however, and the debate over leaving Tiger Stadium continued to rage even as fans began filling up the city's plush new ballpark.

In 1992, in an attempt to keep Tiger Stadium, Detroit voters overwhelmingly passed a ballot initiative prohibiting public funding of new stadiums. But in 1996, they reversed course, passing a pro-posal for a new $300 million ballpark to be built with a combination of public and private funds. Supporters hoped the project would help revitalize blighted downtown Detroit, which for years had been peppered with boarded-up windows as residents and businesses fled for the suburbs. Many, however, felt the new stadium was a slap in the face to working class Detroiters. "It's absurd that we're spending hundreds of millions of dollars on a new ballpark when we can't keep our libraries open regular hours and our kids don't even have safe playgrounds," Frank Rashid, founder of the Tiger Stadium Fan Club, told the *New York Times*.

Miguel Cabrera bats at Comerica Park in his favorite situation: with runners on base. This photo was taken during the 2012 AL Championship Series, which the Tigers won on their way to the eleventh World Series appearance in franchise history.

Controversial or not, when Comerica Park opened, it was a gem. Its entrance was framed by a distinctive pair of snarling stone tiger statues. In left field, a 10-story-high scoreboard, the tallest in baseball, displayed distinctive old-fashioned grillwork. A picture-postcard view of the Detroit skyline was visible beyond center field, and from the correct vantage point one could even spot the city of Windsor, Ontario, across the river. Behind the left field wall were stainless-steel statues of all six players whose uniforms had been retired by the Tigers. A giant Ferris wheel featured twelve baseball-shaped cars and offered rides for $2 a spin. Despite all this, some were disappointed that the park's design lacked any overt references to Tiger Stadium. "There was nothing brought over from the old stadium architecturally," Tigers reliever Todd Jones lamented. "In a brand-new ballpark, you have to put in the soul."

But Jones and other pitchers loved the layout of the playing field. Instead of the massive outfield overhangs that had created cheap homers at Tiger Stadium, Comerica had a vast outfield and comparatively distant fences. In an era when each new ballpark seemed to boost offense by pulling the fences in a little further than the last, Comerica was an anomaly. The left-center-field

Tiger imagery is absolutely everywhere at Comerica Park, including these twin tiger statues at the main entrance gate. Also note the tiger gargoyles ringing the stadium's outer façade, each with a baseball in its mouth.

INSET: Comerica Park is the only major league ballpark with its own Ferris wheel inside. The 50-foot-tall ride features baseball-shaped gondolas and, appropriately enough, these metal tiger heads decorating the entrance.

OPPOSITE PAGE, INSET: This huge cat outside Comerica Park's north entrance is the biggest of the nine giant tiger statues that guard the stadium's various entrance gates. This specimen, measuring 15 feet tall, remains unnamed, although some fans have suggested the moniker Sparky. All nine statues were created by Michael Keropian, a sculptor from Upstate New York.

power alley was 395 feet away, making the park a nightmare for right-handed sluggers. In particular, the park frustrated two-time MVP Juan González, whose home run total dropped from 39 to 22 after signing with the Tigers in 2000. "It's incredible— one of the biggest parks in baseball," González said. "You need to hit it so hard." González hated Comerica so much that he refused to re-sign with Detroit after the season.

Fearful of the park's poor reputation among hitters, team owner Mike Ilitch decided to shorten the left-center field distance by 25 feet in 2003.

Nevertheless, the woeful 2003 Tigers lost 119 games, and only one hitter managed more than 20 home runs. By 2005, though, the Tigers were winning again, and the ballpark was packed for the American League playoffs despite intermittent snow and howling winds. "I found out that it's a beautiful park—when it's full," Ilitch said. "What a difference." Over the next decade, a series of upgrades kept Comerica state-of-the-art, including a new LED video board added in 2012. In 2014, the Tigers joined the league-wide movement toward trendy bar areas, removing some of the right field bleachers and replacing them with an extensive patio featuring barstools, couches, and a 45-foot-long fire pit.

MILWAUKEE

COUNTY STADIUM

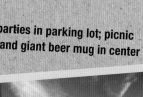

TEAMS: Milwaukee Braves (1953–1965), Milwaukee Brewers (1970–2000)

LOCATION: Corner of N. General Mitchell Blvd. and Interstate 94 E., Milwaukee (adjacent to and northwest of Miller Park)

FIRST MLB GAME: April 14, 1953

LAST MLB GAME: September 28, 2000

NOTABLE FEATURES: Known for tailgate parties in parking lot; picnic area behind left field fence; chalet, slide, and giant beer mug in center field belonging to mascot Bernie Brewer.

MILLER PARK

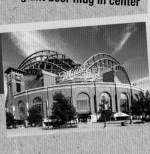

TEAM: Milwaukee Brewers (2001–present)

LOCATION: Corner of Frederick Miller Way and Brewers Way, Milwaukee

FIRST MLB GAME: April 6, 2001

NOTABLE FEATURES: Fan-shaped retractable roof; large bank of windows in outfield; sausage race during sixth inning.

In 1859, Abraham Lincoln gave a campaign speech in Milwaukee about the relationship between labor and capital. "Every man is proud of what he does well, and no man is proud of that he does not well," the future president said. "With the former, his heart is in his work; and he will do twice as much of it with less fatigue." Two months after Lincoln's memorable speech, the grassy field where he delivered it was transformed into Milwaukee's first baseball diamond, and the city's first known game took place there on November 30, 1859.

The city's first enclosed ballpark, Camp Reno, was built nine years later on the Lake Michigan shoreline. It housed the Cream Citys, a popular local team named after the distinctive light color of Milwaukee's locally manufactured bricks. Major league baseball arrived in town in 1878, again in 1884, and then in 1891 and 1901, but each time the team lasted only one season before folding. The 1901 team played at Lloyd Street Grounds, a wooden park with a distinctive tower behind home plate.

For nearly seventy years Milwaukeeans flocked to games at Borchert Field, a horseshoe-shaped stadium built in North Milwaukee in 1887. During its early years, informal custom dictated that Irish fans sat on the first base side and German fans on the third base side. Bill Veeck Jr., who owned the team during the 1940s, once claimed to have installed a hydraulic motor that moved Borchert's outfield fences closer or farther away, depending on who was batting, but that famous story appears to be merely an urban legend. In any case, Borchert Field served as Milwaukee's minor league mecca until the arrival of the big league Milwaukee Braves, who moved into County Stadium in 1953.

Athletic Field was renamed Borchert Field in 1919, when the Double-A Milwaukee Brewers were purchased by Otto Borchert. Borchert had the good sense to know that Milwaukeeans love their beer, and he installed a bar directly behind home plate. (Appropriately enough, two of the five ads visible in this image are for beer.) The Brewers saved on groundskeeping costs by keeping a goat named Fatima at the ballpark to graze on the field during road trips. At night, improbably, she slept on the ballpark's roof.

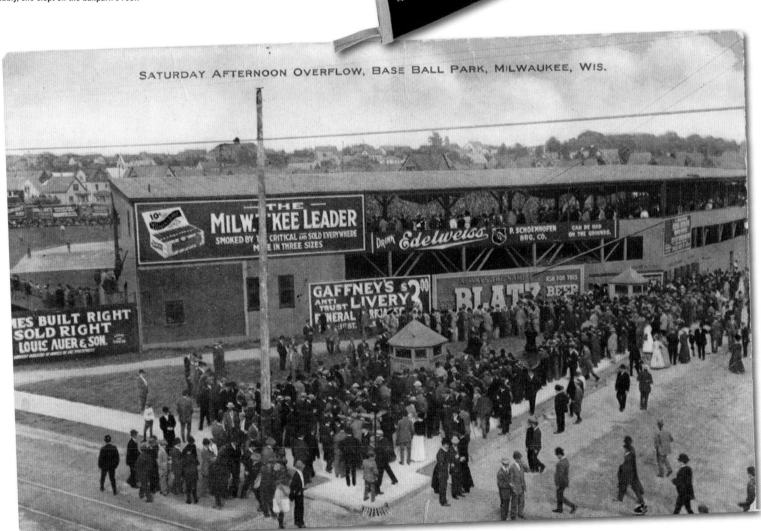

SATURDAY AFTERNOON OVERFLOW, BASE BALL PARK, MILWAUKEE, WIS.

COUNTY STADIUM

MILWAUKEE BRAVES 1953–1965   MILWAUKEE BREWERS 1970-2000

HOME TO THE MILWAUKEE BRAVES for thirteen years and the Milwaukee Brewers for thirty-one, County Stadium was unremarkable in appearance, but bore witness to an impressive array of baseball events during its half century of use. The stadium was originally built as a minor ballpark for the Triple-A Milwaukee Brewers, with construction starting in October 1950. It was one of the first publicly funded ballparks in the country. Three different government entities pitched in, with the city and county of Milwaukee both selling bonds, and the federal government leasing federally owned land to the stadium at $1 per year.

From the beginning, County Stadium was built with major league aspirations. It had an upper deck between first base and third base, large sections of outfield bleachers, and a picnic area in left field that proved to be a popular seating option. At its peak, the ballpark would hold some 55,000 fans and set new league attendance records. As things turned out, the minor league Brewers never played there. Just as the stadium was being completed in 1953, the Boston Braves made

a sudden decision, only three weeks before the season started, to move to Wisconsin and become the Milwaukee Braves.

On April 14, 1953, fans lined up hours before the game, braving the frigid spring weather to get their hands on tickets to the first major league game played in Milwaukee since 1901. "Fans that Opening Day started tailgating, a tradition that continues in Milwaukee," the historian Gregg Hoffmann wrote. "A crowd of 34,357 packed the stadium and thousands more listened on radios outside and in homes and pubs around the town. Fans cheered wildly for every hit, every strike, and everything else. It was all new and exciting."

During their years in Milwaukee, the Braves' roster boasted three of the greatest players of all time—Warren Spahn, Eddie Mathews, and Hank Aaron—and the team finished in the top half of the standings for nine consecutive years. In 1957, the Braves brought home what remains the only World Series championship won by a Milwaukee team. Their most memorable game at County

The main entrance of County Stadium in the late 1990s, during its final years as a major league ballpark. The stadium's capacity had gradually increased over the years, changing its appearance dramatically. When the Braves arrived in 1953 it held just over 28,000 fans, a figure that was later upped to 36,000 and, finally, 53,000 by the time the Brewers moved out in 2000.

Stadium, however, was played two years after that, on May 26, 1959. That day the Braves' bats went into extreme hibernation, as Pittsburgh left-hander Harvey Haddix turned in the best-pitched game in baseball history. Haddix threw twelve perfect innings—three more than anyone else has pitched before or since—only to give up a hit in the thirteenth inning as the Braves won 1-0.

The Braves departed for Atlanta in 1966, but just four years later, a new major league team moved in. A used-car dealer named Allan "Bud" Selig (who had been a die-hard Braves fan) bought the Seattle Pilots, moved them to Milwaukee, and renamed them the Brewers after the old minor league team. County Stadium was a festive place during Brewers games, due in large part to the team's delightful mascot, a strapping blond fellow with a huge handlebar mustache named Bernie Brewer. During the 1980s, the team built a special "chalet" for Bernie on top of a faux beer barrel high above the outfield stands. Whenever a Brewers batter hit a home run, Bernie would celebrate by launching himself down a slide into a giant mug of foamy beer. The Brewers moved into a new stadium, Miller Park, in 2001. While Bernie made the move along with the team, his chalet and giant beer mug, alas, did not. 🍺

TOP: When the Milwaukee Braves sent light-hitting catcher Bob Uecker (right) to the minors in 1961, manager Chuck Dressen told him, "There's no room in baseball for a clown." Uecker spent the next six decades proving Dressen wrong. He was hired as a play-by-play announcer for the fledgling Brewers in 1971, and with his trademark brand of self-deprecating humor, he became perhaps the most beloved personality in Milwaukee baseball history. Along the way he also starred in the comedy classic *Major League*, the campy sitcom *Mr. Belvedere*, and a memorable series of Miller Lite commercials. He's pictured here at County Stadium in 1993 alongside then-manager Phil Garner.

BOTTOM LEFT: A pair of Milwaukee Braves employees show off the team's bullpen cart at County Stadium. The Braves were the first team to adopt bullpen carts, doing so in the late 1950s. After being absent from the baseball scene for twenty-two years, the carts seem to be making a comeback: The Diamondbacks introduced one in 2018.

BOTTOM RIGHT: At a ballgame in Milwaukee, half the fun occurs in the parking lot. Tailgating is so ingrained in Wisconsin's DNA that Miller Park was designed with tailgaters in mind. The stadium's 12,500 parking spaces are more spacious than most, with ample room in between rows. "Tailgating is a Milwaukee tradition that's as important as the game itself," ESPN's Jim Callis wrote. "Or maybe more important. I've gone to Brewers games where we didn't even go inside the stadium until the fifth inning."

OPPOSITE PAGE: Miller Park's exterior—featuring Milwaukee's famous Cream City brick, as well as an inventively shaped retractable roof—is much more attractive than its interior, which resembles a giant aircraft hangar.

MILLER PARK

MILWAUKEE BREWERS 2001-PRESENT

ONE OF THE MOST DISTINCTIVE PARKS in modern baseball, Miller Park is quite unusual in appearance. From overhead the park is shaped like a lopsided football, with the pointed ends located at the foul poles. Viewed from the outside at ground level, two half-moon shapes rise high above the ballpark's walls, an odd horizon line never before seen in a ballpark. The half-moon shapes are the sides of the retractable roof, which opens and closes in the manner of a folding fan or a peacock spreading its feathers. A huge bank of windows in the outfield gives it a greenhouse look, and allows a few rays of sunshine to hit the field even when the roof is closed.

Although outdoor tailgating at freezing Packers games is practically Wisconsin's state religion, the Brewers felt a roofed and heated baseball stadium was necessary to maximize attendance during the chilly spring months. That assessment turned out to be correct. The Brewers drew more than 2 million fans in fifteen of Miller Park's first seventeen seasons, after surpassing that total just once in three decades at County Stadium. "In Milwaukee, the retractable roof has saved baseball for this community, for this state," local columnist Mike Baumann wrote.

While the Milwaukee Brewers acquired a nifty new stadium when Miller Park opened in 2001, the taxpayers of Wisconsin ended up with a huge and unexpected debt. Plagued by mishaps and cost overruns, the troubled ballpark ended up costing double its initial budget of $250 million. Its opening was delayed by a year after a crane collapsed during construction, killing three workers. To make matters worse, the park's much-ballyhooed retractable roof didn't even work properly. Outraged that the state legislature had approved funding for the ballpark after voters turned it down, Wisconsinites mounted a successful recall effort against the legislator who had cast the deciding vote. He was the first lawmaker in state history ever recalled.

KANSAS CITY

MUNICIPAL STADIUM

TEAMS: Kansas City Monarchs 1923–1955, Kansas City Athletics 1955–1967, Kansas City Royals 1969–1972

NAMES: Muehlebach Field (1923–1937), Ruppert Stadium (1938–1942), Blues Stadium (1943–1954), Municipal Stadium (1955–1976)

LOCATION: Corner of W. Euclid Ave. and S. 22nd St., Kansas City

FIRST MLB Game: April 12, 1955

LAST MLB Game: October 4, 1972

NOTABLE FEATURES: Mechanical rabbit behind home plate delivered extra baseballs to umpires; petting zoo behind right field fence included rabbits, sheep, pheasants, and monkeys.

KAUFFMAN STADIUM

TEAM: Kansas City Royals (1973–present)

NAMES: Royals Stadium (1973–1993), Kauffman Stadium (1993–present)

LOCATION: Corner of Lancer Lane and Royal Way, Kansas City

FIRST MLB GAME: April 10, 1973

NOTABLE FEATURES: Lighted fountains in outfield; large center field scoreboard shaped like Royals' crown logo.

Though Kansas City would become a baseball hotbed during the twentieth century, it took a while for the sport to take hold. The town had early dalliances with the major leagues in 1884, 1886, 1888, and 1914, but in all four cases the team lasted less than two years. The 1886 Kansas City Cowboys played in Association Park I, nicknamed "The Hole" because it was built below ground level on a site that had been excavated to provide dirt for the construction of Independence Avenue.

When the Kansas City Monarchs rose to prominence in the Negro Leagues during the early 1920s, they played their games at Association Park II, which was also home to the local minor league franchise the Kansas City Blues. The stadium's owners enforced a rigid segregation policy that restricted African-American fans to the last fourteen rows of the ballpark, even during Negro League games. In 1923, both the Blues and Monarchs left for brand-new Muehlebach Field. This new ballpark was located in a vibrant African-American neighborhood, only a few blocks away from both Arthur Bryant's landmark barbecue restaurant and the Paseo YMCA, where the Negro Leagues were founded. Nevertheless, segregation remained in effect at the stadium until the 1950s.

After Muehlebach was renamed Municipal Stadium, it housed two major league teams for a short time. First the inept Kansas City A's played there for thirteen years, then the expansion Royals moved in for their first four seasons. In 1973, the Royals left Municipal for gorgeous new Royals Stadium (now Kauffman Stadium), a baseball-only facility that was the finest major league ballpark built during an otherwise regrettable era of retro stadiums.

TOP: In 1930, the Kansas City Monarchs became the first pro team to regularly use lights, purchasing their own portable lighting system five years before the first major league night game. Each light standard was mounted on a truck with a telescoping pole attached, and upon reaching the ballpark the pole was extended to its full height of 40 feet. Each light standard held six 1,000-watt lamps.

BOTTOM: The Monarchs and Hilldale (a team from suburban Philadelphia) pose for a formal portrait at Muehlebach Field before Game 5 of the first-ever Negro League World Series in 1924. The game almost started late because Muehlebach was also hosting a high school football game that day, which ended just thirty minutes before opening pitch. The Monarchs' best players that year were pitcher/outfielder Bullet Rogan, shortstop Dobie Moore, and pitcher/manager José Méndez. The Hilldales, meanwhile, were led by third baseman Judy Johnson and catchers Louis Santop and Biz Mackey. The Monarchs prevailed in the best-of-nine series, 5 games to 4.

OPPOSITE PAGE: In 1945, the Kansas City Monarchs signed shortstop Jackie Robinson, a former UCLA football star who had just completed his first season as a college basketball coach. During his lone season as a Monarch the twenty-six-year-old rookie batted .345, .387, or .414 (depending on which source you believe) before signing with the Brooklyn Dodgers on August 28, 1945.

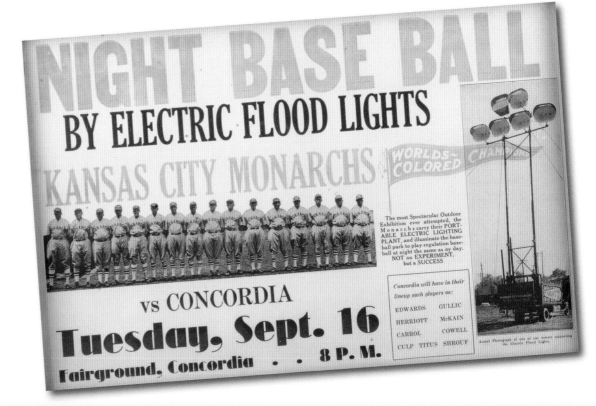

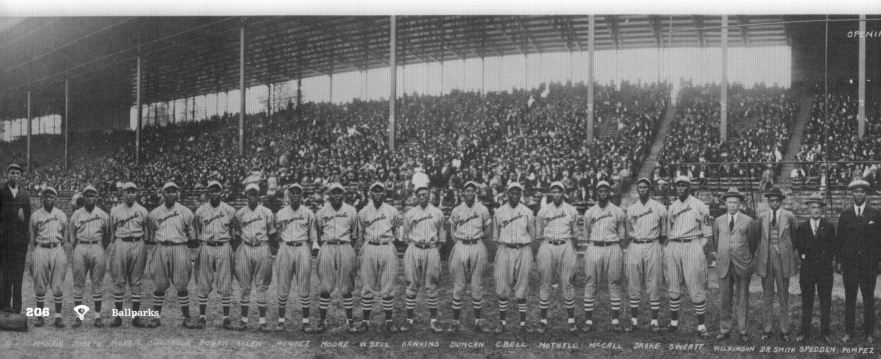

MUNICIPAL STADIUM

KANSAS CITY MONARCHS 1923–1955   KANSAS CITY ATHLETICS 1955–1967
KANSAS CITY ROYALS 1969–1972

AS THE SIGNATURE BALLPARK in one of America's great baseball cities, Kansas City Municipal Stadium served as an epicenter for every imaginable kind of baseball over its fifty-year lifetime. Originally called Muehlebach Field when first constructed in 1923, its name was changed to Ruppert Stadium in 1938, Blues Stadium in 1943, and Municipal Stadium in 1955. The types of baseball it hosted were as varied as the stadium's names. It was first a hub for minor league baseball, then the Negro Leagues, and finally the major leagues, serving as home field for both the Kansas City A's and Royals.

Muehlebach Field was a single-deck stadium when it was first built as the home of the Kansas City Blues, one of the marquee franchises in minor league baseball. It cost $400,000 and seated 17,000 fans. "Between then and its last use in 1972, the dimensions of the playing field and the height of the fences changed more frequently than in any other ballpark," historian Michael Benson wrote. The Kansas City Monarchs, one of the dominant teams in the Negro Leagues, soon began renting the stadium and using it as their home ballpark too. In 1924, the first-ever Negro League World Series was held here. The Monarchs defeated rival Hilldale 5 games to 4, with Game 7 proving to be one of the most exciting contests. Hilldale looked like it had the game well in hand, but Monarchs player-manager José Méndez pitched brilliantly after putting himself in the game as a reliever, and slugger Charles "Bullet" Rogan won it for Kansas City with a walk-off hit in the twelfth inning.

In 1937, New York Yankees owner Jacob Ruppert, seeking a new farm team, purchased both the Kansas City Blues and their ballpark. He immediately changed its name to Ruppert Stadium. During this era, the stands were rigidly segregated, with a few notable exceptions. In 1942, the Monarchs faced a team of white all-stars in

FIRST COLORED WORLD SERIES
ME. OCT. 11, 1924.   KANSAS CITY, MO.

KANSAS CITY MONARCHS

BOLDEN   SANTOP   WINTERS   CURRIE   LEE   CARR   C. JOHNSON   J. JOHNSON   RYAN   MACKEY   ALLEN   CAMPBELL   LEWIS   THOMAS   COCKRELL   BRIGGS   WARFIELD   STEVENS

a benefit game for the war effort. For this game only, Ruppert allowed black and white fans to sit next to each other. "Death claimed segregation, discrimination, and Jim Crow...all pioneer residents of Ruppert Stadium," journalist Sam McKibbe wrote. "There were no mourners, just 6,000 enjoying a baseball drama. The ushers, who are usually rude to Negro patrons, were bubbling with friendliness. That's democracy at work. Whites seated next to Negroes without incident... there was no trouble-making, no vile language, and no fights. The Ruppert management had contended that white patrons would object to sitting next to Negroes at ball games. If it never happens again, it happened Friday night." Alas, it wouldn't happen at Ruppert Stadium again. At the next Blues game, management resegregated the stands.

In 1955, the Philadelphia Athletics, after decades of struggling to make ends meet, moved west to Kansas City. As part of the agreement, Kansas City's municipal government purchased Blues Stadium, added an upper deck, renamed it Municipal Stadium, and leased it cheaply to the A's. After an absence of forty years the major leagues had finally returned to Kansas City, although cynics noted that the team still continued to function as a de facto Yankees farm club. Whenever Kansas City developed a useful young player, that player was mysteriously traded to New York for little in return. Such was the fate of A's stars Clete Boyer, Ralph Terry, and Roger Maris, among others.

The arrival of the big leagues in Kansas City dealt a death blow to the Monarchs. African-American fans began to attend major league games instead of Negro League ones, even though the players on the field were still mostly white, since the American League integrated much more slowly than the National. Nevertheless, in 1955, the A's drew a franchise record 1.4 million fans, while the Monarchs finished $10,000 in the red. The former Negro Leagues juggernaut would limp along for a few more years before finally folding.

The Athletics' years in Kansas City were distinguished by the wacky promotions of owner Charles O. Finley, who purchased the team in 1960 and tried every zany idea he could think of to get fans through the turnstiles. Finley held

Ballparks

cow-milking contests, installed a petting zoo in the outfield, and even paid the Beatles $150,000 to play a concert on the field. None of it worked. The A's annually finished last or next-to-last in attendance, and in 1968 Finley moved the team to Oakland. A new major league team, the Kansas City Royals, moved in the following season, but for them Municipal Stadium was merely a temporary home. The Royals played there for four seasons, leaving once their new stadium in suburban Kansas City was completed in 1973. Municipal Stadium was torn down in 1976 and the site is now a housing development. 🖐

OPPOSITE PAGE, TOP: The upper deck seen here was built when Muehlebach Field was renamed Municipal Stadium in 1955. It proved to be mostly unnecessary, since the A's rarely drew crowds big enough to fill it.

OPPOSITE PAGE, BOTTOM: The left-center field power alley at Municipal Stadium measured 400 feet, making this a difficult ballpark for right-handed power hitters. This photo from 1966 shows right fielder Roger Maris of the Yankees (a former A's star) unleashing a throw to hold Kansas City baserunner Roger Repoz at second. The scoreboard behind Maris, incidentally, was a hand-me-down from Braves Field in Boston. The A's purchased it after the Braves moved from Boston to Milwaukee.

TOP: Although the two teams steadfastly denied rumors of collusion, Roger Maris was one of many stars traded by the A's to the Yankees during the late 1950s and early '60s. Because Maris had a unique ability to take advantage of Yankee Stadium's short right field porch, his home run total exploded from 16 during his final year with Kansas City to 39 in his debut season with New York.

BOTTOM: Athletics fans stream into the newly remodeled and renamed Kansas City Municipal Stadium in 1955, the Athletics' first season in Kansas City. The A's finished second in the American League in attendance that year, but would never again rise higher than fourth.

TOP: The A's locker room at Kansas City Municipal Stadium was vastly different from the lavish clubhouses major league players enjoy today. (Compare it with the one on the bottom of page 22.) Although blue uniforms might seem incongruous for the A's, the team did indeed wear blue from 1955 through 1962.

BOTTOM: Umpire Bob Motley calls out a baserunner at Muehlebach Field on June 6, 1954. A sharecropper's son from Alabama, Motley was decorated with a Purple Heart as a Marine at Okinawa before becoming an umpiring institution in the Negro Leagues. Four years after this photo was taken he was hired by the Pacific Coast League, becoming one of the first African-American umps in the minor leagues. He also served as head umpire for the 1973 College World Series. In 1990, Motley made perhaps his most important contribution to baseball, cofounding the Negro Leagues Baseball Museum in his adopted hometown of Kansas City.

OPPOSITE PAGE: In 2009, the Royals unveiled "The New K," their term for the newly renovated Kauffman Stadium. From 2007 through '09 the team overhauled the stadium while attempting to retain its original charm, an effort that was mostly successful. Among the many additions were an outfield picnic area and a Royals Hall of Fame.

KAUFFMAN STADIUM

KANSAS CITY ROYALS 1973–PRESENT

ALMOST ALL OF THE MAJOR LEAGUE ballparks constructed between 1966 and 1991 were indistinguishable from one another. They were mostly drab concrete bowls with artificial turf, usable for both baseball and football but ideal for neither. The one glorious exception to this cookie-cutter trend was Royals Stadium in Kansas City, a baseball-only facility, which, despite receiving relatively little fanfare, has remained one of the sport's crown jewels for nearly four decades.

In 1967, local voters avoided the multipurpose stadium trap by passing a $43 million bond issue for two new stadiums: one for the Kansas City Athletics and another for the city's new football team, the Chiefs. The A's moved to Oakland anyway, but the American League took advantage of the already-approved stadium by awarding Kansas City an expansion franchise, the Royals. Chiefs owner Lamar Hunt originally proposed that the baseball and football stadiums be built next to

one another and share a single portable roof, which would be placed on wheels and moved to whichever stadium had a game in progress. This audacious dream proved too costly, but the two parks were indeed built side by side at a suburban freeway interchange. The least appealing aspect of Royals Stadium would always be its unfortunate location 10 miles away from downtown, in a spot where the blazing summer sun radiated off an endless panorama of concrete and asphalt.

Royals Stadium was patterned after two ballparks built a few years earlier, Dodger Stadium and Anaheim Stadium. Like them, Royals Stadium eschewed the circular seating bowl that placed fans far away from the action, instead featuring a more natural baseball layout in which the stands hugged the foul lines. The park held more than 40,000 fans despite having no outfield seating. Instead, the team built a picturesque grass berm beyond the outfield wall, accompanied by a spectacular system of lighted fountains which became the park's signature feature. Behind the fountains stood a 60-foot-tall scoreboard cleverly built in the shape of the Royals' crown logo.

The park's most obvious shortcoming was a predictable one for the era: artificial turf. The stadium's 3M Tartan Turf was inexpertly installed, resulting in gaps between the seams, and the warning track was made of a synthetic material, which the outfielders hated. During the 1970s, manager Whitey Herzog stocked his team with fast outfielders, stellar defenders, and base stealers, the types of players who were believed to give a team an advantage playing on the carpet. The 1976 Royals boasted eight players with at least twenty stolen bases apiece, and captured the franchise's first division title. They would go on to win a pennant in 1980 and the World Series in 1985.

On July 2, 1993, Royals Stadium was renamed Kauffman Stadium in honor of the team's ailing owner, who passed away a month later. In 1995, with artificial turf having fallen out of favor, the Royals replaced it with natural grass. In 2006 voters approved $250 million in funding to modernize Kauffman Stadium for the twenty-first century. New bullpens and a press box were built, the concourses were widened, a food court and a Royals Hall of Fame were added, and an HD video board was installed. In an era when most teams were pushing for new ballparks, the Royals instead chose to pour money into their already-classic park. It was a decision for which future generations of fans will surely be grateful. 🌑

OPPOSITE PAGE: A peeved Zack Greinke stands 100 feet tall as pictured on Kauffman Stadium's new video board in 2009. The board, one of the centerpieces of the ballpark's renovation, measures 105 feet tall and 85 feet wide. Greinke had very few occasions to be upset that year, as he won the American League Cy Young Award with an MLB-best 2.16 earned run average.

TOP: The Royals grounds crew drags the infield at Kauffman Stadium. In 2017, the team replaced the entire playing field for the first time in twenty-three years. "Everything below surface, it started to become kind of like an old house," head groundskeeper Trevor Vance told *The Kansas City Star*. "The irrigation is showing some age and it wasn't draining as well as it had. Pipes were getting weak." The new field can drain 20 inches of rain per hour, a fourfold increase over the previous one.

BOTTOM: Kauffman Field's outfield fountains as they appeared after the ballpark's renovation in 2009. The fountains, long considered the ballpark's signature element, were the one aspect of the remodeling that received tepid reviews. Fans decried the removal of the grassy berm that had once surrounded the fountains.

MINNEAPOLIS

METROPOLITAN STADIUM

TEAM: Minnesota Twins (1961–1981)

LOCATION: Intersection of Interstate 494 E. and State Highway 77 N., Bloomington (current location of Mall of America)

NICKNAME: Met Stadium

FIRST MLB GAME: April 21, 1961

LAST MLB GAME: September 30, 1981

NOTABLE FEATURES: Frigid spring weather; "likely the most poorly maintained ballpark ever in the majors," according to historian Philip Lowry.

METRODOME

TEAM: Minnesota Twins (1982–2009)

NAME: Hubert H. Humphrey Metrodome

NICKNAME: The Homerdome

LOCATION: Corner of Chicago Ave. S. and 6th St. S., Minneapolis

FIRST MLB GAME: April 6, 1982

LAST MLB GAME: October 11, 2009 (AL Division Series Game 3)

NOTABLE FEATURES: Unique dome kept aloft solely by air pressure; tall right field wall known as "the Hefty bag."

TARGET FIELD

TEAM: Minnesota Twins (2010–present)

LOCATION: Corner of N. 7th St. and Twins Way, Minneapolis

FIRST MLB GAME: April 12, 2010

NOTABLE FEATURES: Urban location in downtown Minneapolis; buff-colored limestone exterior; right field home run porch lined with flower beds.

efore the Twins brought major league baseball to Minnesota in 1960, the Twin Cities were home to a matched pair of beloved minor league stadiums. Nicollet Park was built in 1896 two miles south of downtown Minneapolis, and served the Minneapolis Millers for sixty years. In its earliest version, it was a simple wooden ballpark, but in 1912, the grandstand was rebuilt in a style reminiscent of a Welsh cottage, complete with red roof tiles and a quaint brick chimney. The distance to the left field fence was only 279 feet, enabling Millers batters to set many home run records over the years. Nineteen-year-old Willie Mays batted .471 during a partial season there in 1951.

Across the Mississippi River in St. Paul, Lexington Park housed the St. Paul Saints from 1897 through 1956. The park was also the home field of the famous St. Paul Colored Gophers, a short-lived but powerful juggernaut in African-American baseball. The Gophers were owned by renaissance man Bobby Marshall, who was also the team's third baseman, an All-American football player at the University of Minnesota, and a practicing attorney. The original Lexington Park burned down in 1915 and was rebuilt in a simple, utilitarian style using steel and concrete.

During their first years after moving to Minnesota, the Twins braved freezing temperatures at Metropolitan Stadium before moving indoors to the Metrodome in 1982. They enjoyed their finest seasons while in the Dome, winning two World Series titles before moving back outdoors to Target Field in 2010. 🖐

TOP: Harmon Killebrew talks hitting with a pair of young Twins fans at Metropolitan Stadium in 1967. Killebrew was nicknamed "Killer," but his reputation was exactly the opposite; he was considered one of the friendliest, most easygoing players in the game. During his career he hit 246 home runs at Met Stadium, far more than any other player.

BOTTOM: A runner crosses home plate during a Minneapolis Millers game at Nicollet Park in 1941. This photo was snapped by Marvin Juell, a janitor at the Minneapolis Public Library who was an avid amateur photographer in his spare time, documenting every aspect of life in the Twin Cities. The Millers won nine American Association pennants during their sixty-five years at Nicollet Park, although they finished fourth the year this picture was taken.

METROPOLITAN STADIUM

MINNESOTA TWINS 1961–1981

A VERSATILE, WORKMANLIKE ballpark, Metropolitan Stadium served the Twin Cities for almost three decades, first as a minor league park, then a pro football stadium, and finally, as the first home of the Minnesota Twins. It opened in 1956 in Bloomington, several miles away from either twin city, surrounded by farmers' fields that would eventually become suburbia. (The summer before construction began, the stadium site itself had produced onions, melons, and sweet corn.) The ballpark was built as a home for the Minneapolis Millers, one of the country's marquee minor league teams, and its triple-decked grandstand held 18,000 fans. Soon afterward, Minnesota was awarded a franchise in the burgeoning National Football League, and the Minnesota Vikings played their first game here in 1961. As it turned out, major league baseball arrived that same year when the former Washington Senators moved in and became the Twins.

With two new major tenants, Met Stadium underwent an expansion that was completed in 1965. An upper deck was built along the first base line, and a huge set of double-decked bleachers provided abundant and cheap—but also bad—seating. "The rest of the park was made up of temporary seating that simply would never go away," the website Pro Football Stadiums noted. "Had the permanent grandstand extended fully down the third base line, Twins owner Calvin Griffith later grumbled, the Twins would never have left the Met." In 1965, the year the renovation was complete, the ballpark hosted one of the most memorable games in baseball history: Sandy Koufax's shutout of the Twins on two days' rest in World Series Game 7. Metropolitan Stadium closed in 1982 when both the Twins and Vikings relocated to the Metrodome. The Mall of America now stands on the site.

The bleachers at Met Stadium were mostly empty for this game on May 13, 1970, despite a marquee pitching matchup between Twins left-hander Jim Kaat and Orioles righty Jim Palmer. This particular set of bleachers in right field was considered the coldest seating in baseball because it offered no protection from the windchill.

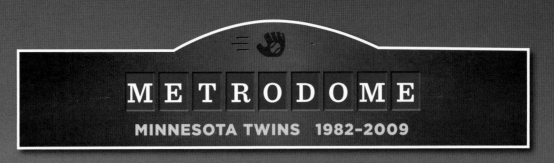

METRODOME

MINNESOTA TWINS 1982–2009

ONE OF THE MOST SURPRISING—and least aesthetically appealing—ballparks in major league history, the Metrodome was the home of the Minnesota Twins, the NFL's Vikings, and University of Minnesota football. With a capacity approaching 65,000, the massive facility also served as a neutral-field host for such jewel events as Super Bowl XXVI in 1992 and the NCAA Men's Final Four in 1992 and 2001. Though the cavernous structure always seemed ill-suited for baseball, the dome's unusual characteristics and the enthusiasm of Twins fans combined to give Minnesota one of the most dramatic home-field advantages ever seen in the sport.

After the Vikings threatened in the late 1970s to move to Los Angeles, ground was broken in December 1979 for a new domed stadium in downtown Minneapolis. The Hubert H. Humphrey Metrodome was different from a normal dome in several ways. Most intriguing was the feat of engineering that kept the roof over the playing field. Instead of the hard roof featured on buildings like the Astrodome, the Metrodome's cover consisted of 10 acres of Teflon-coated fiberglass, one-sixteenth-of-an-inch thick. This flimsy covering was kept afloat with 250,000 cubic feet per minute of air pressure, which meant that any tears required immediate repair to prevent the dome from collapsing. The cream-colored roof also emitted a harsh glare during day games, sometimes rendering it impossible to see pop-ups. While the Twins played there often enough to adapt to this, their opponents did not. The glare from the roof notably contributed to Minnesota's defeat of Oakland in the 2002 playoffs.

One of the Metrodome's signature features, added soon after its opening, was the loose canvas cover on the 23-foot-high right field

wall, known as "the baggie" or "the Hefty bag" because it rippled like one when struck by a batted ball. The left field fence, meanwhile, for many years featured a clear, 6-foot-high Plexiglas extension. This window, which was removed in the mid-1990s, was most notable for its role in Game 6 of the 1991 World Series, when Kirby Puckett crashed into it and made what remains the most memorable catch in Metrodome history. The baggie and the Plexiglas extension were both designed to thwart cheap home runs, since the Metrodome's dimensions were so cozy that it was informally dubbed the "Homerdome."

The Metrodome endowed the Twins with an extraordinary home-field advantage. In their twenty-eight years there, the Twins posted an all-time record of 1,214-1,038 at the Metrodome, a .539 winning percentage. In road games, however, they went 982-1,244, an abysmal .441. One reason for this was the visibility problems created by the roof. Another was the loudness generated by Twins

fans when the park was full, as noise bounced off the underside of the roof. The Metrodome was generally regarded as the loudest stadium in both MLB and the NFL, and a 1999 Vikings playoff game was measured at 128.4 decibels, significantly louder than the loudest rock concerts (which measure 115 decibels).

In 2003, another reason for the Twins' extreme home-field advantage was revealed. The Metrodome's longtime superintendent finally admitted to the long-whispered allegation that stadium workers systematically manipulated the air conditioning system to help the home team. Whenever the Twins were batting, the stadium's fans would be turned on and made to blow toward the outfield fences, helping fly balls carry farther. When the opponents came up to bat, the blowers were turned off. Alas, the Twins lost this home-field edge in 2010 when they moved to open-air Target Field, where no such manipulations were possible. ◑

OPPOSITE PAGE: The Metrodome was one of the largest sports stadiums in the country during the 1980s and 1990s, when it hosted events like the Super Bowl and the Final Four. It was also chosen as the site for the 2012 Democratic National Convention, which renominated Barack Obama for president, but after a major blizzard in December 2010, the dome's roof collapsed under the weight of accumulated snow. The Democratic convention was relocated to Charlotte.

TOP LEFT: An employee of the local newspaper *The Surveyor* distributes copies of a special "Stadium Edition" outside the Metrodome in 1985. The Twins were an exciting young team that year, as star players Kirby Puckett, Kent Hrbek, Gary Gaetti, Tom Brunansky, and Frank Viola were all age twenty-six or younger.

TOP RIGHT: A pair of concession workers boil hot dogs at the Metrodome during the 1980s. Hot dogs actually played a central role in one of the Metrodome's most notorious incidents, when Dollar Hot Dog Night took a violent turn. Twins fans, angry that their former star Chuck Knoblauch had demanded a trade to the Yankees, pelted Knoblauch with the inexpensive weiners throughout the Twins' game against the Yankees on May 2, 2001. Play was stopped in the first and sixth innings as umpires considered forfeiting the game to New York. All nine innings were eventually played, however, and Minnesota won 4-2.

BOTTOM: In December 1981, stadium workers clear snow from the deflated roof of the Metrodome, which had collapsed just a month after it opened. Heavy snowfalls would cause the stadium's roof to collapse again in 1982 (twice), 1983, and 2010.

TARGET FIELD
MINNESOTA TWINS 2010-PRESENT

THE MINNESOTA TWINS FINALLY escaped the Metrodome in 2010. By moving to a new baseball-only stadium in downtown Minneapolis, the team lost the tremendous home field advantage the 'Dome had offered, but gained the ability to play real baseball outdoors on real grass. With a distinctive exterior consisting of white-painted steel and buff-colored Minnesota limestone, Target Field represents a solidly above-average entry in architect Populous's series of retro ballparks.

"Target Field is something of an architectural marvel, in that it sits on a remarkably small plot of land," local journalist Matt Zimmer wrote when it opened. "Its footprint has to be the smallest in major league baseball." Indeed, at 8.5 acres, Target Field does have the sport's smallest footprint, although creative use of overhangs—including one over the I-394 freeway—brings the total usable space to 10.5 acres. Unlike most modern ballparks (but like many classic ones), Target Field's shape is dictated by the city streets surrounding it. It is hemmed in by railroad tracks, a basketball arena, and a freeway, among other things. "Target Field is located on the most complex and urban site of any modern major league ballpark, which presented a defining design challenge," said Bruce Miller, the Populous executive who oversaw the project.

With April temperatures often hovering around 40 degrees Fahrenheit, the Twins' decision to forgo a $100 million retractable roof was both bold and controversial. However, as writer Tom Shefchik accurately pointed out, "It is impossible to have a retractable roof without either having an enormous superstructure or being mostly enclosed by the walls on all sides. That obstructs views outside the park, creates odd shadows during the day, and just is not pleasing to the eye. Target Field's greatest charm is how open it is. The views of downtown are spectacular, and the lack of a roof allowed them to have a really unique and attractive seating situation in the outfield... If you ask me, the occasional weather delay is well worth it to have one of the most stunning parks in baseball."

Target Field has received glowing reviews for its façade of native Minnesota limestone, as well as the intricate urban planning that allowed it to be built on the smallest plot of land in Major League Baseball.

INSET: One delightful aspect of Target Field is a 46-foot-tall reproduction of the vintage logo the Twins used when they first moved to Minnesota. The logo depicts a Minneapolis Millers player and a St. Paul Saints player (named Minnie and Paul, respectively) shaking hands as the Mississippi River flows between them.

Omaha, Nebraska

Rosenblatt Stadium: Home to the College World Series

Rosenblatt Stadium, the quaint old ballpark that housed the College World Series for sixty-one years, was a place where dreams came true and magic happened routinely. "As I remember Rosenblatt, it's full of every color imaginable, wonderful smells, sweat and snow cones, kids and their parents, visitors from every corner of the country and college players, exerting more energy and emotion than at any other moment in their lives," wrote Mike Sherman for ESPN.com.

In 1948, needing a new home for the minor league Omaha Cardinals, the city government carved out a hillside in South Omaha and erected a new stadium there. Cost overruns ballooned the final price to $770,000, and a planned brick façade had to be scrapped—but the city struck gold in 1950 when it lured the College World Series to town. A small-time event at the time, the CWS grew in prestige over the decades, and the stadium grew with it, periodically adding new seating sections that gave the ballpark a charming piecemeal appearance. In 1964, the park was renamed Johnny Rosenblatt Stadium after the politician who had helped bring the CWS to Omaha.

Visually, Rosenblatt Stadium was distinguished by the trusses and cross-bracing beams that held up its huge press box, giving the ballpark a look reminiscent of the cantilevered bridges that connect Omaha to the far bank of the Missouri River. All the steelwork, including eight old-fashioned columns, was painted a festive royal blue. By the early twenty-first century, the ballpark's expansions had increased its capacity to 23,000, making it the largest minor league stadium in the country. Despite this, the sight lines remained outstanding. "One of the beauties of Rosenblatt Stadium is that there is hardly a bad seat in the house," the website Omaha.net noted: "Though some views behind home plate

During the final game ever played at Rosenblatt Stadium—the championship game of the 2010 College World Series—the UCLA Bruins hold a meeting on the mound to discuss how they'll pitch the South Carolina Gamecocks. Whatever they decided, it didn't work, as South Carolina's Whit Merrifield knocked a walk-off single in the eleventh inning to win the title for the Gamecocks.

are partially obstructed, most fans enjoy an intimate experience. Many of the seats are covered, protecting fans from rain, and a gentle night breeze is known to cool down the uncovered fans farther down the foul line and in the general admission outfield."

Architecture aside, Rosenblatt Stadium's most notable feature was certainly the extraordinary memories created here. Many fans remember watching dominant pitchers like Roger Clemens of the 1983 Texas Longhorns or Dave Winfield of the 1973 Minnesota Golden Gophers. Others were drawn to underdogs like the plucky Fresno State Bulldogs, who in 2008 became the lowest-seeded team ever to win the national title. And of course, almost everyone remembers the most exciting moment in college baseball history, which happened at Rosenblatt in 1996. Louisiana State, trailing with two outs in the bottom of the ninth in the championship game, sent light-hitting Warren Morris to the plate as their last hope. If he made an out, the game would be over and Miami would win the title. Instead, Morris hit a low line drive just inside the center field foul pole for a walk-off, championship-winning home run.

Rosenblatt Stadium hosted its final games in 2010, as the College World Series prepared to move to TD Ameritrade Park, a $128 million, 24,000-seat ballpark in downtown Omaha. The new venue was well-received, but it will be decades before it acquires anything like the cachet Rosenblatt had. "Rosenblatt has provided a life-changing experience for more people than the city of Omaha knows," said Texas coach Augie Garrido.

LOS ANGELES

LOS ANGELES COLISEUM

TEAM: Los Angeles Dodgers (1958–1961)

NAME: Los Angeles Memorial Coliseum

LOCATION: Corner of Menlo Ave. and Dr. Martin Luther King Blvd., Los Angeles

FIRST MLB GAME: April 18, 1958

LAST MLB GAME: September 20, 1961 (last MLB exhibition game held March 29, 2008)

NOTABLE FEATURES: Largest stadium in MLB history; oval-shaped field with extremely long distances to right field; left field fence only 251 feet from home plate, topped by 40-foot chicken wire screen.

DODGER STADIUM

TEAMS: Los Angeles Dodgers (1962–present), Los Angeles Angels (1962–1965)

NICKNAME: Chavez Ravine

LOCATION: 1000 Vin Scully Ave. (previously 1000 Elysian Park Ave.), Los Angeles

FIRST MLB GAME: April 10, 1962

NOTABLE FEATURES: Pastel color palette; majestic views of San Gabriel Mountains behind center field; famous for traffic problems and 10-inch grilled Dodger Dogs.

ANGEL STADIUM

TEAM: Los Angeles Angels (1966–present)

NAMES: Anaheim Stadium (1966–1997),
Edison Field (1998–2003),
Angel Stadium of Anaheim (2004–present)

NICKNAME: The Big A

LOCATION: S. Dupont Dr. and E. Orangewood Ave., Anaheim

FIRST MLB GAME: April 19, 1966

NOTABLE FEATURES: 230-foot-tall scoreboard shaped like the team's letter-A logo; fake rocks and waterfall behind left-center field fence.

Though few fans are old enough to remember it, the Chicago Cubs were ubiquitous in early-twentieth-century Los Angeles. Cubs owner William Wrigley built a second Wrigley Field in LA in 1926, when the LA Angels were a Cubs farm team. Chicago also held spring training from 1921 through 1951 on Catalina Island, a resort playland 22 miles off the coast, which was also owned by Wrigley. The California version of Wrigley Field proved popular with moviemakers; the 1942 classic *Pride of the Yankees* was filmed there, as was the television show *Home Run Derby*. The show's title was appropriate, for Wrigley Field's tiny dimensions greatly boosted Angels' hitting stats. In 1956, first baseman Steve Bilko batted .360 there with 55 home runs and 164 runs batted in.

The area's other longtime minor league team was the Hollywood Stars, who played from 1939 through 1957 at Gilmore Field, located next to the famous L.A. Farmers Market. (The stadium was named for business mogul Arthur Gilmore, as it was built on the site where he accidentally discovered oil while drilling for water in 1903.)

Fittingly, the Hollywood Stars were co-owned by several men who matched that description, including Bing Crosby, Gary Cooper, George Burns, and Walt Disney.

Both the Angels and Stars left town when the Dodgers arrived and made Los Angeles a major league city in 1958—although of course the Angels returned in 1961, this time as a major league franchise. After playing one season at Wrigley Field and four at Dodger Stadium, the Angels left the city for the citrus groves of Orange County in 1966. Decades later, however, they would reclaim the LA moniker as part of their longstanding attempt to compete with the Dodgers for the city's affections.

The last time the Coliseum was used for baseball was when this photo was taken, March 29, 2008, when the Dodgers and Red Sox played an exhibition game that drew 115,000 fans, the highest attendance in baseball history.

TOP INSET: NL President Warren Giles inspects the LA Coliseum in January 1958 as the Dodgers were preparing to move in. The Roman arches and distinctive clock seen here were among the park's notable features.

BOTTOM INSET: An overhead view of Wrigley Field circa 1940. The marching band and large American flag on the field suggest a pregame ceremony going on. Though this Wrigley Field had the same name and architect (Zachary Taylor Davis) as its Chicago cousin, it was easily distinguished by the huge clock tower behind home plate.

LOS ANGELES COLISEUM

LOS ANGELES DODGERS 1958–1961

WHEN THE BROOKLYN DODGERS moved to California in 1958, their first order of business was finding a temporary ballpark to play in while their dream stadium was being constructed in Chavez Ravine. Team owner Walter O'Malley flirted with the idea of using Wrigley Field—not the one in Chicago, but its minor league cousin, where the local Triple-A team played. That park was a bit too small, however. He considered the Rose Bowl, where Dodger legend Jackie Robinson had once led the nation in rushing for UCLA, but it wasn't centrally located enough. Finally O'Malley picked the Los Angeles Memorial Coliseum, a massive concrete structure that had been built in 1923 for USC football and expanded for the 1932 Olympic Games.

The ballplayers discovered that it was quite difficult to play baseball in a football stadium. One Dodger pitcher called the Coliseum "the Grand Canyon with seats." The playing field, a giant oval, was entirely the wrong shape for baseball, but O'Malley didn't care. He was more interested in the Coliseum's 93,000 seating capacity. The Dodgers squeezed a baseball field into the space by putting home plate at one end of the oval and situating the left field fence a ludicrously short 251 feet from home plate. This pleased the team's right-handed hitters, but to keep home runs from coming too cheaply, the Dodgers erected a 40-foot-tall chicken wire screen in left field. The screen was an inviting target—so inviting that it changed the way batters approached the game. Lefty sluggers like Wally Moon learned to hit pop-ups to the opposite field, where they would plop over the chicken wire for home runs. The bizarre configuration made a mockery of the game, but Angelenos loved it. When the Dodgers played in the 1959 World Series, more than 92,000 people packed in for each of the three games at the Coliseum. Those remain three of the five highest-attended games in baseball history. The other two were also played at the Coliseum.

Without a doubt, the most special thing about the Coliseum was the thirtysomething redhead in the broadcast booth. Vin Scully had grown up in Manhattan, and he cherished the eight years he'd spent broadcasting in Brooklyn—but it was in Los Angeles that he became a legend. "He has become as much a part of Southern California as the freeways," *Sports Illustrated* wrote in 1964. "Vin Scully's voice is better known to most Los Angelenos than their next-door neighbor's is."

Scully's success was due in part to the fact that the Coliseum was a horrible place to watch baseball. "The closest seats were a long way from the field, and the farthest ones were ridiculous," catcher John Roseboro said. Fortunately, the Dodgers' move into the Coliseum coincided with the invention of the transistor radio. Before the mid-1950s, a radio had been a piece of furniture the size of a cabinet. But now, the new transistor technology enabled companies to produce portable radios. Put a couple of batteries in,

and you could take it anywhere. The first model came out in 1954, and by 1958, they were everywhere.

Transistor radios were a perfect solution to the Coliseum's lousy seats. If you were sitting too far away to see what was going on, all you had to do was tune your transistor to Vin Scully describing the action. At every game, Scully's baritone voice audibly flitted through the crowd, coming from thousands of tiny speakers in unison. You could hear it anywhere—in the restrooms, in the concession line, in the parking lot. "His manner, his style, his voice, really elevated the game to theater," said author Michael Leahy, who grew up in the area and wrote a book about the 1960s Dodgers. "It was as if Scully, his voice, conferred legitimacy on the event. He was sort of a poet, the great bard of the game."

Scully and LA were made for each other. Not only had major league baseball never been played in a stadium as large as the Coliseum; it had never been played in a city as geographically spread out as Los Angeles. Most of the city's six and a half million people commuted to their jobs on the infamous freeway system, and when they were stuck in traffic during evening rush hour, it was Scully's voice that accompanied them home. During the 1960s, 30 percent of all radio listeners in Southern California tuned in to Scully's broadcasts, an astounding ratings number that also helped fuel attendance at the ballpark. When the team finally left the Coliseum for Dodger Stadium in 1962, Scully—and all those transistor radios—followed. ◐

THIS PAGE: Dodgers second baseman Charlie Neal (far left) was a pretty good player, but he seems like an interloper here while chatting with four of the greatest hitters who ever lived: (from left) Hank Aaron, Ted Williams, Stan Musial, and Willie Mays. The quintet was gathered at the LA Coliseum for a 1959 MLB All-Star Game.

OPPOSITE PAGE: Dodgers fans—whose reputation for leaving games early is largely a myth—are still firmly planted in their seats during the bottom of the eighth inning on July 4, 2012. A few months after this photo was taken, the two scoreboards seen here were replaced by larger HD video boards (visible on pages 222–223). The biggest physical change in Dodger Stadium came in 2004, when the dugouts were moved forward and seven new rows of box seats were added in what had formerly been foul territory. If you follow the curvature of the outfield wall past the foul poles, you can see a line of demarcation that marks where the stands used to end.

OPPOSITE PAGE, INSET: A crowd of curious onlookers watches as workers begin the task of leveling Lookout Mountain, the promontory overlooking Chavez Ravine, on September 17, 1959. The building of Dodger Stadium was viewed as a slap in the face by the former residents of Chavez Ravine's Mexican-American community, most of whom had been evicted from their land in the early 1950s, long before the Dodgers were in the picture. A few defiant families, still squatting on the land they'd once owned, were forcibly removed by sheriff's deputies on May 9, 1959, so construction on the stadium could begin.

DODGER STADIUM
LOS ANGELES DODGERS 1962–PRESENT

WHILE THE DODGERS SPENT THEIR FIRST four years in Los Angeles trying to play baseball in a stadium meant for football, team owner Walter O'Malley was busy building a real baseball park in a hilly wooded area a mile north of downtown. Years before the Dodgers came to LA, the city government had destroyed a vibrant Mexican-American community called Chavez Ravine, buying up people's homes to clear the way for a public housing project that never happened. Some of the evictees were descendants of settlers who'd been deeded the land by the King of Spain in 1781; others had moved there because rampant housing discrimination in the area limited their options. By 1957, when O'Malley first spotted Chavez Ravine on a helicopter tour of Los Angeles, only twenty homes in the community remained occupied.

Recognizing that Chavez Ravine was the perfect site for his stadium, O'Malley began buying out the remaining properties, offering as much as five times the appraisal value. However, several homeowners refused to sell, choosing instead to fight the proposed stadium in court. Their legal battle was funded by local theater owners, TV executives, and the owners of the minor league San Diego Padres, all of whom feared competing with the Dodgers for the city's entertainment dollar. O'Malley prevailed in court, but a few stubborn residents, now technically squatters, still refused to leave, so in 1959, they were forcibly evicted as television cameras rolled. This ugly scene became a black eye for the Dodgers franchise, and for years it would hamper the team's relationship with the city's Mexican-American residents.

TOP LEFT: The entire country, Dodger Stadium included, was captivated by "Fernandomania" in 1981, when rookie pitcher Fernando Valenzuela allowed just 2 earned runs over the first 17 games of his career. Valenzuela, who grew up in the tiny Mexican village of Etchohuaquila, helped spawn a generation of new baseball fans in the Mexican-American community. His exploits were narrated by legendary broadcaster Jaime Jarrín on the team's vast Spanish-language radio network, which had stations throughout California, Mexico, and the American Southwest.

TOP RIGHT: Although it didn't quite reach the level of Fernandomania, "Nomomania" arrived in 1994 when Hideo Nomo became the first Japanese player to find stardom in America. The Osaka native led the league in strikeouts as a rookie, and dealt admirably with the spotlight as hordes of media members breathlessly followed his every move. Nomo's signing, like Valenzuela's, was part of a decades-long effort by Los Angeles to market the team internationally. During the 1980s and '90s, the Dodgers also signed the first MLB players from South Korea (Chan Ho Park) and Taiwan Province of China (Chin-Feng Chen), and the first player born and raised in Australia (Craig Shipley).

BOTTOM: The extraordinary Sandy Koufax blows a fastball past New York's Felix Mantilla on June 30, 1962, en route to the first no-hitter of his career. While it was no surprise that Koufax facing the notoriously hapless 1962 Mets resulted in a no-hitter, he would pitch more legitimate no-nos in each of the next three seasons, a feat that remains unmatched in baseball history. From 1962 through '66 Koufax posted a combined ERA of 1.95, leading the league in that category all five years.

The Dodger Stadium site consisted of 325 picturesque acres of rugged hills, scrub brush, and eucalyptus trees—a plot of land seventy-two times larger than that of Ebbets Field. Building the stadium would take three years and become the largest construction project in baseball history. First, the location of the playing field had to be flattened, which involved leveling a 300-foot promontory named Lookout Mountain. Then 25,000 pieces of concrete had to be cast, some of them weighing as much as 32 tons. Since there was no crane in North America large enough to do the heavy lifting, a special giant crane had to be imported, piece by piece, from Germany.

For his architect, O'Malley chose Emil Praeger, who had built the Tappan Zee Bridge in New York and had once renovated the White House. O'Malley, however, was clearly the one in charge. He brainstormed dozens of features he wanted Dodger Stadium to have, some of them more practical than others. Among the ones that never materialized were a retractable roof to cover the infield, a compressed air system to blow constant breeze on the American flag, a Bellagio-style light show featuring fountains shooting water high in the air, and trams that would transport fans from the distant parking lots to the stadium gate—for a small fee, of course. Praeger served as a check on O'Malley's outlandish instincts, and worked with his client to make Dodger Stadium a graceful and classy structure.

O'Malley wisely insisted on a color palette unlike anything seen in baseball before. He wanted to move far away from the decaying Eastern stadiums with their dark wooden seats and dark cloudy skies and dark steel pillars blocking people's views. Dodger Stadium would instead be a burst of color springing forth from a green patch of forest. O'Malley wanted it to be baseball's version of Disneyland, and consulted with Walt Disney himself for advice. Each of Dodger Stadium's four decks was a different pastel shade, with the colors selected to mimic Southern California's landscape: yellow representing sand, orange representing the sun, aqua representing the ocean, and light blue representing the sky. For anyone looking at the grandstand when it was filled with fans in their white shirtsleeves, the effect was one of staring into a huge, brightly colored wedding cake, as broadcaster Vin Scully loved to point out.

It wasn't just the seats. Everything from the outfield fence to the metal railings to the ushers' uniforms sparkled with vibrant color. It seemed impossible to go to a game at Dodger Stadium and not be in a good mood, especially when the sun began to set, casting shadows on the San Gabriel Mountains visible in the distance and painting

TOP: The famous Dodger Dog, manufactured by local meatpacker Farmer John, is 10 inches of tastiness in a blue foil wrapper. The secret to the dogs' deliciousness has always been the fact that they're grilled. During the 1990s, the team tried to cut corners and began boiling the dogs instead, but after a fan revolt, they returned to grilling some—but not all—Dodger Dogs. If you buy one, make sure to get it at a concession stand with the word *grill* in its name; the other stands sell boiled impostors.

BOTTOM: Dodgers broadcaster Vin Scully waves to the Dodger Stadium crowd in 2010, his sixty-first season on the job. By the time he retired in 2016, Scully had been broadcasting for sixty-seven years, more than any other announcer in baseball history. (Second on the list is Scully's good friend Jaime Jarrín, who in 2018 celebrated his sixtieth year as the Dodgers' Spanish-language announcer.) Unlike most broadcasters, Scully has always worked games alone, preferring to have a conversation with the audience rather than with other announcers. His final game at Dodger Stadium, on September 25, 2016, was one of his career highlights, as little-used infielder Charlie Culberson hit a walk-off home run to clinch the National League West title.

the sky a stunning variety of colors. "When you arrived in Dodger Stadium in its early years, it was like going to paradise," said author Michael Leahy. "You would come from different, very hot places in Los Angeles, and you would arrive at the stadium, and if you got there for batting practice and saw the sun set, you'd see this sort of purple sunset in the hills beyond the stadium. This was a slice of California paradise to which people flocked."

Having achieved his desired aesthetic, O'Malley next turned to more practical concerns, such as building enough parking spaces for 17,000 cars. Half the stadium site was reserved for its massive multilevel parking lot, with curved rows of cars radiating out from the stadium, making the whole thing look, from overhead, like a geometric crop circle. Unlike many parking lots, this one wasn't some dystopian hellscape. It was green, with trees and succulents and giant potted plants growing between rows of parking spaces. Even today, Dodger Stadium remains the only major league ballpark that employs a full-time exterior landscaper. And, of course, anywhere you have that many cars in one place, you need gasoline. In exchange for $16 million, O'Malley sold the team's radio broadcasting rights to Union Oil,

and gave the company exclusive rights to advertise inside the stadium, as well as the right to build a gas station on site.

One area of special concern for O'Malley was the toilets. In an era when most ballparks stank faintly of urine, the Dodgers were determined to ensure that their ballpark had no such odors. O'Malley ordered the stadium to be cleaned thoroughly every single day, with particular attention paid to the forty-eight restrooms. Surprisingly, this was perhaps the feature that made the biggest impression on visitors: Dodger Stadium's complete and utter cleanliness relative to other ballparks. "You could eat off the floors," infielder John Kennedy recalled years later. "They kept the thing immaculate." O'Malley also reinvented

TOP: In 2016, the city of Los Angeles renamed Elysian Park Avenue—the street that leads to Dodger Stadium—Vin Scully Avenue. The humble Scully had resisted the move for years, but finally acquiesced during his final season of broadcasting. "I have to thank almighty God to be this old and continue to do something I love," Scully said at the dedication ceremony, which was attended by Dodger fans of all ages. One fan, Moises Flores, carried his three-year-old son on his shoulders. "The cool thing is, my boy is getting the memories now," Flores told the Associated Press. "If the game is not holding you in, it's his voice, his stories and his outlook on the game that you listen to."

BOTTOM: Dodger Stadium is distinguished by its hexagonal scoreboards, zigzagging pavilion roof, and the palm, pine, and eucalyptus trees that line its grounds. It was into these right field stands that Kirk Gibson hit his famous walk-off home run in Game 1 of the 1988 World Series. In 2018, the team put a coat of Dodger blue paint on the seat where the home run landed—section 302, row D, seat 88—and had Gibson autograph it. Fans can sit there for $300 per game, which is donated to research on Parkinson's disease, from which Gibson suffers.

OPPOSITE PAGE: Corey Seager bats against Justin Verlander during Game 2 of the 2017 World Series. "Where do you begin with this crazy, kooky, cuckoo dream of a World Series game?" MLB.com columnist Joe Posnanski wrote after Houston's bizarre eleven-inning victory. You could begin with the fly ball that way caromed off an outfielder's cap to save a run, or the wild pickoff throw that pegged an unsuspecting umpire, or the five—five!—home runs hit in extra innings. To cap things off, a brush fire swept through the hills behind Dodger Stadium late in the game, adding to the general feeling in the ballpark that the end of the world might be nigh.

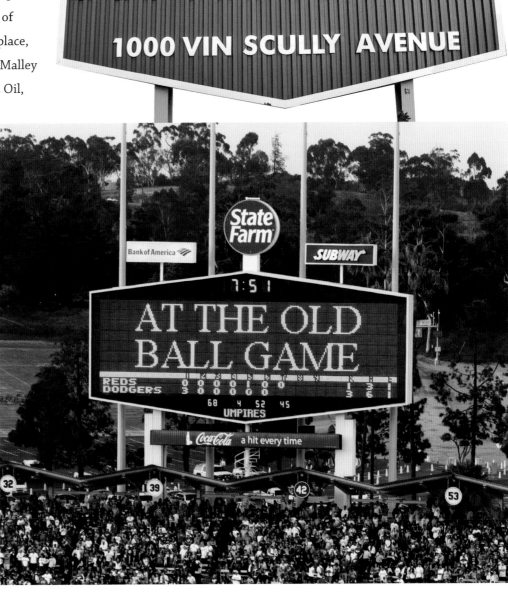

that most basic of ballpark foods, the hot dog. Instead of being steamed or cooked on rollers like at most ballparks, every 10-inch Dodger Dog was grilled, giving it a distinctive taste that placed it head and shoulders above the competition. As of this writing, the Dodger Dog is the only ballpark hot dog that has its own Wikipedia page.

Dodger Stadium is now the third-oldest ballpark in baseball, and has become every bit as beloved in its community as Ebbets Field ever was. It's been the site of innumerable great moments, among them Sandy Koufax's perfect game in 1965, Kirk Gibson's walk-off home run in the 1988 World Series, and the utter craziness of the 2017 World Series. Perhaps no player is more emblematic of Dodger Stadium, though, than Fernando Valenzuela. The exuberant twenty-year-old took baseball by storm in 1981, racing to a 10-0 record and 0.40 earned run average in his first 13 career games. Fans of all ethnicities, but especially Latinos, became entranced by "Fernandomania" and flocked to Dodger Stadium to watch him pitch. In 1982, when the average major league game was attended by 20,766 fans, Valenzuela's games drew an average of 43,312. His success also helped heal the wounds left by the team's long-ago involvement in evicting families from Chavez Ravine. By the time Valenzuela pitched his last game for the Dodgers in 1990, the team's troubles with Mexican-American fans were long extinct. Now, during the twenty-first century, about half of Dodger Stadium's patrons are Latino, and the ballpark draws the most ethnically diverse crowds in baseball.

During its debut season in 1962, Dodger Stadium broke baseball's season attendance record by drawing 2.8 million fans—then proceeded to top that figure thirty-eight more times in the next fifty-five years. All told the Dodgers have sold more than 212 million tickets in their franchise history, which is the largest attendance (by far) of any sports team in the history of the world. A number of factors have helped make Dodger Stadium the most popular stadium ever built: its perfect weather, its convenient location, its aesthetic appeal, its size, and perhaps most importantly, the consistently high quality of the baseball played inside it. ◔

IN THEIR FIVE-PLUS DECADES at Angel Stadium, the Angels have undergone an extensive transformation. Once an also-ran squad content to mimic the nearby Dodgers, the Angels eventually became a powerhouse with the cachet to attract prestigious free agents like Albert Pujols and Shohei Ohtani. Their stadium, too, has undergone a massive metamorphosis, transforming from a modest suburban ballpark into a monstrous football stadium and then back again. Along the way the Angels became the only major league team ever to employ four different geographic designations without actually moving to a new locale. Originally the Los Angeles Angels, they changed their name to the California Angels in 1966, the Anaheim Angels in 1997, and the Los Angeles Angels of Anaheim in 2005.

In 1966, on the advice of Walt Disney (who served on the team's advisory board), the Angels moved from Chavez Ravine to Anaheim, a quiet citrus-growing village that had become a tourist mecca with the opening of Disneyland nine years earlier. Architect Noble Herzberg's design was a transparent attempt to re-create Dodger Stadium, with the same wrap-around grandstand curving gently around the foul poles, the same short metal fences in the right and left field corners, the same slanted roof, and the same palm tree décor. Fans

had unobstructed views of the field from anywhere in the park, a rarity at the time. Anaheim Stadium's central feature was a giant version of the team's logo: a steel letter *A* behind the left field wall with a halo around it and a state-of-the-art scoreboard attached. Visible from five nearby freeways, the 230-foot-tall structure gave Anaheim Stadium its most enduring nickname, The Big A. (After a few name changes, its official name became Angel Stadium in 2004.)

The Angels sold fewer tickets than expected during their earliest years at The Big A, resulting in a financial disaster for the stadium's owner, the city of Anaheim. By 1974, the city had lost more than $1.3 million on the stadium and was trying unsuccessfully to sell it. Relief came in 1979, when the NFL's Los Angeles Rams agreed to move in. A massive refurbishment for the Rams increased capacity by more than 20,000, but also turned the stadium into a faceless mass of concrete. The seating bowl was completely enclosed, views were cut off, and even the landmark Big A structure was relegated to a far-off parking lot.

In 1995, the Rams absconded to St. Louis, and Anaheim Stadium underwent a $117 million renovation to refit it for baseball. The football seats in the outfield were removed, replaced by a Disneyesque waterfall with water cascading over fake boulders. The outside was given an adobe-style façade reminiscent of the Angels' original home, Wrigley Field. The new look was enthusiastically received by fans, transforming the ballpark back into a great place to watch a ballgame. The Angels also found an irresistible symbol in their new mascot, the Rally Monkey. The ubiquitous primate's appearances on the video board were credited with inspiring the Angels to the 2002 World Series title, and a plush version sold at the ballpark became a must-have for young fans. The Angels never did overtake the Dodgers as Southern California's preferred team, but their renovated ballpark helped thrust them permanently into the sport's upper echelon. After their world championship they topped three million in attendance for an impressive fifteen consecutive years, with no end in sight. 🖐

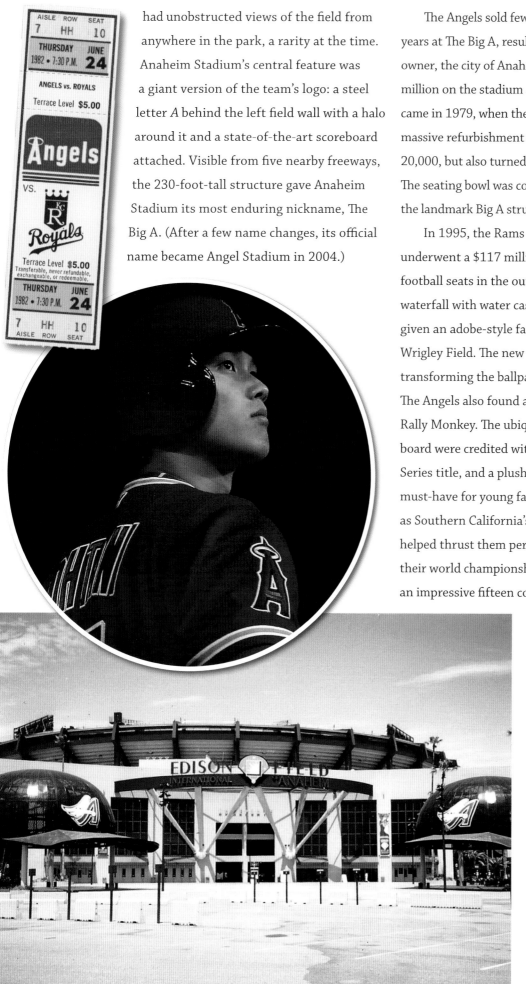

OPPOSITE PAGE: Angel Stadium as it appeared after its highly successful renovation during the 1996–97 offseason. Instead of unsightly football bleachers, fans were now treated to a view featuring a waterfall in left-center field and the Orange County hillside beyond. Things became even more fun here in 2011 when one of the best players of all time, Mike Trout, joined the team.

OPPOSITE PAGE, INSET: This 260-foot-tall landmark is known as The Big A, a nickname which is also often used for Angel Stadium as a whole. From 1966 through 1978, the giant structure loomed behind the left field fence and held the stadium's main scoreboard. When Anaheim Stadium was expanded for NFL football in 1979, the Big A was moved to a parking lot, where it remains today. Whenever the Angels win, the halo on top lights up.

TOP: Before the 2018 season, the Angels scored a coup when they landed Shohei Ohtani, the Japanese wunderkind who was one of the most sought-after free agents in baseball history. A rare two-way player, the twenty-three-year-old Ohtani enjoyed perhaps the best week of any Angels player ever in early April 2018. He won two games on the mound, including a near-perfect game, while also homering in three straight games as designated hitter.

BOTTOM: In 1998, when the stadium was owned by Disney, it was renamed Edison International Field and these giant batting helmets (oddly missing their earflaps) were placed outside the main entrance. The ballpark was renamed Angel Stadium in 2004. In 2017, it was announced that Angel Stadium would be the site of the baseball competition during the 2028 Summer Olympics.

BAY AREA

SEALS STADIUM

TEAM: San Francisco Giants (1958–1959)

LOCATION: Corner of Alameda St. and Bryant St., San Francisco

FIRST MLB GAME: April 15, 1958

LAST MLB GAME: September 20, 1959

NOTABLE FEATURES: California mission-style architecture; site of first MLB game played in the western United States; adjacent to Hamm's Brewery with its famous 13-foot-tall lighted beer glass.

CANDLESTICK PARK

TEAM: San Francisco Giants (1960–1999)

NAMES: Candlestick Park (1960–1996, 2008-2015), 3Com Park (1996–2001), 49ers Stadium (2002–2004), Monster Park (2004–2008)

LOCATION: Corner of Jamestown Ave. and Harney Way, San Francisco

FIRST MLB GAME: April 12, 1960

LAST MLB GAME: September 30, 1999

NOTABLE FEATURES: Cold, biting winds due to location next to San Francisco Bay; known for the aggressiveness and inebriation of its fans.

OAKLAND COLISEUM

TEAM: Oakland Athletics (1968–present)

NAMES: Oakland-Alameda County Coliseum (1968–1998, 2008–2011, 2016–present), Network Associates Coliseum (1998–2004), McAfee Coliseum (2004–2008), Overstock.com Coliseum (2011), O.co Coliseum (2011–2016)

LOCATION: Corner of 66th Ave. and Hegenberger Dr., Oakland

FIRST MLB GAME: April 17, 1968

NOTABLE FEATURES: Pitcher friendliness due to vast amount of foul territory; massive football bleachers in outfield known derisively as "Mount Davis."

AT&T PARK

TEAM: San Francisco Giants (2000–present)

NAMES: Pacific Bell Park (2000–2003), SBC Park (2004–2005), AT&T Park (2006–present)

LOCATION: Corner of King St. and 3rd St., San Francisco

FIRST MLB GAME: April 11, 2000

NOTABLE FEATURES: Proximity to (and views of) San Francisco Bay; 27-foot-tall baseball glove in left field; boaters in nearby McCovey Cove.

B ay Area fans have loved baseball since 1868, when San Francisco's first ballpark was built in the Mission District. Some of the city's early parks met with disaster, however. Recreation Park—located in the SoMa district at 8th and Harrison Streets—was destroyed by the great earthquake and fire of 1906. Eight years later, the San Francisco Seals spent $100,000 to build 18,000-seat Ewing Field, "the most modern minor league park in the country." Unfortunately, they'd failed to properly assess the prevailing climate at Turk and Masonic Streets. Ewing Field was constantly plagued by biting winds; a thick, unrelenting fog often swirled around the field, even cancelling a game; and during another game, a player was so cold he reportedly built a fire in the outfield to keep warm. The lavish but unusable park was abandoned after just one season.

The Seals found a more welcoming home in 1931 when they built Seals Stadium, where they would play for twenty-seven years. The major league Giants also played there briefly before moving to the regrettable Candlestick Park in 1960. Plagued by the same weather problems as Ewing Field, Candlestick was a constant source of frustration until the team abandoned it for magnificent new Pacific Bell Park in 2000, now one of the most beautiful parks in the majors.

Across the bay, meanwhile, Oakland grew its baseball legacy with the formidable Oakland Oaks, who were the Seals' biggest rival. For several years they played at Piedmont Baths, a whimsical structure resembling a medieval castle, located next to the steam baths of the same name at Lake Merritt. In 1913, the team moved to Oaks Park in Emeryville, a suburb tucked between Oakland and Berkeley, where they played until 1957. The Oaks won four Pacific Coast League titles there, including the famous 1948 team known as "Nine Old Men," managed by Casey Stengel. Twenty years later, in 1968, big league baseball finally arrived in the East Bay when the Kansas City A's moved into the new Oakland Raiders football stadium. 🖱

TOP: Willie Mays poses in front of Seals Stadium's marquee in January 1958, a few months before the Giants' first game there. "Seals Stadium had a quirky, fragrant beauty all its own," Mays' biographer James M. Hirsch wrote. "The visiting clubhouse overlooked a bakery, which dispensed a lovely aroma of fresh cinnamon rolls, crusty bread, and pastries. The players couldn't open their clubhouse window without feeling pangs of hunger."

BOTTOM: Ewing Field, built for a then-exorbitant sum of $100,000, is packed with 18,000 fans for its grand opening on May 17, 1914. Unfortunately, the park—located at the base of a hill called Lone Mountain—was so cold, windy, and foggy that ballgames here were a miserable experience. "You ought to call it Icicle Field," one fan complained. After only a year, the Seals returned to their old home, Recreation Field. Ewing Field hosted the occasional sporting event until 1926, when it burned down thanks to a discarded cigarette.

SEALS STADIUM

SAN FRANCISCO GIANTS 1958-59

SEALS STADIUM, HOME OF the venerable San Francisco Seals for twenty-six seasons and the San Francisco Giants for two, was a little gem of a ballpark at the corner of 16th and Bryant Streets in the Mission District. The quarters were so cozy that fans could interact with announcers in the press box. "A fellow would turn around and just say to me, 'Do you have a match?'" Dodgers broadcaster Vin Scully once said. "It was that informal and that close." Built in 1931, the

stadium stood next to the landmark Hamm's Brewery, with its famous lighted beer glass that could be seen for miles. Fans sitting in the horse-shoe-shaped grandstand were treated to views of Potrero Hill behind center field and Twin Peaks down the first base line. Seals Stadium held 23,000 people, and the seats were usually filled when stars like Lefty O'Doul and the three DiMaggio brothers played for the Seals. San Francisco won seven Pacific Coast League championships while playing here, including the ballpark's first season in 1931, its farewell season in 1957, and four straight titles from 1943 through '46.

At Seals Stadium on April 15, 1958, Giants pitcher Rubén Gómez threw the first major league pitch ever thrown on the West Coast, ushering in a new era of big league baseball. But after just two years here, the Giants moved to the newly constructed (and regrettable) Candlestick Park. "Going from Seals Stadium to Candlestick was like going from a Cadillac to a wheelbarrow," one former stadium employee told the *San Jose Mercury News*. Seals Stadium was razed in 1959 and a strip mall was eventually built on the site. The spot where home plate used to be is now Aisle 6 in an Office Depot store. 🖼

Seals Stadium in 1937, when skipper Lefty O'Doul's San Francisco Seals were the city's pride and joy.

CANDLESTICK PARK

SAN FRANCISCO GIANTS 1960–1999

A WINDBLOWN DISASTER of a ballpark, Candlestick Park may be the most universally disliked stadium ever used long-term by a major league team. Its main rival for that distinction is Cleveland Municipal Stadium; both parks were famed for the bitterly cold winds generated by the bodies of water they were built next to. In Candlestick's case, the stadium was hastily conceived, poorly located, and carelessly designed. "Candlestick was trouble from its inception," wrote Robert F. Garratt in *Home Team: The Turbulent History of the San Francisco Giants*. Its construction was marked by "tension, confusion, shenanigans (if not duplicity), underhandedness, and backroom deals between city hall and the builder."

Built on Candlestick Point, a small peninsula jutting out into San Francisco Bay, the stadium was noted for unpredictable weather, which swung wildly between heat and extreme cold, often in the same afternoon. "This kind of weather nightmare is partly due to location... but part of the problem is the wacky thing they call the San Francisco summer," author Michael Benson wrote. "There's a dense fog until noon each day, which burns off and is replaced by a warm but gentle sunshine. At night it's like wintertime."

The extremes of Candlestick were vividly demonstrated for a national television audience at the stadium's first big event, the 1961 All-Star Game. At game time, the temperature was 81 degrees and nearly two dozen fans were treated for heat exhaustion. By the seventh inning, fans were bundled up and drinking hot cocoa to fend off the chill. In the ninth, the National League almost lost the game when its pitcher was blown off the mound by a gust of wind and called for a balk. "Just as I was ready to pitch, an extra gust of wind came along, and I waved like a tree," pitcher Stu Miller told the Associated Press. "My whole body went back and forth about 2 or 3 inches...and I knew it was a balk."

Candlestick's other claim to fame, besides the weather, was the viciousness of its often inebriated fans. One opposing player recalled that "if you were the enemy, the fans would lean over and razz you and cuss you and spit at you and drop things on you every step of the way." One memorable incident occurred in 1981, when a fan threw a helmet at Dodgers player Reggie Smith, who responded by charging into the stands to fight him. "At Candlestick, the wind was a nightmare, but I also thought that the surroundings affected the personality of the audience," broadcasting legend Vin Scully told the *San Francisco Chronicle*. "I could be completely wrong, but it was cold, raw, windy, and I think the people in the stands were unhappy and sometimes would take their unhappiness out."

The Giants, one of the flagship franchises of baseball, somehow failed to win a championship during the forty years they played here, although they did make the World Series twice: in 1962, when the Yankees won a memorable seventh game at Candlestick, and 1989, when the Loma Prieta earthquake interrupted proceedings just as Game 3 was set to begin. Mercifully, the Giants finally decamped for Pacific Bell Park in 2000, moving from one of the worst stadiums ever built to one of the best. 🖐

OAKLAND COLISEUM
OAKLAND ATHLETICS 1968-PRESENT

COMPLETED IN 1966 TO HOUSE football's Oakland Raiders, the Oakland Coliseum added the Athletics as tenants when they moved to the Bay Area two years later. Although it was home to formidable baseball dynasties during the mid-1970s and late 1980s, the Coliseum will always be best remembered by baseball fans for its ruination at the hands of egomaniacal Raiders owner Al Davis.

The Coliseum once had the greatest amount of foul territory in baseball, making it a pitcher's paradise. It was a pleasant place to watch a ballgame, and fans were able to enjoy a delightful view of the Oakland Hills beyond center field. This pastoral atmosphere was brutally destroyed in 1995 when Davis' Raiders, who had abandoned Oakland in 1982, agreed to move back—but only if the government agreed to renovate the Coliseum to seat 63,000 fans. This was done largely by constructing a monstrous set of outfield bleachers that blocked off the scenic view. This hideous hunk of concrete, that towered high above the rest of the stadium, was derisively dubbed "Mount Davis" by A's fans.

Both before and after Mount Davis, the A's always had trouble drawing fans to the Coliseum. Even during their dynasty in the 1970s, the team regularly ranked near the bottom of the league in attendance. The Coliseum's unsuitability for baseball has left the A's in a perpetual state of begging for a new stadium, efforts that so far have proved unsuccessful. During the twenty-first century, the Coliseum has perhaps been best known for its comically frequent name changes, thanks to a series of corporate sponsorships and legal disputes arising therefrom. Between 1997 and 2016, the stadium's name was changed nine times, although as of this writing, at least, it is once again known by its original full name: the Oakland-Alameda County Coliseum.

OPPOSITE PAGE: When Candlestick Park was built, it had open spaces behind the outfield that offered views of nearby Hunters Point. But in 1970, the 49ers announced plans to move to Candlestick, and 20,000 seats were added, resulting in the 63,000-seat, fully enclosed stadium seen here. One might think that erecting a huge wall of bleachers would mitigate Candlestick's wind problems, but that wasn't the case; fans froze just as much as they had before.

TOP: Oakland Oaks manager Charley Dressen waves home a baserunning acorn on the cover of the 1954 Oaks program. For years "Acorns" was a common nickname for the team, used almost as often as the official name, Oaks.

BOTTOM: Like Candlestick Park, the Oakland Coliseum added a gigantic set of outfield bleachers to satisfy the demands of an NFL team. During the ballpark's first twenty-eight years, fans had an outstanding view of the Oakland hills behind the outfield wall. But in 1996, in order to lure the Los Angeles Raiders back to town, the stadium authority built the massive center field structure seen here. Fans derisively dubbed it Mount Davis after Al Davis, the widely loathed Raiders owner. Adding insult to injury, the Raiders eventually left Oakland anyway, moving to Las Vegas for the 2020 season.

TOP LEFT: In 2017, the playing surface at the Oakland Coliseum was renamed Rickey Henderson Field in honor of the electrifying Hall of Famer who played four separate stints with the A's—and who would probably suit up again right now if the team would let him. Henderson, a former All-American running back at Oakland Tech High School, was one of three A's superstars during the 1980s who actually hailed from Oakland. (The others were Dave Stewart and Dennis Eckersley.)

TOP RIGHT: Jim "Catfish" Hunter—whose nickname was bestowed on him for marketing purposes by A's owner Charlie Finley— pitched a perfect game at the Coliseum in 1968 during the eleventh game ever played there. Hunter was one of many colorful characters who helped Oakland win three World Series during the 1970s, a list that also includes Reggie Jackson, Rollie Fingers, and Vida Blue. The Coliseum's most popular denizen, though, may have been a teenage batboy named Stanley Burrell who delighted fans before games with his dancing ability. A's players nicknamed Burrell "Hammer" because he looked like Hank Aaron, and years later he became a rap star: MC Hammer.

BOTTOM: These tarps covering the Coliseum's worst seats illustrate both the Athletics' prestigious past and their challenging present. In 2006, due to low ticket demand, the A's covered up the entire third deck, artificially reducing the Coliseum's capacity from 56,603 to 34,007. But in 2017, after fan complaints, the team removed the tarps in left and right field, bumping capacity back up to 47,170. The only section that remains covered is the top deck of Mount Davis, visible behind center field on the previous page.

AFTER FOUR DECADES at dreary Candlestick Park, the San Francisco Giants finally found a home befitting the franchise's stature when they moved into Pacific Bell Park in 2000. Located in the city's South Beach neighborhood just a few feet from San Francisco Bay, the new stadium was instantly hailed as one of the finest ballparks ever built. With a roster featuring arguably the greatest hitter of all time, Barry Bonds, the Giants immediately turned their ballpark into a moneymaking machine, then used those funds to bolster the team on the field. After failing to win a championship during their forty-year tenure at Candlestick, the Giants won three in their first fifteen years at the new stadium.

For a while in the 1980s, it seemed as if the San Francisco Giants would cease to exist altogether. Between 1987 and 1992, voters rejected a series of proposals for a new ballpark. Owner Bob Lurie threatened to move the team, and in 1992, he actually agreed to sell to a group of investors from St. Petersburg, Florida. Fortunately, a new buyer, grocery store magnate Peter Magowan, swooped in at the last moment and kept the team in San Francisco. Moreover, Magowan announced that despite the rejections at the ballot box, the Giants would build a new stadium anyway—with private funds. Indeed, the city's only contribution to Pacific Bell Park's $357 million budget was $15 million in tax increment financing and $80 million in infrastructure improvements. It was billed as the first time since Dodger Stadium opened in 1962 that a major league park was built with private funds.

An ideal location was found at China Basin, a cove named for the Chinese clipper ships that had docked there in the 1860s. For years, the basin had been a warehouse district where one might encounter the wafting smells of roasting coffee or steamed crabs. Now, the Giants agreed to lease it from the Port of San Francisco. In order to avoid the violent gusts that had made Candlestick so unpleasant, the team commissioned a comprehensive study of wind patterns. As a

AT&T Park has an abundance of great places to sit, including the Arcade section seen here, where only three rows of bleachers separate the right field wall from McCovey Cove. Another excellent place to sit is the 300 level behind home plate, which offers outstanding views of McCovey Cove, San Francisco Bay, and the Oakland hills. (That vantage point can be seen on page 235.)

result, the field faced directly east instead of northeast as Candlestick had. This subtle rotation deprived fans of views of the city skyline, but also decreased the wind inside the ballpark to virtually nothing. Only the top rows of seats were greatly affected, and even those were protected by wind screens.

The Giants and design firm HOK built a near-perfect ballpark, a retro stadium that also looks toward the future. A distinctive right field wall, which separates the stadium from China Basin, features elegant arched windows amid red brick. A giant sculpture of a 1927 model glove, billed as the largest baseball glove in the world, stands behind left field. In right-center, a real San Francisco cable car blows a foghorn whenever a Giants player homers. Even the worst seats offer a panoramic view of San Francisco Bay, with Oakland and the Berkeley hills visible in the distance. There are also countless transportation options to and from the stadium. The park is reachable by car, bus, streetcar, the BART train system, and even by ferry from the East Bay. Fittingly for Silicon Valley's favorite team, Pac Bell was the first ballpark to offer free WiFi in the stands.

Perhaps the only negative is the ballpark's ever-changing name, which has been subject to the vagaries of corporate takeovers and rebranded. Pacific Bell paid $50 million for twenty-four years' worth of naming rights, but when the telecom rebranded itself, the name was changed to SBC Park. Two years later, SBC was swallowed by AT&T, and the name became AT&T Park, as it's known today. Frustrated with all the changes, many San Franciscans began calling it simply "Phone Company Park."

AT&T Park took full advantage of its picturesque location a few feet from San Francisco Bay. A public promenade was built on the narrow strip of land between the right field wall and the water, complete with windows through which ticketless fans could watch the

game for free. China Basin was renamed McCovey Cove after the beloved retired slugger Willie McCovey, and it became a popular spot for boaters who loitered there in hopes of retrieving a home run ball from the water with a fishing net. (A boat dock is conveniently located about a hundred yards from the center field fence.) A statue of McCovey stands next to his cove, while one of Willie Mays graces the main entrance. Adjacent to the stadium is a well-groomed public park featuring a baseball diamond designed for T-ball.

After it opened, the new ballpark quickly became famous for the exploits of Barry Bonds, the controversial slugger who broke baseball's single-season and career home-run records while playing there. It was Bonds who hit the first Giants homer in the ballpark on Opening Day 2000, and who also became the first player to hit a splashdown homer into San Francisco Bay. Although Pac Bell proved to be one of the best pitcher's parks in baseball, and one that was especially tough on left-handed hitters like Bonds, he nonetheless put up astonishing batting numbers. Between 2000 and 2007, Giants batters crushed forty-five homers into San Francisco Bay—thirty-five of them by Bonds. (Through 2017,

117 total homers were hit into the bay, an average of six and a half per year.) In 2006 and 2007, even as nationwide anti-steroid hysteria made Bonds a target of scorn and boos wherever he went, he continued to be greeted by nothing but enthusiastic cheers from the AT&T Park faithful.

After Bonds' retirement in 2007, the Giants built another excellent team based around appealing young stars from their farm system. Tim Lincecum, the diminutive long-haired hurler known as "The Freak," and Pablo Sandoval, the chubby third baseman nicknamed "Kung Fu Panda," both became Bay Area icons whose fame transcended baseball. Improbably, the team became even more successful than it had been during the Bonds era. The Giants won World Series titles in 2010, 2012, and 2014, and they sold out every game at AT&T Park from October 2010 through July 2017—a streak of 530 consecutive sellouts that set a new National League record. From the shop owners of Chinatown to the hipsters in the Mission District, it seems like everyone in San Francisco wears black and orange. 🂠

OPPOSITE PAGE: This sweet swing by Barry Bonds produced the 723rd home run of his career. It was one of 160 he hit at AT&T Park, nearly three times more than any other batter. (As of early 2018, Pablo Sandoval was second, with 55.)

TOP: Much of AT&T Park's beauty is in the small details—although, at 25 feet in diameter, this clock on the center field scoreboard is hardly small.

BOTTOM: In addition to small details, AT&T Park has plenty of large ones, like this 80-foot-long Coke bottle and 32-foot-wide vintage glove. The glove sculpture, an exact replica of a 1927 model mitt, was first 3-D-printed, then fitted with a steel framework and fiberglass coating, and finally the details were hand-sculpted by a team of artists. The stitching was hand-sewn using nautical rope. Incidentally, it's not meant for a four-fingered player—the ring and pinky fingers slide into the same opening.

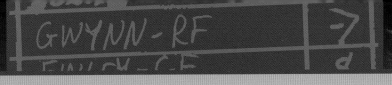

SAN DIEGO

JACK MURPHY STADIUM

TEAM: San Diego Padres (1969–2003)

NAMES: San Diego Stadium (1967–1979), San Diego-Jack Murphy Stadium (1980), Jack Murphy Stadium (1981–1997), Qualcomm Stadium (1997–2017), SDCCU Stadium (2017–present)

NICKNAME: The Murph

LOCATION: Intersection of Interstate 8 W. and Interstate 15 N., San Diego

FIRST MLB GAME: April 8, 1969

LAST MLB GAME: September 28, 2003

NOTABLE FEATURES: First octorad-style MLB stadium.

PETCO PARK

TEAM: San Diego Padres (2004–present)

LOCATION: Corner of Park Blvd. and Tony Gwynn Dr., San Diego

FIRST MLB GAME: April 8, 2004

NOTABLE FEATURES: Buff, white, and navy blue color scheme; located in historic Gaslamp Quarter; use of 1910 Western Metal Supply Company building as left field foul pole.

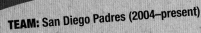

SAN DIEGO PADRES

San Diego's first formal baseball game was played in 1871 at a vacant lot at Broadway and Sixth Streets, seven blocks north of modern-day Petco Park. Other early ballfields were located on the waterfront at Ocean Beach, Pacific Beach, and Point Loma, but the jewel of San Diego stadiums was, without a doubt, Lane Field.

Built by the federal Works Progress Administration in 1936 for a dirt-cheap $25,000, Lane Field was pedestrian in appearance. It was mostly wooden during an era when most other ballparks were built of fireproof steel and concrete, and it "was falling apart from the day it was finished," one local sportswriter complained. Nevertheless, fans of the Triple-A Padres loved it. Lane Field was on the waterfront at Broadway Pier, and the Pacific Coast Highway ran just behind the right field fence. A few feet beyond that, waves lapped up against the pier.

During Lane Field's debut season, the Padres signed a local kid, a gangly seventeen-year-old who would eventually transform himself into the greatest hitter in baseball history. Young Ted Williams batted only .286 during his season and a half with the Padres, but San Diegans would always remember that they'd known him before he was famous. Lane Field was shuttered in 1958 when the team moved five miles north to Westgate Park, and a decade later the major league version of the Padres debuted at San Diego Stadium. In 2015, the city used a $5 million donation—200 times the original cost of Lane Field—to turn its former site into a baseball-themed city park, complete with a monument to Williams and markers where the bases and pitcher's mound once stood.

The sun setting behind Petco Park is one of the most beautiful sights in baseball. Like the ballparks in Baltimore and Houston, Petco incorporated an existing historic building, the Western Metal Supply Company, into its design. It did so even more inventively than those other parks had, adding balconies with seating and a deck of bleachers on the roof, and using the corner of the building as the left field foul pole. Also visible here is "The Beach," a sandy play area for kids behind the right-center field fence. In 2015, it was relocated elsewhere in the ballpark to protect children from home run balls.

JACK MURPHY STADIUM

SAN DIEGO PADRES 1969–2003

WHEN IT WAS COMPLETED IN 1967, Jack Murphy Stadium, then called San Diego Stadium, was used as the centerpiece in a campaign to bring major league baseball to San Diego—and the campaign was a success. In 1969, the Padres began play as an expansion franchise, and in 1981, the ballpark was renamed Jack Murphy Stadium after the local sports editor whose advocacy had spurred its construction. Although it was one of the massive concrete bowls that dominated stadium construction during the 1960s and early '70s, it wasn't a carbon copy of the others. Designed in the Brutalist style by architect Gary Allen, it featured an odd squarish shape more appropriate for football than baseball. Though always best known as a football venue, Jack Murphy would host major league baseball for thirty-five years, spanning the growth of the Padres from hapless also-rans into two-time National League champions.

With attendance sagging in the early 1970s, the Padres almost moved to Washington, DC, but the team was rescued by a new owner, McDonald's mogul Ray Kroc, who treated the team as his personal toy—much to the delight of fans. During his first home game as owner, Kroc took over the public address system to apologize for the Padres' "stupid ball-playing." He also hired a man named Ted Giannoulas to perform at games in a chicken suit. The San Diego Chicken was such a smashing success that most other teams soon hired mascots. With beloved hitting savant Tony Gwynn leading the way, the Padres won NL pennants in 1984 and 1998. The team moved into a new stadium in 2004. Their former ballpark, now known as San Diego County Credit Union Stadium, still serves as the home football field for San Diego State University.

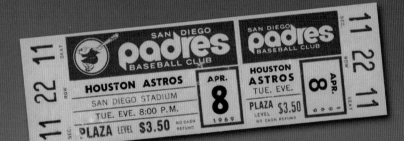

Jack Murphy Stadium's charming exterior included concrete, asphalt, and more concrete. Inside, however, there was often a party going on, usually headlined by the comic antics of either the San Diego Chicken or the Padres' eccentric owner, Ray Kroc.

INSET: It's only two minutes until game time, but Jack Murphy Stadium's bleachers are empty for a Padres-Expos game in 1984. The few who did attend saw Montreal win on a tenth-inning double by Tim Raines. The Padres didn't lose often that year, though, as they captured their first National League pennant.

PETCO PARK

SAN DIEGO PADRES 2004–PRESENT

AFTER SLOGGING THROUGH a seemingly endless series of legal challenges and construction delays, the San Diego Padres finally opened their long-awaited new retro ballpark in 2004. Petco Park proved to be well worth the wait. With a prime bayside location, brilliant architecture, abundant local flavor, and a vibrant neighborhood surrounding it, the Padres' ballpark is one of the true gems of the retro ballpark cycle.

In 1998, San Diego voters went to the polls and approved a new publicly funded ballpark budgeted at $411 million. Ground was soon broken, but construction screeched to a halt for fifteen months while the Padres fought off seventeen different lawsuits filed by taxpayers opposing the use of public funds for a stadium. To make matters worse, a city council member was convicted of accepting bribes from Padres owner John Moores. By 2001, the lawsuits had been resolved, but by then every city alderman who voted for the project had left office, and the Padres were forced to renegotiate terms with the new council. By the time all the hurdles were cleared, the park's opening was pushed back from 2002 to 2004.

Petco Park was the central feature in the redevelopment of the Gaslamp Quarter, the historic district fronting the San Diego Bay waterfront. According to the *San Diego Business Journal*, a total of $1.4 billion had been invested in the district by late 2004, making it the largest redevelopment project in the United States. "While

TOP: The San Diego Chicken has been a constant presence at both Petco Park and its predecessor, Jack Murphy Stadium. The man in the suit all those years has been Ted Giannoulas, who was a college student in 1974 when the radio station he was interning at ran a promotion involving a chicken suit. He got the gig because, at 5-foot-4, he fit into the costume better than anyone else. Giannoulas, blessed with great comic timing, turned out to be a natural entertainer, and he's been making kids laugh at ballparks ever since.

BOTTOM: In 2004, when the Padres urged fans to buy commemorative bricks to be placed at Petco Park's entrance, People for the Ethical Treatment of Animals secretly bought one and had it engraved with the message: "Break Open Your Cold Ones! Toast The Padres! Enjoy This Champion Organization!" To find out why the Padres were less than pleased by PETA's brick, take the first letter of each word in the message and figure out what it spells. The brick can still be seen at the entrance today.

it enjoys success as San Diego's new ballpark, Petco Park serves a bigger role for the city," the *Journal* wrote. "The ballpark breathed new life into Downtown, setting in motion a construction and redevelopment boom." Indeed, the area around the ballpark is teeming with restaurants, bars, and trendy retail shops, making Petco Park one of the most rewarding ballpark experiences in the country.

Better yet, the ballpark itself is gorgeous. Meant to evoke the local setting as well as the Padres' team colors, the seats are navy blue and the exposed steel beams are painted white. The exterior is buff-colored stucco and Indian sandstone, while jacaranda trees and water walls line the walkways leading to the entrance. A pair of 200-foot-tall towers—a tribute to Los Angeles' historic Wrigley Field—house luxury suites with sweeping views of San Diego Bay. Behind right-center field, an elevated grass park provides lawn seating for some 2,500 fans, flanked by a statue of the beloved "Mr. Padre," Tony Gwynn.

Like Camden Yards, Petco incorporated an existing historic building into its design—and did so even more brilliantly than Baltimore had. The four-story Western Metal Supply Company building had been constructed in 1910, and for more than half a century it churned out horseshoes, plumbing supplies, and war material. The building had been vacant since

the company went out of business in 1976. Architect Antoine Predock designed the ballpark so that the Western Metal building fit snugly in left field, where its southern corner cleverly formed the foul pole. Bleachers installed on the building's roof provided seating for 180, while balconies on the second and third floors serve as luxury suites and, the one on the fourth floor, a bar and grill. The ground floor was turned into an entrance plaza and, in 2016, became the site for the new Padres Hall of Fame.

Like virtually every West Coast ballpark, Petco Park was a pitcher's haven. In fact, it took the concept to an extreme. Although nobody was sure exactly why—its field dimensions were not out of the ordinary—Petco in its first four seasons allowed between 18 and 25 percent fewer runs than the average ballpark. "The ball just dies," Padres slugger Ryan Klesko told the local newspaper. "You have to change completely there. You have to take the loft out of your swing. It's not just the dimensions. The ball hangs up in the salt air." After the 2012 season, the Padres moved the right-center field fence 11 feet closer, making things a little easier for lefty power hitters. In the first three years after the change, the home run rate at Petco increased by 19 percent. "Baseball fans want to see the game the way it's intended to be played," team CEO Tom Garfinkel said. "When a hitter gets hold of a ball, it should go out."

Hitting prodigy Tony Gwynn knocks a single to left field during Game 3 of the 1998 World Series at Qualcomm Stadium. The Padres were swept in four games by the Yankees, but Gwynn batted .500 during the series. After twenty major league seasons, all of them with San Diego, Gwynn retired in 2001 with a .338 career batting average. That's the second-best mark of the last eighty years, trailing only San Diego native (and Gwynn's good friend) Ted Williams. After leaving the majors Gwynn served as head baseball coach at his alma mater, San Diego State University, from 2003 until his death in 2014.

Off the Beaten Path...

El Paso, Texas

The Birthplace of Ballpark Nachos and Rock 'n' Roll

Built in 1924, ramshackle Dudley Field was the home of baseball in the El Paso border region for nearly seventy years. Everyone called it the Dudley Dome—not because it actually had a roof, but because its arid location, averaging only 7 inches of rain per year, meant rainouts were few and far between. Because of an irrigation canal running behind the stadium, the field had an inclined slope at the base of the outfield wall similar to Duffy's Cliff in Boston.

Located in a vibrant Latino neighborhood, Dudley Field was only a stone's throw away from the landmark restaurant Chico's Tacos, a popular postgame hangout. It was also the first pro baseball stadium in America with heavily Mexican-American patronage. This was reflected both in the team's roster, which usually included several Mexican-born players, and on the concession menu, which featured such items as burritos and tamales decades before they became trendy. Mexican teams frequently crossed the border to play here, in part because El Paso's remoteness from other American cities meant it often had to look elsewhere for opponents. In 1946, for instance, the El Paso Texans were the only American-based team in the Mexican National League.

During the 1970s, when the minor league baseball industry was waning nationwide, Dudley Field helped save it. A young Vietnam vet named Jim Paul bought the struggling El Paso Diablos in 1974 for $1,000. "That was all the money I had to my name," he said. "If the guy had asked for $1,500, I couldn't have bought the team." Paul turned out to be a marketing genius, and he became the Bill Veeck Jr. of the minor leagues, creating an atmosphere of chaotic fun that drew fans to the Dudley Dome in droves. He hired a zany loudmouth to serve as public address announcer, and every Sunday night hot dogs were sold for just 10¢. Paul revolutionized the ballpark experience by playing rock music over the loudspeakers, hiring cheerleaders, selling nachos, and holding promotional giveaways—all of which seem like standard fare now, but Dudley Field was where they started. Paul eventually founded the El Paso Baseball Seminar, where other team owners gathered every offseason to learn at the feet of the master. When Paul finally sold the Diablos

for $4 million in 1996, it represented a 4,000 percent return on his $1,000 investment.

The venerable Dudley Dome closed its doors in 1990. Amazingly, El Paso has opened two more landmark stadiums since then. Cohen Stadium, which replaced Dudley, has the distinction of being the only ballpark ever featured on the cover of *National Geographic* magazine. And Southwest University Park, opened in 2014, has received rave reviews as a masterful example of urban ballpark architecture. Located just four blocks from the Mexican border, it's squeezed into a downtown city block that's only 5.5 acres, the smallest footprint in all of professional baseball. Populous, the park's designers, couldn't build outward, so instead they built upward, creating the first four-deck minor league stadium ever built. The resulting ballpark, with gorgeous views of El Paso, Ciudad Juárez, and the Franklin Mountains, has been hailed as one of baseball's best.

THIS PAGE: In his book, *Stolen Season*, journalist David Lamb called this ballpark "the wacky Dudley Dome, the very symbol of minor league baseball's second Golden Age." The top photo shows Dudley in 1989; below that is a view circa 1949-53. "Dudley was as grand a park as I had ever seen," Lamb wrote. "It was sixty-five years old, full of odd angles, nooks, and crannies. The grandstands were built with adobe brick, and there was a small hill in center field that covered an irrigation ditch, resulting in marvelous battles between man and ball."

SEATTLE

KINGDOME

TEAM: Seattle Mariners (1977–1999)

NAME: King County Multipurpose Domed Stadium

LOCATION: Corner of Occidental Ave. S. and S. Royal Brougham Way, Seattle

FIRST MLB GAME: April 6, 1977

LAST MLB GAME: June 27, 1999

NOTABLE FEATURES: 23-foot-tall right field fence; wavy appearance when viewed from outside due to zigzagging pedestrian ramps.

SAFECO FIELD

TEAM: Seattle Mariners (1999–present)

LOCATION: Corner of 1st Ave. S. and S. Atlantic St., Seattle

FIRST MLB GAME: July 15, 1999

NOTABLE FEATURES: Open-air retractable roof; extreme pitcher's park; commissioned artworks throughout grounds.

When the Seattle Pilots joined MLB in 1969, they played their first season—and, it turned out, their only season—at Sicks' Stadium, at the corner of Rainier and McClellan Streets, a hallowed location for local baseball. Seattle's teams had played there since 1913, when Dugdale Park was built for the Seattle Giants of the lowly Northwestern League. (The team soon moved up to the much-more-competitive Pacific Coast League.) On the night of July 4, 1932, Dugdale Park was burned to the ground by a serial arsonist named Robert Driscoll, who used discarded game programs as kindling.

In 1938, the Giants were sold to brewing magnate Emil Sick, who renamed them the Seattle Rainiers after his company's flagship beer. That same year, he built a new $350,000 ballpark on the site where the old one had burned, giving it the seemingly unhealthy name of Sick's Seattle Stadium. Behind the left field fence stood a huge, grassy hill where fans could sit and watch the game for free. (It became known locally as Tightwad Hill.) In 1957, Elvis Presley played a memorable concert at Sick's Stadium; among those in attendance was a fourteen-year-old aspiring guitarist named Jimi Hendrix.

By the time the Pilots arrived in 1969, Emil Sick had died and the ballpark name was pluralized to Sicks' Seattle Stadium to reflect ownership by his children. The Pilots moved to Milwaukee after just one season, but Seattle got a replacement team eight years later when the expansion Mariners were born. After twenty-three seasons in the Kingdome, most of them losing ones, the Mariners finally got a proper big league ballpark when Safeco Field opened in 1999. 📷

LEFT: Safeco Field, seen here with its roof open on a rare sunny day, might be the best retractable-roof stadium ever built. Even when the roof is closed, the sides of the stadium remain open to the elements, allowing it to still seem like a real ballpark. The picturesque skyline includes a view of CenturyLink Field, built next door for the NFL's Seahawks in 2002.

KINGDOME

SEATTLE MARINERS 1977–1999

THE KINGDOME, A FORGETTABLE covered stadium that housed the Seattle Mariners during the franchise's early years, is notable mostly for its brief lifespan. Opened in 1977 and abandoned after 1999, its twenty-three years is one of the shortest tenures among parks built specifically for a major league team. The dome's tenants, meanwhile, were the laughingstock of baseball until 1995, when they made a memorable run in the American League playoffs, captured the hearts of local residents, and laid the groundwork for a new ballpark.

Funding for a domed stadium in Seattle was first approved in 1968, but the Kingdome wouldn't be completed for another eight years. The $67 million facility was built to accommodate both baseball and football, although Seattle had a team in neither sport when construction began. The dome was finished in March 1976, in time for an NFL expansion team, the Seahawks, to move in. The expansion Mariners followed in 1977 and the NBA's Supersonics joined them in 1978, making the two-year-old facility the only stadium to host all three major sports at the same time.

After nearly two decades of constant losing, the Mariners finally fielded a formidable team in 1995, led by the exuberant outfielder Ken Griffey Jr. and the hitting machine Edgar Martínez. The Mariners made the playoffs for the first time, and faced the Yankees in a memorable, gut-wrenching division series that would become legendary in Seattle. When Martínez smacked a double into the left field corner to score Griffey with the series-winning run, the future of baseball in Seattle was assured and the Kingdome's fate sealed. A month earlier voters had defeated a measure to fund a new stadium, virtually assuring that the Mariners would move to another city. But in the euphoria that followed the win over the Yankees, state legislators voted to allocate the funds anyway. The Mariners moved next door to Safeco Field in 2000, and the Kingdome was imploded that March.

OPPOSITE PAGE, TOP: This undated photo looks down on the Kingdome's home plate.

OPPOSITE PAGE, BOTTOM: On the inside the Kingdome was pretty much like any other dome, but from the outside it was easily distinguished by the wavy lines of its entrance ramps. The waves served as a tip of the cap to Puget Sound a few yards away.

TOP: This photo of the Kingdome was taken during the 1979 MLB All-Star Game, which explains why there's a giant banner with the National League logo hanging in an American League ballpark. The chandelier-like structure is actually a collection of patriotic streamers installed because the stadium opened in 1976, America's bicentennial year. A fly ball once got tangled up in the streamers, and they were eventually taken down. The stadium's speakers, however, remained suspended from the roof only 102 feet above the playing field. They were also frequently struck by batted balls, leading the *Los Angeles Times* to call the Kingdome "part obstacle course, part pinball machine, and part fun house."

BOTTOM: This swing by Ken Griffey Jr. looks awkward, but it actually resulted in a go-ahead homer during Game 4 of the 1995 Division Series against the Yankees. Just a few weeks earlier, King County voters had defeated a ballot measure to build a new stadium, but the Mariners' epic late-season run mesmerized the city and created countless new fans. "The storybook September, its final chapters yet to be written, has stunned Seattle," the *New York Times* wrote. As it turned out, the final chapter included the Mariners dramatically knocking the Yankees out of the playoffs in Game 5.

SAFECO FIELD

SEATTLE MARINERS 1999–PRESENT

IN 1995, IN THE WARM AFTERGLOW of the first playoff series win in Seattle history, the Washington legislature, giddy with baseball enthusiasm, funded "The House That Griffey Built." The nickname was literal. On March 8, 1997, Griffey himself helped break ground on a site immediately south of the Kingdome, just a block from Puget Sound. Most of the $517 million budget came from state lottery funds and miscellaneous tax increases. Designed by NBBJ, a local architectural firm, Safeco boasted the third retractable roof in baseball history. Although baseball season encompasses Seattle's driest months, the roof gave the team and its fans comfort in the knowledge that every scheduled game would take place as planned.

The roof at Safeco Field contains 11,000 tons of steel—enough to build a 55-story skyscraper—and can be opened or closed in ten to twenty minutes. Like the bleachers you'd find in vintage high school gyms, each roof section simply folds under the other until they are all piled high atop the right field stands. A retro park with natural grass,

Safeco features a traditional entrance rotunda, uniquely scaffolded light towers, and a hand-operated scoreboard. Seattle's best-known landmark, the Space Needle, is visible from various locations inside the park. One delightful feature of the stadium is "Art in the Park," a project whereby forty-three baseball-themed works of art were commissioned for a total of $1.37 million. These paintings, photographs, and sculptures—created by nine Northwest artists—add a welcome touch of beauty to the surroundings. In addition, a pair of museums—the Mariners Hall of Fame and the Baseball Museum of the Pacific Northwest—pay homage to the area's baseball past.

The still-unfinished Safeco Field opened on July 15, 1999, to rave reviews, and Seattle's attendance, which usually ranked last or next-to-last during the Kingdome days, shot up to fourth-best in the American League. In 2001, the stadium became one of baseball's hottest scenes

when the Mariners signed Ichiro Suzuki, the much-heralded Japanese batting wizard. With a well-rounded club built around the electrifying Ichiro, the Mariners won an MLB-record-tying 116 games in 2001. Ichiro energized Seattle's sizable Japanese-American community, and the "Ichiroll," a sushi snack, became so popular that the stadium continued selling it even after its namesake left to play for other teams. (Safeco, known for the inventiveness of its concessions, also sells such favorites as spicy pork wontons, smoked sausage corn dogs, and maple bacon doughnuts—and in 2018 even started serving chapulines—toasted grasshoppers with chili-lime salt.) Another longtime Safeco favorite is the ace right-hander "King Félix" Hernández; on days he pitches, a special section of the left field stands is dubbed "The King's Court."

For its first decade and a half, Safeco was one of the game's most extreme pitcher's parks, reducing hitting numbers by as much as 20 percent in some seasons. The future Hall of Famer Adrián Beltré famously suffered a hitting collapse here after signing with the Mariners in 2005. After the 2012 season, in an attempt to make the park friendlier toward hitters, the Mariners moved the fences closer to home plate, resulting in a small uptick in offense. That winter the team also added the largest scoreboard in the major leagues. After the 2017 season, the entire playing surface was redone, setting up Safeco Field for many more years as one of America's best-loved ballparks. 🌀

OPPOSITE PAGE: Fans take in a game at SafeCo Field with the roof open. Uniquely, the roof doesn't completely enclose the stadium even when shut. Instead, it acts as a sort of umbrella, with wind, rain, and other elements still able to sneak in through the sides.

TOP: Other than the Yankee Stadium with Babe Ruth, no ballpark has ever been more closely identified with a particular player than the Safeco Field is with Ichiro Suzuki. The stylish outfielder is shown here in 2001, the year he became the first hitter to successfully transition from Japanese baseball to the major leagues. That year he won the batting title and the MVP award, inspired a passionate new throng of Japanese-American baseball fans, and led the Mariners to 116 wins, the most in baseball history. Ichiro would later break both MLB's single-season hits record (262, set in 2004) and pro baseball's career hits record (4,257, set in 2017).

BOTTOM: This piece by Seattle sculptor Gerry Tsutakawa, titled *The MITT*, stands outside Safeco Field's left field gate. "Near the center of the glove an aperture appears as an abstract symbol representing a ball nestled in the leather, or a hole where a fastball burned through," the Mariners' website explains. "The sculpture is placed outside the gates to allow fans to touch, lean on, or crawl through the work, giving the public a feeling of ownership of the piece."

DENVER

COORS FIELD

TEAM: Colorado Rockies (1995–present)

LOCATION: Corner of Blake St. and 20th St., Denver.

FIRST MLB GAME: April 26, 1995

NOTABLE FEATURES: Stately redbrick exterior; largest playing field in MLB; humidor to control moisture in baseballs; brewery in right field where Blue Moon beer was invented.

Pro baseball first came to Denver during the 1880s, when the state of Colorado was less than a decade old and Denver was a bustling Wild West city of 35,000. The Denver Mountain Lions played in a wooden ballpark at the corner of Larimer and 32nd Streets, ten blocks northeast of today's Coors Field. A few years later, a majestic, two-deck ballpark known as Riverfront Park was built on the Platte River, on the site now occupied by Commons Park. It was a frequent stop for MLB teams when they barnstormed across the country. Beginning in 1922, the beloved minor league Denver Bears played at Merchants Park in the Platt Park neighborhood. Then in 1948, they moved into 18,000-seat Bears Stadium, which would eventually be renamed Mile High Stadium and become the city's first major league ballpark when the Rockies were formed in 1993. After setting attendance records at Mile High for two years, the Rockies moved to the spectacularly picturesque (but much smaller) Coors Field in 1995.

LEFT: This photo perfectly illustrates why Coors Field is loved by fans but hated by first basemen. While most major league fields face east or northeast, Denver's faces directly north in order to give fans a view of the distant Rocky Mountains behind left field. (Though many mistakenly believe Denver to be in the mountains, it's actually on flat prairie land 17 miles east of where the Rockies begin.) The field's unusual layout means the late-afternoon sun shines directly into the first baseman's eyes, making it extraordinarily difficult to catch throws from infielders. Todd Helton, the Rockies' first baseman for seventeen years, learned to deal with the problem better than most, but even Helton grew so frustrated that he once asked the team to put up a screen to block out the sun. The request was denied.

INSET: A lemonade salesman does brisk business on June 7, 2004, when the temperature at Coors Field reached 98 degrees Fahrenheit. Coors has some of the most extreme weather in the majors, ranging from wintry blizzards to epic thunderstorms to blazing heat. On Opening Day 2004, less than two months before this photo was taken, the game-time temperature was 37 degrees. Several games in the ballpark's history have been snowed out.

COORS FIELD

COLORADO ROCKIES 1995-PRESENT

IN 1995, THE COLORADO ROCKIES opened what immediately became the most infamous stadium in baseball. Though its architecture was excellent and its seats provided scenic views of the Rocky Mountains, it was not these features that drew attention to Coors Field. Rather, it was the stunning frequency with which runs were scored and home runs were hit. When Denver was first awarded an expansion team, everyone was well aware that its altitude would amp up offense, but few were prepared for the overwhelming extent of the effect. Thinner air meant less friction on the ball as it traveled, which wreaked havoc on hurlers' breaking pitches. In addition, most studies concluded that batted and thrown balls traveled between 7 and 10 percent farther at 5,200 feet above sea level. With this in mind, the club made Coors Field's outfield fences among the most distant in baseball. Left-center field was 390 feet away and dead center 415 feet. However, this also dramatically increased the size of the outfield, so singles, doubles, and triples all had

more space to fall in. During the inaugural season of 1995, there were fifty-nine triples hit at Coors as opposed to just twenty in Rockies road games. The total effect was a ballpark favoring batters to a degree unprecedented in baseball history. Pitchers, meanwhile, found Coors Field to be a house of horrors. During the ballpark's first nine years, no Rockies hurler managed to pitch a full season with an ERA better than 4.00. It has become a truism of baseball that no free agent pitcher in his right mind will ever willingly sign with Colorado. In order to stay competitive, the club must assemble an outstanding pitching staff solely using its farm system, something it has never been able to do consistently.

The most interesting solution the Rockies have tried is humidifying their baseballs. Denver's arid atmosphere causes baseballs to dry out and weigh slightly less, contributing to the way they fly off the bat. So in 2002, the Rockies installed a humidor big enough for 4,800 baseballs in the bowels of Coors Field, bringing them more in line with baseballs used at sea level.

While the Rockies' management tries to figure out a way to compete in this roller-derby arena of a ballpark, it continues to be a hit with fans. Originally slated to seat 43,000, the final number was increased to 50,000 after the extraordinary popularity of the Rockies at Mile High Stadium. Although most tickets and concessions were on the pricier side, when Coors Field opened, tickets could still be had in the Rockpile (the far-away center field bleachers) for as little as $1. A brewery was built into one side of the park and the redbrick entrance rotunda that recalls Shibe Park and Ebbets Field. During the 2013–14 offseason, Coors Field underwent an extensive renovation aimed at targeting a specific demographic: young professionals who like to hang out in Coors Field's LoDo neighborhood, known for its nightlife and microbreweries. The club removed 3,500 inexpensive seats in the right field upper deck and replaced them with "The Rooftop," a 38,000-square-foot venue that was billed as the largest party area in professional sports. With new revenue sources, a gorgeous ballpark, and one of the best sports markets in the country, the Rockies seem poised for a bright future at Coors Field—if only they can figure out how to get some pitching.

OPPOSITE PAGE: As a two-sport venue, Mile High Stadium featured the logos of all National League teams on the outfield wall, and the Denver Broncos' retired numbers on the facing of the upper deck. Mile High opened in 1948 as an 18,000-seat minor league ballpark and closed in 2001 as a 76,000-seat NFL stadium. Needless to say, it underwent many renovations over the years, including major ones in 1960, '68, and 1975 to '77. The Rockies played here for their first two seasons, and during their debut year of 1993 they drew 4.48 million fans, shattering MLB's season attendance record by a margin of nearly half a million.

TOP: Coors Field's entrance rotunda was patterned after that of Ebbets Field, visible on page 35. The ballpark's construction was instrumental in the revitalization of Denver's LoDo, or Lower Downtown, district. The area is now bursting with nightlife. As of this writing there are at least sixteen microbreweries within a mile and a half radius of Coors Field, including one, the Sandlot Brewery, that's actually inside the ballpark.

BOTTOM: Coors Field's best-loved player in recent years has been Nolan Arenado, who's known for both his power hitting and his spectacular defense at third base. Arenado piled up 130 RBIs every year from 2015 to '17, winning the Gold Glove award each season as well.

CHASE FIELD

TEAM: Arizona Diamondbacks (1998–present)

NAMES: Bank One Ballpark (1998–2005), Chase Field (2005–present)

NICKNAME: The BOB

LOCATION: Corner of E. Jefferson St. and Randy Johnson Way, Phoenix

FIRST MLB GAME: March 31, 1998

NOTABLE FEATURES: Swimming pool behind right-center field fence; dirt pitcher's path between mound and home plate; retractable roof weighing 9 million pounds that opens or closes in four and a half minutes.

CHASE FIELD
ARIZONA DIAMONDBACKS 1998-PRESENT

Viewed from the outside, Chase Field is as unattractive a stadium as one could imagine. A rectangular box with a half-moon-shaped roof, it resembles nothing so much as a giant discount warehouse. Opened in 1998 for the expansion Diamondbacks, the park features two mainstays of Arizona life—swimming pools and air conditioning—but is surprisingly bereft of a third: sunshine. With high walls, a small roof opening, and steep, distant seating, it makes fans feel as if they're watching a ballgame from the rafters of a colossal airplane hangar.

Although its location in downtown Phoenix seems ideal, all views of the city are blocked by the 180-foot-high walls that support its retractable roof. The roof, made of 9 million pounds of steel, can open or close in less than five minutes, at which point Chase Field's high-powered air-conditioning system, a must in sweltering Phoenix, can lower the inside temperature by thirty degrees in just three hours. At first, the Diamondbacks allowed their starting pitcher to decide each night whether the roof would stay open or closed. Ace hurler Curt Schilling always pitched with the roof closed because he believed home runs came easier with it open. Schilling's instincts were correct. A study by the blog AZSnakepit found that a whopping 21 percent more home runs were hit with the roof open from 1998 through 2015. Eventually, however, the decision to leave the roof open or closed was taken away from the pitchers and is now based strictly on weather reports.

A unique aspect of Bank One Ballpark (as it was called until 2005) when it opened was the pitcher's path, a 60-foot, 6-inch strip

of dirt leading from home plate to the pitcher's mound. Unseen in baseball for decades, it was a throwback to the Deadball Era, when ballparks often featured a naturally worn dirt path between home plate and the mound, due to the frequency of catchers visiting the pitcher. The version here, though meticulously groomed rather than natural, was a well-received tip of the cap to baseball's early days.

Chase Field's signature feature, though, is the swimming pool just beyond the right-center field fence—actually the third major league park to feature a pool behind the outfield fence, after Philadelphia's Jefferson Street Grounds and Montreal's Parc Jarry.

Oddly, the pool was actually the source of the most controversial incident in Chase Field's young history. In 2013, after clinching the National League West at Chase Field, the hated Los Angeles Dodgers jumped into the pool cannonball-style in an impromptu celebration. The Diamondbacks, who viewed it as rubbing it in, were prepared four years later, when the Dodgers again won a clinching game at Chase Field: They had hired hired mounted police to guard the pool until the wee hours of the morning, making sure no unauthorized fun could be had. In 2017, they got to have their own fun, diving into the pool after winning a playoff spot. 🥎

PREVIOUS PAGE: If the Diamondbacks ever leave Arizona, NASA could use Chase Field as a hangar to park a few space shuttles. The ballpark's impersonal atmosphere is a direct result of the high walls required to support its retractable roof. Although that makes it a lousy environment for a ballgame, it's probably better than the alternative, which would be open-air baseball in 110-degree heat.

PREVIOUS PAGE, INSET: A sea of ticket windows makes it easy for Diamondbacks fans to buy last-minute ducats. Attendance at Chase Field usually ranks near the bottom of the National League, but on two occasions— 1998 and 2002—it's risen as high as second. Part of the problem is that there's a plethora of competition for local baseball fans' dollars. Between the National League, the Cactus League, the Arizona League, and the Arizona Fall League, the Phoenix area hosts about 615 pro baseball games per year, far more than any other city in the world.

TOP: If this sea of glass, steel, and advertising wasn't in the way, Diamondbacks fans would have a gorgeous view of downtown Phoenix behind Chase Field's outfield wall. Games are always more enjoyable here when the roof is open, but that only happens when weather permits, which is less than a third of the time. The D-Backs actually have a roof hotline that lets fans know whether the roof will be open or closed that day; if you're thinking of going to a game, give them a call at (602) 462-6262.

BOTTOM: The most popular feature at Chase Field is the swimming pool in right-center field, which can be rented for $5,000 to $7,500 per game. That fee gets you thirty-five game tickets, five parking passes, lifeguard services, unlimited food and soda, and access to private showers and changing rooms. The Dodgers infamously partied here after clinching the National League West in 2013, which didn't go over well with the home team. "I could call it disrespectful and classless, but they don't have a beautiful pool at their old park and must have really wanted to see what one was like," said Diamondbacks CEO Derrick Hall. Four years later, as pictured here, the D-Backs finally got to have their own pool party when they won a Wild Card berth.

Off the Beaten Path...

Tucson, Arizona
Birthplace of the Cactus League

Spring training in the Cactus League has grown into a multimillion-dollar industry, but it began modestly enough in 1947 when the Cleveland Indians moved their training camp to a dusty minor league diamond in Tucson. Team owner Bill Veeck Jr. wanted the camp closer to the Arizona ranch where he spent his winters, but unbeknownst to everyone, he was also planning on integrating his team, and he believed Tucson would be more welcoming to African-American players than segregated small-town Florida. The only drawback was the lack of an opposing team, which Veeck solved by convincing the Giants to move their camp to Phoenix.

Veeck set up shop at Randolph Municipal Baseball Park, where the minor league Tucson Cowboys had played since 1928. (In 1951, it was renamed Hi Corbett Field after the local politician who wooed Veeck to town.) The ballpark was located inside a larger city park that also included a municipal golf course and, eventually, the city zoo. Like many southwestern buildings, Hi Corbett Field was made mostly of adobe—even the outfield wall, which was thick enough for fans to sit on top of during games. Otherwise the park's architecture was pretty standard, consisting of a home plate grandstand covered by a small steel roof, with uncovered bleachers down each foul line. Lights were added in 1939, and renovations took place in 1969, 1972, 1992, 1997, 1999, and 2012.

Hi Corbett Field served as a major league training site for fifty-four springs—forty-six with Cleveland followed by eight years with the Colorado Rockies, and seventy-four Hall of Famers played here during that time. According to legend, Mickey Mantle once hit a *(ahem)* mammoth home run that landed near the elephant habitat in the Reid Park Zoo next door. During the late 1980s Hi Corbett was home to not only the real Cleveland Indians, but also the fictional version depicted in the film *Major League*. All the movie's spring training scenes—including the memorable one where Rick "Wild Thing" Vaughn arrives from the California Penal League—were filmed at Hi Corbett.

The Cactus League has come a long way from its humble beginnings at Hi Corbett Field. Half of the thirty MLB teams now train in Arizona, drawing 1.9 million fans per year and boosting the state's economy by an estimated $579 million annually. Unfortunately, Hi Corbett became a victim of that success, as teams eventually decided to play all spring training games in the Phoenix area rather than busing an extra ninety minutes to Tucson. Hi Corbett Field hosted its final spring training game in 2010. It now serves as the home baseball field for the University of Arizona Wildcats.

TOP: Willie Mays Hayes and Rick Vaughn—played by actors Wesley Snipes and Charlie Sheen—were two of the ne'er-do-well Cleveland Indians in *Major League*. The film company encouraged Tusconians to fill the stands during filming at Hi Corbett Field so they could be used as extras. Years later, Sheen admitted using steroids during the shoot to improve his pitching velocity. "My fastball went from 79 to like 85," he said.

BOTTOM: After Hi Corbett Field was abandoned by pro baseball in 2010, it became the home field for the University of Arizona. It wasn't the first time the school's team played there, as Wildcats players had the non-speaking roles when *Major League* was filmed at Hi Corbett in 1989.

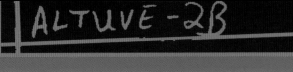

ASTRODOME

TEAM: Houston Astros (1965–1999)

NAME: Harris County Domed Stadium

NICKNAME: The Eighth Wonder of the World

LOCATION: 8400 Kirby Dr., Houston

FIRST MLB GAME: April 12, 1965

LAST MLB GAME: October 9, 1999 (NL Division Series Game 4)

NOTABLE FEATURES: First domed and air-conditioned stadium in MLB history; one of the most extreme pitchers' parks of all time; host of marquee events in football, basketball, and tennis.

MINUTE MAID PARK

TEAM: Houston Astros (2000–present)

NAMES: Enron Field (2000–2002), Astros Field (2002), Minute Maid Park (2002–present)

NICKNAME: The Juice Box

LOCATION: Corner of Texas Ave. and Preston St., Houston

FIRST MLB GAME: April 7, 2000

NOTABLE FEATURES: Retractable roof; historic railroad station incorporated into ballpark's structure; steep embankment in center field known as Tal's Hill.

The most famous ballpark of the recent past, Houston's Astrodome holds a vaunted place as the only ballpark ever billed as "the Eighth Wonder of the World"—and perhaps for good reason, as the US's first domed, air-conditioned stadium and the namesake of AstroTurf. But Houston's baseball history extends much further back than the Astros. In 1884, a group of Houston businessmen decided that their growing city needed a proper ballpark. (After all, with 16,000 residents, Houston was now almost as big as its larger neighbor to the south, Galveston). Called Fair Grounds Park, but known colloquially as Herald Park after the semipro team that played there, it brought barnstorming major league teams to Texas, and soon a full-fledged minor league team was founded. In 1905, it was replaced by West End Park, a wooden grandstand with 2,500 seats located in Freedmen's Town, a section of the Fourth Ward founded by freed slaves after the Civil War. The Houston Buffaloes—named after Buffalo Bayou, which bisected the city—played there, as did a number of early African-American teams. West End Park partially burned in 1911 and later had its roof blown off by a hurricane. In 1928 it was replaced by the 14,000-seat Buffalo Stadium located 2 miles southeast of downtown, which would turn out to be Houston's longest-lasting minor league park.

Houston finally landed a major league team in 1962, named the Colt .45s for three seasons while the state-of-the-art Astrodome was being built. In an era when many games were still played in the afternoon, major league baseball at Colt Stadium never could have worked. Everyone everyone suffered in the summer heat and humidity—except the giant mosquitoes Dodgers pitcher Sandy Koufax once described as "twin-engine jobs." Everyone breathed a sigh of relief when the team moved into the innovative new Astrodome, and although it spawned many imitators and ushered in a new era of stadium architecture, the 'Dome grew obsolete by the late 1990s, when the Astros abandoned it to hop on the retro-ballpark bandwagon, moving into Enron Field, now known as Minute Maid Park. ●

THIS PAGE: The stands are packed and the parking lot is full for a game at Colt Stadium in the early 1960s, as the round footprint of the under-construction Astrodome begins to take shape across the parking lot. Seeing all the grassland and wide-open space in this photo is jarring for anyone familiar with modern-day Houston, as the entire area is now a fully urbanized part of America's fourth-largest city.

OPPOSITE PAGE: The cavernous Astrodome featured the latest in modern conveniences, including opulent office space, cushioned seats, fifty-three luxury boxes, and a $2 million scoreboard that entertained fans with baseball-themed cartoons. Most importantly, it was fully air-conditioned, a necessity for fans trying to escape Houston's sweltering heat.

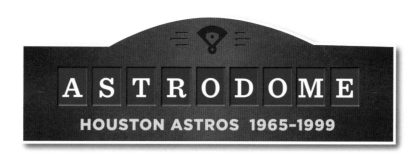

ASTRODOME
HOUSTON ASTROS 1965-1999

WHILE HOUSTON ENDURED three seasons at dank Colt Stadium, the team laid plans for what they called "The Eighth Wonder of the World." The Astrodome opened in 1965 as the first domed stadium ever built, and it rocketed the team from tenth in the National League in attendance to second. Over the next few decades, it became America's most prestigious venue for sporting events and beyond, hosting football and basketball games, rodeos, tennis matches, and several events that would play an important role in American history.

In the 1960s, Judge Roy Hofheinz, a flamboyant ex-mayor, was Houston's most visible political figure and one of its most ardent sports fans. In 1960, he and his partner, oil mogul Craig Cullinan Jr., were awarded an expansion National League franchise (to begin play in 1962) based on the promise of delivering a new ballpark. Before the Dodgers had moved to Los Angeles, their owner, Walter O'Malley, had briefly considered building a domed stadium—designed by famed architect and inventor Buckminster Fuller, no less—in the heart of

Brooklyn. But that dream never came to pass, and it took Hofheinz to finally build baseball's first indoor ballpark. Hofheinz's baseball team, meanwhile, needed a futuristic name to match its futuristic stadium. Although *Colts* seemed the perfect nickname for a Texas team— with a triple meaning of horses, guns, or beer—the team sought to embrace Houston's modern identity as the capital of America's space program. When the team changed ballparks in 1965, it also changed its name to the Houston Astros, leading the new stadium—which was officially known as the Harris County Domed Stadium—to be informally dubbed the Astrodome.

Although the Astrodome was a huge hit, not everything was well-planned. The stadium's roof consisted of metal framework supporting panes of translucent Lucite, which, theoretically, at least, would allow light to shine through and grass to grow on the field. But the Bermuda grass turned yellow and shriveled almost from the get-go. From the moment the park opened, fielders also complained about blinding

reflections from the roof, which made catching pop flies a hazardous adventure. After a year under these conditions, the Astros solved the problem by replacing the grass with a synthetic plastic grass invented by the Monsanto Corporation—it soon became known as AstroTurf. The ceiling panels were also replaced with more opaque versions that blocked sunlight, requiring the team to dramatically increase lighting. In its new incarnation, the Astrodome devoured as much electricity as an average 9,000-person city.

The stadium's gigantic dimensions, combined with the artificial lighting, served to severely depress hitting. The 390-foot power alleys,

TOP: A view from the Astrodome's left field stands in 1968, the "Year of the Pitcher," during which teams scored an average of just 3.4 runs per game there. The Dome was considered one of the most extreme pitchers' parks ever built, decreasing offense by as much as 18 percent during some seasons. This photo was taken the same year the Astrodome hosted college basketball's "Game of the Century," in which Elvin Hayes and the Houston Cougars defeated Lew Alcindor's UCLA Bruins, 71-69, in a game attended by a record 52,693 fans.

BOTTOM LEFT: The Astrodome was a sweetheart deal for the powerful Judge Roy Hofheinz, who paid the county $750,000 per year to rent the stadium, which included full subleasing rights. Shown here at the groundbreaking of the stadium on January 3, 1962, the judge even went so far as to have a luxurious apartment built for himself in the right field stands. Over the stadium's forty-year lease, Hofheinz and his company, the Houston Sports Association, would make a mint subleasing the stadium to anyone who needed a large venue and was willing to pay for it.

BOTTOM RIGHT: A member of the Astrodome's grounds crew chats with a stadium usher during the 1960s, both of them wearing kitschy costumes as ordered by Judge Roy Hofheinz. Between innings the space-suited grounds crew dragged the infield dirt using traditional push brooms, then used vacuum cleaners to tidy up the carpeted portions. The Astrodome's 150 ushers, meanwhile, were dubbed Triggerettes, and were the first female ushers in baseball. Their uniforms were designed by a pair of local fashion designers, Evelyn Norton Anderson and Iris Stiff.

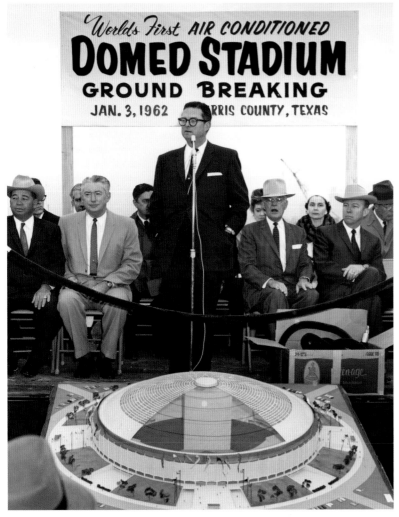

the longest in the league, were where fly balls went to die. Although the Astros of the '60s and '70s featured such outstanding batters as Jimmy Wynn, Joe Morgan, and César Cedeño, the park deflated their hitting stats and made them look less outstanding than they really were. This in turn led Astros management to misunderstand the ability of its own players and to trade many of them, including Morgan, for pennies on the dollar. For pitchers, conversely, the Astrodome was a dream come true. Larry Dierker, Houston's franchise pitcher, was a case in point. In neutral stadiums, Dierker was a mediocre hurler, posting a 50-70 lifetime record with a 4.04 ERA. At home in the 'Dome, however, Dierker was an ace, going 89-53 with a 2.73 ERA. In 1969, Houston became the first major league team to have its pitching staff strike out 1,000 batters in a season. Astros pitchers also hurled six no-hitters here over the park's thirty-five years, including Nolan Ryan's record-breaking fifth in 1981.

From the very beginning, Hofheinz had envisioned the Astrodome as America's premier multipurpose facility, and that is exactly what it became. In 1968, the Houston Oilers of the American Football League moved in, and would remain tenants until moving to Tennessee in 1997. From 1968 to 2003, the 'Dome hosted the Houston Livestock Show and Rodeo, advertised as the second-largest rodeo in the world.

In 1968, it was the site for college basketball's "Game of the Century," the first college basketball game ever to be televised nationally. Over the years, it also hosted University of Houston football, the Bluebonnet Bowl football game, six concerts on Elvis Presley's comeback tour, the 1971 NCAA Final Four, professional soccer, and innumerable other events. One of these was the most famous tennis match of all time, the 1973 "Battle of the Sexes" in which Billie Jean King defeated Bobby Riggs. In 1992, the Astrodome was even the site of the Republican National Convention, which forced the Astros to play twenty-six consecutive road games. In 2005, after the Astros had moved to Minute Maid Park, the stadium became the primary destination for victims evacuated from New Orleans after Hurricane Katrina, serving as a temporary shelter for about 25,000 evacuees for two weeks.

By then, alas, the world's first domed ballpark was a relic no longer being used by any major sports team. The futuristic stadiums of the '60s had fallen out of favor as fans realized that, for all their convenience and practicality, they were sterile and drab places to watch games. In 2000, the team kept the name of their eponymous park but moved into the retro-style Enron Field. The Astrodome has stood vacant since, hosting nothing more than an occasional high school football game. Its future remains in limbo. 🖎

The Astrodome had about 30,000 parking spaces, many of them built on top of what had once been Colt Stadium. The building measured 710 feet in diameter, covered 9.5 acres, and was 208 feet tall, high enough to fit a 20-story skyscraper inside.

IN 1996, AS THEIR NFL TEAM PREPARED to move to Tennessee, Houstonians took action to save their beloved Astros from a similar fate. Voters approved a $250 million baseball-only stadium, which, like other retro ballparks, was marked by both throwback architecture and ultramodern luxuries. Despite going by three different names in its first three seasons, Minute Maid Park quickly became a favorite of Astros fans and a centerpiece in the revitalization of downtown Houston.

The stadium project was deeply intertwined with the soon-to-be-disgraced Enron Corporation, the Bush political family, and the infamous Halliburton Corporation, of which future vice president Dick Cheney was CEO. The contract to construct the ballpark was awarded to a Halliburton subsidiary, and by using partially non-union labor, they were able to finish the project on time and $2 million under budget. The appreciative Astros placed a plaque with Cheney's photograph outside the stadium's entrance gate.

Enron, the energy conglomerate, paid $100 million to name the stadium Enron Field. In 2001, however, Enron imploded amid a scandal in which the company's executives used accounting trickery to line their own pockets, robbing thousands of Americans of their pensions. With the Enron name an embarrassment, the Astros tried to remove the name from their stadium, but the company refused, noting that its payments were still being made on time. The Astros ended up paying Enron $2.1 million for the right to sell the stadium name to someone else. That someone else turned out to be the Coca-Cola Company, which paid $170 million over twenty-eight years to name the stadium Minute Maid Park after one of its subsidiaries.

Minute Maid Park received generally favorable reviews. Perhaps its most important asset was air conditioning, which provided relief from the brutal Houston heat. The Crawford Boxes, a popular seating section behind the left field fence, sat only 316 feet away from home

plate, providing fans with a prime opportunity to catch home run balls. (In order to build these seats, the Astros had to get special permission exempting them from the MLB rule that requires all outfield fences to be at least 325 feet away.) Its bandbox dimensions made Minute Maid Park one of the most notoriously hitter-friendly parks in the game, boosting offense by 14 percent over the average ballpark during its debut season. Strangely, though, that effect dissipated over time for reasons that are not entirely clear. By 2017, Minute Maid Park had swung to the other extreme, becoming a severe pitcher's park that reduced offense by 18 percent.

Union Station, a classical-revival train station built in 1911, sat just behind the left field wall on the stadium site. Instead of tearing down the historic structure, HOK's design cleverly turned it into the ballpark's main entrance gate. As a tribute to the site's railroad heritage, a replica locomotive was mounted on tracks behind the left field wall, tooting its horn whenever an Astro hit a home run. Because high walls mandated by the retractable roof blocked views of the city skyline, the vista of Union Station was the park's most impressive aesthetic feature. However, this view was destroyed in 2015 when the team plastered Union Station with a dozen giant billboards, rendering the historic building virtually invisible and greatly harming the ballpark's atmosphere.

For many years, Minute Maid Park's most controversial feature was a large hill at the base of the center field wall, dubbed "Tal's Hill" because it was reputedly the brainchild of team executive Tal Smith. The hill was a throwback to Cincinnati's Crosley Field and Boston's Fenway Park, both of which had famous embankments in front of their left field fences. Fans liked the hill, but outfielders hated climbing the thirty-degree slope, and over the years it became a constant target of player gripes. Tal's Hill was finally removed in 2016, and the following year the Astros won the first World Series title in franchise history.

OPPOSITE PAGE: Minute Maid Park as seen during a 2004 Astros-Mets game, with Mike Piazza playing first base for New York. On this night Houston's notoriously muggy weather was apparently mild enough to keep the retractable roof open, which always makes for a better atmosphere. The Crawford Boxes, the bleachers behind the left field scoreboard, are some of the most coveted seats in the ballpark because they provide the best opportunity to catch home run balls. The arched doorways behind the Crawford Boxes are part of Union Station, the 1911 train station which was cleverly incorporated into the ballpark's design. In 2015, however, the lovely view seen here was destroyed by the placement of twelve large billboards that obscure most of the historic building from sight.

THIS PAGE: José Altuve, Houston's 5-foot-6 dynamo, celebrates after scoring the winning run on Carlos Correa's walk-off double in Game 2 of the 2017 American League Championship Series. The Astros captured their first World Series title by winning two dramatic seven-game series against two of baseball's most prestigious teams, the Yankees and the Dodgers. Game 5 of the World Series at Minute Maid Park was an instant classic, with the Astros winning despite blowing a three-run lead in the ninth. (The Dodgers went one better, blowing a three-run lead and a four-run lead.) "It's the greatest game I've ever been part of," Astros pitcher Brad Peacock said afterward. "The greatest game I ever watched. You're watching it and you're thinking, 'God dang, this is crazy.'"

Birmingham, Alabama

A Storied Field Charmingly Restored

In 1909, a young boy vivant named Rick Woodward, whose family ran the Alabama Iron Company, became fascinated by the innovative steel and concrete ballparks opened that year in Philadelphia and Pittsburgh. In a move that exasperated his parents, the youthful heir decided to buy his hometown's minor league team, the Birmingham Barons, and build them a new steel and concrete ballpark. Woodward not only modeled his stadium after Forbes Field and Shibe Park; he actually visited Philadelphia to meet with A's co-owner Connie Mack and get his advice on the field dimensions.

Rickwood Field opened in the summer of 1910. With a pricetag of just $75,000, Rickwood didn't compare to Forbes or Shibe in terms of size, but it was the grandest ballpark ever seen south of the Mason-Dixon Line. It sported a redbrick exterior, a green steel roof, and a pagoda-style tower behind home plate. Rickwood's distinctive hand-operated scoreboard, with its clock face and rounded top, was in place by 1929 and seems to have served as the model for the iconic scoreboard installed at Wrigley Field in 1937.

Rickwood's stands were segregated whenever the all-white Birmingham Barons were playing, but during Negro League games it provided a vibrant sense of community for African-American fans. The Birmingham Black Barons played there for four decades, winning back-to-back pennants in 1943 and '44. "The Black Barons were at once a source of deep pride for the city's growing Negro population and a defiant rejection of the racist imagery of blacks as simpletons or savages," the historian James Hirsch wrote.

In 1948, the Black Barons granted a tryout to a local youngster who'd grown up watching the team play. Manager Piper Davis couldn't believe his eyes when he saw what the young man—a sixteen-year-old named Willie Mays—could do on the diamond. Mays quickly became a star, especially among Rickwood Field's female fans, who showered him with pennies whenever he did something spectacular. Just a high school sophomore, Mays was only allowed to play home games so he wouldn't miss school during road trips.

In 1987, after seventy-eight years as Birmingham's primary baseball venue, Rickwood closed when the Double-A Barons moved to the suburbs. In 1992, an organization called Friends of Rickwood raised $2 million to preserve the ballpark, and many of its features have been restored to the

way they appeared in 1910. Rickwood still hosts some 200 ballgames a year, including youth games, high school tournaments, and one Double-A game per season, billed as the Rickwood Classic. Fans are immersed in an old-time baseball experience, complete with obstructed-view seating, vintage outfield billboards for long-defunct companies, and umpires wearing dress shirts and bow ties. As the Friends of Rickwood's website says, "Our dream is for Rickwood Field to be a working museum, a place to actually see and experience baseball as it once was."

TOP: This painstaking replica of Rickwood Field's iconic scoreboard was installed by the preservation group Friends of Rickwood, replacing an electronic version from the 1970s. Rickwood's original hand-operated scoreboard, nearly identical to the one seen here, was on the left field wall by at least 1929, and perhaps even earlier than that. It may have served as an inspiration for the famous scoreboard installed at Wrigley Field a few years later (seen on page 153).

MIDDLE: Rickwood Field's exterior appearance has changed very little since its opening in 1910, although a small tower that once flew the American flag was removed somewhere along the way. The Spanish tile roof seen here was perhaps inspired by D.W. Griffith's 1910 short film *Ramona*, set in 1840s California, which sparked a nationwide craze in mission-style architecture.

BOTTOM: Rickwood Field's light standards, erected in 1936, are like no others in baseball, with the towers cantilevered so that they actually hang over the playing field.

ATLANTA

ATLANTA-FULTON COUNTY STADIUM

TEAM: Atlanta Braves (1966–1996)

NAMES: Atlanta Stadium (1966–1975), Atlanta-Fulton County Stadium (1976–1997)

NICKNAME: The Launching Pad

LOCATION: Corner of Georgia Ave. SE and Pollard Blvd. SW, Atlanta

FIRST MLB GAME: April 12, 1966

LAST MLB GAME: October 24, 1996 (World Series Game 5)

NOTABLE FEATURES: Batted balls carried far due to heat and elevation; site of Hank Aaron's record-breaking 715th home run on April 8, 1974; unique outfield bleachers hung directly over the playing field.

TURNER FIELD

TEAM: Atlanta Braves (1997–2016)

NAMES: Centennial Olympic Stadium (1996), Turner Field (1997–2016), Georgia State Stadium (2017–present)

LOCATION: Corner of Pollard Blvd. SW and Bill Lucas Dr. SW, Atlanta

FIRST MLB GAME: April 4, 1997

LAST MLB GAME: October 2, 2016

NOTABLE FEATURES: Retrofitted as a baseball stadium after use in 1996 Olympics; fans doing the controversial Tomahawk Chop.

SUNTRUST PARK

TEAM: Atlanta Braves (2017–present)

LOCATION: 755 Battery Avenue, Cobb County

FIRST MLB GAME: April 14, 2017

NOTABLE FEATURES: Suburban office park setting; surrounded by several acres of team-owned businesses.

DITCH THE DISH save $400
1-800-COMCAST   comcast

45 MARTINEZ
ERA 3.72

Balls   15
Strikes   31
Total   46

BUD LIGHT

Though the tale of Union soldiers spreading baseball throughout the South during the Civil War is probably more legend than fact, Atlanta's first known baseball game took place in 1866, just two years after General William Tecumseh Sherman burned the city. In a game played near today's Oakland Cemetery, a club called Gate City defeated Atlanta, 127-29. The humiliated Atlanta team disbanded after the game. Two decades later, though, minor league baseball arrived in the form of the Atlanta Crackers, who played at a series of five small wooden ballparks between 1884 and 1906.

In 1907, the Crackers opened Ponce de Leon Park, which would become a beloved local landmark and one of minor league baseball's crown jewels. Built across the street from an amusement park also called Ponce de Leon Park, the ballpark was notable for its lack of a center field fence. Instead of a wall, there was a grassy berm with a large magnolia tree that was actually in play. Over the fifty-eight seasons that baseball was played at Ponce, it was said that only two batters—Babe Ruth and Eddie Mathews—ever hit the tree on the fly.

In 1923, Ponce de Leon Park caught fire in the middle of the night and the all-wood structure burned to the ground in just fifteen minutes. A new $250,000 version, this time built of steel and concrete, opened the next season. In this version of Ponce, the left field fence was actually a long hedgerow, and behind it was a section of bleachers, which was the only place African-American fans were allowed to sit. Nevertheless, the local Negro League team—contradictorily named the Black Crackers—used Ponce as its home field for years.

Ponce became obsolete in 1966 when the Milwaukee Braves arrived and moved into the multipurpose Atlanta Stadium, where Hank Aaron became a local hero. In 1997, the Braves moved to Turner Field, staying there for a twenty-year jaunt before building SunTrust Park north of town in Cobb County. Though pro baseball is no longer played in the city of Atlanta, and Ponce de Leon Park has been torn down for half a century, its famous magnolia tree is still standing. It's now behind the loading dock of a Home Depot.

INSET: Babe Ruth, late in his Yankees career, takes a big swing during an exhibition game at Ponce de Leon Park. This photo probably dates from April 1934, when New York came to town for two exhibitions against the Crackers, winning by scores of 18-9 and 10-5. It may have been the first time Georgians actually enjoyed seeing a bunch of Yankees run roughshod over Atlanta.

Ponce de Leon Park as it appeared around 1956, when it was in its final few years as home of the Atlanta Crackers. The huge building looming behind the grandstand was the southeastern headquarters of Sears, Roebuck and Company, built in 1926 on the site of the former Ponce de Leon amusement park. Today, this historic 10-story building has been repurposed as Ponce City Market, where one can lease office space, shop at upscale stores, or dine on food from around the world. The building's rooftop offers an outstanding panoramic view of Atlanta.

ATLANTA STADIUM, AT JUST OVER a thousand feet above sea level, had the highest altitude of any major league ballpark when it opened in 1966. After never having major league sports, Georgia hit the big time when it landed both an NFL franchise, the Falcons, and an MLB team, the Braves. In 1964, construction began on an $18 million stadium for them to share. Like most multipurpose stadiums, Atlanta Stadium was drab and unrepresentative of its locale—once inside, you could be anywhere. Unlike most of the others, though, Atlanta's at least had real grass. The seating bowl fit about 52,000 for baseball and 60,000 for football, almost all of whom were far away from the action.

Atlanta Stadium quickly became known as "The Launching Pad" thanks to the fly balls that flew over its fences with great frequency. This hitter-friendliness fueled the late-career renaissance of Hank Aaron, enabling him to make a run at Babe Ruth's career home run record. On April 8, 1974, the park was packed for one of baseball's most indelible moments, as Aaron hit homer number 715 to pass the Babe. After Aaron's departure, though, the Braves sank into a morass that saw them finish last eight times in fifteen miserable seasons. In 1991, the franchise finally began to emerge from the ashes. During the stadium's final seasons, when it was known as Atlanta-Fulton County Stadium, it became home to a dynasty the likes of which had never been seen. Led by a pitching staff that writer Bill James called "probably the best in the history of baseball," the Braves appeared in four World Series during the ballpark's final six seasons, winning a title in 1995.

Atlanta-Fulton County Stadium was a prototypical example of the 1960s multi-purpose stadiums. It was designed by a pair of prominent Atlanta architects, Bill Finch and Cecil Alexander. "Bill considered the Atlanta-Fulton County Stadium his finest work," Alexander said when Finch died in 2003. "Even so, he didn't make a fuss when it was torn down.... Bill was a modernist. His hallmarks were functionality and simple, clean lines."

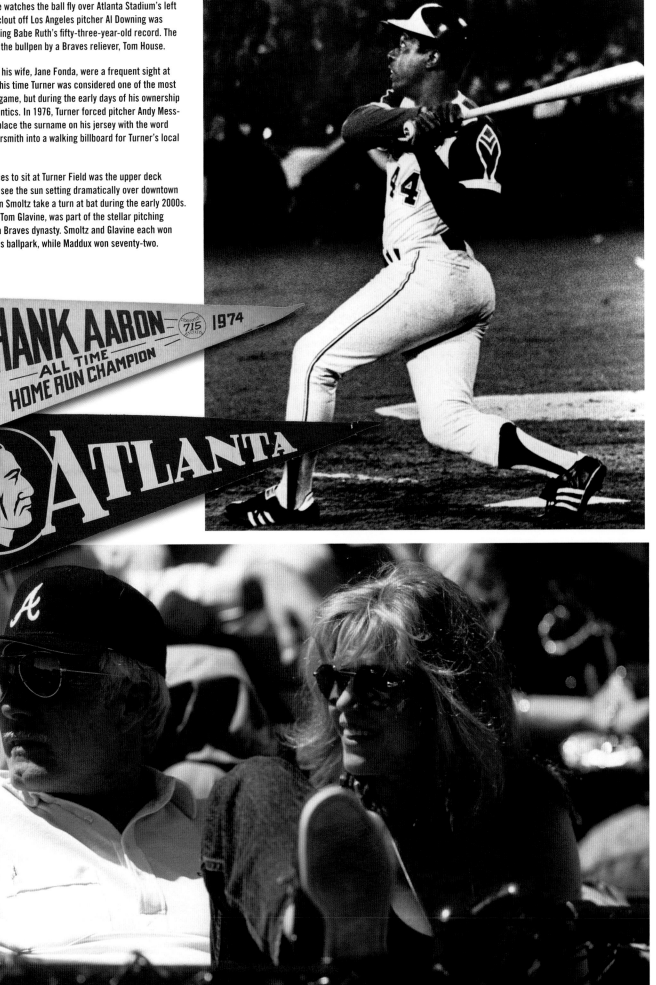

TOP: Hank Aaron looks skyward as he watches the ball fly over Atlanta Stadium's left field fence on April 8, 1974. Aaron's clout off Los Angeles pitcher Al Downing was the 715th homer of his career, breaking Babe Ruth's fifty-three-year-old record. The historic home run ball was caught in the bullpen by a Braves reliever, Tom House.

BOTTOM: Team owner Ted Turner and his wife, Jane Fonda, were a frequent sight at Braves games during the 1990s. By this time Turner was considered one of the most competent and stable owners in the game, but during the early days of his ownership he was notorious for his outlandish antics. In 1976, Turner forced pitcher Andy Messersmith (who wore number 17) to replace the surname on his jersey with the word "channel" — thereby turning Messersmith into a walking billboard for Turner's local TV station, Channel 17.

OPPOSITE PAGE: One of the best places to sit at Turner Field was the upper deck behind home plate, where one could see the sun setting dramatically over downtown Atlanta. These fans are watching John Smoltz take a turn at bat during the early 2000s. Smoltz, along with Greg Maddux and Tom Glavine, was part of the stellar pitching trio that formed the cornerstone of a Braves dynasty. Smoltz and Glavine each won fifty-two regular season games in this ballpark, while Maddux won seventy-two.

TURNER FIELD

ATLANTA BRAVES 1997-2016

WHEN IT COMES TO BUILDING BALLPARKS, following the lead of the Montreal Expos is usually not a good idea. But that's what Atlanta did in 1996, taking a stadium built for the Olympics—which otherwise would have stood as a white elephant—and retrofitting it for baseball. This move had backfired on the Expos in 1976, when Stade Olympique turned out to be not only a bad stadium but also a boondoggle of staggering proportions. Atlanta learned from Montreal's mistakes, though, and Centennial Olympic Stadium was transformed into an enjoyable, if generic, place to watch a baseball game. It served as the Braves' home field for exactly two decades before the team fled the city of Atlanta for the suburbs.

When Atlanta won its bid to host the 1996 Summer Games, the news coincided nicely with the Braves' desire to replace the aging Atlanta-Fulton County Stadium. The Olympics required the building of a new stadium, and plans were announced to turn the facility over to the Braves once the Games were over. It was a coup for team owner Ted Turner, who got a brand-new ballpark constructed almost entirely with money provided by the Atlanta Committee for the Olympic Games. It would be located across the parking lot from the Braves' existing stadium, less than a mile south of downtown Atlanta. Even better for Turner, the building's name would be changed to Turner Field.

To accommodate the oval-shaped field necessary for the Olympics, no permanent outfield seats were initially built. One end of the long oval was located approximately where the first-base dugout would later be. A stand of temporary bleachers, to be torn down after the Games ended, was erected at the other end of the oval, in what would soon be deep left-center field. The bleachers raised the park's capacity to the 85,000 required to meet Olympic demands. In addition to sold-out crowds for the opening and closing ceremonies, the stadium also hosted the track and field competition, in which Carl Lewis won a gold medal in the long jump and Michael Johnson did the same in the 200- and 400-meter races.

When the Olympics were over, the temporary stands were demolished and work began on finishing the baseball portion in time for the 1997 season. Additions included outfield bleachers, a video board, and a gigantic Coca-Cola bottle placed as an advertisement for Atlanta's best-known corporation. A grand entrance plaza in the outfield included the team's main ticket office, as well as statues of Braves legends like Hank Aaron.

Inside, the park featured 28,000 seats at field level, 6,000 at club level, and just 15,000 in an upper deck that was very close to the action. This non-wraparound top deck also meant that a fantastic view of the Atlanta skyline could be seen beyond center field. Though Turner Field attempted to adopt a retro style, this effect was undermined by the colossal amount of advertising, which inundated the senses. It seemed the Braves would slap an ad on anything, including the foreheads of fans who stood still for too long.

More than any of its physical features, Turner Field became famous for its rapacious concession prices. A hot dog cost $6 and a small soda $3.50, prices so steep that even the team owner criticized them. According to the Fan Cost Index—a calculation representing the average cost of attending a game, including parking and concessions—a family of four attending a Braves game in 1997 could expect to pay $129.16, the highest total in baseball. (By comparison, the cheapest stadium, in Montreal, cost only $80.42.) Turner Field was also one of the few stadiums to prohibit fans from bringing their own food, although this policy was rescinded after a public outcry.

The Braves club that moved into Turner in 1997 was in the middle of a full-blown dynasty, enjoying one of the greatest stretches of sustained success the sport had ever seen. However, Atlantans, always more devoted to football than baseball, never showed up to the park in significant numbers. From 2001 through 2005—the last five years in the Braves' record streak of eleven straight first-place finishes—their attendance became an embarrassment, ranking as low as tenth in the National League. Even more astonishingly, they often failed to sell out their playoff games. The dynasty collapsed in 2006, and by the time the Braves played their final game at Turner Field a decade later, they had become perennial also-rans.

Chipper Jones, who collected the first-ever hit at Turner Field in 1997, bats there against rookie phenom Stephen Strasburg in 2010. The switch-hitting Jones smacked 226 career home runs at Turner, far more than any other batter in the park's history. His most memorable homer may have been his final one, when he bid adieu to Braves fans with a three-run, walk-off blast on September 2, 2012. "It was a spine-tingling moment," he told the *Atlanta Journal-Constitution*. "I can't tell you how many times in [the] years since I've been retired I've gone through the archives and kind of relived that moment."

SUNTRUST PARK

ATLANTA BRAVES 2017-PRESENT

TURNER FIELD WAS CUSTOM-BUILT to the Braves' needs, but by 2013, the team was absurdly claiming the sixteen-year-old stadium was outdated and they needed a new one. In reality, it seems the Braves just wanted to follow their fan base, which was gradually fleeing the Atlanta city limits for wealthier, whiter enclaves north of town. The Braves found a willing victim in Cobb County, a suburban community whose government gave the team the ultra-sweetheart deal it was seeking. "While a new stadium built with more high-priced revenue generating seats and suites is likely half-responsible for this decision, the other half is the shifted population center for the region, especially when one considers that most of the money is located in the northern suburbs," the Braves blog Chop County wrote. "The name for this new stadium should be 'White Flight Field.'"

SunTrust Park opened in 2017, but any talk about its merits as a ballpark was wholly superseded by the controversy over its seedy origins. Even in an era when ballpark funding deals are routinely coercive and deceptive, the Braves' wheelings and dealings were shadier than most. Several journalism outlets launched investigations of the deal, including a piece by *Vice Sports* titled: "Cobb County and the Braves: Worst Sports Stadium Deal Ever?" The outlets' reporting cast both

the team and Cobb officials in a poor light. On multiple occasions, for instance, illegal conferences were held in hallways to get around open-meetings laws. The Braves even snookered the county into passing a law outlawing all private parking lots except for those owned by the team. (That particular ordinance was so blatantly corrupt, however, that public outrage forced its rescission.)

The Braves themselves were less interested in the new ballpark than in the many auxiliary businesses on vast tracts of team-owned land surrounding the stadium. After SunTrust Park opened, fans could stay in an Omni Hotel next door, rent an on-site apartment for $3,300 per month, attend a movie, or shop at a seemingly endless number of retail outlets—all ventures owned, at least in part, by the team. In the end, the county official who had violated ethics laws by negotiating a secret backroom deal was booted from office by voters before SunTrust Park even opened. Meanwhile, the ballpark itself turned out to be an aggressively generic structure hardly worth all the trouble it caused. If you're a Braves fan wanting to enjoy a day at the park, it will do the job...you just might have to visit that magnolia tree behind the Home Depot for a real dose of Atlanta's baseball history. ◼

SunTrust Park, essentially a corporate office park with a baseball field hidden inside, opened in 2017 to mixed reviews.

North Carolina

Three Memorable Minor League Stadiums

When it first opened in 1926, Durham Athletic Park (known then as El Toro Park) was a simple wooden ballpark with a small roof, its grounds dotted with trees. But a feat of engineering had made it possible: South Ellerbe Creek had been rerouted underground, directly underneath the pitcher's mound, where it still flows today, under the home baseball field for North Carolina Central University.

After a 1939 fire, DAP was rebuilt with steel and concrete, and later given six light towers (oddly, all of which were located on the field of play, two of them in fair territory). With a distinctive conical tower housing the ticket office, the structure would be home of the Durham Bulls for more than fifty years, until they moved across town to a bigger field in 1995.

In 1988, DAP reached a new level of fame with the release of *Bull Durham*, the classic comedy by filmmaker Ron Shelton, a former minor league ballplayer. Just like in the movie, "the goings-on at this park were legendary in their goofiness," the historian Michael Benson wrote, citing the example of a fan who brought a live chicken to every game. Its memorable giant snorting-bull billboard on the outfield wall was a prop created specifically for the film, but it was based on a real-life outfield ad campaign from 1912 for Bull Durham tobacco (although the bulls didn't snort). It remained in place for years after the Hollywood crew left town.

Another ballpark that makes a cameo in *Bull Durham* is McCormick Field in Asheville—where Kevin Costner's Crash Davis breaks the home run record—albeit a previous, wooden version. Shockingly, the antique wooden grandstand sur-

vived until 1992, when McCormick Field was finally rebuilt in steel and concrete. One of the most picturesque ballparks in the minor leagues, McCormick Field was carved out of a hillside in the beautiful Blue Ridge Mountains in 1924, when Asheville was one of America's great tourist destinations and teams like the Yankees would come down to play exhibition games. Babe Ruth, who once declared McCormick Field the prettiest ballpark in America, suffered his infamous "bellyache heard 'round the world" here, collapsing at the Asheville train station. He spent seven weeks in the hospital due to an ulcer, overeating, or venereal disease (depending on whom you believe).

Even in McCormick Field's newer incarnation, its laid-back atmosphere and small-town charm make it seem like you could be watching a game in 1954, or even 1924. "There is a certain sense of timelessness at a[n Asheville] Tourists game," Kevin Reichard wrote for *Ballpark Digest*. "Watching the crowd I got the sense that a baseball game was a true community activity: Folks were continually running into old and new friends."

Across North Carolina, another minor league ballpark with an intimate atmosphere is nestled into its environs: BB&T Ballpark in Uptown Charlotte. Efforts to build the $55 million ballpark had been derailed by legal wrangling and political bickering for a decade, but it proved worth the wait: The delays gave the team's vice president, Dan Rajkowski, time to visit minor league parks across the country, notebook and camera in hand, documenting the best and worst aspects of each. When the park opened in 2014 (finally giving Charlotte a baseball stadium in addition to the homes for their NBA and NFL teams), *Baseball America* named it the best minor league stadium in the country and *Charlotte* magazine deemed it "Charlottean of the Year"—despite it not being an actual person. 🔺

OPPOSITE PAGE, TOP: Ebby Calvin "Nuke" LaLoosh (played by Tim Robbins) argues with Crash Davis (Kevin Costner) at Durham Athletic Park in the 1988 classic *Bull Durham*. The film, loved for both its realism and its humor, was named the best sports movie of all time by ESPN.

OPPOSITE PAGE, BOTTOM: The concourse of historic Durham Athletic Park as it appeared in 1992, four years after it found Hollywood fame.

LEFT: One of the best aspects of BB&T Ballpark is the view it provides of Charlotte's skyline. During its debut season in 2014, nearly 688,000 fans streamed through the gates, making it the best-attended stadium in minor league baseball.

TOP RIGHT: Asheville's McCormick Field in late autumn, dusted with snow after the end of baseball season. Visible behind it are the historic buildings of Asheville, which attracted so many vacationers during the early 1900s that the local team was named the Tourists.

BOTTOM RIGHT: In Asheville, as at most minor league ballparks, the seats directly behind home plate are usually occupied by an army of scouts wielding radar guns.

ARLINGTON

⚾ ARLINGTON STADIUM

TEAM: Texas Rangers (1972–1993)

NAMES: Turnpike Stadium (1965–1971), Arlington Stadium (1972–1994)

LOCATION: Corner of S. Copeland Rd. and Pennant Dr., Arlington

FIRST MLB GAME: April 21, 1972

LAST MLB GAME: October 3, 1993

NOTABLE FEATURES: Playing field sunken below ground level; largest bleacher sections in MLB; Texas-shaped scoreboard in left field.

⚾ GLOBE LIFE PARK IN ARLINGTON

TEAM: Texas Rangers (1994–2019)

NAMES: The Ballpark in Arlington (1994–2004), Ameriquest Field in Arlington (2004–2007), Rangers Ballpark in Arlington (2007–2014), Globe Life Park in Arlington (2014–present)

LOCATION: Corner of Nolan Ryan Expwy. and E. Road to Six Flags St., Arlington

FIRST MLB GAME: April 11, 1994

NOTABLE FEATURES: "Home Run Porch" in right field; white steel frieze around top of upper deck.

Though Dallasites and Fort Worthers now root together for the Rangers, they spent most of the twentieth century fighting it out in a heated local rivalry. Baseball competition between the two cities dates back to 1888, when the Dallas Hams and Fort Worth Panthers were both charter members of the Texas League. "The game is wholesome and manly barring occasional disfiguration of faces and fingers," the *Dallas News* wrote that year. The Hams won the league's first pennant playing their games at Gaston Park, a ballpark near the Texas State Fairgrounds that they would use for the next two decades. Fort Worth, meanwhile, played at Panther Park along the Trinity River, which was the area's first ballpark to have turnstiles and reserved seating.

The Dallas team—known at various times as the Submarines, Giants, Rebels, Steers, and Eagles—moved to a new facility, Gardner Park, in 1919. The park burned down five years later, but was rebuilt and lasted another forty-two years. Located on the Trinity River in Oak Cliff, fans in the stands could see the river flowing just behind the left field fence. Over in Fort Worth, meanwhile, the Panthers eventually changed their name to Fort Worth Cats and opened a new ballpark, LaGrave

Field, in 1926. Also located on the banks of the Trinity, it was considered one of the nicest parks in the minor leagues, and it was usually full, especially when Dallas was the opponent. "It was one hell of a rivalry," Dallas owner George Schepps once said. "In the '20s and '30s, we never got through a game without a fight."

After eight decades as enemies, the two cities joined forces in 1965 to build Turnpike Stadium in Arlington, halfway between Dallas and Fort Worth. Ostensibly built for a minor league team, the Dallas-Fort Worth Spurs, the real objective was to lure a major league club, which paid off in 1972 when the Washington Senators moved in and became the Texas Rangers. Turnpike was expanded and renamed Arlington Stadium. The Rangers later built two new stadiums on virtually the same site, one in 1994 and another scheduled to open in 2020.

In a surprise twist, the Fort Worth Cats reemerged in 2002 as an independent league team and built a new version of LaGrave Field on the same site as the old one. Alas, the team went out of business in 2014. LaGrave Field is now standing vacant, disfigured by graffiti and looted by thieves. It partially burned in 2017, casting its future into doubt.

The gorgeous Texas sunsets were one of the highlights of attending a game at Arlington Stadium, where the playing field was sunken 40 feet below street level. The lower grandstand seen here was a remnant from its days as a minor league ballpark, while the huge outfield bleacher sections and the upper deck behind home plate were both added afterward.

INSET: Arlington Stadium's most recognizable feature may have been its Texas-shaped scoreboard, which displayed mostly zeroes whenever Nolan Ryan was on the mound.

ARLINGTON STADIUM
Home of the TEXAS RANGERS

ARLINGTON STADIUM

ARLINGTON STADIUM

TEXAS RANGERS 1972-2003

THOUGH IT STARTED LIFE as a sleepy minor league park and ended up as a parking lot, Arlington Stadium witnessed its share of adventures during the three decades it housed the Texas Rangers. The Rangers were so comically awful during the 1970s that they became the subject of a sarcastic memoir—Mike Shropshire's *Seasons in Hell*—but by the time they moved out in 1994, they'd become a consistently winning team. More so than the team's accomplishments, though, Arlington Stadium is probably best remembered as the site of many of Nolan Ryan's finest moments.

In 1965, the Dallas–Fort Worth Metroplex's local minor league team moved into brand-new Turnpike Stadium. Built in the suburb of Arlington halfway between the two larger cities, Turnpike cost the city $1.5 million and held just over 10,000 fans. Its location adjacent to the popular amusement park Six Flags over Texas made it an attractive destination for families. In 1970, the city remodeled the five-year-

old stadium and doubled its capacity in hopes of landing a big league team. The move paid off when the Washington Senators moved to town and rebranded themselves the Texas Rangers. Most of the new seating was in the outfield, giving Arlington Stadium the largest bleacher section in the majors.

The Rangers transformed their image by signing Ryan, a native Texan, in 1989. That year at Arlington Stadium he recorded his 5,000th career strikeout, and in 1991, he pitched his seventh no-hitter. (He remains the only pitcher ever to accomplish either feat.) Ryan's signing made the Rangers vastly more popular, and the team soon added talented hitters like Juan González, Iván Rodríguez, and Rafael Palmeiro. Their success was such that in 1992, construction began on a dazzling new ballpark across the parking lot. The Rangers moved there in 1994, and Arlington Stadium was torn down shortly thereafter. 🍔

Teammates applaud during Nolan Ryan Appreciation Day ceremonies on September 12, 1993, after the last home start of the forty-six-year-old pitcher's career. The team presented Ryan, a noted cow puncher, with a pair of steers named Robin and Ventura. Ten days after this photo was taken, Ryan's elbow ligament snapped while delivering a pitch in Seattle, ending his career instantly.

THE TEXAS RANGERS' GORGEOUS Ballpark in Arlington was a benchmark in the retro-stadium era. As one of the first stadiums to open after Camden Yards, the Dallas-area ballpark sent a clear signal that the days of domes and artificial turf were gone for good. Although it was one of the finest stadiums in baseball, the financing scheme surrounding its creation was one of the more sordid tales in ballpark construction—a backroom bargain whose shamefulness was matched only by the deal made twenty years later that resulted in the ballpark's demise.

In the late 1980s, looking for a business accomplishment that he could tout in future political campaigns, George W. Bush decided to become a baseball owner. Bush spent $606,000, most of it borrowed, to buy a 1.8 percent stake in the Rangers. In return, his partners—who were more interested in his famous name than his business acumen—presented him to the public as the owner of the team. Bush set about accomplishing the task they'd hired him for: getting a new stadium built with taxpayers' money. First, he invoked the time-honored gambit of threatening to move the Rangers elsewhere unless they were given a new stadium. Properly cajoled, the city of Arlington agreed to con-

tribute $135 million. Despite vehement opposition from some, voters nonetheless approved the required sales tax hike in January 1991. "I was like a pit bull on the pant leg of opportunity," Bush later said.

The most lucrative part of the deal took place under the surface. "The idea of making a land play, that's kind of always been the strategy," Bush admitted. With 40,000 people a night coming to the area, the real estate bordering the park was ripe for lucrative development. All along, Bush and his partners had been quietly buying up land around the new ballpark site. Whenever an owner refused to sell, Bush simply directed the city of Arlington to seize the property using eminent domain, then turn it over to Bush and his partners. The end result was, as one economist put it, that "the largest welfare recipient in the state of Texas is George W. Bush."

Its silly name notwithstanding, the Ballpark in Arlington turned out to be a huge artistic and aesthetic success. (It was later given a succession of even sillier names, with the most recent being a mouthful: Globe Life Ballpark in Arlington.) However, while most retro ballparks have been emblematic of the neighborhoods they're in, the Ballpark in Arlington was not. Though located in suburbia, surrounded

THIS PAGE: George W. Bush (right) watches a game in the front row at Arlington Stadium with baseball commissioner Fay Vincent in 1990. Although Bush was presented to the public as the owner of the Rangers, that contained only a kernel of truth, as he actually owned just 1.8 percent of the team. This photo was taken one year after what Bush always lamented as the Rangers' worst move during his tenure: the trade of Sammy Sosa to the White Sox in 1989.

OPPOSITE PAGE: The Ballpark in Arlington is a mishmash of elements from classic ballparks. The right field bleachers echo the famous ones at Tiger Stadium; the white frieze is a tip of the cap to the old Yankee Stadium; the scoreboard resembles old Comiskey Park's, and the center field sections supported by pillars are reminiscent of Wrigley Field and Fenway Park. The amalgamation worked, and The Ballpark was a delightful place to watch a game.

by expansive lawns and vanilla office parks, the ballpark itself had an urban feel. Featuring a redbrick exterior and classical arches lined with Texas's famous pink granite, it towered above the flat landscape so imposingly that one writer compared it to an Athenian palace. However, architect David M. Schwarz was careful to give the ballpark a Texan motif. More than thirty stone longhorn heads, each 20 feet long, adorn the exterior. The grounds are lined with sculptures depicting Texas history. And the wrought iron work on the seating rows features the state's lone star.

The ballpark had a more enclosed feeling than Camden Yards, and unusually steep stairways in the upper deck. Yet in most respects, the Ballpark in Arlington echoed Baltimore's in hearkening back to the classic ballparks built in the 1910s. The playing field was asymmetrical, a manually operated scoreboard adorned the left field wall, and classical latticework lined the edge of the roof. In right field, a "Home Run Porch" reminiscent of Tiger Stadium was constructed, complete with traditional pillars. (The park as a whole was heavily skewed toward hitters, which pleased home-run-loving fans.) "We had to be careful," co-owner Tom Schieffer said. "We didn't want to have ivy on the walls and a green monster and an overhang in right field… Instead, we said, let's think about why those things are special in other parks and build on the ideas generated."

In the mid-2010s, Rangers ownership embarked on one of the stupidest campaigns in the history of ballpark building when they decided their gem of a ballpark, barely twenty years old, was already obsolete and in need of replacement. The team announced that it was seeking to build an indoor, air-conditioned stadium with a retractable roof. Climate control was necessary, they said, to keep fans streaming through the gates during the sweltering summer months. The team initially considered adding a canopy or movable roof to the existing stadium, but dismissed the idea as too expensive. Instead, they opted for a new $1 billion stadium next door.

It was one of the most cynical moves in the annals of ballpark politics. Fans have grown used to baseball teams threatening to move far away if taxpayers decline to build new ballparks. But rarely has a team so successfully played government entities in the same metropolitan area off one another. By threatening to move to Dallas—a whopping 20 miles away—the team spooked the small city of Arlington into funding a new park all on its own, without any help from larger Dallas or Fort Worth.

It remains to be seen whether the Rangers can accomplish their goal of making a ballpark with a retractable roof seem intimate and authentic. No team has ever successfully pulled it off. Retractable roofs require high walls to support their massive weight, making it impossible for the ballpark to offer an intimate atmosphere. But the Rangers insist they mean business. For what it's worth, in architectural drawings their new ballpark essentially looks like a facsimile of Houston's Minute Maid Park. The new Globe Life Field may well turn out to be a spectacular success. But it seems equally likely that the good citizens of Arlington will someday regret voting their classic ballpark out of existence. 🌑

Tennessee

A Fantastic Minor League Park, a Rich Baseball Past

In 1998, a Memphis businessman named Dean Jernigan embarked on an audacious experiment in local ownership: He bought a Triple-A expansion team and turned over its ownership to a nonprofit organization run by seventeen prominent Memphians. The Memphis Redbirds were not only community-owned; they were the first pro sports franchise run by a bona fide, IRS-certified charity, and their first priority was building a new ballpark in downtown Memphis. The team's nonprofit status enabled it to get low interest rates on the $72 million in bonds used to build the stadium, and Autozone Park opened to unanimous acclaim in 2000.

The experiment in community ownership eventually failed—the nonprofit ownership defaulted on its bond payments in 2009 and the stadium was purchased by the city—but the gambit produced a phenomenal minor league ballpark that helped revitalize Memphis's long-dilapidated downtown. Autozone Park proved a worthy successor to a pair of classic stadiums also beloved by locals, Russwood Park and Martin Park. Russwood Park, originally called Red Elm Bottoms when it was built in 1896, was renovated and renamed Russwood in 1921. Because it was situated on an oddly shaped, six-sided city block, it had delightfully quirky

field dimensions. The left field fence was an impossibly distant 426 feet away, while the right field line measured only 301, making it an easy target for left-handed pull hitters. One of those lefties was local favorite Pete Gray, who despite being born without a right hand, batted .333 with 68 stolen bases for the Memphis Chickasaws in 1944. Russwood Park continued to serve as Memphis's primary baseball venue until April 17, 1960, when it burned to the ground.

In 1923, meanwhile, the Memphis Red Sox opened Lewis Park, becoming one of the few Negro League teams to own their own ballpark. The stadium operated until the early 1960s, and for most of its lifetime it was called Martin Park after a pair of African-American brothers, J.B. and B.B. Martin, who bought the team in the late 1920s. The Martin brothers were prominent local dentists who also ran a variety of other businesses, including a hotel next to the ballpark. (They also personally operated the concession stand, which specialized in fried chitterlings.) Although little information exists about Martin Park, fire insurance maps show that it had a steel roof, short foul lines, and a right-angled wall in deep center field. In an era when African-American teams operated on shoestring budgets

Engel Stadium

Home of the "LOOKOUTS" . . CHATTANOOGA, TENNESSEE

and routinely went out of business, Martin Park enabled the Memphis Red Sox to survive for decades as one of the Negro Leagues' most stable franchises.

Notable baseball stadiums of Tennessee past extend beyond Memphis. After the 1929 season, Washington Senators owner Clark Griffith sent one of his top scouts, Joe Engel, on a tour of southern cities to find an appropriate location for Washington's new farm team. Engel ended up in Chattanooga, where he purchased the Chattanooga Lookouts, building them a new $150,000 stadium and naming it after himself. Engel Stadium's grandstand, with eight pillars supporting a large steel roof, was typical for its day, but the field dimensions decidedly were not. The distance to farthest left-center field was 485 feet, making Engel's outfield one of the largest in baseball. Just to the left of this deepest point was a sloping terrace that was in play and featured the word *lookouts* painted on the grass.

Perhaps the most memorable feature of Engel Stadiu was Joe Engel himself. "He was a larger-than-life character," longtime local sportswriter Ray Deering once said. "The richness of [Engel Stadium's] history is in what Joe Engel accomplished and what he brought." Engel installed the world's largest scoreboard, and in case anyone missed the memo, he had the phrase *the world's largest scoreboard* printed on it. In 1931, he traded his shortstop, Binky Jones, to Charlotte for a 25-pound turkey, quipping that "the turkey was having a better year."

The Lookouts played their final season at Engel Field in 1999. In 2003, the ballpark was purchased by the University of Tennessee at Chattanooga, which left it vacant for the next fourteen years. In 2017, the university budgeted $8 million to turn Engel Stadium into an intramural complex for several sports. "We'd always like to see some sort of sports, baseball, softball played there," the university's vice chancellor, Richard Brown, told a local TV station. "But we're gonna talk to the community and kinda pick their brains about what's appropriate."

OPPOSITE PAGE: With three decks, exposed steel, red brick everywhere, and surrounded by historic buildings, Autozone Park was a more intimate version of the best major league retro parks. A colorful 30-foot-tall sculpture of Lou Gehrig at the main entrance gate further enhanced the throwback feel.

OPPOSITE PAGE, INSET: Memphis Red Sox first baseman Bob Boyd (left) and outfielder Pedro Formentál pose at Martin Park in 1949. Boyd would eventually follow Jackie Robinson to the majors, batting .293 over a nine-year big league career. His nephew, Dennis "Oil Can" Boyd, became a famous pitcher with the Boston Red Sox. Formentál, meanwhile, was the Yasiel Puig of his era—a cocky, flamboyant player who would eventually retire as the Cuban League's all-time leader in home runs, runs, and RBIs.

LEFT: Although Engel Stadium was built as the home for a Washington Senators farm team, it ended up outliving the Senators by six decades (and counting). Though the ballpark has been renovated extensively, the redbrick façade and main entrance awning visible here are both still standing.

TOP RIGHT: Memphis's Russwood Park during its early years, when it was still called Red Elm Bottoms. Note the Coca-Cola billboard warning consumers to "beware of imitations." The company removed cocaine from its recipe in 1907, right around the time this photo was taken.

BOTTOM RIGHT: In 1930 and '31, Engel convinced the New York Yankees to travel to Chattanooga for exhibition games. On the latter occasion, he hired a seventeen-year-old girl named Jackie Mitchell to pitch against them. Mitchell, a star pitcher for a local women's team, struck out both Babe Ruth and Lou Gehrig. Ever since, fans and historians have debated whether Engel had arranged for them to intentionally strike out as a publicity stunt. Engel Stadium was also briefly a Negro Leagues venue, serving as home of the Chattanooga Choo-Choos from 1940 through 1946.

TAMPA BAY

UPTON-CF

PENA-1B

FLOYD-DH

AYBAR-3B

TROPICANA FIELD

TEAM: Tampa Bay Rays (1998–present)

NAMES: Florida Suncoast Dome (1986–93), Thunderdome (1993–1996), Tropicana Field (1996–present)

LOCATION: Corner of 16th St. S. and Tropicana Dr., St. Petersburg

FIRST MLB GAME: March 31, 1998

NOTABLE FEATURES: Four rings of catwalks attached to the roof, two of which are in play; 10,000-gallon "petting tank" where fans can touch cownose rays.

RAYS

2008 AMERICAN LEAGUE CHAMPIONS

WORLD SERIES 2008

TAMPA BAY RAYS.

Though major league baseball is a relatively recent arrival to Tampa Bay, baseball itself is not. Cuban émigrés working in Ybor City's famed cigar factories helped popularize the sport in the late 1800s, and Tampa's longtime minor league team, the Smokers, was founded in 1919. They played their games at Plant Field, a large grassy area owned by the Tampa Bay Hotel, which was also used for concerts, auto and horse races, and the state fair. In 1957, Plant Field was replaced by Al López Field, a yellow concrete stadium with a uniquely curved grandstand roof. (It was named after a beloved local ballplayer who starred in the majors for the Boston Braves and Brooklyn Dodgers.) After three decades of use, López Field was torn down in 1989.

Of course, being in Florida, Tampa Bay has a long and colorful history as a spring training site. The Chicago Cubs were the first to arrive, holding their training camp at Plant Field in 1913, but it was actually St. Petersburg across the bay that would prove to be a more alluring spring site. For years López and his Braves teammates trained at Waterfront Park, built in 1919 at St. Pete's downtown harbor. In 1947, the ballpark was torn down and replaced by a new one, Al Lang Stadium, on the same spot. Throughout their glory years the New York Yankees played their spring training games at Lang Stadium, moving to St. Pete in 1925, Lou Gehrig's first year, and leaving in 1962, near the end of the Mickey Mantle era. Today, Lang Stadium serves as a minor league soccer venue.

In 1986, the St. Pete city government placed a huge bet on baseball, breaking ground on the gigantic Florida Suncoast Dome in hopes of persuading a big league team to move there. That paid off when the city landed the Devil Rays, but by then the Dome was out of step with the times, and the franchise has been trying to move elsewhere since the day it moved in. Countless stadium proposals have come and gone over the years, with team ownership currently favoring a site in Ybor City, which would bring baseball in Tampa Bay back to its roots. 🍂

TROPICANA FIELD

TAMPA BAY RAYS 1998-PRESENT

IN 1986, INTENDING TO LURE a major league baseball team to the area, the city of St. Petersburg spent $150 million to build a covered stadium they dubbed the Florida Suncoast Dome. (The name ignored the fact that it rains in St. Pete on almost half the days during baseball season, which is why a dome was necessary in the first place.) Over the next decade, city officials failed in efforts to land the Chicago White Sox, Seattle Mariners, and San Francisco Giants, all of whom used the threat of moving to Tampa Bay as a negotiating tool to get new parks built in their own cities. The Suncoast Dome became not only a white elephant, but also a "symbol of the city's frustrated efforts to reinvigorate itself," a *New York Times* writer observed.

The Suncoast Dome finally gained a major tenant when the NHL's Tampa Bay Lightning arrived in 1993, and the long-awaited baseball club materialized in 1998 when the expansion Tampa Bay Devil Rays were formed. By then the stadium had been renamed Tropicana Field, and it had already become an anachronism in an era when retro ballparks were all the rage. The Devil Rays posted losing records in each of their first ten seasons, and it turned out that few people wanted to watch baseball being played poorly on plastic grass in an indoor echo chamber.

The Rays finally broke through with a pennant in 2008. In 2011, Tropicana Field hosted one of the most memorable games in baseball history, with Tampa Bay mounting an epic late-inning comeback against the Yankees on the final day of the season to clinch a playoff berth. Even during their most successful seasons, however, the Rays continued to rank at or near the bottom of the league in attendance. Indeed, the franchise has spent virtually its entire existence begging for a new taxpayer-funded ballpark. To date those efforts have gone nowhere, and the team seems fated to remain at Tropicana until its lease expires in 2027.

Tropicana Field looks ghostly as the fog rolls in from Tampa Bay at sunrise. One of the stadium's unique features is its lopsided dome, which was intended to save on air conditioning costs by reducing the volume of air inside. The shape also supposedly makes it less vulnerable to hurricanes. The dome can't protect fans from everything, however, in 2012, a stray bullet fell through the roof and hit a fan in the leg during a game.

Vero Beach, Florida

The Birthplace of Spring Training

Branch Rickey, the longtime general manager of the Dodgers and Cardinals, is widely acknowledged as the greatest executive in baseball history. Among many other accomplishments, he integrated the major leagues by signing Jackie Robinson, invented the concept of the minor league farm system, and brought analytics into baseball by hiring the sport's first statistician. In 1948, having already transformed baseball in all those ways, he changed the sport yet again by inventing the spring training complex.

Signing Robinson had made spring training a complicated issue because Florida, where most teams trained, had rigid segregation laws that in some places prohibited integrated teams from even taking the field. Rickey solved this problem by building his own field on private property where Jim Crow laws did not apply. He purchased an abandoned Navy base in the small resort town of Vero Beach, Florida, and named the complex Dodgertown. "The facilities were already there," team official Buzzie Bavasi recalled. "All we had to do was put in the ball fields."

Every spring, several hundred minor league hopefuls would join the major league Dodgers for training camp, with everyone housed in the old Navy barracks. In segregated Vero Beach, the team's African-Americans found themselves unable to do much of anything, so the club turned Dodgertown into a self-contained village with all the services players might need. Local restaurants and golf courses turned African-Americans away, so the team built an integrated dining facility and a golf course. Black players couldn't go to the local movie theaters, so the Dodgers built their own and procured first-run movies to play in it. Dodgertown also had courts for volleyball, badminton, and tennis, billiard tables, and a swimming pool.

Rickey may have invented the concept of the spring training complex, but Walter O'Malley, his successor as Dodgers president, perfected it. "We had more fields, more batting cages, more instructors, more room to practice," former Dodger Wes Parker said. "So many [opposing] players would say 'Gosh, I'd love to play for you guys.'" In 1953, O'Malley built the complex's crown jewel, a little gem of a ballpark named Holman Stadium after the businessman who had enticed the

Dodgertown, baseball's first self-contained Spring Training facility, arose out of necessity in 1948 because it was the only way the organization's African-American players—Roy Campanella, Dan Bankhead, Don Newcombe, Sam Jethroe, and Jackie Robinson (pictured here with Branch Rickey)—could train with their teammates in segregated Florida.

team to Vero. The stadium was notable for its studied informality. It lacked outfield fences, so hard-hit balls would simply roll on the grassy outfield berm until someone picked them up. The dugouts were roofless pits literally dug out of the ground.

Holman Stadium was linked to Dodgertown's other facilities via a network of tree-lined paths named after Dodgers legends. Fans who visited relished the opportunity to watch their favorite team in such an informal setting, and players relished the feeling of unity the self-contained complex provided. "This place is so different from any other park," said George Betscha, a batboy at Dodgertown during the 2000s. "There is so much history here and you can feel it when you walk around."

After the Dodgers moved to Los Angeles, it made little sense to maintain a training facility on the other side of the country, but the team nonetheless continued training at Dodgertown until 2008, when they finally moved their training operations to Arizona. In 2012, the Vero Beach complex was purchased by former Dodgers owner Peter O'Malley and rebranded Historic Dodgertown. It now serves as a training facility and conference center for various baseball, football, and soccer teams.

MIAMI

⚾ JOE ROBBIE STADIUM

TEAM: Florida Marlins (1993–2011)

NAMES: Joe Robbie Stadium (1987–1996), Pro Player Park (1996), Pro Player Stadium (1996-2005), Dolphins Stadium (2005–2006), Dolphin Stadium (2006–2009, 2010), Land Shark Stadium (2009–2010), Sun Life Stadium (2010–2016), New Miami Stadium (2016), Hard Rock Stadium (2016–present)

LOCATION: Corner of NW 199th St. and Carl F. Barger Blvd., Miami Gardens

FIRST MLB GAME: April 5, 1993

LAST MLB GAME: September 28, 2011

NOTABLE FEATURES: Zigzagging outfield walls; left field wall called "the Teal Monster" and contains a hand-operated scoreboard; the only MLB stadium with orange and teal seats.

⚾ MARLINS PARK

TEAM: Miami Marlins (2012–present)

LOCATION: Corner of Northwest 6th St. and Marlins Way, Miami

FIRST MLB GAME: April 4, 2012

NOTABLE FEATURES: Sleek white exterior; Home Run Sculpture behind center field fence; avant-garde artwork throughout the concourse.

As the youngest community in the major leagues by far, Miami may have been a latecomer to baseball, but it has spent the past hundred years making up for lost time. At the start, it had a lot of catching up to do. When the tiny settlement of Miami was incorporated on July 28, 1896, its entire population was 300 people. By comparison, on that very same day in Philadelphia, a crowd ten times that size attended a game between the Giants and Phillies. It wasn't until 1927 that Miami got a minor league team, and even then it was in lowly Class D ball.

In 1949, the opening of a spectacular new minor league stadium signaled that Miami had finally arrived as a baseball town. Miami Stadium, billed as "the most significant ballpark built since Yankee Stadium," was the pet project of José Manuel Alemán, a former Cuban government official. Built with the intention of luring a major league team, the 9,000-seat stadium cost a then-astonishing $2.2 million, which Alemán had looted from Cuba's national treasury before emigrating to Miami. It was a sleek and modern-looking stadium, with a signature rounded roof and eight light towers holding 612 individual floodlights.

Alas, no major league team would ever call Miami Stadium home. Alemán died a year after it opened, and his eighteen-year-old son soon ran the minor league club into the ground. But in 1956, baseball in Miami was rescued by the sport's most eccentric impresario, Bill Veeck Jr. As general manager of the Triple-A Miami Marlins, he drew fans to the ballpark with a series of classic Veeckian stunts, such as signing Satchel Paige and landing him at the pitcher's mound in a helicopter before his first game. When Miami finally did get a big league team in 1993, it was named the Marlins after Veeck's fondly remembered squad. During their first nineteen seasons in the majors the Marlins played their games at the Miami Dolphins' football field, Joe Robbie Stadium. In its baseball configuration Joe Robbie was most notable for its 33-foot-tall left field wall, derisively dubbed the Teal Monster. The team finally moved to a baseball-only stadium, Marlins Park, in 2012. 🖉

OPPOSITE PAGE: Marlins Park's most controversial feature is its bright, 73-foot-tall home-run sculpture behind the center field wall. Many hate the sculpture, but a dedicated few (including this author) love it. The piece is the work of the renowned pop artist Red Grooms. "For nearly fifty years Grooms has combined color, vibrancy, and a generous dose of self-deprecating humor to produce art in all media that provokes and delights," the art dealer Robert Rogal wrote.

INSET: Miami Stadium, noted for its curving cantilevered roof, was renamed in honor of Bobby Maduro, the late owner of the Havana Sugar Kings, in 1987.

JOE ROBBIE STADIUM

FLORIDA MARLINS 1993-2012

THE FICKLE NATURE and brief duration of corporate sponsorships often makes it difficult for twenty-first-century fans to remember stadium names, and nowhere is that phenomenon better illustrated than Miami's Joe Robbie Stadium—er, make that Hard Rock Stadium. Or perhaps you prefer Land Shark Stadium. The erstwhile home of the Marlins changed names ten times during its first three decades of existence, an average of one name change every three years. In addition to the aforementioned three monikers, it has also been Pro Player Park, Pro Player Stadium, Dolphins Stadium, Dolphin Stadium (yes, they removed the *s*), Sun Life Stadium, and New Miami Stadium (a name it acquired when it was twenty-nine years old). As of this writing, it's called Hard Rock Stadium, but by the time you read this it may well have changed again.

Although the stadium was built (and remains best known) as the home of the Miami Dolphins, the Florida Marlins played their first nineteen seasons here. It was a bizarre period in franchise history, with two World Series titles, twelve abysmal losing seasons, and very little in between. The brief moments of glory were always followed by dramatic fire sales, as the other twenty-nine teams in baseball plundered the Marlins' roster for useful parts. Quite understandably, this frustrated the local fans, and after an attendance over 3 million in their first season, the Marlins drew only as many as 2 million just one other time. Fans loved the ballpark's 33-foot-tall left field wall with its hand-operated scoreboard—cheekily dubbed "the Teal Monster"—but otherwise there was little to recommend it as a baseball facility. Few tears were shed when the Marlins moved 14 miles south to Marlins Park in 2012.

The left field wall known as the Teal Monster, seen here with a set of gymnasium-style bleachers folded up behind it, was Joe Robbie Stadium's most notable feature. It once contained a hand-operated scoreboard, which later became electronic, and then in 2010, the scoreboard was removed altogether and replaced with ads. This stadium was intended primarily for football, of course, as evidenced by the Miami Dolphins' retired numbers on the facing of the upper deck. During baseball games, more than half the stadium's 75,000 seats were closed off and not for sale.

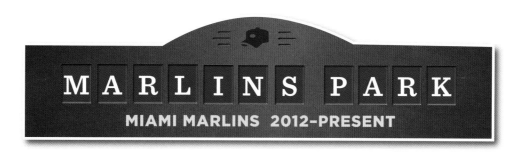

MARLINS PARK

MIAMI MARLINS 2012–PRESENT

IN 2008, THE SENIOR EXECUTIVES of HOK Sport, the dominant architectural firm in stadium building, banded together to purchase the company from its parent firm and renamed it Populous. During its final years as HOK Sport, the firm had fallen into a rut, but Populous' first ballpark as an independent company was a significant departure from the firm's rote reliance on red brick and retro elements. Instead, Marlins Park is an unapologetic ode to modernism, a shimmering white disc filled with glass, steel, bright colors, and unusual artwork. Some people love it, some people hate it—but everyone agrees it's nothing like a rubber-stamp retro ballpark.

The stadium was the brainchild of Jeffrey Loria, the Marlins owner, who had made his fortune as a Manhattan art dealer. One of the most controversial figures in sports, Loria was reviled by many as an arrogant micromanager, but those qualities seemed to serve him well in landing a new taxpayer-funded ballpark, as he combined forces with Major League Baseball officials to negotiate a deal with the city and county of Miami. The new park was budgeted at $600 million, but by the time the borrowed money is paid off in 2048, the final cost of Marlins Park is expected to be $2.4 billion. Miami did get one concession from the team in return, requiring it to change its name from the Florida Marlins to the Miami Marlins. After several more rounds of backroom deals, bailouts, and shenanigans, ground was finally broken in 2009 on the former site of the Miami Orange Bowl, and Marlins Park opened in 2012. There was no red brick, no wrought iron painted in dark colors, no hand-operated scoreboard. The building is sleek and the lines are clean. Loria put his expertise to good use at Marlins Park, even consulting with the family of Joan Miró to design the ballpark's palette. Each quadrant of the building is dominated by a different color: yellow on the first base side, red on the third base side, blue behind home plate, and electric green in the outfield. The concourse is also dotted with works by the likes of Miró and Roy Lichtenstein.

Populous designed the ballpark as an undulating white saucer, although Loria claimed to have sketched out the initial design himself on a napkin. The three-panel 338,000-square-foot retractable roof was designed to be as minimalist as possible; from some angles it appeared to be its own freestanding structure.

The centerpiece of Marlins Park is its home-run sculpture, commissioned from the renowned pop artist Red Grooms for $2.5 million. Directly behind the center field fence, the 75-foot-tall sculpture reacts to every Marlins homer like a pinball machine on acid, with flamingos, spinning fish, and water flying every which way. "It's definitely Miami," Marlins outfielder Logan Morrison said. "There is no need to hold out your bat when you hit a home run and walk down the line anymore, because the stadium will pimp it for you." 🐟

From the outside, Marlins Park is a sea of sleek white lines and repeating patterns. The structure in the foreground is one of two parallel tracks on which the stadium's retractable roof slides open. (For a view of how this looks with the roof open, see the thumbnail inset on page 296.) Marlins Park opened in 2012 "to mostly fawning architectural reviews," Reeves Wiedeman wrote in *The New Yorker*. "Even those who don't like green, or fish, or that thing in center field, had at least one point of praise: Well, it's different! There were no bricks, no green iron trusses. This was gleaming white and shining glass, an homage to Richard Meier, not Honus Wagner."

AFTERWORD
MAJOR LEAGUE STADIUMS AROUND THE WORLD

ALMOST SINCE BASEBALL BEGAN, its supporters have tried to spread it across as much of the globe as possible. Games have been played in the shadow of the Sphinx, on aircraft carriers in the middle of the ocean, and in the rainforests of Uganda. Baseball leagues exist on every continent, even Antarctica, where McMurdo is an annual powerhouse in the Antarctic Internal League. No games have been played on the moon yet, but Jackie Robinson's Brooklyn Dodgers jersey has orbited the Earth while being worn by an astronaut.

An early impetus for spreading baseball across the globe was Spalding's World Tour of 1888 to '89, in which two teams circumnavigated the globe, playing baseball wherever they went. This ambitious plan was the brainchild of Albert Goodwill Spalding, who had once been baseball's greatest pitcher and then became its most influential executive as owner of the Chicago White Stockings and the founder of a burgeoning sporting goods empire. Spalding hoped to popularize baseball worldwide—and, conveniently, sell more sporting goods—by showcasing the game around the world during the winter of 1888 to '89. One of the touring teams was Spalding's own White Stockings; the other was an all-star team of players from the other National League clubs.

Departing Chicago in October 1888, the teams played their way across the country to San Francisco, then sailed for Hawaii—an independent nation at the time—where they were treated to a feast by King Kalākaua. From there they went to Australia, playing games in Sydney, Melbourne, Adelaide, and the gold rush boomtown of Ballarat. The sport was a huge hit down under, with some games drawing more than 10,000 spectators.

After a game in Sri Lanka, the players sailed for Cairo and rode camels to Giza, where they laid out a makeshift diamond next to the Great Pyramid and performed for an audience of 1,200 curious Egyptians. Phillies outfielder Jim Fogarty, playing the role of the ugly American, threw a baseball at the crumbling Sphinx and hit it in the right eye.

After leaving Egypt, the teams toured the great cities of Europe, playing in Naples, Rome, Florence, Paris, Glasgow, Belfast, and Dublin, as well as eight games in baseball's ancestral home of England. The teams then arrived at New York Harbor to a hero's welcome, with a banquet in their honor at Delmonico's attended by Mark Twain and Teddy Roosevelt. In his keynote address, Twain asserted that baseball was "the very symbol, the outward and visible expression of all the drive and push and struggle of the raging, tearing, booming nineteenth century."

Spalding's World Tour had been a tremendous success in terms of generating publicity, but baseball failed to immediately catch on in any of the places where the players had traveled. Still, the signal had been sent that baseball was an ambitious sport whose proponents would go to great lengths to spread it around the globe.

One country Spalding skipped—perhaps because baseball was already popular there—was Cuba. Baseball's roots there date to 1864, when a Cuban student attending college in Alabama brought baseball equipment back home with him. By 1869, there was a Cuban-born star, Esteban Bellán, playing for the Troy Haymakers, one of America's best teams. In 1874, Bellán hit two home runs in what is usually considered Cuba's first official game, played at a ballpark called Palmar de Junco in Matanzas.

For the next ninety years, major league players frequented the Cuban Winter League, using it to stay sharp during the off-season. Sometimes they traveled there as intact teams. When the Detroit Tigers visited in 1908, Ty Cobb was thrown out stealing three times by Havana catcher Bruce Petway, a Negro League star back on the mainland. That same winter a young Cuban named José Méndez threw twenty-five straight scoreless innings against the visiting Cincinnati Reds, propelling him on a career path that would eventually lead to the Hall of Fame in Cooperstown. During the first half of the twentieth century, the Cuban Winter League was the only place in the world where African-American, Latino, and white players regularly played together on integrated teams.

While baseball was played at small ballparks all over the island, most of Cuba's marquee games took place at two large stadiums in Havana. The first was Gran Stadium Cervecería Tropical (Grand Tropical Brewery Stadium)—simply called "La Tropical" by locals—which was owned by (and adjacent to) La Tropical brewery. Built in 1929 on the west bank of the Almendares River, the horseshoe-shaped grandstand was surrounded by palm trees and lush vegetation, and its entrance gate was framed by a pair of 15-foot-tall beer bottles. The stadium complex also included the island's ritziest beer garden, where the upper crust of

LEFT: The Chicago White Stockings and All-Americans pose atop the Sphinx during their worldwide tour. John Montgomery Ward, a pitcher, shortstop, and attorney, is standing in the middle of the Sphinx's chest with a sweater draped over his shoulders. A year after this photo was taken, Ward founded the Players League, a pro-labor major league in which players, not owners, held the clout. Moments after this photo was taken, meanwhile, the players tried to throw a baseball over the 451-foot-tall Great Pyramid of Giza. White Stockings catcher Tom Daly was stationed on the other side so he could catch any ball that made it over, but none ever did.

TOP RIGHT: A pioneer in Latin American baseball, Esteban Bellán was the first Cuban to play professional baseball. One of the many Cubans sent to school in the US by his wealthy parents during the nineteenth century, Bellán caught the eye of a scout from the Troy Haymakers while playing for one of his school teams. A smooth-fielding third baseman, he was nicknamed "The Cuban Sylph" for his graceful play at the hot corner.

BOTTOM RIGHT: The most famous player on Spalding's world tour was Cap Anson, the Chicago first baseman who was the first pro ballplayer to collect 3,000 career hits. Though he was arguably the greatest player of the nineteenth century, he's best remembered for refusing to take the field against African-American players, a stance which helped create baseball's color line.

BOTTOM: Cuba's "Eternal Rivals," the Habana Leones (left) and Almendares Alacranes, pose at La Tropical in 1940. The player laughing fourth from left is Roberto Estalella, who some believe was the first modern MLB player of African descent. When the Washington Senators signed Estalella in 1935 they insisted he was white, "born of Spanish parents in Havana," but rival players hurled racial epithets at him anyway. Estalella, for his part, never seemed to worry about his heritage one way or the other. "It was only an issue for the Americans," he said.

Cuban society gathered in formal wear to drink mojitos among gazebos and faux waterfalls. La Tropical hosted all Cuban Winter League games until 1946 and was frequently visited by major league teams, including the Brooklyn Dodgers, who used it as their spring training headquarters in 1941 and '42. The ballpark still stands, though it was long ago converted to a soccer stadium and renamed Estadio Pedro Marrero.

Cuba's other notable ballpark is Estadio Latinoamericano (Latin American Stadium), the massive facility that has served as the nation's primary stadium since its construction in 1946. Before the Cuban Revolution, Gran Estadio de la Habana (as it was originally named) housed a team in the American minor leagues, the Havana Sugar Kings. After 1960, it became the home field of several teams in the Cuban National Series, including the wildly popular Industriales, commonly referred to as the Yankees of Cuba. Most memorably for American fans, it also hosted two groundbreaking visits by major league teams: the Orioles in 1999 and the Rays in 2016. The ballpark originally contained 30,000 seats in a double-decked grandstand, but in 1971 a drastic renovation expanded that number to 55,000 and its signature leaning light towers were also added. (Cuban ballparks of the Soviet era have a distinctive architectural style, with flying-saucer-shaped exteriors and light towers leaning over the field at a 60-degree angle.)

Not long after baseball reached Cuba it also made its way to Japan, where it was introduced by an American teacher in 1872. Unlike Cuba, where the sport caught fire immediately, baseball in Japan grew at a slow burn for several decades. A series of visits by American players finally cemented its popularity. During the first such visit in 1927, a team of Negro League all-stars led by Biz Mackey played a series of games against a Nisei team from California. "When they got over to Japan and Tokyo, they felt a sense of freedom," Ray Mackey, Biz's grandnephew, told NPR. "The Japanese people met them more or less with open arms." Soon afterward, the Dodgers outfielder Joseph "Lefty" O'Doul, a San Francisco native, began organizing off-season trips to Japan with other big league stars. O'Doul organized tours of Japan in 1931, '32, '33, and '36, at various times bringing along Lou Gehrig, Babe Ruth, Jimmie Foxx, and Connie Mack.

In 1936, O'Doul helped found the Japanese Baseball League and consulted on the construction of its flagship ballpark, Korakuen Stadium in Tokyo. A bowl-shaped, roofless stadium with a capacity of 50,000, Korakuen was the home of the Yomiuri Giants from 1939 through 1987. Because Yomiuri dominates the Japanese baseball scene in much the same way the Yankees once dominated MLB, Korakuen Stadium hosted the Nippon Series (Japan's World Series) twenty-four times in the first thirty-eight years it was played. The park had a ridiculous 295-foot distance down the foul lines, but the rest of the outfield dimensions were more normal. The legendary slugger Sadaharu Oh played his entire career here, tailoring his dead-pull

THIS PAGE: Flag-waving fans cheer on the Cuban National Team as it faces the Tampa Bay Rays in an exhibition game at Havana's Estadio Latinoamericano. (Rays infielder Nick Franklin is about to bat.) The 2016 game was a symbolic breakthrough in relations between Cuba and the United States, and the Obama family attended, sitting in the front row alongside Rachel Robinson, Frank Robinson, Derek Jeter, and Cuban President Raúl Castro. The Rays won 4-1.

OPPOSITE PAGE, TOP: Royals pitcher Dennis Leonard signs autographs at Tokyo's Korakuen Stadium. This was the first game in Kansas City's seventeen-game tour of Japan after the 1981 season, during which they visited fourteen cities.

OPPOSITE PAGE, BOTTOM: The Tokyo Dome is part of a massive entertainment complex, Tokyo Dome City, which also includes a 43-story hotel, a shopping mall, an amusement park, a giant indoor playground, two martial arts venues, and a space museum. The roller coaster pictured here, Thunder Dolphin, is the eighth-tallest in the world.

swing to take advantage of the short right field porch. His 848 career home runs remain the most in professional baseball history.

Korakuen Stadium was memorably used as a filming location for *Stray Dog*, the 1949 noir thriller by Akira Kurosawa that is must-see viewing for anyone interested in old ballparks. Kurosawa filmed one of the movie's most tension-filled sequences during an actual Giants game at Korakuen, and the footage is a priceless document of what the atmosphere was like at a Japanese ballpark in the 1940s.

Korakuen Stadium was eventually bulldozed to make room for the parking lot of the Tokyo Dome, a state-of-the-art facility that the Giants moved into in 1988. At 46,000, its capacity was actually less than that of its predecessor, but its versatility allows it to be used for a variety of non-baseball events, including concerts, basketball games, and mixed martial arts. It also contains the Japanese Baseball Hall of Fame. Like the roof of Minneapolis' Metrodome, the Tokyo Dome's roof is a thin membrane that doesn't stand up on its own; it requires constant air pressure to keep it aloft. The seating decks are steep, which makes for arduous climbs but also closer views. In 2000, "The Big Egg" (as it's known locally) hosted two games between the Cubs and Mets, the first regular-season MLB games ever played in Asia. The experiment was successful enough that it was repeated in 2004, 2008, and 2012. "It was very special to open in Japan," Ichiro Suzuki, the former Orix Blue Wave star, said in 2012. "I loved every minute of it."

In Puerto Rico, the timing of baseball's arrival proved rather ironic, as the first organized game was played in January 1898, just four months before the US Navy invaded the island during the Spanish-American War. Understandably, some Puerto Ricans were reluctant to embrace the national pastime of the occupying force, but several teams were formed over the following decade. In 1900, islanders got a measure of karmic justice when the Almendares club clobbered the US Second Infantry team, 32-18. The Puerto Rican Winter League was founded in 1938 and was an instant success, attracting the best native-born players as well as American Negro League stars. Its biggest ballpark was Estadio Sixto Escobar (Sixto Escobar Stadium), which was home to the league's two most prestigious teams: the Santurce Cangrejeros (Crabbers) and San Juan Senadores (Senators). The stadium's 13,000 seats were extremely close to the playing field, and because Puerto Rican fans cheered more exuberantly than American ones—often making excellent use of artificial noisemakers—Sixto Escobar was one of the most raucous ballparks in the sport. Baseball was "as much a social event as a sporting event," author Jane Allen Quevedo wrote.

"Local fans filled the benches and even climbed into the trees outside the ballpark to secure a good vantage point."

In 1962, Estadio Escobar was replaced by Hiram Bithorn Stadium, designed by local architect Pedro Miranda and named after the former Cubs pitcher who was the first Puerto Rican to play in the majors. Noted for its zigzagging metal roof similar to that of the Dodger Stadium pavilion, it seated 5,000 more fans than its predecessor had. "Fans are rabid," Giants owner Horace Stoneham said in 1963. "From the moment the umpire yells play ball, the stands come alive with hoots, yells, and excitement." In 2003 and 2004, while considering different relocation sites for the Montreal Expos, MLB moved one-quarter of the Expos' home games—forty-four in all—to Bithorn Stadium. The enthusiasm of the Puerto Rican fans impressed everyone, as did the delicious concession items, which included pinchos (kebabs with plantain chips) and alcapurrias (root-vegetable fritters filled with various meats). In 2017, the stadium was severely damaged by Hurricane Maria, including the toppling of the Hiram Bithorn statue at the ballpark's entrance, but it was repaired in time to host a series between the Twins and Indians in April 2018.

In Mexico, meanwhile, baseball's origins are a bit murky, with some claiming games were played as early as the Mexican-American War. While that seems unlikely, the sport had a firm foothold

TOP: Groundskeepers prepare Hiram Bithorn Stadium for the 2013 World Baseball Classic. The ballpark, opened in 1962, displays both American and Latin American architectural features. The accordion-style roof is reminiscent of Dodger Stadium, which opened the same year, while the leaning light towers are a hallmark of midcentury Latin American ballparks. The playing surface was grass during its first thirty-three seasons, but artificial turf was installed in 2005.

BOTTOM: San Diego's Manuel Margot bats against the Dodgers on May 6, 2018, during the second of a three-game series at Estadio de Béisbol Monterrey. The night before, during the first MLB game in Mexico in nineteen years, Dodgers rookie Walker Buehler combined with three relievers to no-hit the Padres. The stadium underwent a $5.2 million renovation prior to the series, including a new video board, audio system, lights, and artificial turf. Visible behind center field is Cerro de la Silla, the 6,000-foot-tall mountain that looms over Monterrey.

OPPOSITE PAGE: The Members' Stand (center) and the Ladies' Stand (barely visible to the left of it) are the two oldest, by far, of the nine stands that comprise the Sydney Cricket Ground. The other seven date from 1980 through 2014. "The sheer weirdness of the two old stands, wedged like a pair of recalcitrant terrace houses into a row of skyscrapers, sets the Sydney ground apart from all others," the *Sydney Morning Herald* wrote. Seats in the Members' Stand are hard to get—spots only open up when a season-ticket holder dies—and attendees follow a stricter dress code than the rest of the stadium. Shorts, T-shirts, sneakers, and team jerseys are banned.

by the time the Mexican League was founded in 1925. During the 1940s, the league made a bid for major league status, paying high salaries to lure major league and Negro League stars from the United States. The white players who crossed the border earned lifetime bans from MLB, while the black players (who, of course, were already banned from MLB) gained an exhilarating sense of freedom. "I came back to Mexico because I've found freedom and democracy here, something I never found in the United States," shortstop Willie Wells said in 1943. "Here in Mexico, I am a man. I can go as far in baseball as I am capable of going."

Baseball's popularity in Mexico, always strongest in the northern part of the country, took off like a rocket in 1981 when Navojoa native Fernando Valenzuela became an overnight sensation with the Dodgers. It was fitting, then, that fifteen years later Valenzuela was the winning pitcher in the first major league game ever played in Mexico, a 1996 contest between the Padres and Mets. The site wasn't Mexico City, whose extreme altitude makes it an unlikely candidate for MLB, but Monterrey, a manufacturing hub near the Texas Gulf Coast. The triple-decked Estadio de Béisbol Monterrey (Monterrey Baseball Stadium) has hosted six more regular-season games since then, including a 2018 series between the Dodgers and Padres.

The sixth (and so far, final) country to host MLB games is Australia, where the Dodgers and Diamondbacks held Opening Day in 2014. This two-game series brought international baseball full circle, as it was held at the Sydney Cricket Ground, the same historic stadium where Spalding's World Tour had played 126 years earlier. One of the world's most prestigious sporting venues, the SCG consists of nine grandstands, each built at different times, surrounding a circular playing field. The two oldest stands, the Members' Stand and the Ladies' Stand, are green-roofed masterpieces dating from 1878 and 1896, respectively. That makes the Sydney Cricket Ground by far the oldest venue to ever host a major league game.

As Major League Baseball continues to lose ground domestically to football and basketball, its officials seem as committed as ever to expanding the sport's international footprint. Exhibitions have recently been played in China, and the Dominican Republic; an official MLB exhibition series has been scheduled at London Stadium, the 66,000-seat home of the West Ham United soccer club; and South Korea has also been bandied about as a possible site for games. Whatever the future holds, it seems certain that major league players will be taking the field at ballparks overseas for years to come. 🏏

BIBLIOGRAPHY

Portions of this book were originally published in *Big League Ballparks* by Gary Gillette and Eric Enders with Stuart Shea and Matthew Silverman. (Metro Books, 2009).

WEBSITES

azsnakepit.com, ballparks.com, ballparkdigest.com, ballparksofbaseball.com, baseball hall.org, baseball-reference.com, baseballresearcher.blogspot.com, bleacherreport.com, bleedcubbieblue.com, brownstoner.com, cbssports.com, chicagobaseballmuseum.org, chicagology.com, cleveland.com, deadspin.com, detroitathletic.com, doubledayfield.com, fenwayfanatics.com, fieldofschemes.com, ghostsofdc.org, gondeee.com, hamtramck stadium.org, hinchliffestadium.org, legends.net, marketplace.org, masslive.com, milb .com, mlb.com, myinwood.net, northjersey.com, oldmetstadium.com, opendurham.org, outsidelands.org, popularpittsburgh.com, sabr.org, savingplaces.org, seamheads.com, si.com, sportspressnw.com, stadiumsofprofootball.com, vice.com, walteromalley.com

MAGAZINES AND NEWSPAPERS

Argus Leader (Sioux Falls, S.D.), *Atlanta Journal Constitution, Atlanta Magazine, The Atlantic, Baseball America, Baseball Research Journal, Boston Globe, Charlotte Observer, Chicago Tribune, Fairbanks News-Miner, Houston Chronicle, Los Angeles Times, Miami Herald, Miami New Times, Minneapolis Star-Tribune, New York Times, News & Observer* (Raleigh, N.C.), *Pittsburgh Post-Gazette, San Francisco Chronicle, San Jose Mercury News, Smithsonian, Sports Business Journal, Sports Illustrated, Sun Sentinel* (Broward County, Fl.), *St. Louis Post-Dispatch, USA Today, Washington Post, Worcester Telegram*

BOOKS

Benson, Michael. *Ballparks of North America: A Comprehensive Historical Reference to Baseball Yards, Grounds, and Stadiums, 1945–present.* McFarland, 1989.

Burgos, Adrian. *Cuban Star: How One Negro-League Owner Changed the Face of Baseball.* Farrar, Straus and Giroux, 2011.

D'Antonio, Michael. *Forever Blue: The True Story of Walter O'Malley, Baseball's Most Controversial Owner, and the Dodgers of Brooklyn and Los Angeles.* Riverhead Books, 2009.

Elzey, Chris, and David K. Wiggins, eds. *D.C. Sports: The Nation's Capital at Play.* University of Arkansas Press, 2015.

Enders, Eric. *Ballparks Then and Now.* Thunder Bay Books, 2002.

Enders, Eric. *The Fall Classic: The Definitive History of the World Series.* Sterling Books, 2007.

Garratt, Robert F. *Home Team: The Turbulent History of the San Francisco Giants.* University of Nebraska Press, 2017.

Golenbock, Peter. *Bums: An Oral History of the Brooklyn Dodgers.* Putnam, 1984.

Hirsch, James S. *Willie Mays: The Life, the Legend.* Simon and Schuster, 2010.

Holway, John. *Blackball Stars: Negro League Pioneers.* Carroll & Graf, 1998.

Holway, John. *Voices From the Great Black Baseball Leagues.* Da Capo, 1992.

Krell, David. *Our Bums: The Brooklyn Dodgers in History, Memory and Popular Culture.* McFarland, 2015.

Leahy, Michael. *The Last Innocents: The Collision of the Turbulent Sixties and the Los Angeles Dodgers.* Harper, 2016.

Lester, Larry. *Black Baseball's National Showcase: The East-West All-Star Game, 1933-1953.* Bison Books, 2002.

Lester, Larry, and Sammy J. Miller. *Black Baseball in Kansas City.* Arcadia, 2000.

Lowry, Philip J. *Green Cathedrals: The Ultimate Celebration of Major League and Negro League Ballparks.* SABR, 2006.

Nowlin, Bill. *Red Sox Threads: Odds and Ends from Red Sox History.* Rounder Books, 2008.

Peary, Danny. *We Played the Game: 65 Players Remember Baseball's Greatest Era, 1947–1964.* Hyperion, 1994.

Repplinger, Matthew Kasper II. *Baseball in Denver.* Arcadia, 2013.

Riley, James A. *The Biographical Encyclopedia of the Negro Baseball Leagues.* Carroll & Graf, 1994.

Riley, James A. *Of Monarchs and Black Barons: Essays on Baseball's Negro Leagues.* McFarland, 2012.

Robinson, Rachel, with Lee Daniels. *Jackie Robinson: An Intimate Portrait.* New York: Harry N. Abrams, 1996.

Snyder, Brad. *Beyond the Shadow of the Senators: the Untold Story of the Homestead Grays and the Integration of Baseball.* McGraw Hill Professional, 2004.

Tygiel, Jules. *Past Time: Baseball as History.* Oxford University Press, 2000.

Wolf, Gregory H., ed. *From the Braves to the Brewers: Great Games and Exciting History at Milwaukee's County Stadium.* SABR, 2016.

Wolf, Gregory H., ed. *Sportsman's Park in St. Louis: Home of the Browns and Cardinals at Grand and Dodier.* SABR, 2017.

Young, William A. *J.L. Wilkinson and the Kansas City Monarchs: Trailblazers in Black Baseball.* McFarland, 2016.

Zinn, John G., and Paul G. Zinn, editors. *Ebbets Field: Essays and Memories of Brooklyn's Historic Ballpark, 1913–1960.* McFarland, 2013.

Connie Mack Stadium, which opened in 1909 as Shibe Park, had been abandoned, looted, and half-burned by the time this photo was taken in the 1970s. During its heyday Shibe was the crown jewel of major league stadiums, and its revolutionary use of steel and concrete construction created a template for all future ballparks. The playing field "looked like the well-kept greens of an expensive golf club," one reporter recalled. During Prohibition, there was a conveniently-located speakeasy across the street that was frequented by fans and A's players alike.

The snowbound Yankee Stadium was demolished in February 2010—though old-school Yankee fans believed it had essentially been demolished decades earlier, during the ill-conceived renovation of 1973–74.

OPPOSITE PAGE: Demolition crews bulldozed Shea Stadium in 2008, but fortunately the ballpark's iconic Home Run Apple was spared. It now sits outside the entrance to Citi Field.

THIS PAGE: The multipurpose Busch Stadium II was demolished in 2005 and replaced by a new version—the third St. Louis ballpark called Busch Stadium—which can be seen under construction in the background.

PHOTO CREDITS

Thank you to the photographers, libraries, and memorabilia-holders whose photographs made this book possible. *L and R refer to left and right; T and B to top and bottom; and i: inset.*

Baseball Hall of Fame & Museum: front cover T, 24 (Ebbets), 31, 32B, 35, 36B, 38B, 40B, 42–43, 44T, 45, 62TL, 68B, 146M, 147, 150B, 151B, 155, 181T, 194TL, 226, 240TL, 240TR, 278T

Shutterstock.com: Joseph Sohm: front cover B, 18, 21, 24 (Shea), 49, 86–87, 161T, 214 (Metrodome), 218, 222 (Dodger), 234–235 & chart, 236, 243T, chart (Camden); James Stuart Griffith: 4M; Everett Historical: 5T; Lunasee Studios: 5M; Photo Works: 6, 185T; Frank Romeo: 4B, 8 & chart (Citizens), 53BL & chart, 53BR, 100 (Camden), 122 & chart (Busch III), 122–123, 138–139, 151, 153 & chart, 158, 198–199, 212B, 213B, 214–215, 215M, 215B, 234 (AT&T), 262T; Aspen Photo: 21i, 22T, 136B; Richard Cavalleri: 24 (New Yankee), 75T, 138 & chart (New Comiskey); Alan Tan Photography: 24 (Citi), 53T; Eugene Parciasepe: 48T; Mary A. Lupo: 48B; Christopher Penler: 52, 86 & chart (Fenway), 96T, 96–97, Debby Wong: Back cover (Mr. Met), 54T, 54B; Daniel M. Silva: 57T, 242; David W. Leindecker: 57B & chart, 58; njene: 60 (PNC); Sean Pavone: 72 & chart; Richard Paul Kane: 73T; Robert Pernell: 73B; f11 photo: 74B; Woodys Photo: 76 & chart (Nationals); Rena Schild: 86T; Marcio Jose Bastos Silva: 92, 96B; Israel Pabon: 93BR; Dan Hanscom: 95T; James R. Martin: 108T; FOTOimage Montreal: 112 (Olympic); Mircea Costina: 112–113; Felix Lipov: 117T; manlio_70: 118 (Rogers); Songquan Deng: 122; GTS Productions: 123T; photo.ua: 138–139; Steve Broer: 140 (Wrigley); Jerric Ramos: 157B; Kathryn Seckman Kirsch: 159BR; Alan Mars: 161T; Steve Cukrov: 163B; Henry K. Sadura: 164–165; aceshot1: 184T, 185B & chart; EQRoy: 184B; anderm: 186 & chart (Comerica), 196–197; Steve Pepple: 186–187; Gerald Bernard: 192T; Melissa Bouyounan: 196i; Gary Paul Lewis: 197i, back cover; Keith Homan: 198 & chart (Miller), 203; David Peterlin: 204 (Kauffman); Natchapon L.: 214, 220 & chart (Target); miker: 215T, Mark Herreid: 220i; Miune: 230T & chart; Eric Broder Van Dyke: 234 (Oakland), 241, 243B; Jeffrey B. Banke: 240B; Paul Coartney: 244 (Petco), 247T; Katherine Welles: 246, 247B & chart, 256 & chart (Coors), 274 & chart (SunTrust), 281; Mark B. Bauschke: 254; Tim Roberts Photography: 260;

Thomas Trompeter: 261; Christian Petersen: 262B; Stephanie A. Sellers: 264 & chart (Minute Maid); Eugene Buchko: 274 (Turner), 274–275, 279; Jason Tench: 280; Dorti: 284 (Globe Life Field) & chart; Ringo Chiu: 289; meunierd: 293L; jejim: 290B; Jamie Waterhouse: 294 & chart; Christopher PB: 303B; Dan Thornberg: chart T (baseballs); cigdem: chart T (bucket); Maurizio De Mattei: chart (Rogers). Backgrounds and icons throughout: Lukasz Szwaj, chrupka, Chantal de Bruijne, primopiano, MaxyM, Picsfive, Kapreski, Johanna Goodyear, Arvind Balaraman

Library of Congress: 1, 4T, 8 (Shibe), 10, 11, 24 (Hilltop, Polo), 26, 27B, 28, 33, 34, 39R, 60 (Forbes), 62B, 63, 64, 65, 66B, 78, 79, 80T, 80BL, 81T, 81M, 83, 88TR, 90M, 93T, 98, 100 (Memorial), 102B, 104B, 106, 110, 126T, 142, 146B, 148, 151T, 162, 166B, 167, 170–171, 176 (Great American), 176–177, 178, 179, 180B, 188T, 206, 207B, 227, 230B, 234 (Candlestick), 236–237, 264 (Astrodome), 267, 272–273, 273, 290T; 301TR, 306, 312

Houston Metropolitan Research Center, Houston Public Library: 2–3, 266; Bert Brandt Collection: 268T, 269, HMRC Collection: 268B

Boston Public Library: 4M, 62T, 75B, 86 (Huntington), 89, 90T, 90B, 99, 191T

Hennepin County Library: 5M, 214 (Metropolitan), 216, 219

New York Public Library: 6BL, 27T, 88TL, 144–145, 169B

© Walter Kadlubowski: 6BR, 138T, 152T, 161BL, 198 (County), 201, 202BR, 213T, 232i, 233B

Alamy Stock Photo: Design Pics Inc.: 7; H. Mark Weidman Photography: 23T, 23B; PCN Photography: 51T; Chuck Franklin: 59T; Philip Scalia: 59B; Maurice Savage: 76–77; Saugus Photos Online: 95B; Amy Cicconi: 174–175; Everett Collection Historical: 209; ZUMA Press, Inc.: 229; Dave Pattison: 250 (Kingdome), 252B; Blaine Harrington III: 256–257; Moviestore collection Ltd: 263T; age fotostock: 274 (Fulton County), 277; AF archive: 282T; Gloria Good: 283T; Jim West: 283; White House Photo: 302; GoAustralia: 305

© Russel Tiffin: 8–9, 22M, 22B, 60–61, 74T, 190B, 192B, 239B & chart, 264–265

Special Collections Research Center, Temple University Libraries: John W. Mosely: 8 (Penmar), 16B, 17P, 41BL; 19TR; Michael J. Maicher: 19B; James A. Craig: 20T; Joseph P. McLaughlin: 20B

Getty Images: Focus on Sport: 19TL, 46T, 71TR, 94T, 103, 183B, 228TL, 278B, 296–297 & chart; NY Daily News Archive: 30; Bruce Bennett Studios: 32T; Bettmann: 40T, 44B, 50, 51M, 93M, 128T, 228B, 268BR; MPI Archive Photos: 43T; George Silk, The LIFE Picture Collection: 46BL, 66T; Ron Galella/WireImage: 46BR; Diamond Images: 47, 118–119; Dan Farrell/NY Daily News Archive: 51B; G Flume: 54–55; Charles "Teenie" Harris/Carnegie Museum of Art: 60 (Greenlee), 67B, 68T; Rich Pilling: 71B, 284 (Arlington), 286; Transcendental Graphics: 8 BR, 301B, 207T; Sporting News: 81B, 191B, 207T; Maddie Meyer: 91; Adam Glanzman: 93BR; Brad Mangin: 94B, 255T; Rob Carr: 100–101; Scott Wachter, The LIFE Images Collection: 109; Michael S. Williamson/The Washington Post: 111B; Rick Stewart: 123B; Francis Miller/The LIFE Premium Collection: 130B; Popperfoto: 150T; Paul Natkin: 152T; Chicago History Museum: 154; John Soohoo/MLB Photos: 156; Chicago Daily News Inc./Chicago History Museum: 157T; LG Patterson/MLB Photos: 159T; Jim Davis/The Boston Globe: 175T; Robert Riger: 181B; W. Cody: 182; Leon Halip: 195; Mitchell Layton: 202T; Stephen Dunn: 204–205 & chart, 253B; Lisa Blumenfeld: 224–225; Andy Lyons/All Sport: 228TR; Matt Slocum: 231; Ronald Martinez: 233T; Ron Vesely/MLB Photos: 248; Dustin Bradford/Icon Sportswire: 259; Elsa: 271; A. Kaye: 298; Mark Rucker/Transcendental Graphics: 291B; B. Bennett: 303T; Roberto Maya/MLB Photos: 304B

Courtesy Larry Lester: 24 (Dyckman), 41BR

123rf.com: © Eddie Toro: 24 (Yankee), 56; © Andrew F. Kazmierski: 24–25; © Jennifer Griffith: 84; Eric Broder Van Dyke: 105, 250–251, back cover B; © Frank Romeo: 158, 229T, 255B & chart; Jonathan Weiss: 159BL; © Dave Newman: 164 & chart (Progressive), 173; © legacy1995: 222 & chart (Angel), 232; © Derrick Neill: 260–261 & chart

Brooklyn Collection, Brooklyn Public Library: 36T, 37, 39T, 39BL

Courtesy Chris Goodwin: 41M

© Jerry Reuss: 60 (Three Rivers), 69, 70B, 121B

National Archives: 76 (Griffith), 82, 85B, 145T, 246i, 284–285 & chart

Harvard Fine Arts Library, Special Collections: 88B

Wikimedia Commons: Thephatphilmz: 93Mi, Wikieditor101: 107; Jleybov, 137; Johnmaxmena2: 140 (Comiskey), 149B, 311; Msr69er: 263B; Aassadi: 270; Kenneth C. Zirkel: 282B; Richiek: 309

Flickr Creative Commons: Danny McKiernan: 111M; Archives de la Ville de Montréal: 112 (Jarry), 114, 115, 117BL, 117BR; Missouri State Archives: 208B; aragh_wolf: 217; King County Archives: 252T, 253T; Todd Dwyer: 299; Erwin Bernal: 310

Maryland Historical Society: 102T

© Robert Strickland: 106B

Toronto Public Library: 118 (Exhibition); 120

Missouri Historical Society: 124 (Sportsman's, Stars, Busch II), 126B, 127T, 128BL, 129, 131T, 131B, 132–133, 134, 135, 136

Historical Society of Missouri: 127B, 128T, 128BR

Michael Schwartz Library, Cleveland State University: Postcards of Cleveland Collection: 164 (League), 166T, 169T; Clay Herrick Slide Collection: 164 (Municipal); Cleveland Press Collection: 168, 170T, 172

Courtesy Brett Streutker: 178T

© Blake Bolinger: 183B

Detroit News: 186 (Mack), 194TL, 194TB

Detroit Library: Ernie Harwell Sports Collection: 188B, 190T

University of Michigan Bentley Historical Library: 189

Walter P. Reuther Library, Archives of Labor and Urban Affairs, Wayne State University: Detroit News Collection: 193

Milwaukee Public Library: 200, 202L

Missouri Valley Special Collections at the Kansas City Public Library: 210

Courtesy Eric Enders: 222–223; 248

© Brad Williams Photography: 231

San Francisco Public Library: 234 (Seals), 236T, 237T

© Christopher Carter: 244–245

Denver Public Library: 257, 258

Kenan Research Center, Atlanta History Center: 276

Memphis and Shelby County Room, Memphis Public Library & Information Center: 291T

Original art by Kevin Baier

Except otherwise noted, all pennant images were provided by PennantKing.com and all ticket stub images were provided by TicketsFromThePast.com. Many of the real objects can be purchased from these sites.

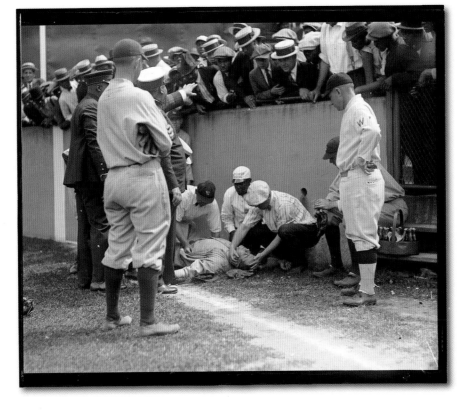

Babe Ruth lies dazed after colliding with the outfield wall at Washington's Griffith Stadium in 1924. The fans were greatly concerned—even a Coca-Cola vendor dropped his soda crate to help—but the Bambino wasn't seriously injured. He not only remained in the game, but he also played the next eighty-two consecutive games.